Australian Literature

AN HISTORICAL INTRODUCTION

John McLaren

Longman Cheshire

Longman Cheshire Pty Limited
Longman House
Kings Gardens
95 Coventry Street
Melbourne 3205 Australia

Offices in Sydney, Brisbane, Adelaide
and Perth. Associated companies, branches,
and representatives throughout the world.

Designed by Mark Davis
Set in 10/12 Century Old Style
Produced by Longman Cheshire Pty Ltd
Printed in Malaysia
by Ling Wah Press Sdn. Bhd., Subang Jaya,
Selangor Darul Ehsan

National Library of Australia
Cataloguing-in-Publication data

McLaren, John, 1932–
Australian literature : an historical introduction.

Bibliography.
ISBN 0 582 71279 3.

1. Australian literature – History and criticism. I.
Title.

A820'.9

CONTENTS

———

The idea of the roundness of the earth is the cause of inventing
this fable of the antipodes . . . for the philosophers having once erred,
go on in their absurdities, defending one another. Is there anyone so
foolish as to believe that there are antipodes with their feet
opposite ours; people who walk with their heels upwards and their
heads hanging down? That there is a part of the world where the trees
grow with their branches downwards; where it rains, hails and snows
upwards?

Lactantius Firmiamus, tutor to the son
of Constantine. Quoted by David
Divine in *The Opening of the World*,
Collins, London, 1973.

PREFACE

———

THE study of literature takes its place somewhere between history and philosophy. History is about events and the people who make them, about the long process by which the human race adapted the earth to its purpose and about the tools, institutions and societies it created as it did so. Philosophy is about the ideas humans have developed to explain themselves and the world. Literature, however, is a branch of cultural studies, a study of the patterns shaped by society, which in turn shape our ways of seeing the world and the ideas we have about it. The student of literature is a *philologist*, a person in love with the word, the idea as it takes form in a particular place and a particular language. Language starts with experience, with perception, and then controls the way we experience and perceive our lives. Language is the ultimate paradox because it is the most intimate part of ourselves, the thing that carries the whole weight of our individual lives, yet its words, with their meanings and the grammatical patterns that hold them together, come entirely from outside us. Our society teaches us our language, and language makes us ourselves. When we study literature, we study works that have been built from words and that therefore take us into the lives of their creators and into the worlds from which they have been created. If we could recover fully what those words and patterns meant to those who wrote them we would have recovered their whole lives, and so would have remade those words

that died with them and yet still live in the language and the literature they have left for us.

A work of literature is therefore not something that has some kind of inherent grandeur or eternal truth, but a piece of writing, or words preserved in some other form, that we can enter into as we read or listen to it, and thus extend our experience into the life of another. It becomes literature not so much because of its own qualities as because of the way we read it. This reading must include the element of pleasure or discovery, because literature and the arts are among those forms of play by which humans discover themselves with delight and horror. There is probably no writing that cannot give pleasure. If we find something tedious it is probably because the way we are reading it — our own context that we bring to it — does not give it any meaning in our lives. Pleasure alone is, therefore, not a test of literature, but of ourselves. The literature we find the best will be that which is most useful to us. This will be the literature that will most extend the patterns of meaning in our lives.

In formal terms, a work of literature is a *discourse*, an extended statement that gives a *message*. This message has been put into its *code*, its pattern of language, by a *sender* or writer. The writer himself is shaped by the *context* in which he writes and the code he uses and which he applies to that part of the context he wishes to clarify, to shape into his writing. The *receiver*, or reader, must *decode* the message.

To do this, the reader must learn the code, but she can do this only within the context of values and experiences she herself has. The aim of reading is to recover the message or *text*, but we can never do this completely because our context is always different even from that of writers from our own time, and much more so from that of writers from times past. Every reading is therefore also an act of creation as we build a new text for ourselves. The further removed in time and place the greater will be this work of building, but greater also will be the novelty, the new meanings in the final structure.

The value of a text for us will depend on the meanings we can take from it for our own use. If it is too remote from us its meanings may not connect with our own lives and it may remain a meaningless game. If it is too close the meanings it adds to us may be trivial. Because our lives and experience are shaped by what has gone before us, and because we create ourselves as we play and struggle with these shaping forces, the works that offer the most meaning will be those that portray the forces that have shaped our world. In Australia, these forces are largely those of European culture, which we can trace back in writing to their dim origins and see still at play in the work of Australian writers today. Australian literature is that writing which brings these patterns most forcefully into an encounter with a 'new' land and the new patterns of society that have arisen in this land. The patterns of this land were shaped in literature long before the first Europeans saw its shores, and those perceptions continue to shape Australian expectations and disappointments today.

The history of Australian literature is a history of the records of this encounter. In this book I have not attempted to record every aspect of the encounter, to consider every writer or even to give a full account of the work of writers who are noticed. Least of all do I intend it as a record of 'great Australian books'. Rather, I have endeavoured to select those writers and those works that provide representative responses to the experience of European civilisation in Australia. This has led to the exclusion of some writers whose works considered individually may hold greater human meaning than some of those I have included, but which do not contribute as much to our understanding of how the experience of Australia has shaped the world's patterns of thought.

The book examines the writing generally in chronological order, using the date of an author's most significant work to fix that writer's place in the chronicle. In places I have departed from this order so that a particular theme can be traced to its natural end. I have not attempted to separate different forms or genres of writing, poetry from prose or creative and imaginative writing from reportage, as all are responses to similar situations. I have, however, for the most part restricted the work discussed to that which was published at the time in book form, as being the most durable and influential, and have mentioned work in journals and newspapers only as it provides context or bears immediately on particular books.

The method of this book is to examine the structure, forms and language of the works in order to determine the part they have played in the overall shaping of Australian literature, and to recover something of the social and cultural context that generated the work. The extent of the examination is limited by this purpose, and it does not pretend to offer complete critiques of the works discussed. The book is intended as an introduction to the works so that they can be enjoyed with some understanding of their place in the whole.

This introduction provides a map to place the works of Australian writers in the context of Western or European culture. Like any other map, it provides no substitute for the experience of the journey, and it necessarily constructs its patterns from its maker's perspective. I hope that its use will give new travellers some idea of the shape of the country they are entering, and show old voyagers some patterns they may have missed. In the end, however, all travellers must construct their own maps to embody the dimensions of their experience.

PROLOGUE

―――――

Aboriginal Literature

LITERATURE in Australia, as in any country, goes back to the time when men and women first walked the land and brought its meaning into their lives in song and dance and story. In Australia, white anthropologists tell us, these first people were black, and came from the north in two waves, starting at least 40 000 years ago. The black people themselves tell us that they have been in this land since the Dreaming. This was when their ancestors, spirit people who combined the qualities of gods and of humans, came to the country and by their deeds and their journeyings created the land and the sky, the seas and the rivers, and all the creatures that dwell in them. In making the world, the spirit people also became a part of it. So the land owns the people who now live in it, and provides the text in which those who have learnt to read it can trace the stories that shaped them and that provide direction for their lives. These stories, and the song cycles and rituals that accompany them, are not just a tradition of folklore and oral history, but a culture embodied in landscape and in art, making humans and nature one.

The cycles of Aboriginal myth shared common forms, creating a common perception of space, time and event. The Aborigines respected the land and lived within its capacities, and they lived well, for to those who understood it, it was a land of plenty. Although their legends include tales of strife and conflict, when human will and passion disrupt the order of nature, the resulting disorder is overcome not, as commonly in European literature, by the imposition or achievement of a new order, but by the re-establishment of natural harmony.

A great deal of this literature has been lost with the passing of many of the communities who were its custodians, and with the displacement or disruption of those that remain. Nevertheless, some has been collected and recounted by white anthropologists and writers. More is kept alive in surviving communities where it is passed on from parent to child, gaining as it goes tales that fit the coming of white settlers into the total pattern. This coming, however, destroyed the wholeness and continuity of the text, and younger Aboriginal writers are more concerned with the struggle to preserve their identity than with the restoration of harmony.

In reading translations of traditional Aboriginal songs and tales we need to remember that these have not only been translated into a different language but into a different kind of text — words on a page in place of a performance that combines words, movement, music and ornament and that refers both to a known landscape and to a known ritual. Professor A. P. Elkin wrote in the Foreword to Roland Robinson's *Legend and Dreaming*, (Edwards & Shaw, Sydney, 1967 [1952], p. 6):

Aboriginal mythology and ritual with the doctrines and philosophy expressed in them, comprise the

DREAMING in its widest meaning. It includes ideas of creation and shaping; of bringing life, natural and human, through the activity of cult heroes; of a past which is recreative in the present through ritual, and of a future which is assured by that same ritual. The Dreaming is always present. Everyone is an expression of it, though he may not realise the implications of this until after his initiation and he has become somewhat grey. Nor do we begin to understand it until we have been present in the great cult-rituals, recorded the chant texts, and so grasped the language and doctrine that we can grasp their esoteric significance.

Needless to say, this can be the lot of very few. The rest of us must be satisfied to hear the exoteric versions of their myths, divorced from the 'high' ritual and chant, and to be told the camp legends about the world and 'all' that is therein.

Robinson, *Legend and Dreaming*, p. 6.

Some indication of the relationship between Aboriginal tales and the landscape, and a contrast with European ways of thought and perception, is given in *Reading the Country* by Krim Benterrak, Stephen Muecke and Paddy Roe (Fremantle Arts Centre Press, 1984). In this book Paddy Roe's stories are transcribed exactly as he tells them. This unfortunately does less than justice to Aboriginal English. The work separates the words from their accompanying tone and gesture, but gives no substitute for this original context. Nevertheless, by juxtaposing the stories with the visual perception of a modern artist and the commentary of a white writer, the book helps us to understand the land as a text that not only provides Aboriginal culture with its meanings but itself holds a complex meaning because of that culture.

The anthropologists Ronald and Catherine Berndt faced similar problems in trying to bring the richness of Aboriginal song to white readers. The songs they have collected and translated for publication in the periodical *Oceania* and elsewhere were originally performed to the acompaniment of dance, clicks and didgeridoo, and involved repetition and clear rhyme, but no punctuation or regular metre. The Berndts sought to keep closely to the form and arrangement of ideas in the original, but to render them in firm metres ultimately derived from the King James version of the Bible.

One of the songs they have translated, the 'Moon-bone Song' of the Wonguri-Mandjigai people (reprinted in Rodney Hall's anthology, *The Collins Book of Australian Verse*, Sydney, 1981, pp. 13–19), shows the close relationship between the daily lives of the people, the wild creatures that share their lives, and the all-encompassing order of nature. It tells of the waning of the old moon and its rebirth as the new.

The song does not begin with the moon, but with particular human activity in a particular place:

The people are making a camp of branches in that
        country at Arnhem Bay:
With the forked stick, the rail for the whole camp,
        the Mandjigai people are making it.
Branches and leaves are about the mouth of the
        hut: the middle is clear within.
They are thinking of rain, and of storing their clubs
        in case of a quarrel,
In the country of the Dugong, towards the wide
        clay plains made by the Moonlight.
Thinking of rain, and of storing the fighting sticks.

The poem is concrete and detailed about place, time and activity. It goes on to specify the people who belong in the camp, classifying them by totem, origin or function: the Morning-Pigeon man, the Middle-of-the-Camp man, the Mangrove-Fish man, two other headmen. The we see the people as a whole:

Sitting there in rows, those *Wonguri-Mandjigai*
        people, paperbarks along like a cloud.
Living on cycad-nut bread; sitting there with white-
        stained fingers,
Sitting there in rows, those *Wonguri-Mandjigai*
        clan . . .

The feeling is one of both peace and plenty. But rest is only a passing phase, soon crowded out by the demands of continuing life:

Wake up from sleeping! Come, we go to see the
        clay pan, at the place of the Dugong . . .
Walking along, stepping along, straightening up
        after resting:
Walking along, looking as we go down on to the clay
        pan.
Looking for lily plants as we go . . . and looking for
        lily foliage . . .

Circling round, searching towards the middle of the
lily leaves to reach the rounded roots.

Aboriginal Bird Painting
(*Photo: Martin Murry*)

The words act out the women's walk to the clay
pan and their search for the roots, and then give
their sense of satisfaction on finding the rich food.
Their joy is shared by other creatures, as the 'birds
saw the people walking along', and they are joined by
the shag-woman and her clan, a kangaroo-rat with
her young and a duck with its eggs, 'Floating along
and pushing the pool into ripples', a leech, a hard-
shelled prawn and 'the tortoise with her young, . .
Swimming along, moving her shell, with bubbles
rising'. All are gathered in the same natural plenty of
the lily plants, the 'Vine plants and roots and jointed
limbs, with berry food, spreading over the water'.
Only when this natural plenty has been established
and celebrated does the poem turn to the events
that sanctify and support the whole — the new moon
that rises as the old moon dies, and the evening star
that accompanies it, hanging in the sky even as the
moon sets:

Sinking down in the sky, that Evening Star, the
    Lotus . . .
Shining on to the foreheads of all those
    headmen . . .
On to the heads of all those Sandfly people . . .
It sinks there into the place of the white gum
    trees, at Milingimbi.

Collins Book of Australian Poetry, pp. 13–19.

The cycles of birth and death, rest and replenish-
ment are complete.

Although we can read this simply as poetry, we
gain more from it if we remember its context in Ab-

original culture. In naming the places and the people,
the poem connects them with their totemic groups
and functions, and with the Dreaming, which brought
them all into existence. It thus renews this Dreaming
in the life of the people today, bringing together the
people and the nature of which they are a part, and
sanctioning the social organisation that arises from
this wholeness of time and space.

The three major cycles of Aboriginal mythology
provide a guide by which the people could understand their unity with the land and its past. The first
is the *totemic* cycle, the classification of the whole of
creation that in turn provides the social structure of
the tribes. This structure is brought into being by
the acts of the heroes of the Dreaming, the spirit
ancestors whose deeds created the landscape and its
meanings and who go on living in the lives of their
successors. Their stories bind the people to the
earth they inhabit. However, two later cycles of
stories, possibly brought from overseas, have
mingled with these stories of the ancestors. Unlike
the earlier stories, which are concerned with the ties
that bind the land and all of its people, these cycles
are about special powers that can be obtained only
by the few through initiation and ritual. They therefore represent a diversification and separation within
Aboriginal society.

One of these cycles tells of the deeds of a sky-
father, a hero who lives in the heavens rather than
the earth. Through proper ritual initiates can approach him and share his wisdom. The other introduced cycle tells stories of the earth mother, who is
often associated with the Rainbow Snake as her
agent, incarnation or partner. These stories are
related to fertility rites, which enable the individual
to share the creative power of this earth mother.

As uninitiated readers we can enjoy the stories of
the Aborigines as literature, but we need to remember that for their authors, and for those who hand
them down in their traditional society, they are not
merely interesting tales or even records of a truth.
They contain also the shamanistic or primitive power
of the word, that connects the things of this world,
the human and the temporal, with the eternal.

A common structure of thought is embodied in all
these retellings of traditional myths. They are at
once spiritual, totemic and historic. They are spiritual in the sense that they deal with a world in which
everything of interest is explained by the existence

of distinct spirits, who may be incarnate or otherwise present for the teller and audience, and who are personified in the events of the story. They are totemic in that they view the human and the natural as sharing a common life and as grouped in a single system of classification. Thus they explain the ordinary, the everyday, rather than the miraculous. Finally, they are historic in that they tell how the tribal customs have been initiated by living heroes who exist in historic continuity as the past is created afresh through initiation rites, ceremony and song. The Dreaming is therefore not only the past from which Aborigines came, but also the present to which they belong.

European Literature

Although the story of European literature written in Australia starts with the beginning of white settlement, the literature itself has its origins in lands far down under, below the northern horizon, lands that had also been inhabited since the dawn of time and that had created their own dreaming for the white man. Yet the experience of these European lands has been one of rough breaks and violent yokings, of invasions, conquests and revolutions, and so, in place of wholeness, its dreaming has conflict, both between humankind and nature and between individual and society. For the European, the land does not own the people, or even the people the land. Some people own the land, and very often have owned other people as well. This puts power at the centre of European culture: the power to dominate nature and make it serve human purposes; the power to dominate others and make them serve the desires and will of the individual. The urge to power produced the questing and turbulent spirit of the renaissance. The ordering and controlling reason of the scientific and industrial revolutions that followed it shaped the thoughts and ideas of the Europeans who first came to Australia and of the literature in which their meanings were expressed.

European literature contains many, often contradictory, traditions. The most important of them come from Jerusalem, from Athens and from Rome. From the Judaic traditions of Jerusalem came the concept of a single God dwelling outside the nature He has created. This tradition teaches humans either to despise this world and seek an eternal destiny beyond it, or to wait for the return of the God who will introduce the millenium, the unending thousand years of peace and prosperity for His chosen people. Yet this otherworldly tradition carried also a high sense of responsibility for the world and those within it. The story of the Fall of humankind explained the disruption between a felt heavenly destiny and our unavoidable worldly responsibilities and ambitions. Sin, in the form of the serpent, turned humanity away from God and so separated us from both God and nature. The attempt to overcome this separation and the guilt that arises from it is a constant driving force in Western culture, as evident in the mystical writers of the Middle Ages as in the writings of the millenarians and visionaries of the seventeenth century and their twentieth century Australian successors. Their common aim is to replant Eden, whether by withdrawing from the world or by transforming it through love and revolution. Australia, the new land, has been an attractive vehicle for their dreams.

Onto this vision the West has grafted the spirit of Athens and the mission of Rome. The Athenians sought the greatest good in their search for the kind of perfection of mind, body and soul that is the aspiration of today's athletes. At the same time, however, they recognised that human passions contradict this desired harmony, leaving us with the alternatives of comedy and tragedy, the Carnival and Lent of the Christian church calender. The Romans in their turn expressed the Athenian ideal of order in the forms of law and engineering, which provided the material and legal basis of the mass state. The economic basis of this state was provided by the ancient institution of slavery, which was in time used by Renaissance Europe as a means of subjugating new worlds and laying the foundations of a new industrial system.

These intellectual traditions emphasised the divisions between the flesh and the spirit, between the human and the natural, between men and women. Among the people, however, an older pagan tradition remained alive in the folklore of fairy stories, herbal medicine and the popular festivals that marked the coming of spring, sowing and harvest, midsummer and midwinter. These customs and tales kept human life in harmony with the world of nature. As Europeans spread through the Americas and across the Pacific, they took these beliefs with them and blended them with the hopes of Christian visionaries for an earthly paradise free from the sins, divisions and oppressions of Europe. These aspirations survive in works as otherwise dissimilar as Patrick White's novel *A Fringe of Leaves*, David Campbell's 'Cocky's Calender' and Christopher Koch's novel *The Doubleman*. They explain the nostalgia for the imagined golden years of the past that characterises so much Australian autobiography.

The Middle Ages brought together these traditions in a single vision of a world united in the glory and wisdom of God. Men and women could share in God's goodness by obeying His word, or they could disobey and be damned for eternity. As no human action could disturb the divine order, this life mattered only as a preparation for the life to come. Nature was valuable only because, as St Bonaventura wrote, it allowed us to come to know God by observing His footsteps in His creation. This vision eventually leads us back to nature in works like Dante's *Divine Comedy* and Chaucer's *Canterbury Tales*.

Yet also in Chaucer we can find the origins of the forces that eventually destroyed this mediaeval unity. These forces were released by the Black Death, which first struck Europe in 1348, sweeping away, along with the lives of nobles and peasants, the ideals of service and mutual obligation that had bound feudal society together. The society that replaced it was based on property and money. Over the next five centuries, the search for wealth drove Europeans across the oceans until they had spread their empires around the globe and united the world in a single economy. This new energy appears first in Chaucer in figures like the Pardoner and the Wife of Bath. The Pardoner knowingly chooses to base his life on avarice, the root of all evil. The Wife of Bath is more complex. Like the early navigators, she fully accepts the mediaeval beliefs, yet finds they cannot contain her energies. She makes a place for herself in society, instead of accepting the one that has been given to her. Yet even Chaucer's Knight, ideal figure of mediaeval chivalry, is caught up in the wars between Islam and Christendom that dominated the later Middle Ages and renewed the mass trade in slavery that financed Europe's expansion overseas. The pressures of these forces disrupt Chaucer's work just as they disrupted Europe.

The expansion of Europe, east, west and south, planted the seeds of the Renaissance and Reformation whereby individuals were to become author of their own fate and measure of the universe. Its first fruits were the discoveries of the East and West Indies, and the attempts to make sense of these discoveries. These attempts included both maps that re-drew the shape of the world and theories that refashioned ideas of the universe. Australia figured on these maps both as a place and as an idea.

The Unknown South Land

The name of Australia appears on maps before the land could be shown as fact. Classical geographers had used the name *Terra Australis Incognita*, the Unknown South Land, to fill in the blank spots at the bottom of their maps. During the Middle Ages maps showed the world as a flat disc centred on Jerusalem, site both of the crucifixion and of the foretold return of Christ to introduce the millenium, His thousand-year rule with the saints. Around this centre are grouped the continents of Africa, Asia and Europe, with the the *Mare Mediterraneum* — Sea in the Middle of the Lands — next to Jerusalem, and the Garden of Eden in the east at the top. Around the borders Oceanus neatly encloses the symmetric masses of the land, and beyond it may be shown heaven above and hell beneath. The intent of such maps is not so much to enable the user to find a way from one place to another as to enable the pilgrim to find the path that leads through the physical world to eternal life.

The neatness and certainty of this world and the simplicity of its purposes and motives were forever destroyed at the end of the fifteenth century by the voyages of Vasco da Gama and Christopher Columbus. Their voyages not only found a new way to the east, a new continent to the west, and a new shape for Africa to the south; they changed the model of the world from a disc facing up to the east and heaven to a globe suspended in the heavens between two poles and their icy surrounds. From being at the centre of things, Europe was displaced to the margins. The land masses of Eurasia and North America stretched across the northern half of the globe, and South America and Africa reached southwards. Between these two yawned a vast gulf of the unknown.

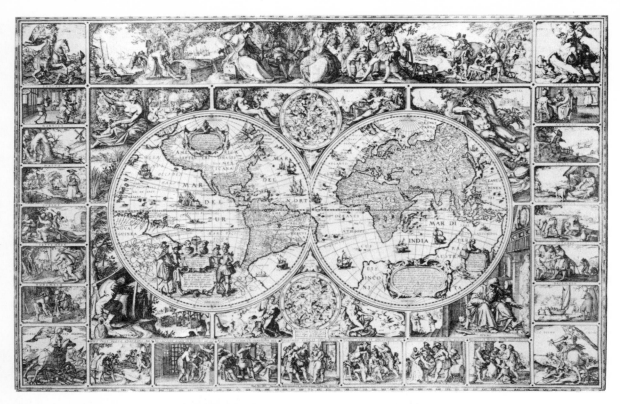

An Early Map showing 'Terra Australis Incognita'

This gap threatened to unbalance the fine poise of the globe, and so geographers decided that it must be covered with another land mass, for which they revived the name of *Terra Australis Incognita*. The search for this land would preoccupy voyagers, venturers and dreamers for almost three centuries. For many, this was still the land where 'here be beestes', where anything might happen and the commonplace expectations of Europe be reversed. For others, such as the visionary Spaniard de Quiros, it was the land where people would redeem the failed hopes of Christianity and which they would make the true *Tierra Austrialia del Espiritu Santo* — South Land of the Holy Spirit. For most, it was the land where the wealth of gold and spices would give them the power and the freedom that they could not find in Europe. Thus did Europe project its own dreams and fears on the new worlds, but before it could test their reality it had to come to terms with the fact of North and South America.

Both America and Asia had already been hazily present in mediaeval consciousness. North America was known to some Western communities through the voyages of the Vikings and the legends of St Brendan, which may have inspired Columbus. The idea of Asia had become more widespread through the tales of such travellers as Marco Polo. These had filled the minds of the people with images of the riches of India, the splendour of the Great Khan in China and the power of the mythical Christian potentate of Africa, Prester John. These wonders lured Columbus so strongly that when he bumped into America he believed he had arrived in Asia. The new world he discovered was from the first established in images brought from the old.

Although the conquest of North and South America led to disaster for the native peoples, it brought vast new wealth to Europe. At first, however, new wealth came from the ventures of the Portuguese in the east rather than from those of the Spaniards in the west. Like their neighbours, the Portuguese were inspired by the hope of extending the glory and empire of Christendom and by the lure of gold. Their voyage established a great trading empire whose network spread as far as Japan, and inspired Luis Vaz de Camoens (1524–1580) to write *The Lusiads* (1572), the national epic that provides both the first modern celebration of the imperial dream and, in its account of Java Major, the first literary description of Australia.

Camoens portrayed his Portuguese as a people called by God to abandon the futile, mutually-destructive quarrels of Europe and win new realms for Christ — in fact, to establish a new, and newly holy, Roman Empire. In order to inspire his countrymen to this task he wanted to recall to them the glory they had already achieved through the exploits of Vasco da Gama and his successors. He wanted to tell a tale of wonders and miracles that was also historically true, so he took a model from Virgil's epic poem, the *Aeneid*, which celebrates the achievement of the first Roman Empire. Just as Virgil celebrated the possibilities of the Augustan peace and ignored the realities of conquest and exploitation, so Camoens turned the history of an imperialist venture into a myth that celebrates its ideal possibilities at the cost of concealing its true nature.

Camoens' vision was indeed splendid, and captured the element of idealism that was to inspire several empires and four centuries of imperialism. It incorporated both the wonders and the riches that people hoped to find in the new worlds. When Camoens grants his voyagers the final reward of a festival of love, in which the nymphs of the sea sate human appetites in the best Roman style, he anticipates the real delights that later mariners were to find on the islands of the Pacific. His vision further anticipates the new world by being given in the form of a working model of the universe, an image of an age when science is harnessed to technology. The empire that is shown in this model passes beyond the boundaries of the known world to the last of lands, which is characterised by peaceful people, idyllic landscape and a wealth of natural fruits and minerals. This last of lands is named by Camoens 'Java Major', the site of the Unknown South Land. The images in this vision were to remain constant in the European dreaming of Australia.

Before the first European settlers arrived to make good their dreaming, other and contradictory images of the new world were to be established. Shake-speare's *The Tempest* conveys the ambivalent combination of both hope and threat these lands offered to the old structures of Europe.

The Tempest is not directly 'about' the new worlds opened by Columbus and Vasco da Gama, and the fictional island of the play's action appears indeed to be in the Mediterranean. The island is, however, outside the known bounds of civilisation, and on it the Europeans of the drama encounter the same forces and challenges as their contemporaries who were trading and settling in America and Asia. The island provides a mythical counterpart for these new worlds.

The characters in *The Tempest* win their new world only by working their way to a new synthesis of the elements of the old. In the first scene, this old world is turned upside-down by its encounter with its opposite, the force of nature. Prospero has been exiled by the overthrow of his social world, but in turn has subjected nature on the island to his magical or intellectual forces. Nature appears in the contrasting images of the free but amoral spirit, Ariel, and the uncouth and threatening Caliban. The image of Ariel was to become the ideal of the noble savage, while the threat to harmony and order represented by Caliban has provided the excuse for the enslavement and subjugation of native peoples down to the present. In particular, Caliban's sexual threat to Miranda represents the savagery Western civilisation transposes from its own core to its subject peoples.

Prospero represents the ideal of the scientist. This ideal achieves its greatest dramatic realisation in the Renaissance figure of Faustus, whose contract to sell his soul for the knowledge that is power symbolises the modern world. Prospero uses his knowledge to impose order on his island, just as Western Europe would use its superior technology to impose its rule on its empires. When Prospero abdicates from his rule of the island and renounces the practice of his magic arts, he acknowledges the limitations of his power. Its contradictions are resolved in the compact of the love freely chosen by Miranda and Ferdinand, but the fruits of this compact can be enjoyed only on their return to Europe.

Propero's island may submit to European power, but it also tests European values. Power is condemned as surely by courtiers who plot against their ruler as it is by the drunken menials who conspire with Caliban in his revolt against Prospero. The opening storm shows the vanity of all social distinction. The insolent and foul-mouthed Sebastian and the courteous but inopportune Gonzales are equally useless compared with the rough-spoken but practical boatswain. The seaman's rebuke 'if you can command these elements to silence, and work the peace of the present, we will not hand a rope more. Use your authority; if you cannot, give thanks you have lived so long, and make yourselves ready in your cabin for the mischief of the hour' (*The Tempest*, I, i, 20–6) echoes through the literature of voyaging as the counterpart to the ideals of profit and glory that inspired the ventures. It can be heard two centuries later on the *Endeavour*, when Captain James Cook refused Sir Joseph Banks' imperious command that he endanger his ship by entering one of the fiords on New Zealand's south coast. Cook wrote:

> . . . it certainly would have been highly imprudent in me to have put into a place where we could not have got out but with a wind that we have found lately does not blow one day in a month: I mention this because there were some on board who wanted me to harbour at any rate without in the least considering either the present or future concequences.

Alan Villiers, *Captain Cook: The Seamen's Seaman*, Penguin, Harmondsworth, 1969 [1967] p. 164.

The woods and meadows of Prospero's island, 'Full of noises, Sounds and sweet airs, that give delight, and hurt not' (*The Tempest*, III, ii, 146–7) represent the ideal pastoral image of the new world that offers hope even to savages like Caliban and churls like his companions. The new world offers the hope of salvation, but if Shakespeare eventually renounces this as dream, it is no more so than any of our hopes of life. Even as he dissolves his visions, pointing out that:

> . . . These our actors,
> As I foretold you, were all spirits, and
> Are melted into air, into thin air

he is at pains to point out that this is no less true of the world itself, which with all its towers and palaces and temples:

> Yea, all which it inherit, shall dissolve,
> And, like this insubstantial pageant faded,
> Leave not a rack behind. We are such stuff
> As dreams are made on, and our little life
> Is rounded with a sleep.

The Tempest, IV, i, 140–58.

Shakespeare thus presents the new world as the theatre on which the conflicts of the old world will be enacted and its dreams fulfilled, and simultaneously renounces it all as illusion. The old world has hovered between these two views of the new ever since. Yet, just as Prospero and his companions return to Milan with new understanding of themselves, so Europe has been irreversibly changed by its encounter with the new world it first called into being from its own imagination.

From this time on the images of the new worlds of Asia and America diverge from those of the still undiscovered *Terra Australis*. Although the East and West Indies were explored, conquered and settled, the South Land remained a goal of European dreaming.

Black Swans, Rottnest Island
(*National Library of Australia*)

But those who sought it were singularly unsuccessful, either missing it entirely and endowing Pacific islands with the burden of their dreams, or stumbling on barren and inhospitable shores that supplied a different and contradictory image from the visions of wealth and wonder that had inspired the earlier voyagers. The first to bring back reports of the island continent were the Dutch, who gave it the name of New Holland but saw only its sandy and desolate coasts. Their only settlement, brief and unplanned, was in the Abrolhos Islands, and was marked by shipwreck, mutiny, murder and savage revenge. Their other contribution to the legend of Australia was the report of the kangaroos, or rather the related species of quokka, first sighted at Rottnest Island — 'Island of Rats' Nests', as they named it, trying to assimilate the strange to the known. The strangeness of these creatures dominated the reports, and established the image of the South Land as the land 'where reside All things in their imagined counterpart', as the Australian poet James McAuley was to express it three centuries later.

The image given by the Dutch was taken over by the English privateer, William Dampier, who described it in his account of his expedition, *A New Voyage Round the World* (3rd edition, London, 1699 [1697]), as a wretched and inhospitable place inhabited by 'the most miserable people' he ever saw, He left the continent as soon as he could, but his record of his encounter helped to establish the image of its people on the model of Caliban rather than of Ariel. Rather than portraying them as brutal, Dampier shows them as simply degraded below any standards of human life:

. . . setting aside their Human Shape, they differ but little from Brutes. They are tall, strait bodied, and thin, with small long Limbs. They have great Heads, round Foreheads, and great Brows. Their eyelids are always half closed, to keep the Flies out of their Eyes: they being so troublesome here, that no fanning will keep them from coming to one's face; and without the assistance of both hands to keep them off, they will creep into one's Nostrils; and Mouth too, if the Lips are not shut very close. So that from their Infancy being thus annoyed with these Insects, they do never open their Eyes, as other People: and therefore cannot see far; unless they hold up their Heads, as if they were looking at somewhat over them . . . I did not perceive that they did worship anything. These poor Creatures have a sort of Weapon to defend their Ware, or fight with their enemies, if they have any that will interfere with their poor Fishery. They did at first endeavour with their Weapons to frighten us, who lying ashore deterr'd them from one of their Fishing places. Some of them had wooden Swords, others had a sort of Lances. The Sword is a piece of Wood, shaped somewhat like a Cutlass. The Lance is a long strait pole, sharpt at one end, and hardened afterwards by heat. I saw no Iron, nor any other sort of metal; therefore it is probable they use Stone-Hatchets, as some *Indians* in *America* do.

William Dampier, *New Voyage*, Vol. i, pp. 464, 466.

Dampier on his second voyage to New Holland had only a fleeting encounter with the inhabitants. This served to confirm the impressions of his first.

The earlier visions of *Terra Australis* do not return to the literature until the eighteenth century, when the fantastic histories of Alexander Dalrymple persuaded the English Admiralty to commission a further expedition to settle the issue. Dalrymple was greatly mortified, however, when they did not give command of the expedition to him, but to James Cook, a man of humble birth who had qualified for command through the tough school of North Sea colliers rather than by birth or in a greedy and anarchic collective of freebooting buccaneers. Cook, the 'seaman's seaman', as Alan Villiers dubbed him, represented the practical rationalism of his age. The reports Cook and the scientist of the voyage, Joseph Banks, brought back completed the image of the real rather than the mythical South Land. These reports were for almost two hundred years known publicly only through the florid version of Dr John Hawkesworth. Cook's own account shows that he had read Dampier, but as a practical man expecting neither saint nor sinner he was able to see the Aborigines on their own terms, and to use his observations to imply criticism of his own society rather than condemn another.

From what I have said of the Natives of New-Holland, they may appear to some to be the most wretched people upon Earth, but in reality they are far more happy than we Europeans; being wholy unacquainted not only with the superfluous but the necessary Conveniences so much sought after in Europe, they are happy in not knowing the use of them. They live in a Tranquility which is not disturb'd by the Inequality of Condition: The Earth and sea of their own accord furnishes them with all things necessary for life, they covet not Magnificent Houses, Household-stuff &c, they live in a warm and fine Climate and enjoy a very wholesome Air, so that they seem to have very little need of Clothing and this they seem to be fully sencible of, for many whom we gave Cloth &c to, left it carlessly upon the Sea beach and in the woods as a thing they had no manner of use for. In short they seem'd to set no Value upon any thing we gave them.

A. Grenfell Price (ed.) *The Explorations of Captain James Cook in the Pacific as told by Selections of his own Journals*, Angus & Robertson, Sydney, 1969, p. 85.

Sir Joseph Banks
(*State Library of NSW*)

The most lasting images conferred on Australia by Cook and Banks were the names they chose. Cook, ignoring its strangeness, gave the east coast the homely name of New South Wales. Banks gave to the place where they were first able to anchor and go ashore to pursue their scientific collecting the name of Botany Bay. This name reflects both the wealth of natural specimens Banks discovered there and his excitement about the find. This discovery, with its rich harvest of plants and its noble harbour, provided a culmination of the enchantment Banks and his companions had felt during their voyage across the Pacific. They had discovered again in Tahiti the dream of a natural world untainted by sin, where nature gave as freely of its fruits as the comely women did of their love. Unfortunately for the future Australia was not as lavish of its gifts, but Banks was not to know this, and even Cook was moved to unusual enthusiasm by the prospects of this new land. The image of the noble savage, the dream of freedom and the hopes of science thus combined in the accounts they brought back, and provided the basis for the hopes that led the British government a score of years later to choose Botany Bay as the site for the penal colony that would rid Britain of its criminal refuse.

The consequences of this decision would bring a quite different set of associations to the name of Botany Bay, which for so long would stand for the whole settlement. For all its consequences, the decision to establish a convict colony embodied the utopian hope that amid new surroundings the villains of England would reform themselves and build a new life as sturdy and independent farmers. Similarly, the image of Australia as a laboratory where nature would reveal its truth and its wonders was kept alive by Flinders and appears again in Charles Darwin's account of his visit to Port Jackson during his round-the-world cruise of scientific exploration on the famous *Beagle*.

The establishment of the settlement at Sydney Cove in Port Jackson brought Aboriginal and European dreamings into direct contact, but despite the romantic and scientific interest attached by Europeans to the natives, it was long before either culture could start to learn from the other. For the Aborigines, the results of white settlement were almost entirely disastrous. Those in the most fertile areas were quickly deprived of their lands and sustenance, their social structure was destroyed and the Dreaming lost. Only now are they able to start the task of re-building a culture from the fragments of two hundred years. Others, left in varying degrees of possession in the wilder and more desolate areas, or given an economic function in areas the whites could not exploit on their own, retained more. Eventually they shared it with others through the efforts of white anthropologists who approached their culture with respect for its own integrity, and through the work of their own artists and story-tellers.

The effects of settlement on European dreaming of the South Land were almost as drastic. Experi-ence in the Americas and Indies had endorsed some of the myths of wealth and wonder, but Australia was largely to deny them. Its strange wildlife sup-ported the idea of a land upside-down — the land of the antipodes, where the people walked with their heads in shoes — but the visions of wealth were never realised. Even the gold-rushes, which prom-ised fortune to many and established a prosperous economy, did not lead to the growth of a new society of equals, but laid the basis for local industries that reproduced the social and economic divisions of the old world. The ideals of brotherhood remained among the excluded, but they were no closer to fulfilment than were those of the few who kept alive the dream of Australia as the Land of the Holy Spirit. Australia became the home neither of a kingdom of saints nor of a human brotherhood, but of an economy con-strained by the bonds of imperialism and existing on the margins of world trade by providing cheap raw materials for the rapidly-growing industrial nations of the old.

Nor did the main ideals of the European dreaming survive transportation unchanged. The Renaissance had already changed the idea of life as a pilgrimage to one of personal pursuit of the goodwill of God, and in the South Land this goodwill was soon seen to be manifest in earthly possessions. The disinterested pursuit of knowledge and beauty was made irrelevant by the struggle to survive. The splendid order of the law became the iron tyranny of the convict age, and Australia's heroes became those who rebelled against it. The natural kinship between humans and nature that had been expressed in folk traditions could find no footing in the new landscapes of a continent that accepted humans only on its own terms. The whites thus found themselves lost in an alien land.

The history of literature in Australia is a story of how writers struggled against that alienation, by denying it, by learning to accept it and by attempting to transcend it. The models for their efforts, like their first audience, were mainly European, and only gradually do new centres of awareness and new tra-ditions in the south become differentiated from the metropolitan centres of the north. In this process the European tradition becomes acclimatised in Australia, its ideals are reworked in terms of new experience, and the ideas and ideals of Asian and Aboriginal neighbours become incorporated as writers bring the old tradition home to the new country. The story is not so much of growth or de-velopment as of the acclimatisation, assimilation and differentiation of a tradition already as old as time.

1

A TAINTED PARADISE

———

OR the first half-century of European settlement in Australia the people concerned were too much occupied by the immediate problems of survival to have energy to devote to imaginative literature. Nevertheless, the work of discovery and exploration was intellectual as much as physical. In setting down their accounts of their experiences in letters, journals and reports the surveyors and settlers placed the new land in its mental as well as its geographic context.

The audiences these first writings were intended for were the officials, scientists and curious general public of England. Such readers were interested in the practical success of their penal experiment, the possible effects of the settlement's development on Britain's prosperity, and the contribution that exploration of the new land might make to human knowledge. These concerns naturally shape the response of the writers to their experience. They did not see themselves in the model of Camoens' Vasco da Gama, as warriors entrusted with the heroic task of extending the empire of Christ. They saw themselves as loyal servants of the English king, strengthening the government and securing the trade of his realm.

Britain at this time was in the full sweep of its industrial revolution. The power of steam applied to the organisation of labour in factories had led to a great expansion of its industrial output, while its merchants, protected by the might of the British

navy, bought and sold on a world market. Yet the misery evident in the highlands and borders of Scotland, the slums of the new English cities, and the whole of Ireland, undermined the confidence of this new society.

Historians debate the extent to which the cottagers expelled from their plots or the labourers penned in the tenements of the new cities shared the increase in national wealth that began in the latter part of the eighteenth century. There is, however, no doubt that, whatever the general standard of living may have been, contemporary observers were persuaded that rural destitution and urban misery threatened the order of society. Manning Clark's collection of *Select Documents* shows the attitudes of the time (Manning Clark, *Select Documents in Australian History*, Vol. I, Angus & Robertson, Sydney, 1950). Optimists believed that the enclosures that deprived the rural poor of their land were justified by their effect in making the country 'much more beautiful' and increasing 'the productiveness of the soil' (p. 1). The pessimists argued that the enclosures themselves were to blame for rural poverty. They left 'the old and infirm [to] fall a burthan on the parish' while 'the young and healthy have dispersed themselves' to North America where they could, even at the cost of selling themselves into bondage, free themselves from hunger. The remainder joined in 'forming troops of the most abandoned thieves that ever disgraced civilized country, and glut the gallows with food, and freighting our ships to the coast of Africa at every returning season, and leaving at the same time a crowded prison to be disposed of in the same manner, or for ballast heaving on the river Thames' (p. 3). Even the independent farmers fell into debt, and eventually were forced to sell up and take the proceeds — their sole patrimony — to the Americas. The land was thus trebly hurt, losing money, youth and skill to the new world while it nurtured vice at home.

The sentiments of the time were expressed by Goldsmith in his literary classic of the enclosures, 'The Deserted Village', published in the year Cook sailed along the east coast of New South Wales:

> Ill fares the country, to hast'ning ills a prey,
> Where wealth accumulates, and men decay;
> . . . a bold peasantry, their country's pride,
> When once destroyed, can never be supplied.

Many Englishmen looked to the colonies to make good the loss, and in fact Goldsmith's grandnephew, born in Canada, in 1825 published in *The Rising Village* a eulogy, a hymn of praise, to the flourishing of transplanted English virtues in the soils of a new land. By then similar virtues were flourishing among the children of the convicts in the antipodean settlements of New South Wales.

The settlement at Port Jackson was intended to relieve the problems of England both by ridding its streets and gaols of the criminals who infested them and by giving these lost souls the opportunity of regeneration in a new land free of the luxury and vice of the old. If, however, the vice was already deeply planted, the convicts would only spread their contamination to the new colony. Henry Fielding had described the general dilemma of the poor in his pamphlet on the *Enquiry into the Causes of the late Increase of Robbers* where he was equally depressed by the conditions of the poor and worried about the threat they posed. They live, he wrote, under conditions so wretched that if 'one considers the destruction of all morality, decency, and modesty; the swearing, whoredom, and drunkenness, which is eternally carrying on in these houses, on the one hand, and the excessive poverty and misery of most of the inhabitants on the other, it seems doubtful whether they are more the objects of detestation or compassion.' (*Collected Works*, Vol. X, pp. 446–8). If

compassion was one motive for establishing the colony, detestation, and the fear it engendered, were the principal factors determining its system of government.

The fears and hopes that industrial England projected on its convict colonies are dramatised by Charles Dickens in his novels. These deal movingly with the circumstances of oppression and the necessary conditions of reform. Repeatedly he establishes islands of compassion where, like the unfortunates of the colony in New South Wales, his characters may recover their spirits and their fortunes away from the cities that represent the evils of industrial England. Yet behind the regenerative theme of his plots lies the fear of the mob, the undifferentiated poor from whom he saves the occasional individual but who collectively threaten the values of human community that he locates within the family. In the only one of his novels that hinges directly on Australia, *Great Expectations*, Dickens dramatises his fears in the single figure of the convict Magwitch. Although Magwitch on his return to England reveals the hypocrisy of his oppressors and earns the sympathy of the narrator, Pip, he remains a figure of dread.

Dickens was accustomed to solving the problems of his less fortunate characters, as he solved the problems of his own improvident sons, by shipping them off to Australia in the closing pages of his books. Once there, his readers were left free to assume, they prospered as they never had in England. But Magwitch is shipped off early in the novel, not to solve his own problems but to direct the novel to its major theme, Pip's great expectations and their falsity. These expectations, as it turns out, come from Magwitch's prosperity, but Pip accepts them in terms of the conventions of gentility and success provided by his society. Magwitch's return destroys these illusions by revealing the true source of Pip's prosperity, and brings in their place the darkness and threat of evil associated with Magwitch, but actually directed at him. This confronts Pip with the moral necessity of rejecting the society he has chosen and embracing the convict and illegality instead. He is unsuccessful in his attempts to rescue Magwitch, for England offers no sanctuary to those it has rejected, but the law of England that condemned Magwitch is shown to be incapable of acting other than as an agent for the evil that finally engulfs him.

Hulk *Success*, Hobart
(*State Library of Victoria*)

worse. Clearly, therefore, the answer was to remove them to an area where the natural resources would exceed their needs. New Zealand was inhabited by cannibals who might resist attempts at settlement, but the natives of Australia had been found by the navigators to be few in number and deficient in technology and so to present no insurmountable obstacle. By establishing a gaol in Australia, the authorities solved the most pressing problem of over-population, that of the gaols and hulks of Britain. They removed to a propitious clime the criminal element of the poor who posed the most immediate threat to society. They provided a deterrent that could terrify others into remaining obedient to the law and they pioneered a settlement that would eventually accommodate large numbers of the surplus population and contribute to British trade and wealth.

There were a few dissenters, notably Alexander Dalrymple, who still smarted with resentment that Cook had been given the command of the expedition that should have been his, and who believed that the South Land was too good for criminals, 'What is the punishment intended to be inflicted?' he asked. '*Not to make Felons undergo servitude for the benefit of others* as was the Case in America: but to place them, as Their own Masters, in a temperate Climate, where they have *every object* of *comfort* or *Ambition* before them! and although it might be going too far to suppose, this will *incite* men to become *Convicts*, that they may be *comfortably* provided for' (Clark, *Select Documents*, Vol. 1, pp. 37–8).

For the supporters of the colony, the opportunities it provided for prosperity and thus the inducement to reform, were its great advantage. Deterrence would be provided for by the thought of the unknown, and the prospect of removal from familiar people and places. Once removed, however, the convicts (except for those beyond redemption, for whom further torments and even execution could be provided on the spot) would be given the discipline of useful toil and see the advantages of leading an orderly life. All would be for the best in that best of all possible worlds once the sole blot on it, crime and disorder, was removed from its sources and healed by the beneficent influences of the new South Land.

The orthodox view of the colony from England was embodied in English poetry even while its first white inhabitants were trying to adjust their expectations to reality. Erasmus Darwin, naturalist and

His only achievement is to have revealed to Pip the truth about himself and his society.

The fears and hopes that Dickens dramatised in this novel had already been projected on Australia by those responsible for establishing the convict colony in New South Wales. They did not, however, foresee how the criminal element, when transported overseas, would survive both as a factor shaping the outlook of the new country and as a nightmare returning to haunt the old country that had attempted to expel it from its midst.

The minds of the governing class had been formed by eighteenth-century rationalism. They believed that once they had identified the problem and the measures to be taken to remedy it, the solution must follow. The problem was poverty leading to crime, and the underlying cause of poverty was clearly overpopulation. Malthus had, in the view of the respectable, demonstrated that the poor inevitably outbreed the resources required to provide them with a livelihood, and that any measures to relieve their suffering can only make the problem poet, friend of Dr Johnson and free-thinking grand-father of the author of *On the Origin of Species by means of Natural Selection*, in 1789 wrote a broad-sheet eulogy of the 'Visit of Hope to Sydney-Cove'. While the colonists faced starvation, Darwin had Hope announce to them her vision that:

> *There* shall broad streets their stately walls extend,
> The circus widen, and the crescent bend; . . .
> Embellish'd villas crown the landscape-scene,
> Farms wave with gold, and orchards blush
>   between.

> Eramus Darwin in B. Elliot and
> A. Mitchell (eds.), *Bards in
> the Wilderness: Australian
> Colonial Poetry to 1920*, Nelson,
> Melbourne, 1970, p. 2.

Darwin's perspective is Regency London and its imagined hinterland, but his vision of a future as English as it is golden was not as influential as Robert Southey's pathetic scene, in his '*Botany-Bay Eclogues*', of the fallen maiden picking her way along Sydney's 'hollow-sounding shore'. Reflecting on the scenes of childhood happiness that her shame has taken her from, she realises she has wilfully made herself 'the slave/Of Vice and Infamy! the hireling prey/of brutal appetite!'. Now, however, that she is 'at length worn out with famine, and the avenging scourge of guilt' and has been sent 'where angry England sends her outcast sons', she 'hails your joyless shores'. For here at last, through work and repentance, she may find peace.

> No more condemn'd the mercenary tool
> Of brutal lust, while heaves the indignant heart
> With Virtue's stifled sigh, to fold my arms
> Round the rank felon, and for daily bread
> To hug contagion to my poison'd breast;
> On these wild shores my Repentance' saviour hand
> Shall probe my secret soul, shall cleanse its wounds
> And fit the faithful penitent for Heaven.

> Robert Southey, 'Elinor', *Poems*, 1797, pp. 2–4.

Southey projects his own fears of passion and degradation onto the fallen woman, and, in his enjoy-ment of her awakening to grace through suffering, makes her the scapegoat for the evils of the society he saw about him in England.

The projection onto the new colony of glorious hopes for the future, combined with the attribution of all moral responsibility for their fallen state to the convicts, made failure inevitable. The golden future existed only in the visions of the projectors. When the human material proved incapable of realising it the convicts received the blame, both from their immediate masters, who attributed it to their incor-rigible depravity, and from those in England who judged that a colony generated in sin could only breed further wickedness. The authorities on both sides of the world were thus encouraged to tighten the con-trols, penal and political, of a system that bred failure by its own rigidity. This contradiction would, how-ever, become apparent only as the consequences of the original decisions worked themselves out in history. In the meantime, the colonists were bur-dened by the cargo of hope and depravity they took with them in the first transports.

The Journals of the Early Settlers

The journals of the early settlers trace both the strength of their hopes and the growing frustration as they were thwarted by the unyielding character of the land and its people, native and newcomer alike. The accounts of several members of the First Fleet were published — the journals of Lieutenant Watkin Tench in 1789 and 1793; Surgeon-General John White in 1790; Captain John Hunter, Phillip's deputy, in 1793; and the Judge Advocate, Captain David Collins, in 1798. Accounts of the experience from the point of view of the convicts were published by James Tuckey in 1805 and ostensibly by George Barrington in 1802. There is some doubt on the authenticity of these accounts because Tuckey was only a boy when he made the voyage and the forger Barrington was almost certainly not the author of the *History of New South Wales* that was attributed to him. An anony-mous work, *The Voyage of Governor Phillip to Botany Bay*, based on the despatches of Captain Arthur Phillip, was also published in London in 1789. The number of these books, and there were many more of them, both genuine and forged, is an indication of the interest that was taken in the new settlement.

The form of these journals is given by the histori-

Captain Arthur Phillip
(*National Library of Australia*)

cal events, and they may seem to be almost purely objective accounts differing only according to the personality of the author or his interests. Thus Phillip explains the circumstances that influenced his decisions and the reasons behind them. He emphasises matters such as the adequacy of supplies or the suitability of convict labour that explain his recommendations to the authorities at home as well as his success, or the lack of it, in meeting their expectations. Collins and Tench are both interested in human behaviour and in the prospects of the colony. White meticulously describes the wildlife. All writers are of necessity most concerned with the hardships caused by insufficiency of food.

Yet all the diaries are clearly products of the eighteenth century, both in their general attitude and in their expectations of the colony. Phillip's role was that of Prospero in Shakespeare's *The Tempest*, to give laws to this little kingdom over which he excercised virtually absolute sway. It may, however, be questioned whether Phillip found the savage Caliban there or took him with him in the convict holds. Neverthe-

less, none of the writers has any doubt about the need to impose foreign laws and to take the land from its native inhabitants, nor does any narrative show any of Shakespeare's ambivalence about the result.

These accounts of the settlement at Sydney Cove have neither the sense of divine compulsion nor even the sense of mere human adventure in the woods that mark the narratives of the North American settlements at a similar stage. For the early Americans, the voyage across the Atlantic was similar to the journey of the Israelites to the Promised Land. The hardships of the voyage became the test of their faith, and they cheerfully endured danger and starvation in the new land as part of their task of building a kingdom for God. Although these sentiments are most characteristic of settlers in the northern colonies, even those in the south — the two Carolinas and Georgia — give their accounts an air of adventure, of establishing a society free of the restraints of the one from which they have come.

By contrast, the Australian accounts are mundane, detached and often prosaic. Although the authors were participants in the events they describe, they write as observers, even of their own feelings. This adds to the analytical and descriptive value of their writings, but absolves the writers from responsibility for their own actions. This may be because, unlike the American settlers, they were agents of a government rather than actors on their own account, let alone souls directly responsible to an unforgiving god. If things went wrong, as they often did, they could blame a government that had failed to make adequate provision, and that government in turn could recall its agents and send others to try a different approach. When the government entrusted the execution of its wishes to private contractors, they might fail to meet their obligations, as did the shipmasters of the disastrous Second Fleet, but the consequences fell most heavily on soldiers and convicts, and the fault could be remedied by closer supervision. This supervision meant that, although the sea voyage to Australia took much longer than the Atlantic crossing to North America, it was always much safer. Certainly, when free migration began the passengers fared worse than had the convicts, who were government property, but even free migration was subsidised and therefore supervised, and the worst horrors of the American migrant ships were avoided.

Watkin Tench, a Marine

The journals of the First Fleet read like a report to a board of directors. Watkin Tench, for example, describes the new country as 'certainly pleasing, being diversified with gentle ascents, and little winding vallies, covered for the most part with large spreading trees, which afford a succession of leaves in all seasons'. He appeals to the sentiments of his day for nature pleasantly ordered and varied, like the parks designed and planted for the country houses of the gentry by the pioneer of landscape architecture, Capability Brown. He continues:

> In those places where trees are scarce, a variety of flowering shrubs abound, most of them entirely new to an European, and surpassing in beauty, fragrance, and number, all I ever saw in an uncultivated state: among these, a tall shrub, bearing an elegant white flower, which smells like the English May, is particularly delightful, and perfumes the air around to a great distance. The species of trees are few, and, I am concerned to add, the wood universally of so bad a grain, as almost to preclude a possibility of using it: the increase of labour occasioned by this in our buildings has been such, as nearly to exceed belief.

> Clark, *Select Documents*, Vol. 1, p. 46.

As observer, the author is at the centre of the landscape, but is not involved in it. It exists to serve him, by affording delight or use. Conversely, the human actors (the convicts who must hew the intractable wood) are present only as an economic calculation — an unbelievable 'increase of labour'.

John White, Surgeon-General

The same attitude of a cultivated tourist and detached observer pervades the journals of John White, the Surgeon General. White spent almost seven years in the colony, and intended to publish a second volume of his journals, but the manuscript for this has been lost. All we have is the account of the preparations for the voyage, the journey itself and his first ten months in the colony. Even so, more than half of this account deals with the journey; with the emphasis falling on the three landfalls — Teneriffe, Rio de Janeiro and Cape Town — and on the social life White encountered in each. In his *Journal of a Voyage to New South Wales* (London, 1790), he takes a justifiable pride in the measures he took to ensure the health of those in his care, including the convicts, but none ever emerges as in individual.

> The weather became exceedingly warm, and close, with heavy rain, a temperature of the atmosphere very common on approaching the equator, and very much to be dreaded; as the health is greatly endangered thereby. Every attention was therefore paid to the people on board the *Charlotte*, and every exertion used to keep her clean and wholesome between decks. My first care was to keep the men, as far as was consistent with the regular discharge of their duty, out of the rain; and I never suffered the convicts to come upon the deck when it rained, as they had neither linen nor clothing sufficient to make themselves dry and comfortable after getting wet: a line of conduct which cannot be too strictly observed, and enforced, in those latitudes.

> To this, and to the frequent use of oil of tar, which was used three times a week, and oftener if I found it necessary, I attribute, in a great degree, the uncommon good health we enjoyed. I most sincerely wish oil of tar was in more general use throughout his Majesty's navy than it is . . .

> In the evening it became calm, with distant peals of thunder, and the most vivid flashes of lightning I ever remember. The weather was now so immoderately hot that the female convicts, perfectly overcome by it, frequently faded away; and these faintings generally terminated in fits. And yet, notwithstanding the enervating effects of the atmospheric heat, and the inconveniences they suffered from it, so predominant was the warmth of their constitutions, or the depravity of their hearts, that the hatches over the place where they were confined could not be suffered to lay off, during the night, without a promiscuous intercourse between them and the seamen and marines.

> J. White, pp. 62–3.

Our reaction to White's moral attitude to the convict women should be tempered by our knowledge that he himself later took a convict mistress, whom he left behind when he left the colony, although he did take their child with him. We may also compare it with White's approving account of Governor Phillip's address to the convicts on the occasion of the first reading of his commission, on 1 February, 1788:

The governor then addressed the convicts in a short speech, extremely well adapted to the people he had to govern and who were then before him. Among many circumstances that would tend to their future happiness and comfort, he recommended marriage, assuring them that an indiscriminate and illegal intercourse would be punished with the greatest severity and rigour. Honesty, obedience, and industry, he told them, would make their situation comfortable, whereas a contrary line of conduct would subject them to ignominy, severities, and punishment. When the Ceremony was concluded, his excellency, attended by all the officers of the colony, withdrew to a tent pitched for the occasion, where a cold dinner was laid out; and, after the cloth was removed, many loyal and public toasts were drank.

J. White, p. 114.

New South Wales is clearly an extension of England and subject to the same universal laws, which prescribe a purely external and utilitarian morality, as well as clear differences in privilege between those in office and their subjects. The same tendency to

reduce everything to a single plane of reality can be seen in the pages where White describes the return of a convict who had attempted to escape, what was learned from his experiences, and his subsequent fate:

Previously to the return of Corbett he must have suffered very severely from hunger; his eyes were sunk into his head and his whole appearance shewed that he had been half starved. While he was absent, he says, he frequently fell in with the natives, who, though they never treated him ill, did not seem to like his company. He informed us that, in a bay adjacent to that where the governor and his party had met with so many of the natives, he saw the head of one of the convicts lying near the place where the body had been burnt in a large fire. This, in all likelihood, was Burn, who was carried off at the time Ayres was wounded, as he has not been heard of since.

The natives of this country, though their mode of subsisting seems to be so very scanty and precarious, are, I am convinced, not cannibals. One of their graves which I saw opened, the only one I have met with, contained a body which had evidently been burned, as small pieces of bones lay in the bottom of it. The grave was neatly made, and well covered with earth and boughs of trees.

The Pennantian Parrot was about this time first noticed. The general colour of the body, in the male, is crimson; the feathers of the back black in their middle; the chin and throat blue . . .

24th. The governor revoked the decree by which Corbett was outlawed, and he was tried by the court simply for the theft that he had committed [of a frock] and sentenced to be hanged.

Samuel Payton, a convict, likewise received the same sentence, for feloniously entering the marquee of Lieutenant Fuzer, on the night of the fourth of June, and stealing from thence some shirts, stockings and combs. His trial had been put off to the present time on account of a wound to the head . . . During the time he remained under my care, I frequently admonished him of the perilous situation he then stood in, and to make known the accomplices whom he was supposed to have . . .

When he and Corbett were brought to the fatal tree, they (particularly Payton) addressed the

Flogging Convicts, Van Diemen's Land
(*National Library of Australia*)

convicts in a pathetic, eloquent, and well-directed speech. He acknowledged the justice of his sentence, a sentence which (he said) he had long deserved. He added that he hoped and trusted that the ignominious death he was about to suffer would serve as a caution and warning to those who saw and heard him. They both prayed most fervently, begging forgiveness of an offended GOD. They likewise hoped that those whom they had injured would not only forgive them, as they themselves did all mankind, but offer up their prayers to a merciful REDEEMER that, though great sinners, they might be received into that bliss which the good and virtuous only can either deserve or expect.

They were now turned off, and in the agonizing moments of the separation of the soul from the body seemed to embrace each other.

The execution of these unhappy youths, the eldest of whom was not twenty-four years of age, which seemed to make a greater impression on the convicts than any circumstance had done since their landing, will induce them, it is to be hoped, to change their conduct, and to adopt a better mode of life than, I am sorry to say, they have hitherto pursued.

J. White, pp. 142–4.

Everything in this passage — the sad condition of the convict on his return, the life of the Aborigines, the appearance of the parrots, the circumstances of the trial, the death speeches and final agonies of the condemned men — is described in the same dispassionate tone. White is concerned to inform his readers and, possibly, instruct them in morality, but by omitting any account of his own feeling he leaves out the whole dimension of reality as we experience it. His writing expresses the taxonomic outlook of the eighteenth century, with its determination to classify everything. Scientists and writers of the time believed that if they described everything and put it in its place they had explained it. The important thing about White's account of Corbett and Payton is his perception that they are convicts who have committed a second offence. They must pay the penalty prescribed by the system, although it is first necessary to rescind the law's previous pronouncement on Corbett to bring him back within its scope, rather

than allowing him the quick death of the outlaw. The colour of the parrots' plumage had the same importance as the burial customs of the Aborigines — these details enable us to classify the birds in their proper species, the Aborigines in the proper sub-species of non-cannibal. The scaffold speeches are not important as statements of any ultimate truth, or as indications of the state of mind of men facing death with no better comfort than the stark judgements of eighteenth-century evangelism to match the stark judgements of an eighteenth-century court. They are included rather as evidence of the salutory effect of public hanging on members of a category of people who have, as the final remarks remind us, not hitherto adopted the mode of conduct prescribed for them by their superiors.

Although White appears to be telling the whole truth, allowing his readers to draw their own conclusions, he in fact lacks the essential spirit of scientific enquiry, the effort to understand the reason behind the events he observes. In anthropology, this involves the recognition that every form of human behaviour has an internal logic. Before this principle was accepted, human societies not accepted as civilised suffered the fate of being allotted a place in the mental scheme of their invaders. The Indians of North America were, for example, first regarded as benevolent creatures of the woods sharing the gifts of nature with the newcomers, and then, when they defended their territory, as agents of the devil attempting to root out Christian communities. The Australian Aborigines were regarded as child-like primitives who must give way to a superior race. If they co-operated in their own destruction, so much the better. The early officials were nothing if not benevolent, but if the 'natives' resisted they were taught a painful lesson until they learned to pass away peacefully.

Attitudes towards convicts

A similar attitude pervades the treatment of convicts in early Australian writing. Like White, the writers feel a duty to care for and admonish the convicts, and there was undoubtedly a need to discipline them if the colony were to survive. But the failure to see them as other than objects meant that the writers were unable to perceive the logic of convict resistance. They were therefore forced to judge this behaviour as either perverse or ungrateful and to trace its causes to the depravity of the convict nature. They were left with only the system to fall back on, and in the absence of any understanding of their own natures could not recognise that the system itself was depraved and self-defeating. This recognition was reserved for the convicts themselves, and for the later generation of writers who built on their experiences.

The early elation of the settlers with the prospects of the new colony at Port Jackson was succeeded by gloom as provisions became exhausted and the realisation grew that the land would yield sustenance only in return for protracted labour, so that Tench eventually decided that, although 'as a receptacle for convicts . . . this place stands unequalled', its appeal to free settlers would be limited to 'men of small property, unambitious of trade, and wishing for retirement . . . To men of desperate fortune, and the lowest classes of people . . . this part of the world offers no temptation' (Clark, *Select Documents*, Vol. 1, p. 50). Yet gradually the colony was established, and its more ambitious inhabitants grew more determined to break its bounds and discover what the country beyond the ranges offered them. Their journals provide the second phase of writing in Australia.

2

EXPLORERS AND VISIONARIES

As the colony at Port Jackson grew, the numbers of free citizens increased. Some had come as free settlers, others had been discharged from servitude on completion of their sentence or by a conditional pardon granted for good service. Others, the currency lads and lasses, had been born in the colony. Meanwhile, by 1840 other colonies had been established around the coast, effectively claiming the whole continent for the crown. New convict settlements had been planted on Norfolk Island and at Hobart Town and Moreton Bay. Planned settlements of free immigrants had been set up on Swan River and in South Australia, although convicts were later sent to Western Australia to prevent the colony from foundering. After the abandonment of an early convict settlement, a collection of freebooters from Van Diemen's Land and overlanders from the north had settled in the Port Phillip District. The first planned white settlement in New Zealand was established in 1840, although sealers, whalers and missionaries from Port Jackson and the USA had already been active on its shores. The main function of Britain's southern colonies had thus shifted from penal to economic, providing land and work for the surplus population and markets for its industries. Whales and seals, and later wool, provided staples for export, and breweries and flour mills supplied the local market. Yet, until the gold-rushes, the Australasian colonies were of minor importance to Britain. The overwhelming proportion of British emigrants during this period went to North America.

Norfolk Island Convict Settlement
(*State Library of NSW*)

Once in the colonies, the settlers sought to create the society they had known at home. However, the very fact that they were making a place for themselves in a new society rather than accepting the one allotted to them in the old gave a new context and new tensions to the forms of the old. Those born as gentlemen struggled to restore family fortunes while maintaining their superiority to emancipated convicts and free settlers who were creating their status through their own efforts. The colonies' pressing needs of labour and skilled services induced Governors to allow freeborn and emancipist alike full scope for their energies and ambitions.

While many saw this development as furthering the settlement's supposed aim of reforming the convicts and making them useful members of society, others feared that it was breaking proper restraints and perpetuating in the south the worst features of Britain's lower orders. Governor Lachlan Macquarie welcomed emancipists into government service and the society of government house, considering this as 'the first step towards a general reformation of the manners of the motley part of the population of New South Wales as it then existed' (Clark, *Select Documents*, Vol. 1, p. 311). In 1812, however, the Select Committee on Transportation was less enthusiastic. It noted that the means by which some emancipists had 'accumulated immense fortunes' were often dubious. The common pattern was first 'keeping a public house, then lending money on mortgage; he then obtains landed property, and large flocks, the latter frequently consisting of stolen cattle which he has purchased'. Although many of these convicts, 'if industrious', were able to make 'an honest livelihood', the Committee observed that they were exposed to 'every description of temptation' and that 'the greater number of them retain the habits of profligacy which first led them into crime', becoming 'still more worthless and dissipated'. Commissioner J.T. Bigge in 1822 extended the scope of his disapproval to those who through Macquarie's patronage had risen to respected positions in society. 'The elevation of these persons to a rank in society which they had never possessed, and for which, without meaning any reflection upon them, their manners give them no kind of claim, has not been productive of the benefits that were contemplated' (Clark, *Select Documents*, Vol. 1, pp. 137–40).

William C. Wentworth

William Charles Wentworth put the case for full citizenship for former convicts and their descendants in his *Statistical, Historical and Political Description of New South Wales* (1819, pp. 348–51). He points out that to exclude them would 'convert the ignominy of the great body of people into an hereditary deformity' and turn 'what was intended as an asylum for repentant vice, not into a house merely of correction, which may moderate with reviving morality and cease entirely with complete reformation, but into a prison of endless torture, where though the sufferings of the body may terminate, the worst species of torture, the endurements and mortifications of the soul, are to end only with existence'. Wentworth concludes

with a moving plea that the former convict should not be required for ever to 'wander a recreant and outcast on the face of the earth, seeking in vain some friendly shore, where he may at length be freed from ignominious disabilities, and restored to the long lost enjoyment of equal rights and equal protection from his fellows' (Clark, *Select Documents*, Vol. 1, pp. 308–9).

It is not irrelevant that Wentworth was born in Australia, although he spent some years in England at school and again later studying at Cambridge and for the law at the Inner Temple. He was concerned not so much to transplant an English society as to create in Australia the conditions that would enable such a society to develop of its own accord. He saw that this required equal rights for all before the law. The language he uses suggests a concern for the emancipated, and indeed the convicts, as fellow humans and not merely as objects of policy. His morality is a personal one based on a sense of identity, not an official one based duty or social utility. He recognised that the necessities of the new society meant that no lasting structures could develop until they were based on a recognition of common bonds and common interests.

Wentworth was a member of the party that played a crucial role in the history of inland exploration. In 1813, with William Lawson and Gregory Blaxland, he led the party that, by finding a way through the Blue Mountains, enabled the colonists to break out of the coastal pocket in which they had up till then been penned.

The Journals of the Explorers

This new phase of history began a different stage of Australian writing — the journal of the explorer. Like the diaries of the first settlers, these works take their form from the pattern of external events and their dramatic force from the qualities of endurance and adaptability required to carry out European purposes in an alien landscape. Although the various explorers were interested in the life of the native inhabitants of the country they traversed, for the most part the Aborigines avoided them, and appear only fleetingly in the narratives. The inland explorers, therefore, found much the same antagonists as the sea venturers — the elements of nature and the discord, or potential discord, within their own parties. Their journals continue the tradition of the discoverers. Like Cook and Banks, they tell of the difficulties encountered, the means taken to overcome them and the novelties discovered. Unlike the diaries of settlement, the accounts of the explorers move in space as well as time. They have a topographic dimension. The geometric survey of the countryside and the resulting maps, together with a discussion of features of scenic, scientific and economic interest, form an integral part of the journals. But the coincidence of the dimensions of time and space also gives the expeditions a purpose. The dramatic form of the journals depends on the achievement or frustration of this purpose.

Blaxland's account of the first crossing of the Blue Mountains was not published until 1823, ten years after the event. By this time he and Lawson had taken up land grants made to them as a reward for their discoveries, and Wentworth was completing his studies at Cambridge. Here in 1823 he had written his nationalistic poem 'Australasia', which he entered for the Chancellor's medal. Meanwhile, the district of Bathurst had been settled, and Evans and Oxley had explored the western slopes and discovered the upper reaches of the Lachlan and Macquarie rivers.

Oxley's speculations on his discoveries, in the journal he published in 1820, established the myth of an inland sea that was to lure explorers for another fifty years, and that still surfaces in Australian dreams of turning the coastal rivers back to water the dead heart of the continent. More pragmatic explorers followed the tangible goal of pastoral settlement. Hume and Hovell pioneered the overland route to Port Phillip in 1824, and in 1827 Cunningham discovered the rich Darling Downs and a route from them to the settlement at Moreton Bay. By 1836 Cunningham, Sturt and Mitchell had completed the main exploration of the parts of Australia that still support the greater part of its population.

The accounts of all these expeditions reflect the utilitarian purpose that drove them — the hope of finding land that would be useful for settlement. Yet behind this practical intent still lay the old vision of establishing a new commonwealth in the south. This vision, which formed the substance of Wentworth's celebratory poem, had already been embodied by Macquarie's emancipist poet-laureate, Michael Massey Robinson, in his effusions to mark royal birthdays. Bigge patronisingly described him as one who, had he remained in England, 'would have had the satisfaction of printing his odes, instead of being raised to the titular honours of poet laureat to the government of New South Wales, and reciting his poetry in the government house on birth days' (Clark, *Select Documents*, Vol. 1, p. 140).

Bigge's estimate of Robinson's poetic skills is just, but the eighteenth-century heroics of the verse helped to construct the image of noble endeavour that enabled explorers and settlers to endure their lot. Where the explorers kept their eye on the detail, Robinson translated their deeds into generalisations of glory. In 'Ode for the Queen's Birthday' (1816), he writes:

Tracts of untravers'd EARTH their Toils explore,
And add new Triumphs to AUSTRALIA'S Shore!

The end of their endeavours is to prepare the way for the triumph of Art over Nature, as human art

Taught the reluctant stubborn Glebe to yield,
And in the Desart sprung the cultur'd field. —
She shar'd their Triumph, and with liberal smile,
Disclos'd the rich Resources of the Soil . . .

Elliot and Mitchell, p. 12.

By contrast, Blaxland describes the momentous climax of his party's trek in the most matter-of-fact manner:

In the afternoon, they ascended its summit, from whence they descried all around, forest or grassland, sufficient in extent, in their opinion, to support the stock of the colony for the next thirty years.

Kathleen Fitzpatrick,
Australian Explorers, OUP,
London, 1958, p. 38.

For another fifty years writers attempted to inflate their observations in the style of Robinson, imposing alien forms on native experience in order to inflate its importance. Wentworth's 'Australasia' (London, 1823) accurately lists the tasks facing the new settlers, but puts them in a language that recalls the neatly ordered scenes of English rural poetry and the classical modes of Virgil. He describes the settlers labouring

. . . to lay with lusty blow
The ancient giants of the forest low,
With frequent fires the cumber'd plain to clear,
To tame the steed, and yoke the stubborn steer,
With cautious plough to rip the virgin earth,
And watch the first-born harvest to its birth

George Mackaness (ed.),
An Anthology of Australian Verse,
Angus & Robertson, Sydney, 1952, p. 375.

He intends his carefully chosen adjectives to confer classical dignity on their task. Instead, by leaping directly to a vision of the finished product, a manufactured landscape, he denigrates its achievement by ignoring the backbreaking labour and frustration the task of settlement actually required.

Behind poetry of this kind is the eighteenth-century concept that the role of poetry, as of science, is to reveal the pattern of reason that underlies the confusing surface of life. But the circumstances of Australian life disclosed no such pattern, and the attempts to impose one rang as false as the attempts to impose English decorum on a society where convicts, gaolers, adventurers and misfits jostled each other up and down the ladders of success. Australia, socially as well as geographically, was England's underworld, where were found 'all things in their imagined counterpart'.

William Wentworth
(*State Library of NSW*)

The labour of herding, clearing and farming, rather than the words of hopeful bards, produced Australians' image of themselves. The dream of settlement finished too often in failure for arcadian heroics to carry any conviction. Although the dream continued to provide bombast for the public orations that became a characteristic part of Australian life, the popular literature of yarn and ballad emphasised the failure. Rather than heroes and yeomen farmers, the currency tradition of the Australian frontier produced the images of the laconic bushman and the un-illusioned battler. These images appear first in the convict songs and laments, which correct the dreams of reformation through honest toil with the facts of forced labour. 'Frank the Poet' spoke for his fellows when he complained:

Growing weary from compulsive toil beneath the
    noontide sun
While drops of sweat bedew the soil my task
    remains undone;
I'm flogged for wilful negligence, or the tyrants
    call it so —
Ah what a dreary recompense for labouring with
    the hoe.

Douglas Stewart and Nancy Keesing (eds.),
Old Bush Songs,
Angus & Robertson, Sydney, 1957, p. 27.

This experience in turn generated the ideal of the bushranger, such as Bold Jack Donohue or the Wild Colonial Boy who wander the ranges only to die in battle against the authorities.

In most cases, the Australian explorers followed the examples of Blaxland and Cunningham and avoided the heroics of the poets. With the notable exception of Major Mitchell, they set down plainly the reality they discovered in the new world rather than trying to force it into patterns learned from the old. Their journals found in England a ready audience that had been influenced by Wordsworth and Dickens. These readers were coming to see the world not so much as a system of ordered classification and rules, but as a unity in which the behaviour of every part influenced every other. They judged action by its results rather than by abstract laws, and believed truth lay in the infinite variety of life rather than in a system behind it.

The conflict between this mode of perception and

the mechanistic mode that reduces all experience to inflexible rules runs deeply through nineteenth-century thought. It arises in Britain, where the industrial, economic and political systems had grown beyond the control of the individual. Australia, by contrast, seemed a new land offering its explorers and settlers the chance to step outside the industrial system and control their own destiny. In practice, it frustrated this promise of freedom with the facts of drought and desert. The journals of the explorers show their patient attempts to find meaning in this alternation of promise and frustration, in the gap between the high hopes with which they embark on their expeditions and the bleak reality of their discoveries.

Interpretations of the Landscape

Frustration looms greater than success in the record of Australian exploration. Evans and Oxley discovered the fine upper reaches of the Lachlan and Macquarie only to be frustrated in their attempts to trace the course of the river. The journeys of Hume and Hovell to Port Phillip, and Cunningham through the Darling Downs, were among the few successes, opening up routes to new pastures. Sturt conducted his expeditions with efficiency and compassion, tracing the Murrumbidgee and then the Murray to its mouth, but the hardships of his last journey led him to desert instead of an inland sea and fertile pastures, and forced him to turn back still short of the geographic centre of Australia that he had hoped to reach. Mitchell's narratives fitted his achievements into the pattern of Camoens' epic poem of Portuguese exploration, the *Lusiads*, which he had translated. He saw himself as a Vasco da Gama discovering a new empire, but those who followed him found too frequently that his triumphant descriptions outran reality. Yet, despite the meagre success of their expeditions, the journals of these explorers show them moving beyond the search for economic opportunity to a fascination with the land itself.

The journal of Hume and Hovell is in much the same pattern as that of Blaxland — a record of hardships endured and problems faced and overcome. When they do eventually reach their destination, 'the so long and ardently-desired bourn of their labours', they comment that the Aborigines appear similar to those of Sydney, that the harbour 'consists of an immense sheet of water', and that the 'soil throughout the plains appeared good, in some places to a considerable extent, and to afford a particularly fine dry sheep pasturage . . .' (Fitzpatrick, p. 78). The pragmatic hope of the last phrase is of a different order of excitement from the enthusiasms of the poets.

Other expeditions were led by government officials who were also, in various senses, scientists. In their accounts we find, as well as notes of material advantages, the scientist's interest in knowledge for its own sake. As they come to accept the land, so they discover its own beauty.

Evans, as well as commenting that the country through which he passes provides plentiful game and is well suited to grazing, repeatedly talks of it as 'handsome' and 'beautiful'. He finishes his account with a plea that he be given the opportunity to join any further expedition to the area, for 'no Country can have a more interesting aspect . . . I am deficient in abilities to describe it properly, but shall endeavour to do so by comparing the country to an Ocean . . . Spaces clear of trees may be imagined as islands, and the Natives Smokes, rising in various points, vessels; it is a clear calm evening near Sunsetting, which shewed every part advantageously' (Fitzpatrick, p. 49). The writer's search for the appropriate simile is an attempt to describe what he sees rather than impose a pattern on it.

Oxley, who had tried to navigate the streams Evans had discovered, was less impressed with the countryside. Rather than accept it for itself, he tried to assimilate it by imposing familiar names, explaining that 'The naming of places was often the only pleasure within our reach; but it was some relief from the desolation of these plains and hills to throw over them the associations of names dear to friendship, or sacred to genius' (Fitzpatrick, p. 61). Yet even Oxley could succumb to the lure of place. He writes of how the 'river expanded into beautiful reaches, having a great depth of water, and from two to three hundred feet broad, literally covered with water-fowl of different kinds: the richest flats bordered the river' (Fitzpatrick, p. 63). The beauty of the river intensified the riddle of its destination, although Oxley was not to have the opportunity of solving it.

Like Oxley, the botanist Allan Cunningham felt the desolation of the countryside, but for him this was in itself a reason to explore it. Unlike Evans, he travelled in a time of drought, so that he found that 'although the land was, generally speaking, rich, and productive of much grass, it was, nevertheless, distressing to meet with tracts, many miles in extent, entirely destitute of water' (Fitzpatrick, p. 82). But even such country he finds interesting, so that, when he at last is able to get an extensive view of the plains to the north, he describes the desolate scene almost with a sense of awe: 'the line of sight extended over a great extent of densely wooded, or brushed, land, the monotonous aspect of which was here and there relieved by a brown patch of plain: of these, some were so remote as to appear a mere speck on the *ocean* of land before us, on which the eye sought anxiously for a rising smoke, as indicative of the wandering aborigines; but in vain: for, excepting in the immediate neighbourhood of a river of the larger magnitude, these vast solitudes may be fairly said to be almost entirely without inhabitants' (Fitzpatrick, p. 83). This sight prompts in him 'an anxious curiosity to explore so extraordinary a region'. Cunningham's account reaches its climax with his discovery of the rich Darling Downs, but just as this discovery is given point by the contrast with the desolate country Cunningham has passed through on his way, so the record of these barren plains and difficult mountains gives the narrative as a whole its particular interest.

The leaders of all these expeditions were practical men whose accounts were given their form by the events of the journeys and the discoveries made. Even the expressions of emotion seem forced from them by their encounter with the land. When we turn to the narratives of the two greatest of this group of early explorers, we find a more self-conscious use of literary models, so that their form is given by the conception of the journey and its results rather than merely by the sequence of events. Major Mitchell, later Sir Thomas Livingstone Mitchell, shapes his account as an epic tale of the opening of a brave new world. Captain Charles Sturt, more conscious of immediate human factors, and of the comparative failure of his expeditions, shapes his two accounts as a tragedy. The works of the two men thus stand for the two aspects of a common Australian experience.

Sir Thomas Mitchell

Mitchell was the most successful of Australian explorers. Not only did his expedition to south-eastern Australia achieve everything he set out to do, but it opened up fertile grazing lands to settlement. His success represented the triumph of a rational plan executed through careful organisation and recorded in maps and narrative that bring the unknown into orderly relation with the old. The land is mapped, its features named, and the whole thrown open for the extension of a society grounded in the civilisation of the Romans.

Official expeditions comprised large parties under the direction of a leader, who was thus involved in a triangular relationship between himself, the party for which he was responsible, and the land they traversed. Mitchell, as a military man, was particularly conscious of his role as commander, and his prose accordingly has a sweep which is detached and comprehensive. He is a surveyor in both senses. He conscientiously measures the land with chain and compass, himself using the compass while his assistants bear the chain. He also looks over the land, comprehending its features in a single view that takes in geography and history, his own role in revealing the features of the countryside, and the future that will follow from it. We see both aspects as he writes of the expedition's southward turn from the junction of the Darling with the Murray: 'We had now got through the most unpromising part of our task. We had penetrated the Australian Hesperides — although the golden fruit was still to be sought. We had accomplished so much, however, with only half the party, that nothing seemed impossible with the whole; and to trace the Murray upwards and explore the unknown regions beyond it, was a charming undertaking, when we had at length to bid adieu, for ever, to the dreary banks of the Darling . . .' (Fitzpatrick, p. 128). Mitchell consciously sets himself in the tradition of the classical hero whose endurance in obedience to his commands will, like that of Hercules, be rewarded with golden fruit to take back as a gift to his masters.

By contrast, in his account of the crossing of the Murray three days later, Mitchell shows that he is a practical man as well as a visionary. His men had failed in their attempts to drive the cattle across the river, explaining that 'the bullocks had been too long in the water to be able to cross before the next day; but having first tried their plan, I now determined to try my own; and I directed them to take the cattle to the steepest portion of the bank . . .' (Fitzpatrick, pp. 128–9). This attempt is successful, as the reader expects, for Mitchell shapes his narrative in detail as well as in the whole to describe his progress through difficulties to a success that he invites the reader to share. This offer was actual as well as metaphorical, and overlanding squatters were quick to follow Mitchell's tracks and establish their flocks on the lands he had opened for them.

Although Mitchell celebrates his own role as leader, he acknowledges the labours of his followers, particularly the Aborigines. He writes that he cannot fairly distinguish these from the the the white, 'for in most of our difficulties by flood and field, the intelligence and skill of our sable friends made the "white fellows" appear rather stupid' (Fitzpatrick, p. 136).

Mitchell's account reaches its climax as he leads his party into western Victoria, which he names Australia Felix, Australia the fortunate. He describes the countryside in ever more glowing terms as he prepares the reader for this event. The prospect in front of the expedition offers promise of splendour in 'a complete view of a noble range of mountains, rising in the south to a stupendous height, and presenting as bold and picturesque outline as ever painter imagined' (Fitzpatrick, p. 139). Then he reaches the moment of triumph:

We had at length discovered a country ready for the immediate reception of civilized man; and destined perhaps to become eventually a portion of a great empire. Unencumbered by too much wood, it yet possessed enough for all purposes; its soil was exuberant, and its climate temperate; it was bounded on three sides by the ocean; and it was traversed by mighty rivers, and watered by streams innumerable. Of this Eden I was the first European to explore its mountains and streams — to behold its scenery — to investigate its geological character, and, by my survey, to develop those natural advantages, certain to become, at no distant date, of vast importance to a new people . . .

Fitzpatrick, p. 139.

The mounting rhythms of this passage convey Mitchell's justified excitement at his achievement, which he relives in his writing. The rhythms also serve to bring together in harmony the various elements of this vision, which we can trace as much to traditional sources as to the particular experience. Every term in the description is general, and takes us away from any specific element of the landscape to a broad category. The view is seen as in perspective, framed by the 'noble range' he has recently passed. In the foreground are not particular kinds of tree, but wood that meets human needs without interfering with the view. From the woods Mitchell moves (by an act of imagination) to a long view that encompasses not only what is actually in sight but the three bordering oceans, the 'mighty rivers' and 'streams innumerable'. Then he passes to the culminating categorisation of the place as Eden, a source of both Arcadian and Utopian imagery, but also, and simultaneously, as a place of scientific interest and of economic use to 'a new people', who are linked to the destiny of becoming citizens of 'the great empire' he has already foreseen. Thus, in projecting the future onto his present discovery, he fits it exactly into a framework of past glory.

Although Mitchell gives a sympathetic account of the Aborigines he encounters on his expedition, and is appreciative of the abilities of Piper, his Aboriginal assistant, he has no doubts that the future destiny of the country is to support a white civilisation. He appreciates the country for what it may be rather than what it is, and sees solitude as waste: 'The scenery around them, the excellent quality of the soil, the abundance of water and verdure, contrasted strangely with the circumstance of their lying waste and unoccupied. It was evident that the reign of solitude in these vales was near a close; a reflection which, in my mind, often sweetened the toil and inconveniences of travelling through such houseless regions . . .' (Fitzpatrick, p. 139). This anticipation gives his narrative its shape and tone, and links him with that part of nineteenth-century thought that believed in the inevitability of human progress.

The self-consciously literary mode and heroic posture make Mitchell's journal exceptional among its contemporaries. The more characteristically sombre and stoic note is struck in Edward John Eyre's account of his journey along the shores of the Australian Bight. The central point of this narrative is his clash with the Aborigines and its tragic outcome. The whole narrative is framed by the dramatic contrast between the proud party that sets out and the sad pair who complete the journey. This melancholy note offsets the triumph of the achievement, and anticipates the dominant tone of the journals of Mitchell's great contemporary, Captain Charles Sturt.

Captain Charles Sturt

Although Sturt shared Mitchell's background and outlook, he had also a compassion that linked him imaginatively with his companions. The misfortunes he experienced denied him the satisfaction of achievement and recognition but also shaped his outlook towards the tragic. He is remembered in history as one of Australia's most courageous and humane explorers, whose expedition traced the destination of the continent's greatest river, the Murray, but his account of this expedition expresses satisfaction only that his 'path among a large and savage population was a bloodless one; and that my intercourse with them was such as to lessen the danger to future adventurers upon such hazardous enterprizes' (Fitzpatrick, p. 92). He does allow himself in his account of the journey down the Murray the satisfaction of knowing that he eventually returned safely, and dwells on the delight of the prospect he found at the mouth of the river:

> It was now near sunset; and one of the most lovely evenings I had ever seen. The sun's radiance was yet upon the mountains, but all the lower objects were in shade. The banks of the channel, with the trees and the rocks, were reflected in the tranquil waters, whose surface was unruffled save by the thousands of wild fowl that rose before us, and made a noise as of a multitude of clapping hands, in their clumsy efforts to rise from the waters. Not one of them allowed us to get within shot . . .
>
> We had been quite delighted with the beauty of the channel, which was rather more than half-a-mile in width. Numberless mounds, that seemed to invite civilized man to erect his dwelling upon them, presented themselves to our view. The country round them was open, yet ornamentally wooded, and rocks and trees hung or drooped over the waters.

Fitzpatrick, p. 122.

This passage, like Mitchell's of Australia Felix, is a set-piece of description. The view of the waters in the centre, with the sun's light above and rocks or trees around the border and water fowl rising from the centre, is composed as carefully as a landscape painting. The mood is conveyed through a precise attention to detail that indicates the romantic desire to achieve truth from fidelity to experience. Yet the picture is not merely romantic — the mood is generated not only by the moment but by the placing of that moment at the culmination of a hazardous and often trying journey. It is modified both by the utilitarian vision of the future settlement that Sturt envisages succeeding his romantic solitude, and by the practical man's implicit admission of his desire to get within shooting distance of the game whose appearance he can still enjoy aesthetically from a distance.

These moments of joy are, like the times of trial, placed by Sturt within the distancing framework of a providence whom he invokes at the beginning of his account:

> Something more powerful, than human foresight or human prudence, appeared to avert the calamities and dangers with which I and my companions were so frequently threatened; and had it not been for the guidance and protection we received from the Providence of that good and all-wise Being to whose care we committed ourselves, we should, ere this, have ceased to rank among the number of His earthly creatures.

Fitzpatrick, p. 92.

Sturt's God is neither the impersonal designer of the universe nor the personal God who examines the soul, but rather a power whose will is revealed only in its outcome. He strengthens the endurance of the individual while absolving him from responsibility for the results of his actions. He is a God for humans confronting circumstances beyond their control, rather than for those who believe they are obeying divine will by making their own fate.

Sturt's belief in providence shaped his view of his journeys as a series of tests of his faith and courage. Thus the narrative of the voyage down the Murray falls neatly into three sections, like the three acts of a drama. The first is his search for the Murrumbidgee and his realisation, on starting to follow its course by land, that he is engaged on a futile endeavour and will instead have to send half his party back and entrust the rest to the boats. The second is his encounter with Aborigines who threaten death to his party. The third is the decision he makes after crossing the lake at the mouth of the Murray to turn back and slog the return voyage against the current rather than risk trying a voyage across the strait to Launceston, a decision he takes, he says, 'as much without hopes of our eventual safety, as I was astonished, at the close of our labours, to find they had terminated so happily'. In each case he weighs the human factors as carefully as the physical, and as a consequence his narrative gives us the feeling of sharing a human drama rather than merely watching a pageant of figures in a landscape.

Sturt is the first of the existential heroes in Australian literature. His faith in God gives him the courage to stand alone, but it was not the faith of Mitchell who was confident that God was on his side. Sturt acted although he was unsure of the outcome, and the emphasis of his narrative therefore falls on human encounters and decisions.

Sturt's encounter with the Aborigines who menaced him from a sandbank as his whaleboat drew inexorably nearer tested him to the utmost. The Aborigines are the great blank of early Australian literature, as they are of Australian history and Australian law, which declared the continent before white settlement as a *terra nullius*, a land of nobody. In the absence of a recognised enemy, white settlers achieved their success by enduring against the elements rather than by winning the kind of victory demanded by both classical and biblical models of heroism. Sturt's encounter was the stuff of just such heroic achievement. Although his description of the

event omits no drama, his emphasis falls on the courage of patience rather than that of conflict:

> The distance was too trifling for me to doubt the fatal effects of the discharge [of his rifle] for I was determined to take deadly aim, in hopes that the fall of one man might save the lives of many. But at the very moment, when my hand was on the trigger, and my eye was along the barrel, my purpose was checked by M'Leay, who called to me that another party of blacks had made their appearance upon the left bank of the river. Turning round, I observed four men at the top of their speed. The foremost of them as soon as he got ahead of the boat, threw himself from a considerable height into the water. He struggled across the channel to the sand-bank, and in an incredibly short space of time stood in front of the savage, against whom my aim had been directed. Seizing him by the throat, he pushed him backwards, and forcing all who were in the water upon the bank, he trod its margin with a vehemence and agitation that were exceedingly striking.

> Fitzpatrick, p. 108.

The drama of this moment depends on Sturt's waiting on events, but this clear confrontation was not to be characteristic of his journeys, and his last expedition in fact ended, in his eyes, in his failure to realise long deferred hope. His antagonist was this time not the Aborigines but the land. Again he led a large party, and was able to find his way in pursuit of the inland sea out beyond the Darling to a creek which proved to be a prison. He could find no water ahead, and there was not enough left behind to make his way back. For six months he waited by the waterhole, watching the water and his supplies dwindle and the wildlife depart. All attempts he made to find a way ahead were unavailing, and his party suffered the effects of heat, monotony and scurvy. When at last it did rain, he sent some of the party back while he again pushed on for the centre with the remainder, but they were overtaken on the first day by a man who reported that his deputy had died on the journey home. He tried again, eventually pushing on through the endless sandhills and gibber plains of Simpson's Desert with only three companions, but was eventu-

Sturt's Party Threatened by Blacks
(*National Library of Australia*)

ally forced to admit defeat and turn home.

The account of this expedition could be as tedious as the country through which he struggled if Sturt had not brought to it the same dramatic sense with which he told the story of the encounter with the Aborigines on the Murray. The introduction to the narrative deepens the stoicism of the first journal by adding to it a tragic sense of the inevitable failure of all human endeavours, so that even the settlement of Adelaide that had followed his successful voyage is shown as a part of the mysterious workings of God rather than a reward for service:

To all who were employed in that undertaking, it had proved one of the severest trial and of the greatest privation; to myself individually it had been one of ceaseless anxiety. We had not, it seems, made any discovery to gild our enterprise, had found no approximate country likely to be of advantage to the Government by which we had been sent forth; the noble river on whose buoyant waters we were hurried along, seemed to have been misplaced, through such an extent of desert did it pass, as if it was destined thus never to be of service to civilized man . . . although at the termination of the Murray, we came upon a country, the aspect of which indicated more than usual richness and fertility, we were unable, from exhausted strength, to examine it as we wished . . . The course of events has abundantly shown how presumptuous we were to question the arrangements of that All-wise Power whose operations and purposes are equally hidden from us, for in six short years from the time when I crossed Lake Victoria [now Lake Alexandrina] . . . that country formed another link in the chain of settlement round the Australian continent . . . Its rich and lovely valleys, which in a state of nature were seldom trodden by the foot of the savage, became the happy retreats of an industrious peasantry . . .

Fitzpatrick, p. 254.

Thus, although he still professes the Arcadian hopes for Australia as a land of happy peasants, he no longer believes that this will be achieved by human endeavour, but only through the will of an inscrutable God.

Just as Mitchell can be regarded as the last explorer from the age of reason, so Sturt can be considered the first to demonstrate that the struggle for the possession of Australia demanded the abandonment of the attempt to impose external patterns on experience. He accepted instead the existence of experience in time, and the way that our experience of events imposes its own patterns on our understanding of them.

New Images

Mitchell's vision of a new golden age and Sturt's image of the lonely explorer struggling with his own doubts in a hostile or indifferent world provided myths that have endured in Australian writing and in the idea of Australia. Mitchell's arcadian vision lacked human passion, leaving only an order that could not adapt to new circumstances. When Mitchell encountered Aborigines who did not fit his vision he shot them. Sturt's explorer, on the other hand, belongs outside society where, like the Israelites in the desert, he struggles with his God, but this God offers a Promised Land neither in this life nor the next. His vision, too, has been stiffened into a code of law, even if this governs the individual rather than society. His tragedy is Roman rather than Greek, the tragedy of the solitary man who endures rather than of the visionary who risks everything and fails.

In the fifty years since settlement Australia had grown from a convict colony to a collection of settlements with a total white population of 150 000. In these settlements, a small governing class sought to impose rule on a society. Settlers constantly moved out to try to grab land and establish their own little kingdoms, convicts and free labourers struggled against the attempts of the law to maintain them forever in a subordinate and docile role, and storekeepers and traders tried to make money from everyone. Australia became neither a Garden of Eden nor a place of rural retreat, but a marketplace of greed. Yet the lure of the unknown remained strong, and explorers continued to set out for the interior and to publish journals of their discoveries.

Later explorers such as Burke and Wills, Leichhardt and Gregory have provided by their fates images that continue to reverberate through Australian literature. The greatest feats of Australian exploration were achieved between 1874 and 1876 by Ernest Giles. His laconic accounts of his travels constitute a fascinating portrait of a man who relied for survival on his own abilities and knowledge rather than on the lavish equipment of an official party. These later explorers were engaged in pushing out the bounds of settlement, and saw the country with the same eyes as those of Mitchell and Sturt and their contemporaries. The journals of the settlers, and the poets and novelists who interpreted their work, provided new images of the country.

3

NEW SETTLEMENTS

If only a receptacle for convicts be intended, this place stands unequalled . . .

Watkin Tench

THE expedition of Lawson, Blaxland and Wentworth opened the way for the settlement of the western slopes of the Great Dividing Range, and those of Hume and Hovell, Mitchell and Cunningham showed the ways south and north. It took a quarter of a century for the inhabitants of the first settlement to find a way across the mountain barrier, but in the next twenty-five years virtually all the areas of Australia that were to be settled had been opened to Europeans. The overlanders followed the explorers, the city businessmen made money by advancing the necessary capital, and convicts and subsidised immigrants provided their labour, sometimes with the reluctant assistance of the native-born, whose upbringing had taught them that work was a penalty imposed by a penal system. Yet these different classes held the common aim of making homes for themselves in the new land. Only slowly did it dawn on them that this meant making the new land their home.

For a minority of colonists, making a home in Australia was only the preliminary step towards making one in England. Whether they intended to remain in the colony or return to the north, all accepted the northern model of what was desirable.

Female Factory, Parramatta
(*National Library of Australia*)

They designed their buildings, public and private, on European models. They cleared the native scrub and planted gardens and parks with European trees. But the written word, like the social life that generated it, went beyond European rules of decorum and gentility. The earliest newspapers are filled with vitriolic attacks on the government and bitter diatribes among the local politicians. Apart from memoirs of settlement and exploration, the early local publications include histories with the polemical purpose of arguing a political case. The writers include such noted controversialists as W.C. Wentworth, whose *Statistical, Historical and Political Description of New South Wales* appeared in 1819, John Dunmore Lang, whose *Historical and Statistical Account of New South Wales* came out in 1834, and Caroline Chisholm, whose *Female Immigration* was published in 1842.

These works were intended to develop pride in the community and encourage its development along the lines their authors believed desirable. Other writers, however, were more interested in highlighting the lurid and unique, the qualities that inspired interest in the colony at the expense of respectability. As early as 1818, Thomas Wells published *Michael Howe, the Last and Worst of the Bushrangers*, which was followed by the autobiographical *Memoirs of James Hardy Vaux* in 1819. There was also a host of broadsheet literature in the same vein as its English counterparts, with bloodthirsty confessions and piteous speeches from the scaffold by prisoners about to be executed.

While this debate and reportage created a lively undergrowth of literature in Australia, the poets, rather in the fashion of the gardeners and architects, sought to give the colony true dignity by making the highest of the arts at home there. We have already considered the laudatory verse of Wentworth and Robinson. The Chief Justice, Barron Field, went further than occasional verse, and in 1819 published his collection as a book, *First Fruits of Australian Poetry*. In these poems Field, who spent only seven years in Australia, attempts to shed an air of romance over its native life. In 'Botany Bay Flowers', he hopes to rescue Australia's flowers and insects from Science, by which they have been

> gather'd and dissected, press'd and dried,
> Till all their blood and beauty are extinct;
> And nam'd in barb'rous Latin . . .

> Elliot and Mitchell, p. 14.

and restore them to their proper realm of poetry. Science, Field claims, seeks facts rather than truth, but his own powers are inadequate to his aim. At best he succeeds only in casting a net of fancy rather than of imagination over the creatures he tries to recruit for Queen Mab's fairy train. John Dunmore Lang had great fun at Field's expense, and claimed that his 'Botany Bay Flowers' were suitable only as physic, for 'one grain for a doze/Would make a

badger vomit, I suppose'. Yet it is difficult not to mock a poet who could commence a poem, even one written in the spirit of jollity, with lines such as these from 'The Kangaroo':

> Kangaroo, Kangaroo!
> Thou Spirit of Australia,
> That redeems from utter failure
> . . . this fifth part of the earth

> Elliot and Mitchell, p. 17.

Charles Tompson

When we turn to the work of the first native-born white poet, Charles Tompson, whose collection *Wild Notes, from the Lyre of a Native Minstrel* appeared in Sydney in 1826 while he was still under twenty we find the same assumptions both about the function of poetry and the future destiny of Australia. Tompson writes of what he sees and knows. His diction is correspondingly more direct, but his perceptions are still shaped by the vision of Australia as 'The brightest gem in Albion's crown'. In 'A Song for 26 January 1824', this is the place where

> Peace lifts her olive sceptre high,
> Brown Industry assumes the plough,
> Commerce expands her canvas wings,
> Wealth points where honour guides the prow;
> These, happy Australia, these
> Proclaim thee 'Queen of Southern Seas!'

> Mackaness (ed.), *Anthology of Australian Verse*, p. 365.

The vision of the future leads immediately to generalisation. Even his slighter poems, on love or on an Australian winter, fall into the accepted modes of poetry as a repository of higher feelings rather than a search for truth. When he writes in 'Black Town' of the abandoned mission to the Aborigines, there is no doubting his good will, but the whole falls into the mode of pathetic pastoral made familiar in England by Goldsmith in 'The Deserted Village' or Burns in 'The Cotter's Saturday Night'. The poem conveys the sense of lost opportunity, but the opportunity he envisaged remains completely detached from the lives of those to whom it was offered:

Ill-fated hamlet! from each tott'ring shed,
Thy sable inmates perhaps for ever fled . . .
Seek, with the birds, the casual dole of heaven,
Pleas'd with their lot — content with what is giv'n.

Time was, and recent mem'ry speaks it true,
When round each little cot a garden grew,
A field whose culture serv'd a two-fold part,
Food and instruction in the rural art.

Elliott and Mitchell, p. 26.

Were it not for the reference to 'the sable inmates' and later to the 'darkling child', the account could equally refer to the gardens and hopes of a convict settlement, or to one of the deserted British villages that Tompson had never seen. The novelty is in including the Aborigines in the rural vision, and thus recognising them as human rather than as a problem. However, the pious climax of the poem, with the 'sable proselyte's' progress from salvation through learning to true manhood as Britannia consummates her plan to 'Christianize the world!' reduces the apparent subjects of the poem once more to objects, the instruments of another's ambitions. Both the vision and the philanthropy get in the way of any recognition of the actual plight of the people who were being dispossessed, just as the myths of the future distort the dispossessors' views both of the society they were building and of the land they were trying to tame.

Yet Tompson has at times a directness that is the reverse of the inflated rhetoric of his predecessors. His elegy on 'Winter in Argyleshire' (in NSW) begins with lines that quickly place his conventional gloom in the southern hemisphere:

With cheerless gloom and storm-portending clouds
    Rude Winter brushes from Antarctic wilds,
The front of Heav'n, in murky vapours shrouds,
    Then bursts his sounding freightage o'er our isles.
No more are heard the thrush's mellow notes,
    No more the plover mounts the ev'ning breeze,
No more the soaring lark on aether floats,
    Spoil'd of their honours, mourn the leafless trees.

Elliott and Mitchell, p. 28.

The subject of the poem is the conventional gloom of winter, but amid the poetic trappings the Antarctic and the plover remind the reader that the place is Australia. While Robinson and Wentworth, like their English models, impose a northern view on their Australian subject, Tompson starts with the local subject, but his attempt to confer poetic dignity on it restricts him to a language that fashions his experience back into an English form. Like the artists, the poets had to learn to see before they could compose.

Literature of the Convict System

While the poets manufactured elevated images of life in Australia, the writers on convictism were all too happy to wallow in its depravity. They conferred an awesome if false dignity on their subjects while giving their readers both the pleasure of reading about vice and the sanctimonious delight of disapproving of it.

The literature of the convict system gives voice to those elements of human nature and society that the system had been intended to eliminate from England and to reform or control in Australia. The memoirs of convict experience by Joseph Holt and James Hardy Vaux, and the tale of the bushranger Michael Howe, like the broadsides sold after executions and purporting to give the felons' last words, express the violence and brutality that was the common lot. Their protest is, however, limited by the concentration on the sensational and the bizarre, and controlled by a framework of morality. The experience of the convicts themselves finds only a faint voice in the literature.

The broadsides, with their tales of bushranging, cannibalism, massacre by land, and piracy and mutiny by sea, express the fears that underlay the system. One aspect of these is the belief in the inherent savagery of the underclasses, who can be controlled only by the most rigorous discipline and morality. The confessions on the scaffold therefore emphasise both the brutality of the crimes and the repentance of the criminal. So we are told of Edward Broughton that:

Whilst the executioner was pinioning the arms and adjusting the rope of the unfortunate *Broughton*, the following statement was read at his express desire, as a full confession of his awful crime.

Broughton said . . . He more than once endeavoured to rob his own mother, and his horrible conduct was the means of breaking his father's heart, and hurrying him to the grave . . .

> Geoffrey C. Ingleton, *True Patriots All*, Angus & Robertson, Sydney, 1952, p. 125.

The warning offered by the fate of Broughton and his companions appears even more strongly in the first book about a convict, Thomas Wells' *Michael Howe, the Last and Worst of the Bushrangers of Van Diemen's Land* (facsimile with introduction by C. Craig, Platypus Press, Hobart, 1966 [1818]). Howe and his confederates are described as unregenerate villains. The tale of pillage, arson and murder reaches a proper climax as Howe flees alone, feeling himself 'too much a traitor and a villain for the safe admission of a companion or confederate . . . '. The author's description of Howe's lonely flight anticipates Marcus Clarke, who had read this account:

> Thus we find the crimes of this man lead him on, step by step, till he is reduced to prefer the desperate situation of standing opposed to all mankind; compelled unceasingly to watch for his life; certain of seeing an enemy in every face; certain that to suffer himself for a moment to sleep might terminate his miserable existence; certain, too, that in that sleep his enormities would at least visit him with horrid retrospective visions, anticipations of torture, despair, and death . . .

> Wells, p. 23–4.

The nightmares conclude when Howe is eventually taken by deceit and, clubbed by musket butts, 'expired without speaking the last of a lawless, murderous banditti! — exhibiting in his career and end the strongest proof of retributive justice . . .' (p. 33).

Yet behind the pamphlet's account of Howe's brutality we can glimpse a more rational figure. His background and youth were respectable. His early career of crime parallels the activities of the English rickburners who protested in the name of Captain Swing against the injuries done to them by the enclosing landowners who were depriving them of their livelihoods. Howe's letter to the governor and the oath by which he swore his companions similarly follow the precedents of English labourers joining in combinations to protect themselves against the powerful. Finally, the author mentions Howe's 'sort of journal of dreams, which shew strongly the distressed state of his mind, and some tincture of superstition' (p. 31). This diary, written in kangaroo blood on kangaroo skin, suggests a mind broken by isolation and outlawry rather than one sunk in its own brutality.

The description of savage deeds draws attention away from both the sources of convict grievances and the fear that they might combine in effective rebellion. This fear was particularly acute in the case of the Irish convicts, many of whom had been transported for political crimes and all of whom had reason to detest their English masters. It appears in the confession of 'General' Joseph Holt, and the broadside account of the insurrection at Castle Hill, with its references to the rebels' 'concealed directors' and 'secret contrivers'. (*True Patriots All*, pp. 22–3). The description of the savage punishment of the rebels, later to form the subject of Robert Fitzgerald's poem 'The Wind at Your Door', indicates the fear they inspired.

The broadside accounts of contrition on the scaffold reflect the hopes of the audience rather than the feelings of the supposed speakers. We have, perhaps, a more authentic voice in the broadside that tells the story of a merchant's son who has returned to London 'after Suffering Fourteen Years Extreme cruelty'. Although this document concludes with the usual moral appeal to others not to follow the author's example, it seems to have the strength of personal experience in its rejection of the argument of those who believed that transportation was too good a fate for criminals. The author declares:

> . . . should youth but know the sufferings or dreadful afflictions, attached to that of being transported to New South Wales, that many would prefer immediate death, rather than submit to commit such violations as subject felons to that awful doom, and moreover declareth that to be transported to New South Wales is no less than lengthening a torturing death, through which there is but very few out of the vast number which are sent there that liveth out their time, or surpasseth their inhuman, cruel and most barberous punishment . . .

> Clark, *Select Documents*, Vol. 1, p. 150–1.

Such writings fixed in the public mind the image of New South Wales and the other penal colonies as places of suffering rather than hope.

The experience of the individual convict appears to have depended as much on chance as on anything else, although the majority of them seem to have done as well as we might expect of people who in general came from the most depressed and turbulent elements of British society, and who lacked any experience to help them in the new colony. Governor Phillip complained that among his convicts there were 'few who are inclined to be industrious, or who feel themselves in any ways interested in the advantages which are to accrue from their labours' (Clark, *Select Documents*, Vol. 1, p. 54). Many convicts from the First Fleet must indeed have felt like the one whose letter was published in the *Gazetteer* on 29 December, 1790. The letter, of course, refers to a time when conditions in the colony were at their worst:

God only knows what our Governor thinks of it . . . but for my part, from the highest to the lowest, I see nobody that is so contented as they were at first. We fear the troops, and they are not content with seeing those who live better than themselves, nor with us who live worse . . . We have heard of some convicts at home, who might have been pardoned for capital crimes, have chosen their former sentence rather than come here; and which, though it was contradicted, we cannot help thinking it is true . . .

> Clark, *Select Documents*, Vol. 1, p. 53.

Although conditions were to improve later, this letter identifies the essential evil of a closed system that makes everyone suspicious of everybody else.

That the convict system succeeded at all was because outside it a society grew that offered some hope to those convicts who eventually obtained their release, and to those assigned to a position that gave them some opportunity to pursue their own affairs. One such was Henry Tingley, whose letter home was printed with the report of the Select Committee on Transportation in 1835:

I have a place at a farmhouse, and I have got a good master, which I am a great deal more com-

fortable than I expected. I works the same as I were at home; I have plenty to eat and drink, thank God for it . . . Of a night, after I have done my work, I have a chance to make a few shillings . . .

> Clark, *Select Documents*, Vol. 1, p. 131.

Yet the writer was conscious that his contentment depended on remaining in favour, and that the penalties of failure were absolute:

All a man has got to mind is to keep a still tongue in his head, and do his master's duty, and then he he is looked upon as if he were at home; but if he don't he may as well be hung at once, for they would take you to the magistrate's and get 100 lashes, and then get sent to a place called Port Arthur to work in irons for two or three years, and then he is dislike[d] by everyone.

> Clark, *Select Documents*, Vol. 1, p. 131.

The individual might have the fortune to create for himself an area of comparative security, but outside it the system remained absolute. In his book on the subject, Governor Phillip argued that this was the essence of the system, as no encouragement would work unless the alternative were 'a short cut, to the government gang or the penal settlement, where he will be subjected to every privation compatible with the maintenance of his health' (Clark, *Select Documents*, Vol. 1, p. 149). The chilling utilitarianism of the final phrase demonstrates the power of the system to destroy the perception of its officials as much as the bodies of its victims.

Captain Maconochie, who saw the results of the system at its end point on Norfolk Island, where he attempted humanitarian reform, in his book described the operations and results of the system:

1400 doubly-convicted prisoners, the refuse of both penal colonies . . . were rigorously coerced all day, and cooped up at night in barracks which could not decently accommodate half the number. In every way their feelings were habitually outraged and their self-respect destroyed . . . the men's countenances reflected faithfully this description of treatment. A more demoniacal looking assemblage could not be imagined, and nearly the most formidable sight I ever saw was the sea of faces upturned to me when I first addressed them.

Clark, *Select Documents*, Vol. 1, pp. 142-3.

In prefacing his description, Maconochie cites with approval the remark made by a convict to the Revd Dr Ullathorne about Norfolk Island: 'When a prisoner was sent to Norfolk Island he lost the heart of a man, and got that of a beast instead' (Clark, *Select Documents*, Vol. 1, p. 143). This was the point to be taken up by later novelists. In the meantime the free settlers preferred to create a replica of English society on the basis of a convict system whose existence they affected to ignore.

Henry Savery

The manners and morals of this replica of English society were described by Henry Savery in *The Hermit of Van Diemen's Land*, a book of sketches published in Hobart Town in 1829. These employ the device of an observer recently arrived in the colony and describing its society from the detached viewpoint of the outsider. This enables Savery to satirise the identities of his day, and gives the work an irony that reveals the gap between the pretensions of colonial society and its real basis.

The Hermit expects to find a 'a population who, either not having found old England good enough for them, must themselves be the purest of the pure, or who having been purified of their sins by punishment, must now have repented, and . . . become the most virtuous of the virtuous!' (p. 48). He does indeed find that Hobart Town provides a scene of 'bustle and activity', and is distinguished by 'a commodious Wharf, fine Stone-buildings, a Chamber of Commerce, and three Newspapers' (p. 49). His expectations of finding 'a pure and innocent race of beings' (p. 55) are, however, quickly disappointed. The first people he meets are inflated with the importance of their own affairs, his watch is nicked, and the officials he encounters combine the officiousness of their English counterparts with a colonial boorishness of their own.

The colony the Hermit finds has the pretensions of English society without the basis of authority and learning needed to support them. Thus he shows us examples of magistrates completely ignorant of the

law, gentlemen of property incapable of elementary courtesy, stockholders seeking only their own profit in the name of the public interest, landowners looking to the law only to justify their own tyranny, and farmers incapable of properly husbanding their wealth of ploughland and pasture. Most telling of all, he describes 'striplings who . . . have been invested with a petty, subordinate post under Government, and consequently think fit to display their imaginary consequence by assuming a garb, similar to that worn by some of the Royal household in England' but whose real status is that of persons who 'happen to enjoy the privilege of superintending a parcel of unfortunates, doomed to labour in irons, whilst they break stones for the high roads . . .' (p. 157).

Savery's standard was an idealised English countryside, and he allows the Hermit a journey during which he discovers, among the rural idiocies, one household that holds to his ideal. His satire is, however, more convincing than his pastoral. He is savage in delineating the callousness of colonial society. Savery describes the rebuff the Hermit receives when he pleads on behalf of a friend who has fallen into debt. To the argument that nothing is to be gained by the 'cruel process of imprisonment, separating the debtor from his wife and children', the lawyer replies:

> I know nothing of wives and children, Sir — my duty to my client is all I have to think about. People have no business to have wives and children, if they cannot pay their debts. I have but one rule, Sir — I always say in reply to the question, what is to be done with so and so, let him go to gaol, and I say so now.

Savery, pp. 93–4.

The lawyer's words anticipate Dickens's condemnation of the reduction of human obligation to the single vision of the law. Most of Savery's descriptions are, however, less dramatic. By implication he compares his characters with the standards of London society. The comparison reduces Hobart to the provincial, and so redirects his satire from the evils of society to the follies of the individual.

Savery's novel of transportation, *Quintus Servinton* (edited by Cecil H. Hadgraft, Jacaranda, Brisbane,

1962 [1830–31]) avoids confrontation with Australian society by concentrating on the hero's disaster in England, on the details of his trial, imprisonment and voyage, and on moral reflections about his fate. The account of his life in the colony is concerned with personal intrigue and overshadowed by his return to England, a happy ending Savery was not himself to enjoy.

Like Charles Tompson, Savery wanted an authentic local culture rather than an imitation of English models. The failure of their work shows the impossibility of their aspirations in a colony still dependent on servitude imposed from abroad. While the masks of gentility hid the corruptions of power, writers could only satirise folly or hide from reality in pastoral follies of their own.

Louisa Ann Meredith

The writers who followed Savery and Tompson tended to address an English audience, and their work may be properly considered a part of English literature rather than the beginnings of an indigenous literature. Nevertheless, they contributed to fixing the image of Australia in the minds of both English and local readers.

Louisa Ann Meredith grew up in Warwickshire, but in 1839 she married her Australian cousin and sailed with him to New South Wales. Her account of this voyage and her experiences during the next four years in NSW was published in London in 1844 as *Notes and Sketches of New South Wales* by Mrs Charles Meredith. She explains her modest aims in her preface:

> Knowing that very many persons at 'Home' are deeply interested in the distant Colonies, as being the residence of dear friends and relatives, . . . I believed that a few simple sketches from nature . . . would be a welcome addition to the present small fund of information on common every-day topics relating to these antipodean climes.
>
> Meredith, p. vii.

But writing is never so simple, and whatever her intentions Mrs Meredith succeeds rather in conveying her reactions to a startlingly different land and society than in adding to simple information. Her experience is conditioned not only by her English upbringing, but also by her situation as the wife of a successful squatter whose authority and practical skills give her a privileged shelter from which she is able to encounter the country in safety. Nevertheless, despite her habitual deference to her husband, the judgements she expresses are her own.

Meredith's ability to be both involved and detached gives her work its particular quality. Her social position involved her in the life of the colony, but because her own situation is secure she is not driven either to adapt herself to the conditions or to change the conditions to suit herself. This work has already been done for her, mainly by her husband. Although like Savery and her other predecessors, she brings expectations of propriety determined by English circumstances, these remain for her standards of private judgement rather than a pattern to which she attempts to make the colony adhere.

At times this makes her infuriatingly judgemental, as when she takes Australians to task for adapting the English language to their use, and calling a brook a creek and a saltwater channel a river. She shares

Louisa Ann Meredith
(*State Library of Tasmania*)

the attitudes of her class to workers, whom she considers suffer in the new country by being overpaid, and so able to waste their lives on liquor rather than labour. She finds it difficult to adapt to Australian weather and landscape, but the wildlife gradually fascinates her despite herself. If her work helps to fix such images of Australia as the heat, drunkenness, drought, burnt-out forests, strange animals, illiterate squattocracy, insolent workers and untrustworthy natives, it also accepts the colony on its own terms, rather than as either a successful or a failed new world. Paradoxically, this acceptance comes because she takes it quite naturally as a part of England, distant and peripheral indeed, but essentially working out its destinies in the same way despite some harrowing circumstances. Thus, in her preface, she can refer to it both as the 'Antipodes' and as 'here'. She becomes completely Australian, without either accepting Australian standards or ceasing to be an English gentlewoman.

Her experience is perhaps summed up in the lyrical accounts she gives of two trees that grew on her Homebush property. The one was

> a common English pear-tree; a crooked, wide-spreading, farm-house-garden sort of tree, that won my especial love, from the good old-fashioned sort of pictures of gable-ended houses and neat garden-orchards it brought into my mind, and the glory and delight of its spring-time blossoms was an earnest and most child-like joy to me . . . telling of blooming fragrant gardens, with velvet turf paths, and shady arbours, and singing birds, and little running brooks, *one* of whose silver threads near our thirsty home would have been a priceless treasure . . .

> Meredith, p. 140.

The vision combines the English past with memories of childhood, and represents an ideal that was to inspire many Australians who had never seen England, and is in essence not different from ideals of American rural life from Washington Irving to Norman Rockwell. Meredith could also write of the native plants in the surrounding bush with a certain respect, restrained only by the persistent sense that they do not quite belong in civilised company:

> The trees called by the Colonists 'he-oak' and 'she-oak' . . . are usually of rather handsome forms, with dark, rough, permanent bark, and brownish-olive foliage, resembling in structure the 'horse-tails' of English brooks, consisting of long tufts of jointed grassy branchlets, hanging down like coarse hair, or a horse's tail . . . Perhaps none of the novel trees in this colony have so completely strange and un-English an aspect as these; and in a moderate breeze the tones uttered amongst their thousands of waving, whispering strings are far from unmusical, and reminded me of the lower, wailing notes of an Aeolian harp . . .

> Meredith, pp. 141–2.

Yet Meredith's experience was not entirely detached and serene. As well as the morally disturbing Aborigines, bushrangers and convicts haunted the edges of her imagination. She tells tales she has heard of audacious attacks on pastoral homes by bushrangers, but she sees the convicts herself:

> We passed several 'chain-gangs' working on the road; these are convicts, who, from their great and repeated crimes, are sentenced for various periods to work in irons in the service of the government; and the villainous countenances of the greater number, the clank of the chains, and the thought of how awful an amount of crime has led to this disgraceful punishment, made me positively dread passing or meeting a band of the miserable wretches . . . they do frequently evade the vigilance of their guards, and, 'taking the bush' . . . often become formidable in their attacks on travellers in the lonely roads up the country. Not long ago, I saw an account of *eleven* murders having been committed by one of these desperadoes, and accompanied by such horrors of mangling, burning and otherwise disposing of his victims, as far exceed all the fearful tragedies of a like kind we read of in the English papers.

> Meredith, pp. 58–9.

Meredith has no doubts about the treatment of the convicts. She rationalises that they are treated better than they deserve, as they 'do not perform on average the third part of the labour which any English mechanic or labourer does gladly and cheerfully'. England is not brought in here as a standard so much as an alibi, a talisman to banish the threat of the convict and the unruly labourer that jeopardises the future of this extension of the old world. Meredith tries to take the new country on its own terms, noting its faults although believing they will be corrected with time, but she cannot so easily repress or exorcise the fears England exported to its antipodes. Unlike the heat of an Australian Christmas or the philistinism of colonial society, they corrupt the heart of her world.

Alexander Harris

Harris also saw the canker that rotted colonial society, but he experienced it from the opposite end of the social scale from Mrs Meredith. Although he came out as a free labourer, he had to make his own way, mixing with the ex-convicts and itinerant workers and sharing their rough huts and hard drinking. His book, *Settlers and Convicts*, MUP, Melbourne, 1953 [London, 1852], is an example of the literature that was written for the English market to encourage migration and to offer useful advice to migrants to ensure their success. The novel offers an optimistic tale, apparently autobiographical, showing not only the difficulties that must be faced but also how, with endurance, they can be overcome. For Harris the colony is a place of opportunity. The difficulties are largely those of hardship and isolation, but they also include the upper classes who have been corrupted by convictism:

> The fact is, the upper classes of New South Wales settlers have so long been used to deal with the poor wretched convicts, and to tell them that they have no rights, and to taunt and mock them if they talk about redress for any ill treatment, that the habit and the feeling at the bottom of it have become rooted in their very nature . . . supercilious intolerance pervades the whole feeling with which the upper class in New South Wales generally regard the lower . . .
>
> Harris, pp. 163–4.

Harris's experience of the lower classes supports Mrs Meredith's impressions of general drunkenness, but he regards the phenomenon in a somewhat different light. At worst it is evidence of foolishness rather than moral depravity and at best it is the accompaniment of good fellowship. Not long after his arrival, Harris finds himself in a public-house in Sydney, where 'almost everybody was drinking rum in drams, or very slightly qualified with water', and the company is clearly of 'the very lowest class'. Even so, Harris notes that:

> I could not however, even at this early period of my acquaintance with this class of people, help observing one remarkable peculiarity common to them all — there was no offensive intrusiveness about their civility; every man considered himself just on a level with all the rest, and so quite content either to be sociable or not, as the circumstance of the moment indicated as most proper.'
>
> Harris, p. 5.

In the same spirit he describes a settler's hut where he later finds hospitality:

Incidents in the Life of a Selector
(*National Library of Australia*)

Situated on the main track and alone in the midst of the wilderness . . . The hut was well built of slabs split out of fine straight-grained timber . . . Our hosts were two Irishmen, brothers, who had got a little bit of good land cleared here in the wilderness, and refused nobody a feed and shelter for the night . . . Merrily sped the couple of hours betwixt our arrival and going to bed. One sang a song, another told some tale of the olden time . . . My share was to answer all the questions . . . and to pocket with the best grace I could (for most of these men had been convicts) the jokes they not very sparingly, but I must say with very good humour, cut on me for having come to the colony 'to make a fortune' or for being 'a free object', or for having 'lagged myself for fear the King should do it to me'.

Harris, pp. 22–4.

Although Harris' book is much concerned with the physical characteristics of the colony, the theme of people adapting themselves and their customs to the needs dictated by circumstance, and of creating new forms of human fellowship in the process, runs right through it, culminating in his reflection on the bonds developed through work and loneliness:

There is a great deal of this mutual regard and trust engendered by two men working thus together in the otherwise solitary bush; habits of mutual helpfulness arise, and these elicit gratitude, and that leads on to regard. Men under these circumstances often stand by one another through thick and thin; in fact it is a universal feeling that a man ought to be able to trust his own mate in anything.

Harris, pp. 180–81.

The original concept of mateship may have arisen among the convicts, and, together with its associated feelings of hostility to the boss, been transferred to free labour. Harris is the first writer not only to relate it to the social and environmental factors which bred it, but also to recognise it as a human value transcending the deprivations that cut Australia off from its European precedents. Although he writes for an English readership, Harris is the first Australian prose writer to establish in his work a specifically Australian sensibility as the point of moral reference.

4

FAR HORIZONS AND
DARK CLOUDS

ALTHOUGH history, and particularly cultural history, can rarely be divided by precise dates into neat periods, the year 1851 marks a turning point in Australian history. In that year Port Phillip was separated from New South Wales, the right to establish their own legislatures was granted to the four south-eastern colonies and offered, when they should want it, to the settlers in Western Australia and Moreton Bay, and gold was discovered in New South Wales and Victoria. These events shifted the focus of colonial politics from London to the provincial capitals, brought a great influx of immigrants and a new source of wealth, and generated a confidence in the colonies that the long delayed dream of a new nation, or at least a new England, in the south, could at last be realised.

Within a period of twenty-five years, Sydney, Melbourne and Adelaide had all established the universities, museums, libraries, churches and public gardens required by their new status as colonial capitals. Yet these changes had little immediately discernible effect on Australian writing. The new national confidence arose from the debates during the depression of the 1840s rather than from the influx of goldseekers in the 1850s.

Although the gold-rushes did not appeal to writers as a subject until some years later, the prosperity brought by gold spread widely through the community, and induced a general feeling of expansion and promise, which is reflected in the writing. This confidence rested not only on the new wealth of the gold-fields, but on the tradition of vigorous, often violent, political debate that had taken place in newspapers and the NSW legislative council since the turn of the century. This debate had raged about land policy, the relation between British and colonial governments, the powers of governors, the transportation of convicts, the place of the different social classes and the nature of the rising Australian society. Although the depression of the 1840s dampened self-confidence, the movement for self-government kept pressures high. When, during this period, Charles Harpur conceived the ambition of establishing him-

National Art Gallery, Sydney
(*State Library of NSW*)

self as a national poet, it was natural that he should write political poems and publish them in *The Empire*. This paper was owned by Henry Parkes, who used it as a vehicle for his passionate advocacy of Australia's place as a free member of the British Empire. Parkes published his own political verses, in which he condemned both British and Australian governments for their treatment of the poor, and expressed his hopes that Australia would welcome them into a commonwealth of independent farmers he hoped would be built from the wealth of the gold-fields.

The gold-rushes directly inspired practical and more controversial polemical writing. John Sherer's *The Gold-Finder in Australia* (London, 1853) combines practical information with a romantic emphasis on the dramatic incident and colourful character. John Dunmore Lang's polemical essays, *Freedom and Independence for the Golden Lands of Australia* (London, 1852), from the title onwards use the golden age in its double sense of wealth and well-being to advance his argument for a republic in the south. Antoine Fauchery's *Letters from a Miner in Australia* (Paris, 1857; translated by A.R. Chisholm, Georgian House, Melbourne, 1965) described life and opportunities in Victoria for the benefit of a French audience. Likewise, Raffaelo Carboni writes from a European perspective in his account of the miners' revolt against licence fees in his book, *The Eureka Stockade* (Melbourne, 1855). This endows the diggers' act of defiance with the heroics of European revolution, and so establishes the event in the national consciousness as a symbol of popular rebellion that has remained potent even when other revolts have faded from memory.

The chroniclers of this period portray a turbulent society that belied its aspirations to civilisation by its crass materialism. Although the gold discoveries brought about a vast influx of free immigration, and provided the financial and industrial foundations of the newly independent colony of Victoria, they neither generated uniform prosperity nor destroyed the social power of the squatters who, according to Fauchery, were 'Australia's true savages' (p. 99). Just as individuals experienced sharp swings from poverty to riches and back again, the economy of whole colonies was subject to violent alternations between prosperity and depression. Even at the best of times, the promised wealth flowed only to the few, and independent diggers soon found their

hopes of fortunes reduced to the realities of wage labour. The chroniclers were content to record their personal experiences and observations of this environment, and the balladists furthered the image of the rough bushmen as they expressed the hopes and resentments engendered by the new frontier. The writings of authors who aspired further seem forced and superficial. Minor versifiers looked back nostalgically to English childhoods in those moments when the sight of a daisy or the smoke of a campfire distracted their attention from the work of the day. This mode was adopted even by more talented authors who sought in their work to create an indigenous tradition and sensibility. To prove the authenticity of their Australian experience, they distort it into a shape that can be assimilated to the cultural expectations derived from England.

Charles Harpur

The distortion of the Australian experience affected Harpur's earlier political satires. In his major work, 'The Creek of the Four Graves', his attempt to give a heroic dimension inflates the language and, by removing it from the commonplace, diminishes it to fable or fantasy.

In the earliest published version, this poem opens straightforwardly with the lines:

> I tell a settler's tale of the old times,
> As told to me by our friend, old Egremont,
> Who then, with four of his most trusty men,
> Went forth into the wilderness — on foot,
> For horses then were cattle of too great price
> For the rough usage of its trackless depths . . .
>
> Elliot and Mitchell, p. 42.

Yet even here the words direct our attention away from the episode that is the subject of the poem into the context in which the poet wants us to read it. The metres and the words belong to the special discourse of heroic poetry, with overtones of Milton and connotations of the search for an earthly Paradise. 'Egremont' is not a likely name for a friend, and not even Major Mitchell, let alone a stockman concerned about such practical matters as the price and endurance of horses, would be likely to say he 'went forth into the wilderness' and its 'trackless depths'. The literal figure of Egremont cannot bear the metaphoric weight the poem places on him. Harpur intends the episode to symbolise the price paid to found a new civilisation, but its images endure as metaphors for the way that Australians came to see their occupation of the land.

First of all, the poem provides images of the bushlands — not the dry bush of the inland, but the silent and overpowering forests of the coastal ranges, with 'circling forest trees' that lead the eye on to 'shaded and enormous mountains' beyond, and from there to 'the whole universe . . . coiled in vast rest'. This solemn setting leads Egremont, as he keeps lonely watch, to

> . . . thoughts of home
> Ingathered to his heart, as by some nice
> And subtle interfusion that connects
> The cherished ever with the beautiful
> And lasting things of nature . . .

> Elliot and Mitchell, p. 44.

The impulse to the sublime is eighteenth-century, but the link the speaker makes between nature and his innermost thoughts comes from Wordsworth and the romantics. Whereas Wordsworth turns to nature to restore the human wisdom ravaged by the industrial revolution, Harpur finds in it confirmation of the civilised spirit Egremont is able to preserve even in the wastes of Australia:

> Egremont's moment of cultivated reflection is
>   shattered by
> A yell so horrible as now affrights
> And upward sends the shuddering air
> . . . a semi belt
> Of stript and painted savages . . .

> Elliot and Mitchell, p. 44.

The poet gives the gruesome details of this savage onslaught from which Egremont is barely able to escape, leaving the place where now

> . . . four stark corpses plundered to the skin
> In brutal mutilation, seemed to stare
> With frozen eyeballs up into the pale
> Round countenance of the moon; who, high in
>   heaven,

> With all her multitude of stars, looked down
> As peacefully as on a bridal there
> Of the warm living . . .

> Elliot and Mitchell, p.46.

This stark image of nature calmly contemplating savagery, omitted from later versions, contradicts the earlier Wordsworthian sentiments of sympathetic nature. The murderers who strike from the dark of the woods symbolise the menace of a nature that must be tamed before the settlers can possess the land for civilisation. This also contradicts Harpur's own rationalisation that God had designed creation to look with sympathy only at the 'offices of Unity and Love'. These offices are singularly lacking in his poetry.

Unlike the explorers, the imaginative writers had not been forced to the realisation that the only way to endure nature in Australia was to submit to it. Despite their best intentions to civilise it, therefore, they succeeded only in projecting on it and on its Aboriginal inhabitants the fears and guilts that they still carried for the European invasion of the land. Even when Harpur does allow himself to be overcome by nature, in 'A Midsummer Noon in the Australian Forest', the imagery remains general or confused — what is a dragon-hornet? The moment remains one of temporary retreat from 'noon's scorching eye'.

Harpur speaks for the towndweller for whom the bush is a source of income and an object of contemplation rather than a matter of daily struggle. Although he was born in Australia, the son of a schoolmaster, and worked for a time as a farmer, his career was that of a man of letters who obtained government employment from time to time in order to support himself and his family while he got on with his true vocation. His poetry is therefore involved with literature and politics rather than with the work of making the land serve European functions.

Catherine Helen Spence

The most significant response to the materialism of the Australian colonies at the time of the gold-rushes is in the work of Catherine Helen Spence. Her work reveals not only the illusions of male domination, but also the contradictions of a society that sought to build a new order on the same basis of economic discrimination as the old.

Spence's first novel, *Clara Morrison* (reprinted in *Catherine Helen Spence*, edited by Helen Thomson, Australian Portable Authors series, UQP, St Lucia, 1987 [1854]), tells of the emigrant experience from the viewpoint of a woman who is initially its victim rather than its beneficiary. Clara, the heroine, has, like Spence herself, been brought up in Scotland in a respectable and educated family. After the death of her parents, Clara's uncle disposes of the inconvenience she represents by sending her to Adelaide. Here she is forced to go into service as a household drudge, losing all social status as she works seven days of each week for a wage of five shillings. Eventually, however, she discovers cousins who accept her into their family. Through them she is drawn into the political and economic life of the colony at the time when its ideals of free settlement and its economy of agriculture and mechanics are being threatened by the Victorian gold-rushes. After several changes of love and fortune she marries a respectable grazier, thus finding the security and acceptance she had been denied in the old world by her lack of parents and in the new by her lack of money.

Catherine Helen Spence
(*National Library of Australia*)

Although the novel adapts the established pattern of Victorian fiction to the migrant experience, it differs from its fellows by its feminine viewpoint, its lack of attention to such stock excitements of colonial life as bushfires and bushrangers, and its largely urban and domestic ambience. The emphasis is not on the novelty of life in the colonies but on the possibilities it offers of allowing people, particularly women, to become independent of the forces of patriarchy and snobbery that continue to oppress them. The discovery of gold threatens these hopes by strengthening the values of vulgar materialism rather than those of the intellect by which alone the potential of the new land can be realised.

The latter part of the novel is encumbered by the conventional machinery of the plot, as the artificial barriers to true love are gradually removed. Spence does not present love and marriage as the only desirable end to a woman's life. A bad marriage, or marriage to an unsuitable man, is presented as one of the worst of fates. The strongest character in the novel, Margaret Elliot, like Spence herself, deliberately chooses not to marry. Clara's marriage is portrayed as a marriage of intellectual equals, and concludes the novel satisfactorily only because it rescues her from the economic dependence that would otherwise have been her lot in a society controlled by businessmen.

The conventional plot of the novel is a vehicle for the disclosure of social structures that sustain hypocrisy and cruelty. The keystone of this structure is not the patriarchy itself, but the deception that clothes itself impermeably in words that conceal the truth. Mastery of this art is diffused among many of the male characters, but concentrated in the person of Miss Withering. Her condemnation of fiction and praise of fact and her ruthless self-seeking epitomise the rejection of compassion in the name of reason:

'I like to get information from what I read,' said Miss Withering, taking up a book containing the driest chips of information . . .
'I think time is too valuable to be frittered away over novels,'

Clara Morrison, p. 95.

Clara Morrison, like her author, rejects the tyranny of a society bound to this tyranny of fact.

Henry Kingsley

When we turn to Henry Kingsley we find ourselves safely back in the world of male supremacy and European assumptions. Kingsley was himself a visitor to Australia, and although he had to make his own way in the country he was, unlike Alexander Harris, cushioned by a web of contacts and introductions that ensured that he never fell out of the ranks of gentility. Although he tried his hand at various jobs, he was, like Charles Harpur, essentially a writer, and so was at a distance from the physical struggle with the land. His characters come to Australia to restore fortunes ruined in England, and have every intention of returning to their native land once they achieve their material ends. Kingsley became fascinated with the land and its people, and identified completely with the task of settlement, which he saw in terms at once heroic and pastoral. His characters may be, as Furphy was to complain, overgrown English schoolboys, but their attitudes, or the attitudes their author displays through them, represent the European enthusiasm for a golden age made real amid the southern alps.

Kingsley's novel, *The Recollections of Geoffrey Hamlyn* (Lloyd O'Neil, Hawthorn, 1970 [1859]), is not so much about Australia as about the impact of the Australian dream on members of English society. The novel describes the establishment of cattle stations in Australia in the 1830s, but the story actually commences in a Devonshire village 'Somewhere between the years 1780 and 1790', and its main characters do not reach Australia until the eighteenth of his forty-eight chapters.

Unlike Catherine Spence, Kingsley rejoices in the success with which English society is replanted in the antipodes. Yet even so, he rejoices in the space and light the new land offers. His characters find, near the headwaters of the Murray, Murrumbidgee and Snowy rivers, the land freely given by God that they need to restore their family fortunes. This land, however, welcomes them not just with the promise of riches but with a vision of Eden. Kingsley's description leads the eye of the reader out from this vision to still further opportunities spreading to the edges of the sky and the sea that alone bound human endeavour:

> A new heaven and a new earth! Tier beyond tier, height above height, the great wooded ranges go rolling away westward, till on the lofty skyline they are crowned with a gleam of everlasting snow. To the eastwards they sink down, breaking into isolated forest-fringed peaks, and rock crowned eminences, till with rapidly straightening lines they fade into the broad grey plains, beyond which the Southern Ocean is visible by the white sea-haze upon the sky.

> Kingsley, p. 149.

The centre of this scene remains empty, awaiting the human industry that will assimilate it to civilisation. This soon appears in the form of travelling stockmen and cattle, followed by drays bearing household goods. Kingsley explicitly likens their advent to Abraham's journey to the Promised Land:

> so we sat and watched them debouche from the forest into the broad river meadows in the gathering gloom; saw the scene so venerable and ancient, so seldom seen in the Old World—the patriarchs moving into the desert with all their wealth, to find a new pasture ground. A simple primitive action, the first and simplest act of colonisation, yet producing such great results on the history of the world as did the parting of Lot and Abraham in times gone by.

> Kingsley, p. 151.

The story that follows tells not of the work but of the romance of settlement. The plot becomes a series of deeds in which the hero, Sam Buckley, fights against natural and human evil until he wins both his land and his lady. The work of shearing becomes an occasion for a Christmas celebration, and the task of branding the cattle gives Sam the opportunity to display the skill and courage that entitle him to have 'a big three-foot of blue steel in his hand, and her Majesty's commission to use it against her enemies' (p. 281). The battles against Aborigines, bushfires and bushrangers validate the settlers' claim to the land they have found.

The settlers are not, however, able to make the land completely their own. The tale of the child lost in the bush, who is eventually found 'dead and stiff, one hand still grasping the flowers he had gathered on his last happy play-day, and the other laid as a pillow, between the soft cold cheek and the rough cold stone' (p. 287), conveys in its pathos the aspect of this new land that refuses to yield to human aspirations.

If the indifference of the land itself remains untouched, Kingsley nevertheless shows the defeat of human evil. The Aborigines, symbols of savage malice, are defeated in a set battle, and Kingsley allows only a hint of the terrible retribution the whites habitually wreaked on those who opposed them. A greater threat comes from the villain of the novel, George Hawker, who menaces the new land with the evils of the old. Through his gypsy mother, Hawker represents the primitive fears of the unknown that lie at the heart of European folklore and that have no place in the clean lands of the Snowy Mountains. Further, as one of the dispossessed whom society has sought unsuccessfully to subjugate by law and exile, he represents the social evils from which the new settlers are seeking to escape. Although he is eventually defeated by the manly courage of the gentlemen, his affinity with the gloom and melancholy of the bush qualifies Kingsley's vision of the new land exempt from human weakness and evil.

Journals of Later Explorers

By the end of the 1840s, the boundaries of settlement had virtually been established, and later explorers encountered more determined resistance from the Aborigines and a landscape that became more discouraging to dreams of European settlement the further they journeyed into it. Mitchell wrote another triumphal journal to commemorate his explorations towards Carpentaria and Leichhardt rejoiced in some of the prospects he found between the disasters of his expedition through what is now the Northern Territory, but the age of victorious exploration was now succeeded by one of heroic endurance. Most of the journals report either matter-of-fact travels through country of no particular interest, or epics of survival in the tradition of Eyre and Sturt.

Burke and Wills

The most famous of these was the disastrous journey in 1860–61 by Burke and Wills from Cooper's Creek

Return of Burke and Wills to Coopers Creek
(*National Library of Australia*)

to Carpentaria. This journey was recorded in the journals of William Wills which gain their power from the contrast between their laconic tone and our knowledge of their tragic conclusion. Wills emerges from his account as an interested observer who accepted implicitly the authority of his leader and the orthodoxies of the social hierarchy that made it impossible for them to see that Charles Gray was dying in front of them or to learn from the Aborigines how they could live in this forbidding land. As they face their own fate, the journal becomes more moving. Wills reflects on their inability to realise that 'Poor Gray must have suffered very much when we thought him shamming', and then faces his own death with stoic faith and undiminished loyalty to Burke.

Ernest Giles

The accounts of exploration reach their culmination in the journals of Ernest Giles. Giles was born in England but came to Australia at about the age of fifteen. He came to know the country almost as well as the Aborigines. Unlike most of his predecessors, he led only small parties, which meant that he had to work with the land rather than attempt to impose his will on it. Giles was the first white man to cross the country from east to west and back, but his greatest exploit was his crossing of Gibson's Stony Desert in 1874. He named this wasteland after his companion, whom he sent back with their only surviving horse to seek help. Giles followed him on foot, carrying a water cask on his shoulders for much of the way, and even turning aside in a vain attempt to track Gibson into the wilderness where he had gone astray. Altogether Giles covered 175 kilometres without fresh supplies of food, and 95 kilometres without any water except what he carried with him. Yet the account of this journey is quite detached. It makes clear the author's sufferings and feelings but indulges neither in heroics nor in moralising:

> I was in such a miserable state of mind and body, that I refrained from more vexatious speculations . . . I stayed here, eating and drinking, until about ten a.m., when I crawled away over the stones down from the water. I was very footsore, and could go only at a snail's pace. Just as I got clear of the bank of the creek, I heard a faint squeak, and looking about I saw, and immediately caught, a small dying wallaby, whose marsupial mother had evidently thrown it from her pouch. It only weighed about two ounces [57 grams], and was scarcely furnished yet with fur. The instant I saw it, like an eagle I pounced on it and ate it, living, raw, dying — fur, skin, bones, skull, and all. The delicious taste of that creature I shall never forget. I only wished I had its mother and father to serve in the same way. I had become so weak that by late at night, I had only accomplished eleven miles [17 kilometres], and I lay down about five miles [8 kilometres] from the Gorge of Tarns, again choking for water.

> Fitzpatrick, *Australian Explorers*, p. 474

This is as close to an unmediated account of experience as it is possible to get. The writer puts his emphasis entirely on the circumstances that press on him and the will with which he struggles to survive them. The only touch of literary ornament is in the name he has given to his place of refuge, but the romantic associations of the name are smothered by the reality of his struggle to attain his goal. The country strips the individual to his essentials. When, on reaching his base, he realises that his companion is gone, his thoughts point to the vanity of human aspirations in the face of that unyielding reality:

> It was impossible for him [Gibson] to be still in existence in that fearful desert, as no man would or

could stay there alive . . . The days had not been excessively hot, Mr Tietkens said 96° [35°C] to 98° [36°C] had been the average, but today it was only 90° [32°C] . . . That evil spirit of this scene — Mount Destruction — frowned upon us, and now that Gibson was dead, exploration was ended; we had but to find his remains . . .

> Fitzpatrick, pp. 475–6.

Giles writes his names on the desert, but the names he chooses pay tribute to the destruction of human hope. Yet, in enduring and in writing he, unlike Gibson, achieved the only victory the land would allow — the assertion of his own existence.

The accounts of exploration provide the images of the dead heart of Australia and the lonely individuality of human existence. Within the boundaries of settlement, however, women and men still struggled to adapt the land to their purposes and realise the dream of a society with room for everyone, only to find the dream repeatedly frustrated by human weakness or natural adversity. The golden years of hope were succeeded by decades of hardship in which the rich consolidated their power while the poor found hope ever more elusive. While the explorers sought their answers outside the confines of society, poets and novelists tried to find the causes of their frustrations in the conditions of social existence.

Henry Kendall

Kendall followed Charles Harpur in his aspiration to create a poetry that would add a cultural dimension to Australian society, and allow it to take its place among the nations of the world. Like Harpur he projected the failures of society onto the land it sought to civilise. Taking the cue from such episodes as that in which Gilbert, the naturalist on Leichhardt's expedition, had been killed during a night attack by hostile Aborigines, Kendall personified the threat of the landscape in the form of its indigenous inhabitants. His long poem 'The Glen of Arrawatta' is almost a reworking of Harpur's 'The Creek of the Four Graves'. Kendall's victim is, however, a sole wanderer, whose meditations run from his own pastoral success to the 'lonely tracks' of Burke and Wills and then to soft thoughts of childhood in England, until

. . . far beyond the home of pale red leaves
And silver sluices, and the shining stems
Of runnel blooms, the dreamy wanderer saw,
The wilder for the vision of the moon,
Stark desolation and a waste of plain,
All smit by flame and broken with the storms;
Black ghosts of trees, and sapless trunks that stood
Harsh hollow channels of the fiery noise,
Which ran from bole to bole a year before . . .

Elliot and Mitchell, p. 73.

The contrast of gentle England and harsh Australia, a reversal of early hopes, was already a convention. Kendall describes England in literary terms, while he gives an accurate and detailed description of the Australian bushfire with which he contrasts it. The emphasis of the poem therefore falls on nostalgia and on the defeat of hope as much as it does on the threat that erupts from the landscape as the traveller falls asleep:

Thereafter grew the wind; and chafing depths
In distant waters sent a troubled cry
Across the slumb'rous forest; and the chill
Of coming rain was on the sleeper's brow,
When, flat as reptiles hutted in the scrub,
A band of fierce fantastic savages
That, starting naked round the faded fire,
With sudden spears and swift terrific yells,
Came bounding wildly at the white man's head . . .

Elliot and Mitchell, p. 73.

The 'savages' belong to a nightmare, but the growing unease in the earlier lines is again precisely observed and placed. Nor are Aborigines the only threat within the landscape — the bush in his poems is equally haunted by the ghosts of convicts, murderers and the unknown dead. In several poems, including 'The Last of His Tribe', the dispossessed Aborigines themselves become a part of a nostalgic landscape that comes to stand for a universal loss of human hope rather than a specific threat.

Kendall did at times write of the things that engaged the attention of the ordinary people of his time. His ballad on the Melbourne Cup links him both with the folk writing that had developed alongside the formal literature of the new country and the work of his friend, the literary balladeer, Adam Lindsay Gordon.

Adam Lindsay Gordon

Gordon was an Englishman who came to the colonies to redeem a misspent youth, only to find that Australia offered as many chances of going to the bad as did England. A superb horseman, he had a variety of jobs, from mounted trooper to keeper of livery stables.

Gordon wrote his ballads as an aside to his life of action. His first published work, *The Feud* (Mount Gambier, 1864), was a series in the Scottish ballad tradition, but he then turned to Australian subjects, particularly those concerned with horses. Although they are more suited to the drawing room than the campfire, their fast moving pattern of rhyme and rhythm involves the reader in the action without too much concern for detail, and the combination of popular subjects with easy sentiment ensured their wide appeal.

The best known of Gordon's works, 'The Sick Stockrider', demonstrates these qualities at their best. The opening lines, with the bushman helping his mate 'All through the hot, slow, sleepy, silent ride', prepare for the nostalgia of the following verses where the speaker recalls all the highlights of his life, which simultaneously contains all the elements of what Australians regarded as their authentic experience:

Adam Lindsay Gordon

Twas merry at the glowing morn, among the
gleaming grass,
To wander as we've wandered many a mile,
And blow the cool tobacco cloud, and watch the
cool wreaths pass,
Sitting loosely in the saddle all the while.

Elliot and Mitchell, p. 83.

This is poetry that flatters the readers by enabling
them to identify with both the freshness of morning
and the relaxed control of the horseman. The poem
builds on this mood by recalling alternate images of
action and rest — chasing cattle or bushrangers,
singing, yarning and drinking in the pub. The nostalgia
is intensified as the speaker recalls those he has
known at work or play and who, after good lives or
ill, have died before him. As he prepares to join them,
he reflects on his own life, arriving at the comfortable
conclusion that

I should live the same life over, if I had to live again;
And the chances are I go where most men go.

Then, as the mists close round him, he asks that he
be allowed to:

. . . slumber in the hollow where the wattle
blossoms wave,
With never stone or rail to fence my bed;
Should the sturdy station children pull the bush
flowers from my grave,
I may chance to hear them romping overhead.

Elliot and Mitchell, p. 85.

The images of wattle and children join to soften the
alienation of the empty bush into a homely freedom,
just as the nostalgic mood of the whole poem draws
our attention away from the implicit hostility of the
landscape in which even the support of his mate
through the long, hard ride is finally unable to defeat
death. The contradiction between the freedom the
land offers and the harsh demands it makes is resolved in the easy sentiment that we all have to die
and that nothing matters much. The golden dawn of
promise when 'the sun shot flaming forth' ends in a
grey dusk where 'sickly, smoky shadows through
the sleepy sunlight swim'.

Bushrangers

Kendall and Gordon in their ballads drew on the folk
tradition that had been established in convict times.
In the 1850s the songs of the 'Wild Colonial Boy' had
celebrated the same qualities of courage and defiance
found in 'Bold Jack Donohue'. Later ballads added
other elements from the experiences of the small
miners, selectors and travelling workers, all of whom
shared the convicts' hostility to the authority that
sought to keep them in the place it had ordained for
them. The bushranger was a natural symbol of their
own feelings of rebellion. Even a brutal marauder
like Morgan could attract sympathy when the balladist
gave him some of the aura of a Robin Hood and emphasised the treachery that had encompassed his
death rather than the cruelty by which he had lived:

Oh, Morgan was the traveller's friend; the
squatters all rejoice
That the outlaw's life is at an end, no more they'll
hear his voice.
Success attend all highwaymen who do the poor
some good;
But my curse attend a treacherous man who'd
shed another's blood.

Douglas Stewart and Nancy
Keesing (eds.), *Australian Bush
Ballads*, Angus & Robertson,
Sydney, 1955, p. 34–5.

The travellers are, of course, those who had to tramp
the bush tracks in search of food and work, and who
were not troubled by the bushrangers' assaults on
those who travelled in coaches with purses of gold.
By identifying with this group, the anonymous balladist
extends his antipathy to authority to include their
chief enemy, the squatter. The prosperity brought
by gold apparently enabled the squatter to achieve
the dream of wealth that had first brought Europeans
to Australia. He had been able to re-establish the
English society that had rejected him and driven him
forth into new lands, but the achievement of his
dream excluded those who came later, as well as
those who had not been able to match his luck. The
bushranger was his nemesis, the fate that brought
the revenge of those who found themselves as powerless in the new land as they had been in the old.
    The qualities perceived in the bushrangers came
together in the rebellious figure of Ned Kelly. His

speech from the dock represents the demand of the Irish peasant to be allowed to get on with his life, and his defiance of those who would interfere with him. The legends that accumulate about him, however, belong to a new world. Even when a ballad takes an Irish form:

> Oh, Paddy dear, and did you hear
> The news that's going round . . .

it quickly assumes an Australian tone:

> To rob the bank of all its gold
> Was their idea that day,
> Blood-horses they were mounted on
> To make their getaway.

The aims are purely material, and the emphasis is on individual prowess. This is not the language of community, where the individual who defies convention finds a tragic fate, but of class, where there are laws but no standards and the individual is absurd:

> The farce was here repeated,
> As I've already told,
> They bailed up all the banker's clerks
> And robbed them of their gold,
> The manager could not be found,
> And Kelly, in great wrath,
> Searched high and low, and luckily
> He found him in his bath.

> Stewart and Keesing, pp. 42–6.

The resolution of Kelly and his gang does not affirm any higher morality or loyalty, but reduces all the laws and conventions of the old world to the same plane of absurdity.

Not all parts of society reacted to the exploits of the bushrangers in the same way. Another ballad celebrates the courage of the police who were gunned down by the gang, and rejoices in the eventual fate met by the outlaws. Even this writer, however, cannot entirely save the police from their own absurdity:

> The sergeant's horse raced from the camp alike
>   from friend and foe,
> And McIntyre, his life at stake, sprang to the
>   saddle-bow

> And galloped far into the night, a haunted,
>   harassed soul,
> Then like a hunted bandicoot hid in a wombat hole.

> Stewart and Keesing, pp. 41–2.

The Australian environment was hostile to the conventions of the old world, and consequently the attempt to make authority, rather than outlaws and outcasts, heroic inevitably finished by making them look ridiculous.

Rolf Boldrewood

It was this problem of making authority rather than outlaws heroic that faced Thomas Browne, who was a Police Magistrate when he sat down to write *Robbery Under Arms* (Lloyd O'Neil, Melbourne, 1970 [1882–83]). Under the pseudonym of Rolf Boldrewood, he attempted to write a heroic tale of the Australian bush a little more than a year after Ned Kelly's hanging. His staunchly conservative views were formed by his present employment and his squatting past, and his literary tastes by his reading of Walter Scott, whose novels provided the pattern for his own work. Scott's novels invariably find resolution within the established system, which proves able to accommodate dissenters, just as his fiction offers a means of accommodating Scottish energies and loyalties within the framework of British capitalism. But whereas Scott's heroes are driven by conflicting loyalties, Boldrewood's have no stronger motives than the desire for easy wealth and the love of horses and adventure that indicates moral weakness.

The heroic framework of Boldrewood's novel distracts our attention from any social conflicts that might underlie the pastoral community it portrays. The bold action of the story, and the heavy moralising in which the narrator, Dick Marston, wraps the tale of his adventures, concentrate our attention on the particular incidents rather than the causes that produce them. The bushrangers are eventually restored to the system not by any acknowledgement of their legitimacy but by their surrender or death-bed repentance. Starlight, the leader of the gang, is not a resentful settler like Ned Kelly but an English aristocrat mysteriously banished to the colonies. The gang he leads reproduces the social distinctions of the society imagined by the squatters. The authority of the gentleman earns the loyalty of his free followers and restrains the surly nature of the menials.

The heroics of action distract attention from the underlying conflicts of the pastoral community. The fears felt by the whites towards the dispossessed Aborigines are projected on to the half-caste, Warrigal, who eventually betrays the narrator, Dick Marston. The resentments that drove men like Ned Kelly appear only in the misanthropy — the dislike of other people — shown by Marston's father, and in the brutality of his associates, Wall and Moran. In these ways the novel contains the radical implications of its bushranging heroes within a framework that legitimises the pastoral order. Noble squatters like Mr Knight or Mr Falkland guarantee a society in which good men like George Storeyfied and the reformed Dick Marston are able to win land and prosperity, and good women like Grace Storeyfield maintain the moral order.

Despite its author's intentions, elements of the novel undermine the social order its structure upholds. The patience of Marston's wife or of Grace Storeyfield cannot match the vitality of the Barnes girls. The rough democracy of the Turon gold-fields has a liveliness absent from the gentility of the squatting households and the dull respectability of George Storeyfield. The outlaws' retreat in Terrible Hollow has an ambivalence of freedom and menace that cannot be contained by the English models of gentility adopted by both Starlight and his antagonists, or tamed by Aileen Marston's domesticity. The last sight she and Dick have of it reveals what it could be:

> Just then, as if he'd waited for us, the sun came out from behind the mountain; the mists lifted and rolled away as if they had been curtains. Everything showed clear out like a playhouse . . . From where we stood you could see everything, the green valley flats with the big old trees in clumps, some of 'em just the same as they'd been planted. The two little river-like silver threads winding away among the trees, and far on the opposite side the tall gray rock-towers shining among the forest edges of the high green wall.
>
> Boldrewood, p. 331.

The vision is of the pastoral idyll that has been realised in social terms by men like Mr Falkland, and

that Aileen has managed to bring for a short time to the Hollow. But the circumstances that have brought the Marstons to the Hollow prevent them from making its promise a part of society. As long as they are there, they are safe, but their wealth is useless to them. They turn back to drink and violence. The words with which Dick Marston concludes his description place the Hollow in its true perspective:

> Somehow the sun wasn't risen enough to light up the mountain. It looked black and dismal as if it was the nightfall coming on.
>
> Boldrewood, p. 331.

Despite himself, Boldrewood has invested the Terrible Hollow with popular images of hope and rebellion, but these eventually collapse in savage despair. It finally passes from the Marstons through an act of betrayal, and it is left to the gold-seekers to recover it for the civilised world. In opening the Hollow to society, they destroy the hope of refuge it represented, the dream of freedom it offered on behalf of the continent. The diggers, by settling it, make it merely another part of civilisation.

Marcus Clarke

Although Boldrewood celebrates the ideals of pastoral life, most Australians by this time lived in the coastal cities where they were building an urban society based on trade and manufacture. They enjoyed bush romances just as they took a pride in financing expeditions to the interior, but their daily lives were bound up with the new world of the industrial revolution rather than the old dream of rural independence.

These cities produced a different kind of literature from the yarns and ballads of the bush. This work appeared in the newspapers and magazines that had been established to meet the needs of a growing society for news, comment, gossip and stories. The writers came from the world of journalists and lawyers, businessmen and jobbers who flourished in the cities and had more in common with the citizens of London or Manchester than with the settlers and workers of the bush. Although some of these writers, like Francis Adams, were concerned with the particular nature and problems of Australian

Marcus Clarke
(*State Library of Victoria*)

society, as a whole they were more interested in illustrating the general principles of human conduct. Their writings belong in the general tradition of travel literature and reportage, and are a part of the process that was incorporating Australia into a Greater Britain.

Among these writers was the young Marcus Clarke, who had come to Melbourne when his father's premature and penniless death dashed his hopes of a prosperous career in England. For a couple of years he worked in the Victorian Wimmera. During this time Clarke contributed some bush sketches to the *Australian Monthly Magazine*. When he returned to Melbourne, he embarked on a career as a journalist, writing variously for the *Argus*, its weekly stablemate the *Australasian*, and the *Age*. These essays are in the tradition of Addison, offering polite commentary of manners and morals, and flattering his readers that their prosperous colony was a part of the world's most advanced civilisation. However, in his 'Lower Bohemia' column he examined the other side of prosperity by exploring the lives of those

whose poverty was lit by no hopes of selling a story or obtaining a safe government place. In these columns, he shows how the lives of the poor form an integral part of the whole structure of society.

At the conclusion of his ramble 'In Outer Darkness', where Clarke takes the reader among the derelicts bedded down for the night along the Yarra, he comes across the hangman, whose reason for 'living in the stone-heaps is that if criminal Bohemia knew that he had a settled abode, they would annoy and maltreat him'. Clarke then concludes his essay with a generalisation that both turns the hangman into a metaphor of society and stands on its head the dream of a society free from the terrors of the old world:

> It struck me as a curious comment upon capital punishment that the executor of justice should be forced to live like a dog by reason of his office. The man who pulls the bolt does no more than the judge who sentences, or the jury who decide upon guilt or innocence. Yet the spectacle of the old man with laughing mouth, eager eyes, and white locks streaming, half buried in that dismal pit, in such a bleak wild night, made me shudder. I was in the midst of the Crusoe's desert island of modern civilization, and I had suddenly come upon that Footprint — instinct with a terrible significance which was alone wanting to make the parallel complete.

> Michael Wilding (ed.), *Portable Australian Authors: Marcus Clarke*, UQP, St Lucia, 1976, p. 666.

The footprint found by Crusoe warns of the intrusion of the savagery of cannibalism, but this laughing old man symbolises the savagery at the heart of the civilisation that founded Australia as a place of both hope and exile.

This unease in Clarke finds its full expression in the novel *For the Term of His Natural Life* (serial version, Stephen Murray-Smith (ed.), Penguin, Harmondsworth, 1970, [1870]; book version in Michael Wilding (ed.), *Portable Australian Authors: Marcus Clarke*, UQP, St Lucia, 1976 [1874]). The original version, published as a serial, 'His Natural Life', in the *Australian Journal*, begins with Dickensian scenes in London, and lays an elaborate plot of crime and concealment. The story gathers intensity when its hero, Richard Devine, now known as Rufus Dawes, finds himself on a prison transport bound for Australia. It traces his fate within the system until he is eventually saved by his love for Dora and achieves some prosperity on the Ballarat goldfields. The book version, however, eliminates most of this plot and concentrates on prison life and the brutalising effects of the System, which becomes a metaphor for the act of injustice on which Australia is founded. Dawes is still freed from despair by his love for Dora, named Sylvia in this version, but dies with her when the ship on which they are escaping from Norfolk Island founders in a storm.

In modelling his work on Dickens rather than Scott, Clarke showed his awareness that Australia's promise of the freedom in which individuals can make their own lives is an illusion. Australians, both as individuals and as a society, were at the mercy of forces outside themselves. While Dickens constructs elaborate plots which eventually allow the individual to escape into a haven from society, Clarke, in the final version of his novel, abandons all such contrivance. The early elaborations of his plot are forgotten in his relentless description of the power by which the System takes over completely the lives of its victims, destroying convict and free alike. The only escape is the death the convicts eventually choose in preference to continued bondage. While Dickens brings Magwitch back to threaten society with the terror it had sought to banish, Clarke follows his convict through the hell of his banishment until this constitutes his only reality.

Clarke went to considerable trouble to ensure that his novel was historically accurate, although later research has shown that the experiences it portrays were by no means characteristic. It matters little that most convicts, unlike Dawes, were unregenerate rogues, and that despite this the majority of them served their sentences quietly and found peaceful livelihood, and even prosperity, in Australia after their discharge. Nor is it pertinent that physical conditions on the ships taking them to Australia were better for convicts than they were for the later free settlers. Clarke may take the worst case, but through it he shows the relentless logic on which the whole system rested. The innocent victims like Dawes or the men like Gabbett and Mooney, driven to utter despair and brutality, may have been extreme cases, but they were a necessary part of the whole. Without such final sanctions enforced with an inexorable rigour that could allow no possibility that it might be wrong, no part of the System could function properly.

In Clarke's novel, not even nature offers prospects of freedom. Instead, it provides the walls of the prison, isolating the human society and so reinforcing the absolute power of the commanders. It allows violence and betrayal to follow their inevitable course. When a group of convicts escapes into the bush, it inflicts on them the hardships that drive them to cannibalism. The only idyll the novel allows, when the isolation of the bush allows Dawes for a brief period to become Sylvia's protector, makes his subsequent betrayal and servitude the more bitter.

The logic of the System is the logic of the law taken to its ultimate conclusion. In a community isolated from the wider society that generated it, the logic underlying that society is revealed more starkly, and by being revealed is condemned. It is the logic of a society that makes human beings its objects and ties them to the rules of a structure that judges them 'objectively', regardless of what they actually do. In detaching his convicts and gaolers from England, Clarke reveals without circumstantial distraction the inner logic of industrial capitalism. In identifying this logic, Clarke also looks ahead to the twentieth century when the logic of capitalism has been extended to the whole globe in the form of economic and ideological systems that deny any authenticity to individual hopes and experience. Clarke's world was produced by industrial capitalism, but in it lie the foundations of Kafka's courts, Solzhenitsyn's Gulag, and the random terror of groups who refuse all human restraint. In declaring his independence from the System that created Australia, Clarke also declares his loyalty to that wider human community that exists despite the law.

A LITTLE RADICALISM

The one powerful and unique type yet produced in Australia is that of the Bushman.

Francis Adams, *The Australians*, London, 1893, p. 165.

The *Bulletin*

IN January 1880 a new weekly paper appeared on the streets of Sydney. For the next quarter of a century, the *Bulletin*, as this paper was named, challenged with cheeky energy all that was held worthy by the great and good of the land. J.F. Archibald, its founding editor and partner in the enterprise, encouraged a mixture of gossip, comment, news and anecdote, short paragraphs and long essays that cut across the safe divisions of life and art into which his conservative competitors divided their columns.

From the first, Archibald encouraged his readers to write for his paper. It thus became a medley of voices speaking the life of a far-flung land rather than the product of professional writers describing and commenting on their surroundings. The serious press lectured the public through editorial sermons, and the popular press concentrated on information and sensation. The *Bulletin* instead invited its readers to join it in the jostle of hectoring, story-telling, comment and quip with which it created a society in its own image. The features of this image were those of the bushman, and its dimensions the colonies of Australia and New Zealand, but its pattern was conceived and constructed in the urban world of Sydney. The bush fed the city, and the city responded by giving back the bush as the image of the true Australia.

Despite its exuberance, the world of the *Bulletin* had at its centre the same bleak sense of oppresson

Conflict in Society
(*Bulletin, 16 August 1890*)

that Marcus Clarke had embodied in *For the Term of His Natural Life*. While a reporter in Melbourne, Archibald had met Clarke, and his report of the hanging of a petty criminal by the name of Joseph Weechurch, who had been condemned to death for his second attempt to kill a warder, reads like an episode from Clarke's novel. He later demonstrated his opposition to capital punishment by attempting to steal the hangman's rope when he was sent to report the hanging of an Aborigine at Mudgee. His reports of the execution emphasise the disintegrating effects of the due process of the law on the gaol governor as well as the grim comedy and grisly conclusion of the actual hanging. Archibald makes the law a symbol of 'inhuman rectitude', blind to the causes of human behaviour and impervious to human sympathy, and portrays the Aboriginal victim as a symbol of the injustice wreaked on his people. This hostility to the cruelties of the system became characteristic of his editorship of the *Bulletin*.

From the first issue, Archibald campaigned in the *Bulletin* against capital punishment. Two pages of fierce argument about the hanging in Sydney of the 'Wantabadgery bushrangers' show the contradiction between the act of execution and the human basis of the society it is supposed to protect. A portrait of the hangman at home, playing the role of host and pious father, contrasts unnaturally with the grotesque details of his public duties. Archibald's report horrifies and fascinates, as it evokes the force with which society, trying to purge itself of evil, incorporates it in its own structure. The hangman corrupts all, perverting even the central festival of Christianity with the reminder to the prisoner that 'his Christmas box was to be a coffin'.

The hangman and the hanging judge become symbols of the alliance of power and respectability against which Archibald's *Bulletin* directed its campaign of satire and invective. Other images included Mr Fat the businessman, the politicians, newspaper proprietors and churchmen who abetted him, and behind these the British establishment of governors, generals and monarch that kept Australia in bondage to overseas interests and ideas. In contrast to these toadies and timeservers, the *Bulletin* exalted the images of an innocent and independent Australia represented by the 'Little Boy from Manly' of its cartoonists and the bushman of its balladists and storytellers.

Although the people the *Bulletin* chose as images of Australia are powerless, they are also young.

J. F. Archibald
(*State Library of Victoria*)

They represent the future of an Australia purged of the oppressions of money and Empire, and of the accompanying taint of lesser races. The *Bulletin* sympathised with the Aborigines as victims of oppression, but believed they lacked the capacity to survive in the new society and hoped only that their passing would be painless and speedy. The Chinese and southern Europeans, on the other hand, were regarded as intruders who threatened both working conditions and standards of decency, and must therefore be altogether excluded. By denying the principle of human community, this racism contradicted the principles on which the paper built its ideal of commonwealth.

This contradiction runs through the work of the writers the *Bulletin* nurtured. On the one hand, they champion the ordinary man against the oppression of the powerful. On the other, they portray him as persecuted by the troublesome behaviour of those weaker than himself, women, Chinese and Aborigines, who provide a standard butt for Bulletin humour. Their men suffer from the feeling of being imprisoned by a system in which wealthy men combine with harsh nature to condemn the individual to lifelong toil. The only refuge they can find is the boozy society of the grog shanty.

Poetry and short stories appeared in the *Bulletin* as a part of the whole miscellany of writing, rather than as something set apart for special attention. They were subjected by Archibald to the same general principles of selection — Australian relevance and economy of words. The work published ranged from a maundering English serial, included by Archibald's partner Haynes against Archibald's objections, and similarly romantic Australian stories, to brief sketches in verse and prose. A poem by Kendall was published as early as 1881. In 1890 the first contributions from Price Warung (William Astley) appeared in the *Bulletin*. His 'Tales of the Convict System' carried on Archibald's theme of the injustice embodied in the System which formed the basis of society. Astley's kind of documentary fiction was to be one of the *Bulletin's* major contributions to Australian literature. Price Warung's stories lack the symbolic resonances of Marcus Clarke, but their roots in historical actuality enable Warung to avoid both the melodrama and the insistence on an innocent victim that obscure Clarke's purposes. Warung condenses historical incident in pursuit of literary truth, and only the grimmest humour leavens the general gloom of his stories. They constitute a powerful indictment of a System that corrupts all who are involved in it.

Warung's work is not, however, characteristic of the *Bulletin's* general populism, which clothed the hardships of the world in humour. The brief paragraphs of readers' anecdotes, the cartoons and the ballads pricked pomposity with irreverence. From images of swaggies and horsemen, struggling farmers and hard-drinking shearers, the paper constructed for its readers the ideal of the true Australian as a battler.

Ballads and Yarns

It was the bush ballads and yarns that articulated the ideal of the true Australian as a battler. The *Bulletin*, along with its contemporaries such as the Queensland *Boomerang*, took these ballads and yarns from the campfire to become for a generation the dominant form of Australian writing. Their easy egalitarianism, their preference for action over ideas and their sense of the outdoors shaped the way Australians came to think of themselves.

At its best, the freedom and self-reliance of the bush tradition is found in a song like 'The Maranoa Drovers' by A.W. Davis:

> The night is dark and stormy, and the sky is
>   clouded o'er;
> Our horses we will mount and ride away,
> To watch the squatters' cattle through the
>   darkness of the night,
> And we'll keep them in the camp till break of day.
>   For we're going, going, going to Gunnedah so
>   far,
>   And we'll soon be into sunny New South Wales,
>   We shall bid farewell to Queensland, with its
>   swampy coolibah —
> Happy drovers from the sandy Maranoa.

> Douglas Stewart and Nancy
> Keesing (eds.), *Old bush Songs
> and Rhymes of Colonial Times,
> [Old Bush Songs]*, Angus &
> Robertson, Sydney, 1957,
> p. 130.

The place names with their Aboriginal derivations give a sense of being at home in the countryside, the easy rhythm matches the spaciousness of the drove. Even when the anonymous author speaks of the hardships of the track as storms interrupt their sleep, the speed of the rhythm and cheeriness of the chorus gloss over the difficulty. The song presents the image the men like to have of themselves.

This relaxed good humour in the face of adversity moves easily into the broad slapstick humour of the tall stories of bush heroes and the yarns of dreadful thirsts and binges, which in turn merge easily into the horrors of madness and death. These themes come together in a ballad like John Philip Burke's 'His Last Stage', where the figure of the swagman is both a figure of fun and a pathetic reminder of a life now nearly past:

> His dog toddled on by his side,
> He was wall-eyed and mangy and old,
> His voice, shrill and cracked, had been broken at
>   'graft',

In yelping the sheep to the fold —
  Jog, jog, jog,
With his load on the sundowner's course,
For sharers in labour were master and dog,
And sharers in damper and 'horse'.

Douglas Stewart and Nancy
Keesing (eds.), *Australian
Bush Ballads*, Angus &
Robertson, Sydney, 1955,
pp. 255–6.

In due course the sundowner's brain 'grew puzzled and queer', and he rushes desperately into the empty bush, falls down a cliff and dies, where

. . . crows were to him, as to hundreds before,
The only ones there for his sake.

Stewart and Keesing, *Australian
Bush Ballads*, pp. 255–6.

The relentless metre keeps the verses at the level of a joke, and so enables the narrator to keep at bay the images of starvation, madness and death in an utterly alien land. This is the final reality beyond the freedom of droving or the laughter and mateship of the pub.

The indifference of the country became active when it was embodied in the hostility of Aborigines who attacked the lonely men trying to build their own kind of life in the wilderness. The balladists projected both their fears and their sexual guilts on those they perceived as threatening or destroying their dream of home and family. Some of the writers were content to make the Aborigines mere figures of fun who could safely be disregarded. In a ballad of an Aborigine cuckolded by the white miner who takes his wife, H. Head solves the problem by frightening the Aborigine with a revolver shot until he is no longer quite black, so that the:

. . . next fool that looks on that child
Maybe they will think it is his son.

Stewart and Keesing, *Australian
Bush Ballads*, p. 104.

The cruelty and irresponsibility of this joke pale into insignificance beside the gloating self-righteousness of the ballads of revenge. In 'Lex Talionis', Francis

Myers writes of an attack on a bush settler in his home, and the boy who escaped to bring an avenging party. They arrive at the homestead too late, however, and the boy is marked as the avenger:

. . . his lips were sealed as by deadliest drouth
With the kiss of his mother's fire-charred mouth;
Baptized in blood and confirmed by fire,
His whole soul dark with one fell desire . . .
'Twas to kill and to kill, and in killing pay
His debt to the devils in the proper way.
He is dead, God rest him, and all his tracks
Are marked with the bones of the cursèd blacks.

Stewart and Keesing, *Australian
Bush Ballads*, pp. 101–3.

The frustration of settlement and the loss of home led to the death of all human feeling except that of hatred, and of all fellowship except the bond of vengeance.

Women and children have little place in the world of the ballads. In the ballads about Aborigines, they are the objects of pity and guilt, left at the mercy of savages by their absent menfolk. In the bushranging ballads, they appear as allies of the outlaws against the police, like the heroine of 'The Bloody Field of Wheogo', who shares the inversion of moral values produced by the conflict with authority:

And twinkling bright in the shadowy night
A lonely taper shines,
And seated there is a woman fair
Who in amorous sadness pines.

For her lord is gone, and she sits alone,
Alone in her mountain home!
But 'twas not her lord that she deplored,
For she liked to see him roam.

The joy of her heart is a bushranger smart
Who, lion-like, prowls in the night . . .

Stewart and Keesing, *Australian
Bush Ballads*, p. 13.

The ambiguity of the ballads is that the home which is the central symbol of security and independence, the object of the long struggle with the land, is also a place of bondage for the free spirits who prefer to wander the land at will. The bushranger here is admired rather than the selector but, unusually, marriage is seen as a bond also on the free spirit of the woman. The ambiguity remains, however, because the home where she waits 'with supper all spread, and a four-post bed', has been staked out by the troopers who are using her as a bait to trap her lover.

The bushranger's girlfriend merges easily into the figure of the wanton barmaid who entertains the wanderers in the shanties while she joins with the keeper in depriving the workers of their hard-earned cheques. The attitude to these women is casual, except in the occasional ballad like 'The Devil on the Rock', where the shanty becomes an image of death. More usual is the attitude of Breaker Morant's drovers:

> We've drunk the wine, we've kissed our girls, and
>   funds are sinking low,
> The horses must be thinking it's a fair thing now
>   to go . . .
> Then back again — I trust you'll find your best
>   girl's merry face,
> Or, if she jilts you, may you get a better in her
>   her place.

Stewart and Keesing, *Australian*
Bush Ballads, p. 169.

The girls are mentioned in the first and last lines of the poem as a kind of frame for its real business — the droving trip — and they have slightly less importance than horses, drink and tobacco.

A different image of women as the long-suffering heroines of men's struggles was produced by the literary balladists. Victor Daley in 'Woman at the Washtub' salutes the woman labouring while men forget her: 'From birth till we are dying/You wash our sordid duds', (Russel Ward (ed.), *Penguin Book of Australian Ballads*, Penguin, Ringwood, 1964, pp. 219–20).

George Essex Evans in 'Women of the West' creates the image of the pioneer:

> In the slab-built, zinc-roofed homestead of some
>   lately taken run,
> In the tents beside the bankment of a railway just
>   begun,
> In the huts of new selections, in the camps of
>   man's unrest,

> On the frontiers of the Nation, live the Women of
>   the West.

Ward, *Australian Ballads*,
p. 105.

In both of these pieces the women are seen from outside. Daley tries to turn the signs of deprivation into marks of honour. He produces an image that denies the woman even consciousness of her own, and rewards her only with a dream-time future. The thumping rhymes add to the falsity of the whole. Evans avoids this condescension, and provides women with an image that they could endorse, but at the cost of generalisation and idealisation. While the ballads about the work and play of men involve the reader in the experience, Evans' poem holds up the lives of women as an example to be admired. It thus keeps them safely in the place of the poet's making.

The ballads were complemented in the *Bulletin* by the yarns and cartoons that arose from the same world and expressed the same values. This world, founded on the life of the bush worker, is not comparable with that from which the folk songs and ballads of Britain emerged. The British balladists recorded a history they shared with their listeners. The Australian folk writers used the columns made available to them in the *Bulletin*, and its contemporaries such as the *Worker* and the Brisbane *Boomerang*, to define themselves as a class. Their songs and yarns express the values their authors share with others in a similar situation, and thus separate this group from outsiders such as bosses, new chums and city dwellers. At the same time they provide for these others the ideal of the true Australian. The urban publication and urban readers are therefore as important to them as is the audience of bush communities from which they arise.

'Banjo' Paterson

The essentially public purpose of the bush ballad means that there is no real difference between those composed as an incidental activity by bush workers and those produced by more consciously professional writers. In fact, Andrew Barton 'Banjo' Paterson, the most representative writer to emerge within this tradition, lived for most of his life in the city, and was once labelled by Henry Lawson the 'city bushman'. Yet

'Banjo' Paterson
(*National Library of Australia*)

he was both completely at one with his bush audience and the most polished practitioner of the balladist's craft. Paterson became and remains Australia's most popular poet, and is still known and quoted in pubs and homesteads throughout the country. His work expresses every element of the bush legend, and his 'Waltzing Matilda' has become a symbol of national identity. Yet the limitations of his writing arise from this very representativeness that has made it so popular. Paterson's work enables the reader to enter completely into the author's feelings, and to identify them as his own. The stereotypes impose themselves on our consciousness without really altering it. The images idealise and simplify experience, but do not at all objectify it so that we can inspect it, criticise it and adjust to it.

We can see how this happens in one of his best-known poems, 'Clancy of the Overflow'. This poem sets up distinct images of 'the dusty, dirty city' and the 'language uninviting of the gutter children fighting', and contrasts these with Clancy's life where

. . . the bush has friends to meet him, and their
     kindly voices greet him
In the murmur of the breezes and the river on its
     bars,
And he sees the vision splendid of the sunlit plains
     extended,

And at night the wondrous glory of the everlasting
     stars.

Ward, *Australian Ballads*, p. 161.

The internal rhyme and assonance combine to fix the images in our minds at the same time as they take us on at a pace that allows no room for questioning.

Paterson's verse creates memorable images of the Australian character. The modest, wiry but daring man from Snowy River is one; the shrewd and ingenious Saltbush Bill, with a native cunning that outwits the conceit of the Englishman, is another. He places these people within the framework of anecdotes that endorse his model — the Man from Ironbark confronted with the 'gilded youth' of the city: 'Their eyes were dull, their heads were flat, they had no brains at all' — the crescendo is irresistible. The stories, with their rough but shrewd humour, flatter us into identification with their bush heroes, and thus with the easy-going but proudly independent Australian. The works flatten out the problems of real life into the sentimentality of a sunlit bush where, if only the cities and their banks would keep out, all problems can be solved with a quick wit and a firm hand on the reins.

A similar mood pervades his stories in prose, although these contain more of the genuine hardships of bush life. They have within them, however, an element of cruelty — the jackaroo who finds himself the victim of an avaricious property owner finishes up dying in the horrors of drink, the butcher's dog is slaughtered by the cook, and a peaceful police sergeant is drowned as the climax of a farcical piece of satire. Despite some lyrical descriptions of the countryside, this element creates a basic unease.

Paterson may have felt this unease himself about the country in which he travelled so widely and which he made the subject of popular and lyrical mythology. In his 'Song of the Future' he celebrates the achievements of the white race in building a nation in a land that 'But yesterday was all unknown', and in which 'The wild man's boomerang was thrown/Where now great cities stand.' This achievement he describes as the culmination of the Biblical efforts of the pioneers who 'saw the land that it was good . . . and gave their silent thanks to God'. But now he feels that this achievement is endangered:

But times are changed, and changes rung
From old to new — the olden days,
The old bush life and all its ways,
Are passing from us all unsung . . .
Our willing workmen, strong and skilled,
Within our cities idle stand,
And cry aloud for leave to toil.

The stunted children come and go
In squalid ways and alleys black;
We follow but the beaten track
Of other nations, and we grow
In wealth for some — for many, woe.

> A.B. Paterson, *The Collected
> Verse of A.B. Paterson*, Angus
> & Robertson, Sydney, 1951,
> pp. 135–6.

Paterson's writings reveal his dismay that Australia is becoming like other nations—the dream of a new world has not been realised. His only response is an appeal to a nostalgia for a pioneering past that not only opened up the bush to the world but needed the markets and capital of the wider world to ensure its success. By ignoring this, the bush myth-makers turned from confrontation with the factors destroying their dream and turned their rage instead against imagined enemies like the Aborigines and the Chinese. This is most obvious in Paterson's 'Bushman's Song'. His marvellous celebration of the free life of the shearer runs against the fact of coloured labour being used to break the unions:

> 'We shear non-union here,' says he. 'I call it scab,'
>   says I.
> I looked along the shearin' floor before I turned to
>   go —
> There were eight or ten dashed Chinamen
>   a-shearin' in a row.
> It was shift, boys, shift, for there wasn't the
>   slightest doubt
> It was time to make a shift with the leprosy
>   about . . .

> Paterson, *Collected Works*, p. 65.

The appeal to solidarity in the first line is contradicted by the racism of the next. The union brotherhood could not become a human brotherhood because it was based on the exclusion of white women and all

coloureds. The free man who travelled alone destroyed his own freedom by his independence.

There is indeed an air of parochialism about the nationalism and radicalism of the *Bulletin* school. The older establishment papers may have appeared provincial by their insistence on the British connection and English standards, but they recognised that Australia did not exist on its own. The *Bulletin*, for all the attention it gave to European and American political and intellectual movements, tried in effect to shut the world out from Australia, and in doing so imprisoned the bush myth within the borders of the nation. In trying to portray a commonwealth based on bush values and free of the oppression of the System, it instead imprisoned its readers in their own fears and ideals. The rural bitterness of the magazine's later years is not entirely due to its loss of radicalism following Archibald's departure in 1903. It arose from the failure of an impossible dream.

Henry Lawson

In no Australian writer does the contrast of bitterness and idealism emerge so clearly as in Henry Lawson. The first poem he published begins with the cry 'Sons of the South, awake! arise!', but immediately goes on to talk of the 'old-world errors and lies' which make a hell in the 'Paradise/That belongs to your sons and you'. Ten years later, recalling the past with some bitterness, Lawson wrote of himself that he 'started a shy, ignorant lad from the Bush, under every disadvantage arising from poverty and lack of education, and with the extra disadvantage of partial deafness thrown in', yet with 'implicit faith in human nature, and a heart full of love for Australia, and hatred for wrong and injustice'. Both passages have the same idea of the individual trapped by social and personal circumstances in a country that should be able to offer to everyone the chance to grow freely to human fulfilment.

All of Lawson's work can be read as a testimony of his concern for men and women reaching for their potential only to be frustrated and to fall back into a stubborn resistance to their fate. In general his verse, for which he was best known in his lifetime, carries the reader on the highest flights of hope, while the prose confronts the bitterest frustrations of reality. Yet, because his characters are not crushed even when all illusions are destroyed, the hope he

Henry Lawson
(*State Library of Victoria*)

the fence — the ultimate result of ten years', fifteen years', and twenty years' hard, hopeless graft by strong men who died like broken-down bullocks further out. And all the years miles and miles of rich black soil flats and chocolate slopes lay idle, because of old-time grants, or because the country carried sheep — for the sake of an extra bale of wool and an unknown absentee. I watched old fossickers and farmers reading *Progress and Poverty* earnestly and arguing over it Sunday afternoons. And I wished that I could write.

> Henry Lawson, *Collected Prose*,
> Vol. 2, edited by Colin Roderick,
> Angus & Robertson, Sydney,
> 1972, p. 109.

These bitter images and characters appear time and again in Lawson's writing. The last sentences explain why this work struck a chord with his readers. Lawson recalls that the droughts and other troubles of the early 1880s finally broke many of these selectors and sent them to menial labour in the cities, but he remembers also the time when there was hope that they would achieve the dream. The despair is tinged with a paradoxical nostalgia for a bush that possessed the dream even if it withheld it. The writing functions in the gap between aspiration and failure.

In 'Pursuing Literature', Lawson distinguishes the three periods that provided the sources of his work. The 'roaring days' of the gold-rushes constitute a heroic age when the promise of wealth offered hope to all. This hope was blighted in the second period, when the diggers became selectors, using the wealth they had won from gold in the endeavour to establish themselves on the land. Finally, he writes of the time of defeat, when the selectors have abandoned their farms to join new rushes, fossick over old fields, tramp in search of casual work, or accept the ultimate defeat of labour in the cities.

Each of these periods elicits a different response in Lawson's writing. He knew of the roaring days from yarns in which his father's mates recalled the days of their youth through the golden haze of nostalgia. They appear in his work in nostalgic sketches like 'An Old Mate of Your Father's' and heroic ballads like 'The Lights of Cobb and Co'. Their spirit provides the title of his first book of verse, *In the Days when*

discovers in his prose endures beyond that which he vaunts in his verse.

At the beginning of his article 'Pursuing Literature in Australia', from which come the remarks about his start in life, Lawson gives an account of the social background against which he lived his early years:

In the first fifteen years of my life I saw the last of the Roaring Days of Gulgong goldfield, NSW. I remember the rush as a boy might his first and only pantomime. 'On our selection' I tailed cows amongst the gullies of a dreary old field that was abandoned ere Gulgong 'broke out'. I grubbed, ring-barked, and ploughed in the scratchy sort of way common to many 'native-born' selectors round there; helped fight pleuro and drought; . . Saw selectors slaving their lives away in dusty holes amongst the barren ridges: saw one or two carried home, in the end, on an old sheet of bark: the old men worked till they died. Saw how the gaunt selectors' wives lived and toiled . . . Noted, in dusty patches in the scrubs, the pile of chimney-stones, a blue-gum slab or two, and the remains of *the World Was Wide* (Angus & Robertson, Sydney, 1896), where we read of a time:

> When finds of wondrous treasure
>   Set all the South ablaze,
> And you and I were faithful mates
>   All through the roaring days!

and when

> The brooding bush, awakened,
>   Was stirred in wild unrest,
> And all the year a human stream
>   Went pouring to the West.

> Henry Lawson, 'The Roaring
> Days' in *Henry Lawson: Poems*,
> edited by Colin Roderick, John
> Ferguson, Sydney, 1979,
> pp. 28–30.

The promise of treasure is associated with the human solidarity of mateship. The 'roaring days' include both a time when physical strength enabled the speaker and his listeners to go roaring about the world, and a time when the world itself roared with work and the wealth it gained. This activity wakens the 'brooding bush' so that, instead of the horrors of isolation and dread that had been found in it by Harpur, Clarke and even Boldrewood, it gives birth to a world of excitement, companionship and riches.

This roaring world is already framed, in Lawson's poem, by images of loss. The opening couplet puts it nostalgically in the past:

> The night too quickly passes,
>   And we are growing old . . .

> Lawson, *Poems*, pp. 28–30.

Associating the roaring days with the youth of the individual makes their passing a natural and inevitable process rather than a part of history that is subject to human control. The poet and his fellows are defeated before he speaks. The final stanza confirms the air of nostalgic powerlessness when he makes the achievement of the promise and material progress itself the reason for the loss of the human presence:

> But golden days are vanished,
>   And altered is the scene;
> The diggings are deserted,
>   The camping grounds are green;

> The flaunting flag of progress
>   Is in the West unfurled,
> The mighty bush with iron rails
>   Is tethered to the world.

> Lawson, *Poems*, pp. 28–30.

The images of men and action in 'The Roaring Days' provide a standard of contrast to the miseries of the present, which Lawson knows from his own experience. He notes the wretchedness of the city, where the 'Faces in the Street' cause him to complain that

> . . . cause I have to sorrow, in a land so young and
>   fair,
> Too see upon those faces stamped the marks of
>   Want and Care.

> Lawson, *Poems*, p. 4.

As bad is the suffering of the wretched in the bush whom he laments in such poems as 'Past Carin'', and sketches like 'A Day on a Selection'.

The easy rhymes and rhythms of these verses are an effective means of sharing an emotion, whether of nostalgia, pity or excitement, but they also lend themselves to easy solutions. Just as Lawson weeps at the thought of golden hopes that are lost, he is easily swept up in tides of revolutionary action that will sweep all difficulties before it. He welcomes the 'lurid clouds of war' that will dissolve contradictions and unite the men of Australia to:

> . . . fight for Right of a Grand Mistake as men
>   never fought before;
> When the peaks are scarred and the sea-walls
>   crack till the furthest hills vibrate,
> And the world for a while goes rolling back in a
>   storm of love and hate.

> Lawson, 'The Star of
> Australasia', *Poems*, p. 120.

The excitement of the long seven-beat lines sweeps the images and emotions on without the check of thought or moral discrimination.

The same excitement marks his call to revolution in 'Freedom on the Wallaby'. After observing that:

> Our fathers toiled for bitter bread
>   While idlers thrived beside them

he prophesies that the sons of bush hardship will

> . . . make the tyrants feel the sting
>   Of those that they would throttle;
> They needn't say the fault is ours
>   If blood should stain the wattle.

Lawson, *Poems*, p. 51.

The poem enlists the images of bush and mateship against tyranny. Its power, however, arises from the division it creates between *us*, the readers, who are defined as the heirs of the roaring days, and *them*, the ill-defined enemy, which is anything we care to blame for our problems. The imagery and the emotions were available to be harnessed to any cause, as Lawson was to demonstrate in the patriotic rants he wrote during the First World War.

Significantly, when Lawson deals with the gold-diggers and their contemporaries in his prose works, it is usually in the context of their later struggles. We see them in the days of struggle rather than hope, and without the softening of nostalgia, although this is replaced at times with sentimentality. Even the famous story of 'The Loaded Dog' takes place on a gold-field so nearly exhausted that fishing has become one of the main occupations.

This period, of exhausted gold-fields and impoverished selections, provides the subject matter for Lawson's most significant work. He recalls it from his own childhood, but without nostalgia. The reminiscent sketches in 'A Day on A Selection', 'A Child in the Dark and a Foreign Father' or the famous 'Drover's Wife', as well as his 'Fragment of Autobiography', all telling of marriages strained by desperate poverty, define the elements of the time. They are filled with images of entrapment, whether of the child by his deafness or his constant chores, the woman by isolation, or the man by the constant struggle against drought and the banks, and by the responsibilities of the wife and children whom he is unable to sustain.

The sense of entrapment is bleakest in the sketch 'Crime in the Bush', published in the *Bulletin* (see *Collected Prose*, Vol. 2, pp. 32–6). Here Lawson takes the convict theme of Marcus Clarke and generalises it to the entire bush society, which he portrays as so encumbered with poverty, ignorance and isolation that all human decency is extinguished in a welter of brutality, incest and crime. The unrelieved gloom of the story is, however, as sentimental in its uncomplicated view of human life as is the pathos of innocent and brave little Isley in 'His Father's Mate'. Lawson avoids these extremes in his early classic 'The Drover's Wife', where Tommy's heartfelt promise, 'Mother, I won't never go drovin'; blast me if I do!' has the warm sincerity of Isley's support for his father. This promise is, however, qualified by the colloquial vigour of its grammar, which gives Tommy his own independence of personality, and by our knowledge that this Tommy will become the reluctant and exhausted Tommy of 'A Day on a Selection' who will be forced by manly spirit and economic necessity to follow his father and go droving after all.

In 'The Drover's Wife' (Henry Lawson, *Collected Prose*, Vol. 1, pp. 47–57) the selection, the little piece of land that embodies the dream of rural freedom, has itself become the prison. The endeavours of the woman to resist the spirit of the place, by dressing the children and taking them on the Sunday walk through the monotonous bush, and by lingering over the fashion plates in the *Young Ladies' Journal*, only emphasise her isolation, which is not relieved by any confidence that her easy-going husband will ever fulfil his good intentions and make enough money to take her back to town. Yet the fact that the best success she could hope for is an escape into town indicates the failure of the bush dream.

The absent husband in 'The Drover's Wife' links these stories with those in which Lawson draws on his trip to Bourke and his tramp to Hungerford, when he met the itinerant bushmen who provided the models for Mitchell, Peter M'Lauglan, Joe Wilson and his mates. These characters belong to his third period, the time of failure. They have a past but no future. They have been driven off their farms by the failure of their marriages or their finances, and now support themselves by whatever work comes their way. Their attitude is not, however, the heroic defiance of the verse, but the cynical detachment of Mitchell, the man whom nothing more can surprise. The mateship that holds them together is not so much a source of strength as a refuge from despair, from the solitude that gives its space to madness, like the shepherd in 'The Bush Undertaker'. The figures of 'Awful Example' and 'Gentleman Once' who haunt the shanties represent their only alternative fate. Lawson brings these themes together in his sequence on the courtship and marriage of Joe Wilson, from the collection *Joe Wilson and His Mates*

(Blackwood, Edinburgh, 1901). This was published during his London sojourn from 1900 to 1902 although some of the stories in it had been written in Australia.

The portrait of Joe Wilson can be easily taken as autobiographical, and indeed a 'Going on the Land' sketch only recently discovered in Lawson's papers, underlies the resemblance in its close parallel to the events Lawson describes in his more deliberate autobiography (in Brian Kiernan (ed.), *The Essential Henry Lawson*, Currey O'Neil, Melbourne, nd). He explains in a note that 'Wilson' is 'Olsen' anglicised, a parallel with the way his father had changed his name from 'Larsen' to 'Lawson'. Although Joe's character resembles Lawson's own, even to his romantic view of himself as a poet and therefore too good for this world, the events belong to his father's generation of miners who try to settle themselves on the land, only to find, as Joe does, that they become trapped there by poverty, debt and family.

The sequence of stories is cast in the past tense, with constant asides from Joe as narrator in which he berates himself for not having valued his good fortune while it lasted. The three paragraphs that open the sequence with the happiest of all the tales already have an air of elegy that warns us that the happiness will prove fleeting:

> There are many times in this world when a healthy boy is happy. When he is put into knickerbockers, for instance, and 'comes a man today', as my little Jim used to say . . .
>
> I wasn't a healthy-minded, average boy: I reckon I was born a poet by mistake, and grew up to be a Bushman, and didn't know what was the matter with me — or the world — but that's got nothing to do with it.
>
> There are times when a man is happy. When he finds out that the girl loves him. When he's just married. When he's a lawful father for the first time . . . I'm happy tonight because I'm out of debt and can see clear ahead, and because I haven't been easy for a long time.

> Lawson, *Collected Prose*, Vol. 1,
> p. 537.

The story of Joe Wilson's successful courtship, and his subsequent precarious success as a farmer, is shadowed by the lives of the people among whom he lives. Even Black, the squatter at whose home Joe finds Mary in the first story, 'could be bitter sometimes in his quiet way' when he considers that his own marriage has finished with him being displaced from authority by his wife and son. But worse shadows fall as the sequence unfolds. In 'Brighten's Sister-in-Law' Joe finds succour for his desperately ill son at a wayside shanty where the sister has taken refuge with her dissolute relatives from her own failure in the city. Still more haunting is the gaunt neighbour, Mrs Spicer, whose desperate efforts to preserve her family and decency are symbolised by the threadbare napkins with which she sets the table when Joe and Mary visit, and the few spindly geraniums that with her dying breath she commands her children to water. These are the reminders of the fate that awaits Mary if she is left isolated in the bush. Joe reveals in himself the weakness that will doom Mary to this fate if she survives.

In the final story of the sequence Lawson shows the possibility of developing in marriage a relationship strong enough to resist the disintegrating effects of isolation and hardship. For a time at least, Joe's luck changes Lahey's Creek, keeping at bay the images of the 'gaunt, brick-brown, saw voiced, hopeless and spiritless Bushwomen', each in her 'lonely hut on a barren creek in the Bush' and establishes instead a positive sense of hope.

Lawson's work shows both faith and tolerance towards humanity. The tolerance, the belief that there is some good in every human being, and that we must stick together in the adversity that is life, is the basis for the mateship that is the creed of the bush and the only barrier to despair. But this barrier is not enough when faced with life's most bitter denials of common humanity. Only the women in his stories have the strength to face the emptiness of the lives in which they are imprisoned and find in themselves the love, humour, and courage from which they create human communion and value.

Henry Lawson is the first Australian author to write without European illusions and with complete confidence in the judgement of his Australian audience. His work assumes that the writer shares the experience and assumptions of the reader, although he may seek to correct ideas that he knows his audience holds but that his experience proves wrong. The dream of a golden age in a new land has become

Drought in the Far North of South Australia
(*National Library of Australia*)

a nightmare in a land so old that it rejects all human hopes. Instead of a fierce Jehovah, his characters encounter a landscape in which they can call only on the strength they discover in themselves. Law itself is futile in this environment and home a precarious refuge. The structures of civilisation are maintained by bush custom and the endurance of women. The gods and icons of the old world are alike found missing.

Lawson's charts of this world had no need of the carefully constructed plots of conventional novels and short stories. These were the products of a scientific and industrial revolution that had promised humankind a control over nature that the experience of Australia had shown to be illusory. His yarns and sketches instead show a world in which individuals can take nothing for granted. They must build their lives from what is available rather than on the basis of their own wills. The image of the bush in his work, with its overtones of mateship and its nostalgia for the roaring days, presented his bush readers as they liked to see themselves, and assured those who had been driven to the cities that the values on which they had tried to build their lives did endure. In his best work, he goes beyond the sentimentality that is a defence against despair, and discovers the values people create through work with their fellows. His work thus continues to speak to an industrial society in which the individual can maintain integrity only by resistance to the environment. His writing foreshadows a new world, but it is a new world built in spite of the old.

Lawson's Contemporaries

Two of Lawson's contemporaries divided his image of the alienating bush into two separate aspects. Barbara Baynton describes a bush where horror is scarcely redeemed by any human value. Arthur Hoey Davis, better known as Steele Rudd, writes of the same world of natural and human disaster, but overlays its frustrations with the bitter humour of farce, occasionally lightened by the glimpse of a human face behind the clown's mask.

Barbara Baynton's *Bush Studies* (Angus & Robertson, Sydney, 1981, [1902]) presents six situations that completely isolate the individual in a hostile environment. In the first, 'A Dreamer', the bush itself is the isolating factor. It actively seeks to destroy the pregnant woman as she struggles along a lonely track and through storm and flooded river to reach the safety and warmth of her childhood home. When she arrives, however, she finds that the home is now in the possession of death, and that even the family dog has become her enemy. In 'Scrammy 'And' and 'Squeaker's Mate' the isolation of the bush gives power and opportunity to the enemy. In the first, a former mate besieges the old shepherd in an attempt to find where he has hidden his gold. In the second, the man flaunts his new mistress before his former mate, the woman who now lies crippled from the blow of a tree she had been felling while clearing their selection. Both stories reverse human values, as the mate becomes an enemy, and the woman takes the man's place as toiler only to find her place as woman usurped as a result of the man's physical and moral weakness. Only the dog in each story remains loyal and preserves the victim from complete isolation.

In the next two stories, Baynton presents the bush as the agency that isolates the individual and brutalises society. In 'Billy Skywonkie' the refusal of the men to have anything to do with the half-Chinese girl who has been sent as housekeeper is a greater sexual degradation than any physical assault could be. She is reduced not only to an object, but to an unwanted object. The parson in 'Bush Church' is, similarly, merely an object of derision, but is as much a victim of his own uncomprehending religion as of his uncouth congregation. The society the writer portrays in these stories has lost even the most elementary decency or courtesy.

The last of Baynton's studies, 'The Chosen Vessel', is also the most terrible. Ignorance and brutality conspire with the bush to bring about the murder of the mother with her child still in her arms. Whereas the woman in Lawson's 'Drover's Wife' has her dog and her own courage to defy the threat of the swagman, the woman in Baynton's story is completely at the man's mercy. The satirical portrayal of religious superstition only makes more dreadful the story's ending, which denies the woman the help she believes is at hand.

Baynton's novel, *Human Toll*, (in Sally Krimmer and Alan Lawson (eds.), *Portable Australian Authors*: *Barbara Baynton*, UQP, St Lucia, 1980 [1907]), develops these themes into a story that culminates in madness and death, as a woman flees through the trackless heat and thirst of the bush. Although the success of the novel as a whole is undermined by the melodramatic plot, the almost unreadable colloquial dialogue of the opening chapters, and the futility of the devotion the two sympathetic men show to the heroine, it contains memorable images of obsession, tenderness, vulnerability and callous brutality. The final sequence transforms the conventional pathos of the child lost in the bush into a symbolic descent into hell as the woman flees through the parched bush with an already dead child in her arms. Yet even this flight, vivid as are its terrors, remains too unmotivated, and its resolution too arbitrary, to bear the symbolic weight placed on it. Like the stories, the novel remains a study in horror relieved only by the maternal instinct that is the one human value to survive the brutalisation of the bush.

By contrast, Arthur Hoey Davis, writing as Steele Rudd, uses farce to keep in check the potential horror of his stories. The earlier stories of *On Our Selection* (UQP, St Lucia, 1987 [1899]) have the authenticity of bush experience. In 'The Night We Watched for Wallabies', for example, the farce does not conceal the desperation of the family trying to protect its crops. The kids' attempts to avoid their share of the work emphasise the grimness of the struggle, but the birth of a new baby symbolises, at least for the moment, a renewal of hope. The same idea of continuing life combines in 'Kate's Wedding' with the theme of neighbourliness to show the making of a community. Dad's struggle with the manure, the incongruity of the parson, and the petty feuds that are the commonplace of life are subsumed in a greater unity.

This sense of creation is absent from the later stories, where Davis exploits farce for its own sake. When the Rudd family achieves some success, and Dad goes off to Brisbane as a Member of Parliament, the satire directed at urban pretensions lacks the sense of shared experience that the author brought to his accounts of early struggle. The characters of these early stories use humour as a defence against the cruelty of fate. Removed from this environment, it becomes merely entertainment, as the figures of Dad and Dave become crude caricatures in folklore of the bushman as yokel.

In both Rudd and Baynton, the dream of love and security finds itself in conflict with the realities of deprivation and isolation. In one, the dream is overcome by horror, in the other it survives through humour, but often of so cruel a kind that only those trapped in the same situation have any right to join in the laughter. The two authors view Australian life through very different frameworks, but neither transcends the framework to provide a wider perspective. They leave the reader to view the bitterness of their experience from the outside.

Joseph Furphy

When Joseph Furphy's novel *Such Is Life* (Angus & Robertson, Sydney, 1948 [1903]) was first published by the *Bulletin*, the publishers described the book as 'being certain extracts from the diary of Tom Collins'. These supposed extracts had already been reduced by the editor, A.G. Stephens, who had excised the two great chunks that later became the separate works *Rigby's Romance* (serialised 1905–06, C.S. De Gavis, Melbourne, 1921) and *The Buln-Buln and the Brolga* (Angus & Robertson, Sydney 1948). From the first, readers of the novel were confused by the illusion that the events it contained were selected at random by an actual narrator. They read it as an autobiographical report of life in the Riverina towards the end of the nineteenth century, and missed the deliberate structure the author, Joseph Furphy, had ordered beneath the apparently casual notes of the narrator, Tom Collins.

This narrator has held a slightly privileged position as Deputy-Assistant-Sub-Inspector in the government service, with the 'reversion of the Assistant-Sub-Inspectorship itself' if his superior officer should die. He could therefore enter easily into the society

Joseph Furphy — 'Tom Collins'
(*National Library of Australia*)

of travelling stockmen and teamsters, small selectors, swagmen and boundary riders, even if he was not quite on the level of the squatters themselves. His stance as diarist enables him both to share the lives he describes and to stand slightly apart from them as commentator. In commenting, however, he intrudes his own personality, sharing with the reader the fruits of a lifetime of formal but undirected reading. He interrupts even the yarns told by the people he meets to comment on their stories and to draw attention to the lurid speech he forbears from reproducing. Thus he distances people and events, placing them in the framework of his personal philosophy. The confusions in this philosophy become apparent only when we recognise the distinction between narrator and author. From the viewpoint of the author, the elaborate patterns the narrator constructs to explain life are themselves merely a part of the fiction we compose to make life endurable.

Collins' addiction to philosophising inflates the trivial and the commonplace to the level of the portentous and universal. Rather than enabling him to see the world in a grain of sand, his literary parallels mock the heroic dimensions with which he invests his account. If Collins becomes a figure of comedy, the patterns Furphy weaves relate the lives of even the meanest characters to issues of justice and responsibility. For example, the episode when Tom loses his clothes in the Murray and is forced to cavort naked among the respectable citizens along the Victorian bank is introduced by a long meditation on the fate of nations. Its most serious outcome is not Tom's embarrassment but the fate of a swagman whom he has momentarily befriended.

Although Collins may at first appear as another version of Lawson's bush philosopher Jack Mitchell, Furphy is playing a much deeper game than Lawson. Collins' absorption in his own speculations imposes on his experience a pattern which blinds him both to what is going on around him and to his own responsibilities for what happens. Furphy's concern is, despite the title of his novel, not just with what life is, or even with how we interpret it, but with how, given that we can never know the ultimate causes or the future consequences of our acts, we can ever produce a society in which justice will triumph over greed and ignorance.

Furphy throws his problem at his readers in the opening words of the book, 'Unemployed at last!'. The implicit sense of achievement challenges both the conservative who believes that work is a duty and the liberal who believes it is a right. Collins' subsequent speculation, after a decorous line of dots, as to whether his state is part of the pattern of the universe, the result of his own conduct, or merely a device of the devil to lead him into evil, sets the ostensible philosophic framework of the book, with its clear alternatives of fate, freewill and a perversely dangerous universe.

Collins' speculations quickly lead the reader, apparently by his casual choice of a page from his diaries, into the flat plains of the Riverina. These seem to deny all possibility but that of chance meetings and partings, and therefore to reject the possibility of either human or divine responsibility. Yet, as soon as we meet a party of people in this landscape, we find ourselves among teamsters for whom its details carry a wealth of meaning for life and death. They are involved in a class struggle for the resources of food and water. Their achievement is to keep themselves and their beasts alive. Beside this Collins' vague official duties are quite meaningless. His self-imposed task of going back to his diaries to find meaning in his experience and in the lives of those he meets is, on the other hand, a most valuable form of employment. The extracts challenge the whole scheme of things implied by the distinction made in the opening words. In turn, the pattern revealed through the diaries challenges all the kinds of patterning we attempt to impose on experience through language or reason.

The problem of reading the book is not merely one of discerning the author's pattern beneath the narrator's, but of deciding how to read the language itself. For example, when we replace the bracketed words in the speech of the bushmen that he records with what we can assume was in the original, we get fine specimens of Australian colloquial. But Furphy, rather than using mere euphemism or paraphrase, reports the supposed originals in a manner that draws attention to their departure from respectable modes:

> I'm a great believer in Providence, myself, Tom; an' what's more, I try to live up to my (adj.) religion. I'm sure *I* don't want to see any pore (fellow) chained up in fire and brimstone for millions o' years, an' a worm tormentin' him besides; but I don't see what the (adj. sheol) else they can do with Alf. Awful to think of it. Mosey sighed piously, then resumed. 'Grand dog you got since I seen you last. Found the (animal) I s'pose?' 'No, Mosey, bought him fair.'

Furphy, Such is Life, p. 7.

The phrases in brackets halt the flow of the language and compel us to notice the fact they we have a transcription of speech, not the original. They also draw attention to Mosey's mode of speech, and thus to the way he enjoys his own words as he quite deliberately constructs a drama in which he and the target of his abuse, Warrigal Alf, occupy the places he as the author of the drama allots to them. We have to read the passage on two levels: the lurid speech of the bullocky, and the distanced report of the narrator. The juxtaposition of the two levels enables the author to show the characters dramatising their lives as they speak them.

The distinction between the roles we play in our own eyes and in the view of others is evident from the first chapter when, as the teamsters sit around yarning after tea, each one in turn has to leave the company and go to the water tank for a drink. As he leaves, he ceases to be a participant in the discourse and becomes an object for the unflattering comments of the others. While Tom's diaries provide one narrative scheme, and the author another, we are made aware that there are as many possible patterns in the events as there are participants.

In having Collins deny that the book has any plot, while at the same time giving the reader clues to any number of plots and interpretative schemes, Furphy signals his disbelief in a world subject to human purposes. Yet, in allowing both the narrator and the characters he meets to select characters and incidents more or less as they will, Furphy asserts the human need to interpret experience. At the same time, as he follows a plot unwinding without the connivance or even the recognition of its narrator, he shows how misleadingly false any interpretation can be, serving only to conceal from the narrator what is plainly before him.

The narratives in the book are rarely allowed to flow without interruption. They are interrupted by digressions, by events and by the listeners. This interruption of the linear sequence of events links apparently unrelated incidents to each other and so introduces themes and sequences of action that are further unwound and interwoven throughout the novel and outside the consciousness of the participants. Despite the realism of characters and events, this patterning has more in common with the mediaeval romance than it does with the nineteenth-century novel. The characters of romance tell their own stories, but they are also part of a story of which only God knows the plot. In Furphy's novel, even the author of the universal plot is unknown, but, like the storyteller of the Middle Ages, he anticipates an audience that will recognise that every event forms a part of several patterns at different levels of significance — narrative, personal, moral and cosmic. His world is finally unknowable, and he resolves its contradictions only by reiterating Ned Kelly's last words, 'Such is Life!'.

The characters in *Such Is Life* are trapped in lives of search and pursuit. The search varies from Tom Collins' pursuit of meaning to the teamsters' constant quest for grass; from the pursuit for escape from the malevolent fate that stalks Steve Thompson to the efforts of the predatory widow Mrs Beaudesart to ensnare Tom in matrimony. At its most comic, the epic of search and pursuit is embodied in Tom's efforts to find a pair of trousers to cover his nakedness; at its most pathetic, in Mary Halloran's search through the bush for her father and the desperate race of the bushmen to find her before death finishes her quest.

The novel's philosophical framework is provided by the three propositions Tom Collins offers in his meditations. The first is his theory of fate as the outcome of critical choices that lead to unknown ends. Once having chosen, even between apparently trivial alternatives, we are irrevocably committed. So Tom's chance decision to cross the river before having a smoke leads to the incarceration of an innocent swagman, just as his later decision not to awaken a man resting against a tree leads to two deaths. Although the novel shows the inextricable tangle of events and decisions, its irony undermines Tom's easy philosophy. Characters are shown as responsible for their own actions. Sollicker and Barefoot Bob uphold an unjust system by merely carrying out orders, just as Stewart ameliorates it by his compassion. Tom's philosophic speculations blind him to the truth before him and lead him to behave with unconscious cruelty to Nosey Alf, and distract him from his double failure of duty towards the swagman Andy. The death of Mary Halloran is due ultimately not to Collins's random act of courtesy, but to the inveterate bigotry and obstinacy of her mother. Chance may decide the circumstances, but people determine their own fates.

By undermining the central point of Tom's philosophy, the novel demonstrates the truth of his other two propositions. People's moral stature is revealed through their actions rather than their stations, valuing practical compassion and showing how the petty and the mean-minded damage themselves. This endorses Tom's belief that any system other than egalitarian democracy is an affront to humanity. This in turn leads to the proposition that Australia provides the opportunity to build a society based on justice and free from the superstition, intolerance and hierarchies that distort life in the old world. This possibility is inherent in the beauty the book reveals within the superficially drab landscape:

> . . . the monotonous variety of this interminable scrub has a charm of its own; so grave, subdued, self-centred; so alien to the genial appeal of more winsome landscape, or the assertive grandeur of mountain and gorge. To me this wayward diversity of spontaneous plant life bespeaks an inconfined,

ungauged potentiality of resource; it unveils an ideographic prophecy, painted by Nature in her Impressionist mood, to be deciphered aright only by those willing to discern through the crudeness of dawn a promise of majestic day. Eucalypt, conifer, mimosa; tree, shrub, heath, in endless diversity and exuberance.

. . . this recordless land — this land of our lawful solitude and imperative responsibility — is exempt from many a bane of territorial rather than racial impress. She is committed to no usages of petrified injustice; she is clogged by no fealty to shadowy idols, enshrined by Ignorance, and upheld by misplaced homage alone.

Furphy, *Such is Life*, p. 81.

The emptiness of the land offers freedom, and its hidden wealth promises plenty. It requires only human vision untainted by superstition to realise its potential. The narrative, with its ironic refusal to acquiesce in the delusions that blind its characters, offers the clarity necessary for this realisation.

Furphy's awareness that no human design can cover the variety of human fortune and character accounts for the persistent irony of the novel, but in contrast to the pessimism of Thomas Hardy, with his idea of the president of the immortals playing with human lives, or even with Henry Lawson, Furphy's irony is optimistic. He ruthlessly condemns systems of rule and thought that keep people in bondage or exclude them from their share in the common heritage. Furphy also condemns individual conceit that blinds people to the consequences of their own actions, as Collins' delight in his own speculations and wisdom blinds him to the cruelty of his behaviour to Nosey Alf. More generally he finds that people's actions are determined by the roles they are given. So Barefoot Bob as boundary rider can be villain, but as bushman is close to being a hero. This perception frees Furphy from the racism that infected most of his contemporaries. While Bob condemns the Chinese boundary riders as 'opium and leprosy', Furphy sees them as merely asserting a human dignity within the role they have been allotted by the whites. Similarly, he regards the Aborigines with the same tolerance he extends to the whites. Furphy takes the side of the half-caste Toby rather than that of the Scotsman who condemns him for having been dispossessed, and favourably compares the behaviour of the supposed Aboriginal king with the pretensions of European royalty.

Like Lawson, Furphy writes without strain for an Australian audience. He takes the Australian experience for granted, and brings to it the whole English literary tradition. Furphy revalues this tradition in the light of the new world, discovering in it the broad humanity he finds among his bushmen, but rejecting from it the rigidity of hierarchy and authority that stunts the individuals it involves. His humour is directed at the human pretension that is embodied in all systems, and even in the language we use to interpret our lives, so that his belief in the power of rationality is qualified by the levelling effect of universal absurdity. This rational stance means that his work does not attain the power of Lawson at his best, but it prevents him from ever descending into the deceptions of sentimentality or nostalgia. Although he may not transcend the experience of the Australian bushmen, he does succeed in illuminating their lives with a broad light of sanity and tolerance that suggests that if we cannot have a heaven, we need not build a hell on earth.

Christopher Brennan

While Lawson and Furphy, and their fellow-contributors to the *Bulletin*, were developing the image of the bush as the distinctive Australian experience, other writers, including *Bulletin* figures like Edward Dyson, turned to the city for their material. For the poet Christopher Brennan the whole of Australia was a provincial prison. The son of an Irish Catholic family, he had no love of England and turned instead to the continent, to Germany and particularly to France, for his inspiration. He was, however, a spiritual exile who would have been a misfit in any country. His misfortune was to live in a colonial society that provided him with friends, but without the language and interests to sustain his development as a poet. Uninterested in Australia, he created a world of disembodied mythology. His contemporaries did not even achieve that much in their verse, writing either nationalist and proletarian bombast or emaciated echoes of their English models.

In some of Brennan's earliest work we find the image of the city as the place of evil, where

The yellow gas is fired from street to street
past rows of heartless homes and hearths unlit,
dead churches, and the unending pavement beat
by crowds — say rather haggard shades that flit

round nightly haunts of their delusive dream
where our paradisal instinct starves:
till on the utmost post, its sinuous gleam
crawls in the oily water of the wharves;

where Homer's sea loses his keen breath, hemm'd
what place rebellious piles were driven down —
the priestlike waters to this task condemn'd
to wash the roots of the inhuman town!

Christopher Brennan, 'Towards the source' (1897), in *The Verse of Christopher Brennan*, Angus & Robertson, Sydney, 1960, p. 73.

The mood is the general world-weariness and disenchantment with human achievement that was charac-

Christopher Brennan
(*State Library of Victoria*)

teristic of the later European romantics. The original associations of every image are reversed. The gaslight that banishes dark becomes instead a sick yellow, revealing only homes, hearths and churches that have lost their reason for being. The crowds become shades, their dreams destroy paradise. The wine-dark sea that gave Homer's heroes the path to freedom and adventure washes only piles that have vainly resisted their imprisonment. The 'moving waters at their priestlike task' of Keats's sonnet 'Bright Star' are condemned to futility, while the town, ultimate symbol of the human achievement of civilisation, has become an image of inhumanity.

Against the degradation of the social world, Brennan sets love and, later, an inward spirit. The circumstances of his marriage, with a long interval between his return from Germany and the arrival of his bride to join him, lend a peculiar poignancy to his poems of love — first, the presence of the beloved recalled in absence, then the quieter joy of reunion:

Four springtimes lost: and in the fifth we stand,
here in this quiet hour of glory, still,
while o'er the bridal land
the westering sun dwells in untroubled gold . . .
all is content and ripe delight, full-fed.

Brennan, *Verse*, p. 91.

The mellow glow is already an elegy for a lost perfection.

The marriage was in fact to prove a disaster, but its moments of fulfilment provide the standard of perfection that Brennan both seeks and mourns in his later poetry. The poems of love and marriage are literary projections of experience, but as he moves further away from this period in his life, his poetic emotions become tied to more empty conventions. So, when the speaker woos Undine rather than any bride of flesh and blood, he seeks only

. . . there to drowse the summer thro'
deep in some odorous twilit lair,
swoon'd in delight of golden dew
within the sylvan wiches' hair . . .

Christopher Brennan, 'The
Forest of the Night' (1898–1902)
in C.J. Brennan, *Poems*,
G.B. Phillip, Sydney, 1913,
p. 110.

The dialectic between literature and experience has given way to experience constructed entirely out of poetic phrases. This robs his poetry of any sense of resistance to a world that imposes its experiences. Brennan seeks to find a retreat from the world, not to change it.

Only in Brennan's 'Wanderer' sequence (1902) does he again capture a myth in a web of language that places it in the context of experience other than the purely self-referential emotions of 'Lilith'. This sequence of poems goes beyond the constraints of any particular culture, yet still creates a quite specific context as the Wanderer passes through a landscape of closed houses and chill winds. The language of his journeying creates the values that drive him on.

The images of this sequence do not suggest a particular place. They serve instead to bring together the desolation of the Wanderer of Anglo-Saxon poetry, the nightmare landscapes of poems like Browning's 'Childe Harold', and the loneliness of continental Australia in a structure that isolates the individual from all human fellowship leaving him only with his own endurance:

O desolate eves along the way, how oft,
despite your bitterness, was I warm at heart!
not with the glow of remember'd hearths, but warm
with the solitary unquenchable flame that burns
a flameless heat deep in his heart who has come
where the formless winds plunge and exult for aye
among the naked spaces of the world,
far past the circle of the ruddy hearths
and all their memories . . .

Brennan, *Verse*, p. 164.

The poem does not rob home and hearth of their value, but makes them more potent symbols of human worth by their contrast with the Wanderer who must first leave them to set out on his way, and then refuse to allow them to distract him from his unspecified quest. Yet the value they hold emphasises the achieved strength of 'the wanderer of the ways of all the worlds' who is able to contain these values within himself

. . . because he knows
no ending of the way, no home, no goal,
and phantom night and grey day alike
withhold the heart where all my dreams and days

might faint in soft fire and delicious death:
and saying this to myself as a simple thing
I feel a peace fall in the heart of the winds
and a clear dusk settle, somewhere, far in me.

Brennan, *Verse*, p. 165.

Louis Stone

Unlike Brennan, who in his verse sought to ignore
Australia and create a universal context of culture,
his Sydney contemporary, the novelist Louis Stone,
wrote quite specifically of Sydney. Stone took his
characters from the larrikin pushes in the same way
that Lawson had chosen his from the bush workers.
The larrikins were a sub-group produced by poverty
and distinguished by a brutality that Lawson notes
only in the bleakest of his bush sketches. The pushes
had their own cameraderie, but as Stone shows early
in his novel *Jonah* (Angus & Robertson, Sydney,
1945 [1911]), this was used to enforce a brutal uni-
formity and to punish outsiders rather than as a form
of mutual support. The push is not even in potential
an alternative form of society, but is the direct product of the savagery Stone sees as the essence of
city life. The two contrasting characters of the book,
Jonah and Chook, the leaders of the gang, learn from
it the skills of survival in the city, but they eventually
succeed in their different ways only as they break
away from the gang.

Stone sets against the brutal life of the city not the
gang but the family. The old shoemaker befriends
the orphaned Jonah and virtually adopts him as a son.
Mrs Yabbsley, mother of Jonah's eventual wife Ada,
offers a street hospitality. Her natural goodness,
aided by the sight of his child, wins Jonah to his marriage and brief reformation. Success finally eludes
Jonah, however, because he is unable to give anything of himself. He destroys the old man who has
helped him, then neglects Ada and spoils the child by
the indulgence he shows in place of love.

Even in his prosperity, Jonah remains trapped in
the slums from which he has come. His deputy,
Chook, succeeds in escaping by leaving the gang to
marry Pinky. Although this marriage is based on the
security of mutual love, it is nearly destroyed by
their poverty. It endures only because Chook has a
run of good luck when he defies Pinky and risks
everything on a game of two-up.

C.J. Dennis

The figure of the larrikin is finally tamed and acclimatised in literary terms by the popular rhymer
C.J. Dennis. In his *The Songs of a Sentimental Bloke*,
(Angus & Robertson, Sydney, 1957 [1915]), Dennis
creates him in an idiom taken from the colloquial but
exaggerated for comic effect to give an Australian
version of the rough diamond with the heart of gold.
The combination of homely vocabulary and plain
feelings undoubtedly elicited a ready response from
Australian readers. It gave his readers an image of
themselves as unpretentious and practical, but above
all decent. At the same time this image softened the
hostility most readers would have felt in practice had
they met the originals of Dennis's city larrikins:

Life 'as got me snouted just a treat,
Crool forchun's dirty left 'as smote me soul,
And all them joys of life I used to think so sweet
Is up the pole.

Dennis, 'A Spring Song', p. 4.

In reducing the ordinary Australian to the lowest
common denominator in this way, Dennis was in fact
pushing to the margin those aspects of Australia that
were distinct, making them a subject for local indulgence rather than a part of the evolution of European
culture. Separating the Australian element, his work
weakens the resistance to European domination that
had been provided by the work of Lawson, Furphy
and Stone. In so doing, Dennis encourages the absorption of Australia within the global culture from
which it had struggled to find independence.

'The Sentimental Bloke'
(*National Film & Sound Archive*)

$$\underline{\quad\quad}\bigcirc\!\!6\!\!\bigcirc\underline{\quad\quad}$$

RECONSIDERATIONS

Early Twentieth Century

THE Commonwealth of Australia, which came into existence on the first day of the twentieth century, paid tribute to republican hopes in its name and to the realities of power in its constitution. Australia remained a loyal member of the British Empire, and local power remained in the hands of state governments and their financial backers.

The imperial loyalties of the new country were confirmed in the Great War. Eager volunteers enlisted in an Australian Imperial Force. Their experiences in the epic defeat of Gallipoli, the desert warfare of Palestine and the grim trenches of France forged a new sense of national identity that was centred on the image of the digger. This term, deriving from a tradition of endurance stretching back to the gold-rushes, suggested also the irreverent yet capable individual who could be depended on when the bullets were flying. The theme was taken up by English writers like John Masefield, who wrote of the unsurpassed 'physical beauty and nobility of bearing' of the Australians who had stormed the unconquerable heights of Gallipoli. This legend received its definitive expression in the despatches and war histories of C.E.W. Bean.

At home, patriotic enthusiasm hid deep divisions. The Prime Minister, Billy Hughes, who had adopted the nickname of 'Little Digger', deserted his party and split the nation over his campaigns for conscription. Patriotism turned into the extreme nationalism of xenophobia, as foreigners were persecuted and old ethnic communities like the Germans were suppressed, their languages forbidden and their memories erased. Although these divisions were not directly expressed in Australian writing at the time, the

Two young diggers

search for a basis of national unity became a major force behind the literature of the years after the war.

The writers of this period seem engaged on a process of reassessment. Bean himself had written before the war about everyday life in western New South Wales. Although his war histories contributed to national myth-making, they also constitute a serious examination of the conditions of modern warfare and of the way that Australians adapted to them. Among the novelists of the 1920s, Katherine Susannah Prichard went back to the bush settlements in search not of heroes but of the circumstances that produced community, and M. Barnard Eldershaw wrote about the generations of a Sydney merchant family to examine the ways in which the promise of a new land was thwarted, even in its apparent fulfilment, by the limited sensibilities brought from the old world. Frank Wilmot expressed in his poetry the reactions of the war-weary, and sought in his writings of life in the city to find images of universal experience. The 'Vision' group around Norman and Jack Lindsay and Kenneth Slessor tried to find the universal by entirely abandoning the present for eternal images of joy and delight. But the most searching reassessment of both Australian and British ideals is to be found in the trilogy of novels by Henry Handel Richardson. These appeared between 1917 and 1929, and were then published in a single volume as *The Fortunes of Richard Mahony* (Heinemann, London, 1930).

Henry Handel Richardson

Henry Handel Richardson was the professional name used by Ethel Richardson. After a childhood and education in Australia, she went to Germany to study and, after her marriage, spent the rest of her life in England. Ethel Richardson returned to her native country only once to confirm some of the background of her fiction.

Her first novel, *Maurice Guest* (Heinemann, London, 1908), deals with the lives of music students in Leipzig. Her second, *The Getting of Wisdom* (Heinemann, London, 1910), is about the experience of adolescence among the boarders at Melbourne's Presbyterian Ladies' College, where Richardson herself went to school. *The Fortunes of Richard Mahony* trilogy follows in many details the story of her father's

Henry Handel Richardson
(*National Library of Australia*)

life. While she may draw the materials of her novels from actual events, it is a mistake to read the books as either history or biography. She thoroughly transmutes her sources into fiction, which is to be read as a response to events, not as a record of them.

Richardson's central work, the trilogy, is built on the simple structure of a family chronicle spanning three generations. The first volume, *Australia Felix*, traces Mahony's fortunes from shortly after his arrival on the gold-fields through marriage to Mary Turnham, failure as a storekeeper and success as a doctor, to the point when he becomes disillusioned with the colony, sells everything up and returns to set up practice in England. In the second volume, *The Way Home*, Richard encounters the warmth of Mary's mother and the cold pride of his own family. He fails in his practice but comes into wealth through a lucky investment. Mahony returns to Australia and sets up house in Melbourne where he becomes involved in spiritualism. At the end of the volume, he again sells out everything and, having entrusted his wealth to a speculator, returns to Europe for a grand tour. While in Venice Mahony learns that the speculator has absconded and that he is ruined. In the final volume, *Ultima Thule*, he and Mary return to Australia, where Mary is forced to endure his professional failure and steady mental disintegration. Finally, she is reduced to taking a position as postmistress, where she is able to care for him for the few months remaining in his life. In this volume, his young son's observations and reactions, shorn of any adult context of explanation or interpretation, make Mahony's fate more stark.

The themes of the trilogy are encapsulated in its Proem. This description of a cave-in on the Ballarat gold-fields is a prose-poem paraphrasing the experience of Australia. It opens with the bleak statement, 'In a shaft on the Gravel Pits, a man had been buried alive'. It cuts to a picture of the hapless miner, 'his ribs jammed across his pick, his arms pinned to his sides, nose and mouth pressed into the sticky mud as into a mask' as 'over his defenceless body, with a roar that burst his ear-drums, broke stupendous masses of earth' (p. 7). The words not only vividly imagine the mode of his death, but portray the way in which the material weight of the earth negates the human attributes of tools, strength and respiration. In the face of this disaster, the dead man's mates make a brief survey that ascertains that nothing can be done, and the crowd melts away 'with a silent shrug. Such accidents were not infrequent'. The party who had worked the mine 'made off for the nearest grog-shop, to wet their throats to the memory of the dead, and to discuss future plans'. The narrative then focusses on the one figure who is left, the dead man's closest mate, Long Jim, who sits, 'pannikin of raw spirit in his hand, the tears coursing ruts down cheeks scabby with yellow mud' as he weeps, 'not for the dead man, but for himself'. This lone figure of failure, whose face is a metaphor for the land he has destroyed and which in turn is destroying him, provides in his past and future history a kind of variation in a minor key of Mahony's own.

In his misery, Long Jim reflects on the contrast between the ordered comfort of England and the indiscriminate savagery of Australia. This provides one of the polar oppositions of the book, yet even Jim's maudlin reflections cast some doubt on the terms of the comparison. The comfort he recalls is rather cosy, self-enclosed in its lamplight and mist. It is tied to a past that was already vanishing, even in England. In the raw mix of people pouring along the roads to Ballarat there is not only crime and brutality, but also a crude vitality that Jim, with his sentimen-

tality and prejudice against foreigners, is unable to recognise. Already in Jim's musings we can hear the first sounds of the phrase that is made explicit only in the time of Mahony's first prosperity, but that echoes as a *leitmotif* through the book: '*Coelum, non animum, mutant, qui trans mare currunt*' (those who flee across the oceans change only their sky, not their souls). Both England and Australia are what they are made by those who use them for their own purposes. The revenge Australia takes on its exploiters comes not from any inherent quality in the land but from the actions dictated by their own natures:

> It was like a form of revenge taken on them, for their loveless schemes of robbing and fleeing; a revenge contrived by the ancient, barbaric country they had so lightly invaded. Now, she held them captive — without chains; ensorcelled — without witchcraft; and, lying stretched like some primeval monster in the sun, her breasts freely bared, she watched, with a malignant eye, the efforts made by these puny mortals to tear their lips away.
>
> Richardson, *Richard Mahony*, p. 13.

Although the land 'contrives', its malignancy is not action but waiting, revealing people for what they are as they destroy themselves by their unwillingness or inability to change to meet its demands, to learn to love it. In fact, the inability to love anything is the source of the tragedies in the novel.

The novel moves between the poles of Britain and Australia, which represent opposing sets of values. Britain represents the restrictions of mind and energy that Mahony is unable to tolerate. Australia is free from the prejudices and inhibitions of British society, but the freedom it offers is only the opportunity for material gain. Mahony finds himself equally imprisoned in each country. His pride is equally affronted by the narrowness of Britain and the materialism of Australia. His tragedy is that in his search for the gifts of the spirit he destroys the professional abilities that alone could sustain him in the search.

The novel is constructed around a series of dichotomies or polar opposites. Mary and Richard Mahony are alike torn between Britain and Australia. While Mahony embodies the contradictory ideals of the two countries, Mary copes with their practicalities. The opposition between these two is symbolised by Mahony's affinity with an ever-restless sea that nevertheless makes no demands on him, and by Mary's ability to meet the unrelenting demands of the land. It comprises oppositions between the desire for change and for permanency, between male and female, and between the spiritual and the material. The gold that lures people to Australia becomes the symbol of these oppositions, representing at once the wealth that can free them from material worries and the delusive hope that keeps them bound in its pursuit until the earth engulfs them. It is a symbol of both matter and spirit, of bondage and freedom.

Richardson reverses the traditional significance of gold as a symbol of sterility. Mahony spurns the search for gold and instead seeks the values of the spirit, but by neglecting the needs of the material world he becomes professionally sterile and eventually destroys himself and his family. Mary, who at first treats his intellectual aspirations with respect, comes to deride them when he pursues them into the ludicrous practice of spiritualism. Even when she has doubts about her attitude they are quelled by the vigorous commonsense of her friend Tilly. It is only Mary's neglect of the spirit for the practical that saves the family from the total ruin that Mahony's material incapacity would otherwise have brought on it.

In tracing the vicissitudes of Mahony's fortunes, Richardson shows the dependence of well-being on wealth. Mahony is deluded not in trusting the gold from the earth that gives him his years of prosperity, but in becoming absorbed in a world of the spirit to the exclusion of the people around him. When, at last, he loses one of his own children, his belief that he can overcome death and talk directly with her spirit confirms the opinions of the townspeople that he has lost his senses, and destroys his remaining chance of earning a material sufficiency. Finally, believing that Mary's materialism is preventing his spiritual release, in a frenzy he burns the family's last securities. This attempt to escape from all material bonds brings about his complete loss of freedom. He is incarcerated in a mental home from which only Mary's material and social skills are able to free him for the last few months of his life.

Although Richardson herself was a lifelong adherent to spiritualism, which was the subject of respectable intellectual interest in the period covered by the novel, her fictional treatment of its practice is consistently satirical. The action of the novel endorses Mary's view that, as a result of Mahony's obsession with spiritualism, 'from a tolerably clear-headed person he had turned into a bundle of credulous superstition' (p. 545). Increasingly unable to deal with the world as it is, he turns to a deceptive faith to escape from its complexities.

While Mary is obviously right in her clear-headed rejection of the impostures of spiritualist practice, her refusal to take seriously the questions these address implies a limitation in the sensibility of the commonsense society she represents. She herself recognises this deficiency in the Bishop who represents that society's highest spiritual ideals, and whose visit provokes from Mahony the foolishness of public indiscretion. The Bishop behaves perfectly as a 'genial, courtly gentleman', but he has nothing to offer to Mary in her grief except the same empty formula of words he offers to everyone in like circumstances:

'. . . so *very* sad . . . Still! . . God's ways are not our ways. His Will, not ours, be done!'
. . . It was not so much tact and civility on his part, as a set determination not to scratch below the surface. He didn't want to spoil his own comfort by being forced to see things as they really were.

Richardson, *Richard Mahony*, pp. 721–22.

Just as only the miner who risks burial by scratching below the surface can hope to discover the hidden gold, so only those who, like Richard, risk their sanity and even their lives by asking ultimate questions can ever hope to find truth. The professional men of the spirit are as barren as the land itself.

The tragedy of Mary and Richard Mahony does not arise from a union of incompatibles, but from circumstances that divide their essentially complementary natures. Mahony's pride prevents him from sharing with her the details of their business affairs, while her impatience with abstract ideas prevents her from sharing his thoughts. He fails to recognise the love she expresses in looking after his pets, neighbours and assistants, in managing her numerous and troubled family, and in using her tact and social aplomb to ensure the success of his medical practice. Impatient of 'fiddling detail', he leaves it in her hands, thus further isolating himself from his surroundings. This isolation is compounded by the black Irish pride that hounds him with fear of poverty and debt, and by the years of childless marriage that deny them a bond in which their two natures might find a common purpose. When the children do arrive, they become only a further cause of division, establishing independent relationships with their two parents. Finally, Mahony's repeated upheavals of the household destroy any basis of security. They destroy Mary's confidence in him and drive him further into the prison of self.

Mahony's spiritualist practices are more a search for escape from this prison than an attempt to evade the finality of death. Mary, absorbed through family and society in the needs of others, has no need of such escape, and her lack of sympathy for Mahony's attempts merely adds to his sense of confinement. As she engages herself with her friends, he is angered that 'Never had she seemed so deadly practical, and lacking in humour; so instinctively antagonistic to the imaginative and speculative sides of life' (p. 482). Unable to recognise his dependence on Mary's practical skills, he is like the miner in the Proem. His

Eureka Stockade
(*National Library of Australia*)

failure to attend to material supports leads to his being buried alive.

Mahony is contrasted with the figures of Purdy Smith, the boyhood friend with whom he first comes to Australia, and Mary's brother John Turnham. The two between them have the qualities Richard lacks. Both are thrusting and self-confident, able to mix easily with all levels of society and born politicians, but there the resemblance ends. Purdy begins and ends his political career in the Eureka uprising, in which he engages as opportunist rather than radical. He harbours a grudge for Mahony's early favours, and precipitates both his financial disaster and his eventual mental collapse. Turnham, on the other hand, is a loyal friend, whose confidence in himself and in the future of Australia gives him the success that evades Mahony. This confidence springs, however, from a lack of sensitivity to the needs of others. He achieves public success at the cost of domestic disaster. Only in the agonies of his death does he find a courage that takes him beyond the bound of self. John's suffering and death unites Richard and Mary again in their common concern for him. This unity, however, disintegrates when they have to sort out the muddle of business affairs John leaves behind him. Richard retreats again from practical involvement to the enchantments of spiritualism, and becomes easy prey to Purdy's ill-judged financial advice.

Turnham's death breaks Mahony's last link with practical affairs. Henceforth, he moves steadily apart from Mary. He abandons his business adviser and entrusts his affairs to Purdy's agent while he takes his family off on a restless journey to Europe. Here the cruel death of the cat, which Cuffy witnesses in Venice, prefigures the way the world treats Richard, and prepares us for the news of his final ruin.

The last volume of the trilogy traces Mahony's disintegration as poverty deepens his isolation and destroys his capacity to build the medical practice that alone could free him from entrapment. His consequent sense of failure drives him further from the support that Mary could offer. The scream of the mill whistle, the increasing hostility of the locals in Barambogie, the unceasing heat, the physical pain and the taunts of the children add torture to imprisonment. Only in the moment of his collapse does he make a last attempt at escape, throwing out his fist in a gesture that could be either an appeal for help or a final act of rejection. The resolution of his conflict will come only in his final words, 'Dear wife!' which offer Mary her only reward. With these words, signifying his acceptance of her caring love, Mahony restores the complement of their opposites. This allows his burial in 'the rich and kindly earth of his adopted country' to bring him at last release from the imprisonment it had meant to 'his wayward, vagrant spirit' (p. 990).

The central opposition of the novel is between Richard and Mary, spirit and earth, but there is also a conflict between the different earths of England and Australia. In the first volume, the chemist Tangye offers the proposition that those who flee across the oceans change only their skies, not their souls. Restlessness is internal, not a product of circumstance, and cannot be cured by a new country. So Richard is as uneasy when he attempts to establish a practice in England as in his efforts to settle in Australia. Mary's soul belongs to her adopted Australia, but she is nevertheless able to create a home in either country for as long as Richard will allow it. Despite these continuities, places do matter. While the violence of the Australian climate, and the corresponding crudity of its society, violate Richard's sensibilities in a way that England never could, he finds on his return home that the freedom he has enjoyed in Australia has so changed his spirit that he can no longer tolerate the restrictions of England. Finally, a denigrating remark about Mary reveals to him the moral offensiveness of a society that prides itself on its own stagnation.

The contrast of the two societies is dramatised by the supper-party Mary offers to the people of Buddlecombe. She has thrown herself into the preparations with enthusiasm and Australian generosity, only to find that she has offended the costive local standards. Her guests, accustomed to the slender fare of an Abernethy biscuit and barley-water or inferior sherry, are shocked by the profusion of a supper-table on which 'jellies twinkled, cold fowls lay trussed, sandwiches were piled loaf-high'.

A laden supper-table was an innovation: and who were these newcomers, hailing from God knows where, to attempt to improve on the standards of Buddlecombe? It was also a trap for the gouty — and all were gouty more or less. Thirdly, such profusion constituted a criticism of the meagre provisions that were the rule. He grew stiff with embarrassment; felt, if possible, even more uncomfortable than did poor Mary, at the refusals and head-shakings that went down one side of the table and up the other. For none broke more than the customary Abernethy, or crumbled a sandwich. Liver-wings and slices of breast, ham patties and sausage-rolls made the round, in vain. Mrs Challoner gave the cue; and even the vicar, a hearty eater, followed her lead . . .

Richardson, *Richard Mahony*, pp. 446–67.

The icy exclusiveness and servility of provincial England, and the absence of any charitable spirit to ameliorate Mary's embarrassment, are contrasted with the food which symbolises her free spirit. Even Mahony, overhearing her casually insulted by one of the local dignitaries, recognises how Australia has formed her in a mode more spacious than England can contain:

Her manner had a naturalness, her gestures a spontaneity, which formed only too happy a contrast to their ruled and measured restraint. Indeed as he studied her, it began to seem to him that into all that Mary did or said there had crept something large and free — a dash of the spaciousness belonging to the country that had become her true home.

Richardson, *Richard Mahony*, p. 492.

This spirit, which Richardson specifically likens to the spirit of the Christ 'who had broken bread with publicans and sinners', gives Mary the strength she needs to endure the later collapse of their fortunes.

Yet the novel insists that neither virtue nor the spirit is enough. Money remains the measure in both countries. Mahony is as much excluded from the clubs of Melbourne in his days of poverty as he has earlier been from the society of Buddlecombe. The gold that lures men to Australia corrupts them and the society they build. The wealth that flows to Ballarat and Melbourne in the earlier books of the trilogy is obtained by raping the land, and the society it supports is distinguished by its intellectual pretensions and emotional triviality. Its achievement ends in the depression to which Mahony returns in the final volume. The only virtues that survive are Mary's practical generosity and his own endurance.

Richardson's novel is not only about Australia or even the conflicting values of the old and new worlds. It is also about a response to the turmoil of the early twentieth century. The first book of the trilogy was finished during the First World War when Australians had enthusiastically embroiled themselves in the conflicts that were tearing apart the old world and the known forms of society. It was published in 1917, the year of the Russian revolution. The later volumes were published in the time of the Weimar republic in Germany and the growing conflict of Nazism and Communism, when the ancient faiths of Europe were collapsing and people were desperately seeking new gods. Richardson's account of Mahony's spiritual search is as much a response to these twentieth-century needs as it is a recreation of experience in nineteenth-century Australia. Mahony's slow mental breakdown is the counterpart of T.S. Eliot's journey through the Waste Land, and the search of Richard and Mary for wholeness is the same venture on which D.H. Lawrence's characters embark in their flight from a disintegrating urban civilisation. While Lawrence seeks wholeness by going back to the elemental, Richardson seeks it by looking forward to a new start in a land untainted by the constrictions of the old.

Although Richardson understands the emptiness of the Australian bush and the hollowness of its people, she is also able to find in both the possibilities of renewal. Mahony responds to the promise of the wattle bloom, and although on his third landing in Australia he finds himself doubly alienated from 'its dun and arid landscape', Richardson places his disillusion against her realisation that Australia, like any landscape, must be learned:

It was left to a later generation to discover this: to those who, with their mother's milk, drank in a love of sunlight and space; of inimitable blue distances and gentian-blue skies. To them, the country's very shortcomings were to grow dear: the scanty, ragged foliage; the unearthly stillness of the bush; the long, red roads, running inflexible as ruled lines towards a steadily receding horizon . . . and engendering in him who travelled them a lifelong impatience with hedge-bound twists and turns. To their eyes, too, quickened by emotion, it was left to descry the colours in the apparent colourlessness: the upturned earth that showed red, white, puce, gamboge; the blue in the grey of the new leafage; the geranium red of the young scrub; the purple-blue depths of the shadows. To know, too, in exile, a rank nostalgia for the scent of aromatic foliage; for the honey fragrance of the wattle; the perfume that rises hot and heavy as steam from vast paddocks of sweet, flowering lucerne — even for the sting and tang of countless miles of bush ablaze.

Richardson, *Richard Mahony*, p. 585.

Likewise, while Richardson sees the limitations of Australian society, she also sees its potential for creating a new harmony. Although the populist election campaign waged by John Turnham in Ballarat is every bit as sham and vulgar as the political conspiracies Lawrence portrays in *Kangaroo*, the politician Turnham reveals in the face of death a clear-sighted courage that wins for his life a value its merely material achievements could not give it. Sir Jake Devine is the image of the successful colonial politician, dropped aspirates and all, but he has the compassion and practical generosity of a natural goodness. Even the cynical lawyer, Henry Ocock, is finally shocked into acts of selfless support for Mary. The society is shown as capable of generating virtue from its materialism.

The wholeness Mary and Richard finally achieve transcends mere self-fulfilment. Mahony's rejection of the material and physical in his search of a disembodied spiritual ideal alienates him from society and from Mary. Eventually he is forced to learn to trust her, and she in turn learns from him to perceive the unchanging fact of death and to go beyond the denial of life that it offers. In this trust of the giving self, enduring to the point of death and needing nothing beyond, the novel discovers its answer to both the divisions of self and the disintegration of society that were the products of the early twentieth century.

This disintegration is illustrated in episode after episode in the novel, as incidents in the old world mirror the violence of the new. Richardson gazes not just at the brutality on which Australia was founded, but at the collapse of values in the world she saw about her. In the end, her answer to this denial of humanity is the courage of Mahony, the family that Mary represents, and the hope of renewed life she finds in the repeated symbol of the wattle. 'An End of Childhood', later published as *The Adventures of Cuffy Mahony* (Angus & Robertson, Sydney, 1979 [1934]), follows the train of events to their worst possible conclusion. This story, in which Mary dies and Cuffy is taken from his sister, closes with a vision of the wattle in full and fragrant bloom. Against the greatest odds, the fiction affirms life.

The Crisis of Belief

Henry Handel Richardson's work responds to the crisis in European values that led in the arts to modernism, and in politics to the carnage of the First World War and the subsequent obscenities of fascism. While earlier romantics had opposed the ideals of nature and human feeling to the oppressions of the industrial revolution, by the end of the nineteenth century the hopes of liberal democracy and scientific progress had foundered. In Germany, the philosopher Nietzsche had expressed the new mood in his proclamation that God had died and that the future belonged to the overman who would transcend circumstance to create himself. Richardson, who was deeply influenced by German thought, dramatises these ideas in her first novel, *Maurice Guest,* set among the music students of Leipzig at the turn of the century. The talented and idealistic Guest is driven to despair and suicide when he realises that the natural blooming of his love for Louise is powerless against the force of the amoral genuis, Schilsky. The creative force embodied in Louise and Schilsky mocks Guest's gentler ideal of responsibility, but in separating them from the community it becomes sterile and destructive. Their pursuit of their own perfection reduces both music and love to the exercise of power over others. Guest's death is as much a demonstration of this sterility as of his own futility.

Such writers as Kafka, Joyce and Proust responded to the collapse of belief with works in which the individual is driven to reconstitute meaning and society from the fragments of words and perceptions that are the sole reality in his isolation. In the new worlds of Australia and the USA, however, writers saw the crisis in social rather than existential terms. Their work remains naturalistic as it traces the collapse of the promise of freedom and the tragedy of the individual driven into isolation and destruction by a society that has separated the self from community.

Only in *The Getting of Wisdom* does Richardson present a character, Laura, who learns sufficient confidence in herself to transcend her circumstances and accommodate to society without destroying herself.

Even in Europe modernism constituted only a small part of the writing being published, and the general lag in popular taste accounts for its slight immediate impact in Australia. The distance from the major cultural centres, as well as the differences in historical hopes and disillusions, were factors in the conservatism of Australian writing between the wars. It was equally important that Australia was a considerable distance from the war itself. Australian society was profoundly affected by the wartime casualties — 220 000 killed or wounded from a population of five and a half million — and by postwar economic troubles. Although these troubles disrupted traditional values and loyalties, their causes seemed remote. In Australia the urgent task seemed to be to restore an old order rather than to build a new one. The problems of society seemed to be associated with specific causes, such as the greed of unionists or business, the prostitution and corruption of politicians or the heedlessness of British commanders, rather than with a general collapse of civilisation. Writers, therefore, used traditional forms of verse to establish worlds of natural beauty to correct human brutality, or traditional structures of fiction to discover ways of reconciling the individual with society. They had to possess themselves and their past in their own country before any would be ready to make an assault on the citadels of global culture.

John Shaw Neilson

Most traditional and modest in his aspirations, although strong in his subtle achievement, was the poet John Shaw Neilson. Neilson, whose first work had been published on a country press in Nhill in 1893, had been nurtured through the *Bulletin* by its literary editor, A.G. Stephens, but his work has neither the overt nationalism nor the easy romanticism of many of his *Bulletin* contemporaries. His lyrical forms are intensified by clear observation reduced to essentials of sound and colour, often interchangeable.

The Australian element in Neilson's work comes not from any specific landscape but from the quality

John Shaw Neilson
(*State Library of Victoria*)

of the light, which becomes a symbol of love and joy in contrast to the ever-present threat of death. Love is not so much a passion in these verses as a light that fills the whole human frame. The light, however, is fleeting, threatened not only by the dark of night and death but also by the excess of heat and drought in the Australian summer that burns away life and hope. Love is both an awakening into new life, the 'slow delight/that tells the birth of day' (*Collected Poems*, Lothian, Melbourne, 1934, p. 87), and the nurturing love whose fruit is marriage and the creation of home and children. The children, however, appear as frail and as threatened as love itself. Neilson creates the lightness, the seeming detachment from the earth of his verse within the harsh truths of poverty, hunger and death: 'Down in that poor country, no pauper was I.' (p. 161) He discovers his delight in defiance of an accusing God and threatening death. His love is symbolised not only by light, but by the nest the blind girl fashions as a gift for him:

. . . lined with a love as warm as a man may find:
Out of the blackness light is called — and Dolly is
    lame and blind.

           Neilson, *Collected Poems*, p. 921.

At times Neilson seems like Blake, fleeing from the town with its 'crying, cruelty, every tone' to the 'green fields where the tired eyes go' and

The leaves have listened to all the birds so long:
Every blossom has ridden out of a song:
Only low with the young love the olden hates are
    healed:
Let the tired eyes go to the green field!

           Neilson, *Collected Poems*, p. 113.

At other times he is like Wordsworth, producing complete identification of the human and the natural, as in the way he sees the early-flowering almond:

Still as a bride thou art
   In a bride's gown:
See! an uplifted heart
   Beats in a clown.

           Neilson, *Collected Poems*, p. 119.

Most commonly, however, the human is at the centre of his attention, either transforming the merely natural through love, or taking consolation from it for sorrow, like the woman whose children are taken from her before she can show them the sea:

The tall man spoke in lover talk
   To blind her for the day,
But the Sunlight was more merciful:
   It had no more to say.

           Neilson, *Collected Poems*, p. 63.

The heat of sun and north wind has burnt from her her love, her children, her hope, but it can still give the last consolation of silence.

Neilson's poetry is filled with pity for the weak and the bereaved, and with a preference for play and fancy to labour and law. This outlook carries with it the danger, not always avoided, of sentimentality. The elves and fairies who sometimes stumble into his woods obscure the clarity with which he normally views the world. The random cruelty of fate seems at times to overwhelm the poetry.

The other side of Neilson's pity was a bitter rage against the humans whose callousness caused the suffering of sterile cities and generated poverty and war. The contrasting images of green and stone in 'Out to the Green Fields' have the intensity of Blake, but the redemption of 'Stony Town' by play and song offers an alternative grounded in common activity rather than visionary zeal. In 'The Soldier is Home' he writes with bitter irony of the soldier who comes home 'Hating the shriek of loud music, the beat of the drum', and mourning 'the good legs he left in the desert behind' — 'Oh! yes, the soldier is home' (p. 150). In 'Take Down the Fiddle, Karl' (published in *Collins Book of Australian Poetry*, p. 101) he proclaims the brotherhood of song against the hatreds of war. In 'The Ballad of Remembrance' (*Collected Poems*, pp. 169–75) he cancels England's claims of justice and valour with the single image of the back of the convict scourged by the law of England to maintain the squatter's rule in the land.

Finally, however, it is a poem like 'The Orange Tree' that captures the vision Neilson offers against all the pain and squalidness of the world. In this ballad, the young girl is constantly interrupted by the speaker trying to account for the miracle she simply perceives in the tree. His explanations represent imagination working to create images of joy, of madcap love, of unknowable beauty, but the girl surpasses him, dismissing all his imaginings as dross in the face of the truth she discovers purely through attention:

> — Listen! the young girl said, For all
>   Your hapless talk you fail to see
> There is a light, a step, a call,
>   This evening on the Orange Tree . . .
>
> — Silence! the young girl said. Oh, why,
>   Why will you talk to weary me?
> Plague me no longer now, for I
>   Am listening like the Orange Tree.

> Neilson, *Collected Poems*, pp. 100–101.

Truth comes from total attention to the other. The greed and fear with which humans seek to bind life destroys it. The light comes from outside this world, but it will be seen only by those who, with the innocence of the young girl, listen like the orange tree.

Frank Wilmot

A slightly younger contemporary of Neilson was Frank Wilmot, who wrote as Furnley Maurice, a name he adopted when he established a magazine to attack A.G. Stephens, who had declined to publish his work. Wilmot, a socialist and pacifist, published during the war a collection entitled *To God: from the Weary Nations*, which employed the inflated rhetoric of its time, not unlike the jingoistic verses published during the same period by Brennan and others. Later, however, he published verse that used the free rhythms of the moderns, but which, unlike them, is content to describe the surface of life. At its best, this verse has an exuberance that captures the bustling life of the city, and at the same time contrasts the plenty it promises with the poverty it contains.

Most successful of his city poems is 'Upon a Row of Old Boots and Shoes in a Pawnbroker's Window' (*Melbourne Odes*, Lothian, Melbourne, 1934; published in *Collins: Poetry*, pp. 115–19). The poem contrasts images of poverty and plenty, and the harshness of toil with the beauty it creates.

Melbourne is built:

> From rock and trouble and grumbling toil,
> Or out of the sliding slush the churning concrete-
>   mixer
> Spews into a hideous iron-befangled mould . . .

The products of this labour, however, are turned by the blaze of sunset into

> . . . floating towers with their bases muffled in trees
> And the trees cooling their feet in the water,
> And behind, long splashes of cloud.

Such beauty, he implies, is the right of all humans both by their birth and by their labour. This continuing optimism places him firmly in the mainstream of that belief in human and scientific progress that elsewhere had been shattered by the First World War.

Occasionally, as in 'Apples in the Moon', or the image at the end of 'The Victoria Markets Recollected in Tranquility', where

> The old horse with the pointed hip
> And disillusioned under-lip
> Stands in a drift of cabbage-leaves
> And grieves

> Judith Wright (ed.), *A Book of Australian Verse*, Oxford University Press, Melbourne, 1956, p. 52.

Wilmot suggests a sadness at the heart of existence, but normally he engages more robustly with the activity of life. In his most ambitious poem, 'The Gully' (*The Gully and other Poems*, Melbourne University Press, Carlton, 1944 [1929]), this engagement leads him to a vision of a future Australia that will match its natural beauty with the justice of its rule. However, when he turns from the tranquil observation of natural beauty at the beginning of the poem to the vision at its end, the work collapses into abstraction. Like Bernard O'Dowd, he was unable to integrate the vision with the experience that generated it.

Although Wilmot's work is modern in style, it affirms a traditional view that the problems of individual happiness can be solved by adjustments to the social order to ensure that the products of its vitality are shared by all. He neither plumbs the depths of despair that Mahony experiences nor achieves Neilson's strength of affirmation. In his attempt to ground national feeling in the sense of place, he looks forward to the Jindyworobaks of the following decade. Like them, he recognises that the problem of establishing political and cultural independence rests first on discovering an appropriate language. His work is a kind of poetic counterpart to the social realism of Australian fiction after the Second World War.

RENAISSANCE AND REVOLUTION

After the First World War

THE end of the First World War had left Australia a divided nation. The radical nationalist tradition that had been expressed by the writers associated with the *Bulletin* divided into separate and conflicting streams, variously emphasising mateship and bush independence. The labour movement had been split over the issue of conscription, which in part reflected the wider divisions between Catholics and Protestants. There was conflict between returned servicemen and between the servicemen and others. The conservatives were divided within themselves. They felt a nostalgic loyalty to the British Empire that had led them to their sacrifices in battle. They resented the affront given to their pride by the disdain with which the English establishment had treated their efforts and aspirations. Simultaneously, they were united in their fear of bolshevism. The consequence was a form of aggressive nationalism that sought to harness the patriotic zeal forged in war to the task of uniting Australians against the enemies within, and in defence of property and the rights of business and industry. Writers and artists felt themselves caught between the threat of social disintegration below and the aggressive materialism of capital above.

In Europe this struggle between forces that threatened to dissolve all order and tradition and those that denied the possibility of any independent life had spawned the modernist movements in art and literature. From the distance of Australia, however, these movements seemed merely new forms of degradation. In trying to cast off the chains of the Australian philistine, therefore, the most influential writers did not join forces with Joyce's cunning exiles but tried to recreate the older, and for them more fully human, world of the European renaissance. Rather than verse and narrative emphasising the primacy of form and image, and denying the possibility of a content separate from the manner in which it was expressed, they tried to renew the image of a world hospitable to the expression of human passion and emotion. Their work had the paradoxical effect of emphasing the unique nature of Australia while denying its reality.

This paradox marks the work of writers associated with the journal *Vision*, particularly Norman Lindsay and his son Jack. These writers sought to produce a renaissance in Australia by freeing its culture simultaneously from the narrowing thrall of nationalism, from the utilitarian and materialist values of their surrounding society, and from European decadence. The results of their work opened new possibilities to Australian writers, freeing them from the drab assumption of realism and naturalism that the writer's task is to show the world as it is and reveal the laws underlying its development. Their work, however, was flawed at its source by the belief that artists could free themselves completely from society and create

Norman Lindsay
(*Angus & Robertson*)

a self-sustaining world of their own. Rather than offering a criticism of society or a higher possibility for
life, their writing, like their art, became merely a form
of entertainment and escape. Where they escape
from this dilemma, they do so by holding firm to a
base of felt experience.

Hugh McCrae

The leaders of this group were the poet Hugh
McCrae and the artist and novelist, Norman Lindsay.
McCrae's first book *Satyrs and Sunlight: Silvarum
Libri* (John Sands, Sydney, 1909) had provided
poetry that soared away from the everyday world to
sing of a life of the senses in a world of passion and
beauty. This book contained decorations by Norman
Lindsay who, even more than McCrae, became the
intellectual leader and chief inspiration of the group.
His polemic essay, *Creative Effort: an Essay in Affirmation* (*Art in Australia*, Sydney, 1920), with its
view of the artist as visionary, making permanent in
beauty the sense of the moment, provided the unifying doctrine of the group.

McCrae's erotic, fanciful lyrics challenged both the
earnest morality and the nationalism of prevailing
fashions with a vision of a world charged with magic

and delight. Although he writes of Australian
seasons, his images are drawn from the worlds of
European myth and faery, his lawns decorated with
daffodils, his woodlands populated with nymphs and
centaurs, his nights occupied with the sighings of
Pierrot and Columbine. When he recalls the farm on
which he was raised, the memories of his parents are
gently affectionate. The conclusion of the poem,
however, totally rejects the traditional environment
of 'thirsty sheep, hay yet sweet and she-oak tall':

> I hate the farm-house on the hill, its windmill top
>   Slow girding at the sky;
> I think and think upon it still without one drop
>   Of weakness in mine eye.

> 'Memories', from *Satyrs and
> Sunlight*, 2nd ed., Lothian,
> Melbourne, 1911 [1909],
> pp. 69–70.

As Lawson had recognised, rural Australia destroyed mind and spirit. McCrae gave his life to
creating from old world tales and legends an Australia
that existed in the spirit rather than in any physical
location. In his best work he achieves delicacy, but
too easily the images become decorations and the
poems more whimsy:

> Pierrette and I took supper on the grass,
> And like a globe of silver in her wine,
> She drank the moon, then laughed to see it shine
> Still i' the sky, despite the empty glass.

> Pierrette and I, gay lovers, full of bliss,
> Made merry in the shadow of the lime,
> And, fondling me, she laughed a second time:
> 'My heart's mine yet, despite your empty kiss'.

> R.G. Howarth, (ed.), *The Best Poems
> of Hugh McCrae*, Angus &
> Robertson, Sydney, 1961,
> pp. 38–9.

The image of drinking the moon captures the lovers'
delight, just as its transformation into a metaphor for
their love defines its shallowness. Yet, like the love,
the whole idea is shallow, a turning away from life,
producing just the kind of entertainment Lindsay
deplored as the aim of art. Even when McCrae deals
with darkness and death, his imagery seems to have
this same quality of illustration or diversion rather

than involvement. The poem 'The Murder Night' builds an atmosphere of death, with images of a sick man's window, a swallow fluttering and dying, and a silent gutter of blood under the barn door, only to dissipate it in the last verse, where:

> . . . up on the bald wet hill
> A gibbering madman stands.
> And sniffs his horrible fill
> Of the rose in his shaking hands.

Howarth, p. 31.

Instead of dramatising the contrast, the rose and the madman remain mere stage properties. As the poem presents no human situation the images fail to carry any emotional impact. The same is true of his poems of love, where the lovers remain mere phantoms, like the woman in 'The Phantom Mistress', who provokes a murder and is locked up in a madhouse before she is allowed any merely human emotion. The images replace rather than define the human element in the situation. The affirmation of life becomes avoidance.

Norman Lindsay

McCrae's poetry is the verbal equivalent of Norman Lindsay's art. Lindsay was a member of a talented family of artists from Creswick on the Victorian gold-fields. This town, which provided the setting for three of his novels, is just a few kilometres east of the city of Ballarat that had first lured Richard Mahony's restless spirit with its deceptive promises of wealth. However, like Lawson on Gulgong, the Lindsays grew up in the declining years of the gold-fields, and chased their vision of achievement to the cities and to an older world. As artists, they tried to recreate the nature of this world before it was affected by industrialism, yet their liveliest work was in the drawings and cartoons celebrating the little towns of an Australia already 'with iron rails . . . tethered to the world'. Norman Lindsay's novels deal mainly with the male search for pleasure, particularly food, drink and women. His greatest literary achievements were the irrepressibly larrikin spirit of his children's classic, *The Magic Pudding* (Angus & Robertson, Sydney, 1918), and the immortality he conferred, in his novels *Redheap* (Ure Smith, Sydney, 1959 [1930]) and *Saturdee*, (Ure Smith, Sydney,

1961 [1933]) on the sources of this spirit in his native town and its surrounding bush.

For all its image-breaking vigour, the world of Lindsay's fiction is in effect merely the reverse image of the society he rejects. The kids in his books appear convincing because he understands that they reject the rules of the adult world only to impose their own. Pudding owners and pudding thieves in *The Magic Pudding* are alike bound by strict conventions that make their behaviour absolutely predictable. Even when they confront each other in court, they follow protocol, and the humour arises because they so completely subvert the adult world by using its own rules. Thus Bunyip Bluegum and the other pudding owners are free to follow their own imperatives of eating, singing and knockabout play. The honesty to follow rather than repress their desires distinguishes them from the judge and usher, the mayor and the constable who represent adult society. The strength of the fiction is that this behaviour represents pragmatic reality rather than the idealism of Lindsay's doctrines.

Five years before *The Magic Pudding*, Lindsay's first novel, *A Curate in Bohemia* (Bookstall, Sydney 1913), presented a similar picture of rebellion against respectability. This time it was among the penniless artists of the Melbourne of the 1890s to which Lindsay himself had escaped from his small-town upbringing. Like the later Barnacle Bill and Sam Sawnoff, the students are interested in satisfying their desires, which in this case are chiefly for wine, women, tobacco and song. The curate, who stumbles as unwittingly into this scene as he apparently has into the church, is less embarrassed by his own naivety than he is by his companions. He lapses from virtue, but soon makes himself socially acceptable by providing a source of ready cash, and in return learns to appreciate worldly pleasures. At the end of the novel he has abandoned the church and joined the others in insolvency, but not without worry. '"What am I to do – to earn a living"', he wonders, only to be told '"Do!" said Cripps, summing up the business of life in a sentence, "what's the good of trying to earn a living! You'll be all right. Go in for Art" ' (p. 248). This is in fact the same attitude as that of the middle-class respectability they reject. Art may be the most important thing in life, but it is a form of leisure for those who do not have to work. The workers are lesser mortals who exist to support the artists in their pursuit of pleasure.

Lindsay expressed the philosophy he developed in these student years in his early polemic essay, *Creative Effort*, and in his later autobiographical novel, *Rooms and Houses* (Ure Smith, Sydney, 1968). The essay argues that art is the supreme expression of man's existence and depends on the artist freeing himself from the restrictions imposed by society. The novel expounds the same idea through the debates between its characters, young artists in the Melbourne Bohemia of the 1890s. The flimsy plot revolves around their pursuit of pleasure and love, but the novel's substance is contained in their attempts to create an art that will offer an alternative to a sterile society.

Civilisation, the painter Jim Flack proclaims, 'exists on our capacity for expression' (p. 12), but this expression terrifies society and attracts the rage of the wowsers. True art can be achieved only by dedicated work, as opposed to the easy distraction of 'talk which made concrete the illusion of life brought to reality by words, of creation achieved without toil' (p. 15). The task of the artist, the novel asserts, is to create a true art free of the rottenness of Europe and the repression of Australia. This art will constitute a new paganism grounded in the earth and expressed in the movement of work in which, as in medieval illumination, the picture carries the full meaning of its implicit text. Good and evil are subsumed in the single image of delight, 'a gay, naked lady, crowned with roses. A gay, libidinous lady' (p. 61).

Yet, for all its philosophy, the novel celebrates a flight from life rather than an engagement with it. Lindsay seems compelled to seek refuge in the past, whether in the simpler struggles and hopes of his own childhood and student days, or in classical and fanciful medieval romance. His most successful novels are the three that escape into the real past of his childhood and youth, when responsibility could still be avoided. The country town in which they are set, Redheap, is recognisable in its smallest details as Creswick. It becomes the focus of both resentment and nostalgia as Lindsay recalls the frustrations and continually resurgent hopes of youth.

The first of these novels, *Redheap*, was banned in Australia for twenty-nine years after its first publication in 1930, presumably because it admitted that sex is practised outside marriage even in country towns. It deals with the troubles old Robert Piper has with his god-fearing family of country grocers, his formal education, and his girlfriends and sisters. The

second, *Saturdee*, was based on stories published in *The Lone Hand* between 1908 and 1919. It looks at life in the small town through the eyes of Peter Gimble, aged eleven. Peter is worried by the menace of rival gangs, his mother's heedless restrictions on his freedom, the boredom of Sundays and his pressing needs for time, money and watermelons. The third, *Halfway to Anywhere* (Angus & Robertson, Sydney,, 1947) deals with the amorous problems of Peter's 15-year-old brother Bill and his friend Waldo.

The three novels are characterised by Lindsay's insight into the workings of boys' minds, knockabout comedy and the swift verbal caricatures that create instantly recognisable figures complete with the roles they are set to play. These can give even a paragraph the qualities of a fully-rounded story, as in the opening of 'The Age of Flint' in *Saturdee*:

From the peace of pecking and clucking the backyard of the Bull and Mouth Hotel was suddenly ruffled into a fluster of squawking and quacking by the arrival of stones hopping among the poultry. To fowls, a meteoric discharge of unknown origin; to the groom of the Bull and Mouth, a phenomenon not so difficult to explain. He stuck his head out of the stable to bellow 'I'll warm your hide, young Pointer'. Five heads bobbing behind the back paddock fence shot out of sight, and five pelters in ambuscade ran swiftly across the road to hop the Grammar School fence and scoot behind the school. They were Bill and Waldo, Peter and Bulljo, and Pointer Brindle, son to the Bull and Mouth, and a sometime Saturday friend of Bill's, because by yodelling out from his front gate, Bill could bring Pointer Brindle yodelling out to his backyard; and because he had an extra large-sized stable to entertain friends in. Besides, he was a boy much denounced by mothers, and therefore well worth going with. For himself, he had a sharp foxy face looking out between a large pair of ears, which had got a start in the race for life, and arrived at manhood before the rest of Pointer Brindle.

Lindsay, *Saturdee*, p. 44.

Saturdee is a series of sketches or short stories that individually give glimpses of the town from the viewpoint of Peter Gimble, the schoolboy just emerging from the last stage of childhood to begin the transition from the freemasonry of gangs to the gaucheries of courtship. The comedy arises from the contrast between the magnitude of his hopes and the lack of his resources to realise them in the face of the malignancy of fate and adults.

The perspective of *Saturdee* is very similar to that of Bancks' 'Ginger Meggs', the comic strip that had started its popular career in the Sydney *Sun* a few years earlier. Peter and his friends show the same ingenuity as Ginger in outwitting adult authority and local bullies while still recognising that they can never win. Peter and Ginger both represent the irrepressible battler who gave Australia a comforting image in the depression years. However, while Ginger is merely mischievous, Peter is implacably opposed to all authority. The adult world he encounters is uncaring and repressive, and in opposing it Peter is not merely getting about his own business but asserting a right to his own life that no amount of after-school bread and jam can buy from him. Unlike Ginger Meggs, Peter and his companions are not eternal children, but grow up in the course of the novel. The narrator expresses the theme of the novel in his observation that 'All decisive gestures are acts of growing up. An act done by you; a bunged eye or a bunged-up love affair. Each allows the ego to burgeon by self-esteem or self-contempt: each completes one cycle and forces you to begin another' (p. 190).

The language of the novel takes the comedy beyond the slapstick humour of the action. It detaches the reader from the events and points to the comedy at the heart of human affairs. Its pretensions mock the boys' activities and at the same time make them a parody of adult affairs. While the action shows the gulf between the worlds of child and adult, the language shows the patterns that shape both, to which the boys are already tied even while they are still growing up. The 'process of equity' by which they judge their own case is no more pompous or less self-interested than the processes by which adults mete out judgement and punishment to their children, or than the more remote processes that determine prosperity and failure in the wider world. The patterns revealed in the boys' activities cover all aspects of behaviour, and thus provide a set of stereotyped roles into which people's behaviour must fit. Men and women, old and young, whites and Chinese, schoolmasters and bankers, the holy and the unholy constitute everchanging parts of a whole that always remains the same.

This view of life produces the central ambivalence of Lindsay's fiction. Although he purports to show the processes by which people learn to understand life and thus free themselves from it, he portrays a world in which the only true freedom is enjoyed by those who have yet to accept their responsibility for themselves, let alone for others. While his satire is telling it is ultimately grounded in an irresponsibility that can offer only escape as a solution to the problems of mature life.

Jack Lindsay

Norman's son Jack joined him in Sydney for five years from 1921, a period Jack Lindsay describes in *The Roaring Twenties*, the second volume of his three-volume autobiography collected as *Life Rarely Tells*, (Penguin, Ringwood, 1982 [1950–1962]). The ambience of cheap cafes and cheaper rooming houses in this book is reminiscent of Norman's Melbourne Bohemia, but Jack pursues art more seriously than any of Norman's fictional selves. He had been inspired by the argument of Norman's essay *Creative Effort* that the artist lives at a qualitative level above the masses and that 'only the creative image was dynamic, concrete, able to hold the universe together' (*Life Rarely Tells*, p. 175). Jack spent his time in Sydney, and his early years in London,

Ginger Meggs
© *Jimera Pty. Ltd.*

attempting to live these ideals out as a creative artist making concrete in words all the experiences life brought to him. The style of this life as much as its product was a rejection of the materialism and divisions Lindsay and his colleagues saw in the world about them.

As part of his project, Jack, with Norman, the bookseller Frank Johnson and poet Kenneth Slessor, established the magazine *Vision* to bring to the world the ideals of their artistic renaissance. Similarly, he worked with John Kirtley on his press to publish poetry by himself, Slessor and others, in fine editions with appropriate art work, often by Norman, aimed at matching words to images in a form that would speak to the creative elite. Jack has since written in 'Norman' (in Lin Bloomfield (ed.), *The World of Norman Lindsay*, Macmillan, Melbourne, 1979, p. 121) that his commitment to his father's views at this time, although excluding the idea of social action, preserved his own total opposition to the existing world. The last volume of Jack Lindsay's autobiography describes how he fought his way back to a philosophy that reconciled social commitment with artistic purpose.

The trilogy as a whole provides a subjective cultural history of Australia in the first three decades of the twentieth century. In it we can trace the process by which the environment forms the first consciousness, European culture provides the means of interpreting it and the individual then has to reconcile these and take possession of the land. In this process, contradictions reveal themselves between the sense of an independent Australia and the reality of its economic dependence and between the individual's realisation of what life could be and his knowledge of what it is. Finally, this newly shaped sensibility returns to Europe and is incorporated in the mainstream of European thought.

Like Australia itself, the autobiography reveals the very limited way in which European ideas were used by writers selecting from the past rather than examining the way tradition was being modified in the present. Thus the assertion of artists during the 1920s becomes a form of provincialism, pretending that only in Australia can the true spirit of Europe be reborn. It was only when Lindsay returned to the source in Europe and became immediately involved in its struggles that he could reconcile the conflicting impulses he took from his Australian upbringing. The autobiography recreates his Australia from this European perspective.

The first volume of the autobiography tells of Jack Lindsay's childhood and youth in Brisbane, the second is set in post-war Sydney where he pursued his artistic destiny with his father and associates, and the third describes the expatriate life in England amid the artistic and intellectual ferment of the late 1920s and the 1930s. The migration of the Fanfrolico Press from Sydney to London at the end of the second volume constitutes a symbol of the uneasy relationship between the metropolitan centre and an assertive but still provincial Australia.

Lindsay had already dealt with the Brisbane of his youth in *The Blood Vote*, a political novel written in 1937 but not published until 1985 (University of Queensland Press, St Lucia). Brisbane in both books is portrayed as an overgrown country town and as a terminus for thirsty overlanders. The images of mangrove swamps, day trips to the ocean beach or Bribie Island, houses on stilts, harlots sitting out on display in Albert Street, speakers on street corners

The Blood Vote
(*Education Department, Victoria*)

and strolls through the Botanic Gardens appear in both works. So too does the image of the sad cattle in the holding paddocks outside the abattoirs, waiting to be killed. The use of this image in the two works, however, indicates the difference between them in purpose and perspective.

In the novel, which deals with the conscription referendums and the debates about revolution and political change, the cattle become an image both of the men waiting to be sent by parents and politicians to become victims of the bloodbath in Europe, and more generally of a world dominated by capitalism (pp. 277–8).

In the autobiography, the same scene appears in the first chapter as one of the childhood images that still haunt the author as the scope of his recollections narrows down from a panoramic view of Brisbane to the particular memory of a 'vast herd of red cattle . . . Standing dejected with bloodshot eyes and a sort of hellish patience amid the fine brown dirt and the few meagre scraped trees' (p. 1). The image locates the narrative firmly in a child's perspective, so we know we are encountering history as reconstructed through deliberative memory. The image thus relates not just to a particular threat, but to the child's more general fear of a world in which destruction is barely contained.

The autobiography opens in Brisbane with the dawning of the narrator's consciousness as fragments of the external world crowd in on the child and produce the self that interprets them. This experience is particularly disjointed as a consequence of the continuing upheavals and central disruption of Lindsay's family life as his mother's marriage breaks down and she shifts constantly from one home to another. Then, through books and poetry, the author comes to make sense of the world around him, bringing Marlowe and Spenser, Keats and Shelley to bear on the great spaces and brilliant light of Australia. But this world proves treacherous, dividing inner from outer and essence from experience.

The wider world is borne in upon him through war abroad and political controversy at home. The contradictions of the outer world, the upheavals of his family life, and his own awakening sexuality gradually bring him to realise the turmoil heaving beneath the placid domestic surface his aunt contrives to impose on her sister's household. Life becomes a struggle between his creativity and his fear of death.

At this point Lindsay's personal search becomes merged with his public involvement. The first volume ends with his early love affairs, his rediscovery of the harsh Australian landscape, his discovery of his father and Nietzsche, and his departure for Sydney. The second tells of his involvement with his father, learning the life of the artist.

In Sydney Jack Lindsay moved amid a circle of writers, musicians and artists who saw themselves as engaged in the task of producing an Australian renaissance that would be free alike from nationalism and colonial subservience. They shared a revulsion against the previous war and a conviction that a similar holocaust was in the making. Jack Lindsay identified the cause of this evil with the city, symbol of the alienation of humanity from its own nature by the operations of mechanical logic, science and industrialism. Against these he posed the creative forces of love and art, but recognised that as these become instruments for the self they too become destructive. The volume records his struggle against both external and internal forces of destruction to achieve a harmony that would transcend both.

In the third volume, *Fanfrolico and After*, we follow Lindsay's gradual involvement in the issues of the day through the people he meets in London, and the long and painful relationship that forces him to rework his whole philosophical position. The narrative takes the form of a chronicle of people and events, focused on Lindsay's efforts to establish and conduct the Fanfrolico Press in London. However, the global economic crisis that led to the end of the press in 1930 also precipitated a personal and philosophical crisis for Lindsay. As the remainder of the book focuses on Lindsay's involvement with Eliza de Locre, the narrative changes from a chronicle to an analytical account of the deepening crisis in his personal relationship. His eventual breakdown and consequent self-analysis lead him on a philosophic journey from existentialism to Marxism.

Jack Lindsay resolved his artistic dilemma by placing the personal literary creation of the artist in the context of the material production by which society creates its own structures. He chose to use his skills as a writer to produce work that would give a vision of liberation to the masses. At the same time he explained his personal dilemma by relating it to the wider politics of society. Power and property constrain the individual within the bounds of the past, and the resulting tensions produce psychological conflicts that mirror social divisions.

Just as Lindsay's road to Marxism was difficult, he avoids presenting Marxism as an easy solution. In the epilogue he added to the trilogy for the 1982 edition, he remains unshaken in his beliefs in the potential for human liberation of the Russian Revolution but looks without illusion at the actual performance of Lenin's heirs. His Marxism was not just another mechanical system, a means of providing a ready answer to every dilemma, but a method that directs attention to the material and social conflicts underlying the immediate problem, and that resolves conflict dialectically, that is, not by seeking a middle position but by working through the opposites to find a unity on a higher plane of understanding or action. For example, the apparent conflict between reason and imagination becomes a search for an integrating reason, just as the resolution of the opposition between self and society becomes the endeavour to create a society in which the self is fulfilled through community.

Lindsay's autobiography is not merely important as a declaration of faith, but as an account of the path to that faith from the nightmare in the Brisbane abattoirs of long-horned cattle simultaneously doomed and threatening, through the menacing excitements of inter-war Sydney and London and the horror of isolation and breakdown, to a Britain finding wartime solidarity in the face of the repeated betrayals of its leaders.

In writing this work at the end of the 1950s, Lindsay was also returning the account of his life to the mainstream of Australian literature. The book is a record of the early decades of this century, but the importance of the record is to the developing sense of national independence in post-war Australia. Lindsay reminds the reader that, while the writers of the 1920s may not have achieved the renaissance they sought, implicit in the problems with which they grappled were the issues that still engage Australian writers.

Kenneth Slessor

In Australia the influence of Norman Lindsay and the *Vision* group was expressed particularly in the poetry of Kenneth Slessor. In a 1955 essay 'Norman Lindsay' (in *Bread and Wine*, Angus & Robertson, Sydney, 1970, pp. 111–27), Slessor wrote that Norman Lindsay provided him with a model in the 'moral and aesthetic' rebellion represented in his art, and a doctrine in the idea of *Creative Effort* that art 'reveals its own vision of the passion, beauty and pain of life, forces the realisation of these things on us. It drags us out of all inertia of mind, of all Nirvana of entertainment' (p. 121).

Slessor derived his poetic themes from the example of Hugh McCrae's poems of sensual pleasure in a legendary world of the past. However, Slessor from the start preferred longer lines and stanzas, which give him room for more solidity of detail than McCrae's lilting ballad metres. Consequently, rather than a world of faery his poems provide pictures that, although idealised, recognisably belong in the Middle Ages, the Renaissance or the eighteenth century. When he chooses to write of a Greek myth at home in Australia, he takes a real statue of Pan in a Lane Cove estate.

Slessor's early poems give the sense of a world that, highly coloured though it may be, has a material existence. The 'Good roaring pistol-boys, brave lads of gold' who frequent his 'Thieves' Kitchen' (Kenneth Slessor, *Poems*, Angus & Robertson, Sydney, 1957, p. 25) come from the company of McCrae's knights and vagabonds who drink and love in defiance of the knowledge that 'soon, soon your flesh must crawl/And Tyburn flap with birds, long necked and swart!' (p. 25). But if the poet in his picture of the kitchen itself transfigures the historical reality of poverty and vice into a romantic image of pleasure and freedom, his description keeps contact at least with physical reality. The general image of 'roistering easy maids' is made substantial, even if still only as an object, in the arms and legs of a particular girl, Joan. Unlike McCrae's, Slessor's verses shape the concrete experience as well as the images of debauchery and death.

Like McCrae and Lindsay, Slessor felt that the modern world was impoverished by its separation from the mythologies of Greece and Rome. Australia lacked even a landscape given meaning by these myths. Slessor's early poems seek to restore continuity by incorporating the European past in Australian culture. Unlike the American poets in Europe, such as Pound or Eliot, who were attempting a similar task by rewriting the myths, Slessor sought rather to relocate them. In 'Earth-Visitors' (pp. 1–2) he takes us back to a timeless and placeless past when the gods still 'came gusting down/Cloaked in dark furs, with faces grave and sweet'. The inn to which the gods come, although existing only in a time and place of the imagination, is given a material bustle where 'Post-boys would run, lanterns hang frostily, horses fume, /The strangers wake the inn', but the gods themselves leave no more than a thread or a feather as trace of their visit. In an attempt to bring them back, Slessor concludes his poem with a vision of Venus visiting Norman Lindsay with her inspiration at Springwood, but this remains an assertion, splendid in its claims and its vision of the beauty of 'the shining of her naked body', her breast 'berries broken in snow', but lacking the concrete detail with which to convince the imagination. She is no more than a vision, whereas the earlier visitors remain as memory. Yet for all the colour of their visit, they too remain in an imaginative world contained by the poem itself, lacking the connection with actual striving and conflict that would enable the vision of the gods to supply the deficiencies Slessor felt at the heart of everyday life.

The poems that describe this world have the same material detail as the scenes of myth and legend, and they have a similar sense of a spectacle in which the poet remains an observer excluded from any participation in the action. In 'The Night-Ride', the bustle of the railway resembles the innyard on the arrival of the gods, as the speaker notices 'Gas flaring on the yellow platform; voices running up and down;/Milk-tins in cold dented silver' (*Poems*, p. 31). But no gods appear to give meaning to this world of crowding materiality.

Slessor's early poems thus present a dilemma. Either we inhabit a sterile world of meaningless activity, or we retreat into a colourful but self-subsistent world of the imagination that may compensate for the emptiness of actual life but cannot change it. The earth visitors steadfastly refuse to return.

The escape Slessor found from his dilemma was through the figures of the seafarer and explorer. These figures in his poetry come from a recent past where heroic action was still possible, and they are presented to us as larger than life. In their lives they create through their achievement the meaning the gods once gave to human activity. They work amid seas that are everchanging but always the same, and that conceal and mock all human action. The sea as an image of time, the flood that takes and covers

all, becomes the dominating note, raising the question of whether we can discover any meaning in a world empty of gods. In exploring this world, the seafarer engages with a real world of material problems, but at the same time he represents the artist creating meaning in a world outside common existence. The success or failure of his exploration provides the answer to his question.

Slessor's first significant sea venturer is Captain Dobbin, who

> . . . having retired from the South Seas,
> In the dumb tides of 1900, with a handful of shells,
> A few poisoned arrows, a cask of pearls,
> And five thousand pounds in the colonial funds,
> Now sails the street in a brick villa, 'Laburnum
>   Villa',
> In whose blank windows the harbour hangs
> Like a fog against the glass,
> Golden and smoky, or stoned with a white
>   glitter . . .

> Slessor, *Poems*, p. 42.

In this retirement he continues the active life of his past, through his mementoes,, through the log in which he records movements of ships in the harbour, and through the books that keep alive the deeds of the great seafarers of the past. So past and present, the sedentary and the journeying, are combined in the unity of a single life.

The retrospective explorations of Captain Dobbin continue in the poems of 'The Atlas', in which again the chronicles and charts of the past give permanent form to the lives of their authors. The work expresses the human ambivalence that enables us to find, even in the slaughter of a sea fight, a joy that overcomes the indifference of ocean and time. The deliberate killing in a battle is an example of the way humans, alone among the species, force their meaning on the world by destroying each other, but such meaning is unalterably negative.

Only in the 'Five Visions of Captain Cook' (*Poems*, pp. 57–62), does Slessor find a figure who can bear the weight of his concerns, whose achievements outweigh even the futility of his death by the agency of a knife forged on board his own ship and traded for pigs to sustain his company. The visions are twofold. Each gives a vision of Cook as seen by others,

The Landing of Captain Cook
(*National Gallery of Victoria*)

but each also presents a vision Cook offered to others. The first presents Cook as the demi-god seen by the ordinary sailors who voyaged with him:

When captains, you might have said, if you had been
Fixed by their glittering stare, half-down the side,
Or gaping at them up companionways,
Were more like warlocks than a humble man —
And men were humble then who gazed at them.
Poor horn-eyed sailors, bullied by devils' fists
Of wind or water, or the want of both,
Child-like and trusting, filled with eager trust —
. . . Those captains drove their ships
By their own blood . . .

Slessor, *Poems*, p. 57.

The captain is picked out as the more than human being who by his spirit sustains his crew against both their weakness and the physical buffeting of the universe. The picture is completed with densely-packed imagery of sprung yards and masts overboard on the one hand, magic potions, strange sortilege with books and alphabets in stars on the other. The passage culminates in a change from description to action as Cook 'came to the Coral Sea/And chose a passage into the dark'. The verse creates the hero, who then creates history, so that now 'men write poems in Australia'. Deed and word become one.

The second vision, where the reef of 'Flowers turned to stone' threatens the voyage and reminds the reader of Captain Dobbin's vision of watery depths where 'Flowers rocked far down' and 'white, dead bodies . . . were anchored' (p. 45). In this vision, however, as seen by his officers, Cook goes calmly to bed amid the dangers. When the ship does slide 'towards a reef that would have knifed/Their boards to mash', his calm so transmits itself to the officers that they continue taking their sightings for longitude.

> Men who ride broomsticks with a mesmerist
> Mock the typhoon. So, too. it was with Cook.

Slessor, Poems, p. 59.

While the first vision was of man creating his destiny in the teeth of nature, this is of nature itself subdued and fitted to the calm order of science.

The third vision, of the two chronometers, shows the instruments by which Cook tamed distance even while time kept relentlessly marching on. This is reversed in the fourth, which shows Cook from the viewpoint of the midshipmen with whom he shares his knowledge while he escapes in the jolly boat for an interval from the demands of both nature and time.

The final vision shows Cook's death as recalled by blind Captain Alexander Home, now, like Captain Dobbin, finally moored in an inn in Scotland. Time has flowed past him, yet just as Cook continues to live in his tales, so his own past remains alive in his memory. The poem affirms that while time cannot be stopped it can be measured and used, and the life created within time remains in it. The sea, image both of time and of the nature from which humans make their lives, the 'old, fumbling, witless lover-enemy', has taken Cook's last breath, but in doing so it has rendered him the 'last office of salt water'. Fate determines the time and mode of death, but until that moment man is his own fate. In washing Cook's dead body, the sea makes his life complete and, in that sense, immortal.

Cook as hero gives the world back a god to take the place of those who have departed. However, for those who find no hero to sail with, life remains empty and incomplete. The nameless dead are lost in the waters of time. In 'Five Bells', the poem Slessor chose to end his collection of poems, he explores the life of such a one, and so preserves his name (*Poems*, pp. 103–6). This poem also marked the end of Slessor's career as a publishing poet, with the exception of two wartime poems. One of these is a bitter satire on a vainglorious Australian general, whose men 'gave him everything, in fact,/Except respect'.

The other is a delicate elegy for the dead sailors of all forces whose names are forever lost. In it grief is intense but has been subdued to stoical acceptance. 'Five Bells' represents the journey to this acceptance.

'Five Bells' is again concerned with the sea, but this time with that part of it enclosed within Sydney Harbour. The quiet waters of the harbour are alive with the beauty of reflected light, but the darkness at their heart represents the oblivion of time. Within the poem, Slessor reclaims from time the life of Joe Lynch, who was alive and is dead. By retelling it, the poet seeks to find out the meaning of Joe's life, 'why you were here/Who now are gone, what purpose gave you breath . . .?' (p. 106).

The five bells that sound out from the dark warship on the harbour represent the second part of a nautical watch, but the figure five, also the number of Cook's visions, and of the poems of 'The Atlas', may have had further significance for Slessor. Traditionally, the figure five represented Man and the operation of essence on matter. The 'Five bells coldly ringing out' across the harbour provide an interval from time during which Slessor lives the whole of his late friend's life. The essence of man, in the form of Joe living or the poet recalling him, acts on time through words to create a life.

The narrator presents first a discussion of two kinds of time — that which is 'moved by little fidget wheels' and his own time, 'the flood that does not flow' (p. 103). The poem is an *oxymoron*, a contradiction of a flood that does not flow, time that is timeless. It tells of the life of Joe, which has been carried away on the flood of time, but continues to exist in the memory that occurs in the instant of time between the five bells. During this interval, the speaker lives another man's life, only to emerge at the end into an unchanged world. By implication, Joe has lived and died without any effect on his world.

The narrator's immersion in Joe's life does change his world, as it recreates that life in brilliant imagery which gives tongue to the dead man squeezing his face 'In agonies of speech on speechless panes' (p. 103). The poem gives an image of him both as a dead man desperately trying to force himself back into the world of the living, and as a living man constituted from fragments of the words, phrases and enthusiasms.

Like Joe Lynch, Slessor's poetry exists through images. These images do not constitute a body of thought, nor do they replace on earth the gods they mourn. But the work is not, as has been claimed, nihilistic or despairing. It pays tribute to the creative power of humanity by creating its own world in which men continue to live in the words with which they defy inevitable death. Starting from the shallow epicureanism of Norman Lindsay and Hugh McCrae, that sought to live through sheer delight, he created for himself a stoic faith that, while accepting the world as unchangeable, nevertheless found in it rich possibilities of enduring life.

Robert FitzGerald

Whereas Slessor's poetry starts from the power of words and their ability to create in images a world that would withstand time, the poetry of his contemporary Robert FitzGerald, who was also associated with *Vision*, concentrated on human action. His poems are shaped to convey an idea or state of mind as shown in action. He thus appears more hopeful than Slessor, but his poetry is equally a response to the disintegration of the individual by the flow of time and the brutality of society. The product of this response is not, however, creation of the fruit of action, but the knowledge of being that comes from doing.

FitzGerald stated his problem and its answer early, in 'The Greater Apollo' where he speaks to dead Caesar and Cataline:

But I look out and watch a bud
burst in renewal on the bough —
O sweating selves, O men of blood,
this too was yours; what have you now?

and answers them:

I think in your unanswering tombs
you feel through me today's known bliss
because you, living, saw such blooms
in coloured springtimes far from this.

> Robert FitzGerald, *Forty Years'*
> *Poems*, Angus & Robertson,
> Sydney, 1965, p. 12.

The doctrine is a simple one of experience, that does not change through his forty years of publication. The expression is direct, the simple form of the verse

pointing the reader to the object rather than to the words that express it.

FitzGerald's early books are concerned with the constant flux of matter and human attempts to make sense of it, through the senses and through reflection on experience. A central image is moonlight, which divides the world into dark and light, is constantly changing but also continually recurring. Against change the poet sets images of the beauty of flowers and music, the binding force of love, and the natural order created from chaos but revealed by human thought. These poems coalesce in the two major poems he produced during the 1930s, 'The Hidden Bole' [1934] (*Collected Poems*, pp. 61–7), and 'Essay on Memory' [1937] (*Collected Poems*, pp. 71–82). In the first of these, he seeks a pattern at the heart of the unchanging time of nature, and in the second he searches for meaning in the sweep of time and the constant change that constitute both the individual life and human history.

In 'The Hidden Bole' FitzGerald contrasts the constant renewal of nature with the fragility of the individual life. The former is symbolised by the banyan tree, in which every tendril that touches earth becomes a trunk, so that no single bole can ever be discerned as its centre, the source of its being. Yet, at the same time, even the branches that fall at the edges are a part of the whole, and the single dropped bud is the purpose of the whole, 'what spun hours have worked for and last aim/of evolution' (p. 65). This flower belongs with light and the dance that FitzGerald uses as the image of beauty, seeing it embodied specifically in the dance of Pavlova. Beauty he sees, in terms that recall Norman Lindsay's *Creative Effort*, not as the child of nature but as the finest product of intellect. It distils art from nature, and the supreme form of art is the dance, which dies in the moment of its creation, for permanence is death. The poem opens and concludes with a tribute to the supreme dancer Pavlova, herself now dead:

So does she crown our thought, all thought involve —
as all sweet tones resolve
into the twilight chiming of a bird.

> FitzGerald, *Collected Poems*, p. 67.

The philosophic problem of the poem is thus resolved not into an idea but into an image. The fading of the beauty of dance and music, symbolised by the song of the bird, into the darkness of time is also a rebirth, in memory and in the renewal of subsequent artists who will once more create the fair.

While in 'The Hidden Bole' FitzGerald presents beauty as the answer to change, the imagery of 'Essay on Memory' presents time as destroyer and memory as the cruel reminder of a dreadful past, a madman who:

> peers
> from the brown mottled ruins, shrieks and gibbers
> among the fallen fragments of lost years . . .

> FitzGerald, *Collected Poems*, p. 72.

The imagery does not suggest a place but symbolises the state of mind from which the speaker attempts to escape.

Memory appears first as rain knocking with chill knuckles at the door of consciousness, but it is further defined through a sequence of images that show it destroying all peace in the present and hope for the future. These images show it first as the personal memory of the events that shape our lives, then as the greater memory of the race that can reach back to the dawn of life, but finally as the fearful memory that brings only knowledge of dissolution.

The poem examines the conflicting nature of memory and thought, memory and hope, and the relation of past and present. It deals with philosophic issues of human continuity, the nature of time, and individual identity, through a series of symbolic scenes rather than through argument. Finally, it overcomes the threat of dissolution by the transformation brought about through generations of our encounters with the Australian continent. This experience changes the rain of memory from skeletal knuckles to a shower of gold:

> Rain in the clean sun falling — riches of rain
> wash out the dusty fear, the air's dull stain;
> ay, Memory is a shower of gilded darts
> which pins today's delight on our healed hearts . . .
> How should we hold us from wild enterprise,
> who use the limbs of the past and its quick eyes . . .

> FitzGerald, *Collected Poems*, p. 80.

The clear statement of these lines convinces by experience beyond the reach of argument. This gives the speaker the strength to exhort his fellow Australians to take up the task of building a destiny worthy of their forebears, undeterred by worry of what may happen to our achievement after we have gone. Memory, the poem concludes, links 'all of gone with all-to-come', and thus we cannot be defeated. At a time when the approach of yet another war in Europe threatened the end of civilisation, FitzGerald succeeded in creating from the past a sustaining confidence in humanity. The imagery does not transcend reality to find a new world of the spirit, but sanctifies it as the source of hope.

Fitzgerald's later poems deal rather with the past in action, in dramatisations of scenes like Tasman's reflections after escaping the Heemskerck Shoals in New Zealand or the fifth day of Warren Hastings' prosecution before the House of Lords, than with the past as idea. He does, however, treat the furthermost past as such in his remarkable poem 'The Face of the Waters' (*Collected Poems*, pp. 102–4), which returns us to the instant when time or consciousness emerges into existence.

The opening of this poem is built from images that suggest a nightmare, as feet scurry across black granite, laughter sounds cruelly in pursuit and a harpspring or trap springs behind. The disembodied images carry horror, but the free movement of the lines answers the fear with a sense of energy. The poet is expressing the inexpressible moment before anything begins, either the individual life or life as a whole or the universe itself. In this moment of emergence the poet finds the whole of life, 'light and the clear day and so simple a goal' (p. 104). He finds affirmation not in overcoming nothingness, but in the mystery that the whole splendour of being and action emerges from nothing.

FitzGerald's narrative poems show individuals constructing their own world from the circumstances they are given. The central characters of these poems are all, in a sense, failures. 'Fifth Day' (*Collected Poems*, pp. 104–9) takes a scene from Hastings' trial to portray the actors as in a canvas caught from time. The day was merely one of hundreds in a case that went for seven years and ended with Hastings' acquittal, but FitzGerald is interested in how it lives into the present. For Burke the day was a failure, and

Hastings was eventually acquitted, but these outcomes have nothing to do either with Burke's later triumphant career nor with the eventual fate of the empire Hastings had governed in India. What survives is the gesture that remains caught in time:

it concerns all men that what they do
remains significant unbroken thread
of the fabric of our being . . .
Attitude matters. Action in the end
Goes down the stream as motion, merges as such
with the whole of life and time; but islands stand:
dignity and distinctness that attach
to the inmost being of us each.

FitzGerald, *Collected Poems*, p. 106.

This is the same position reached at the end of *Essay on Memory*.

The idea of life as the gesture rather than the consequence of action appears again in 'Between Two Tides' (1944–52, *Collected Poems*, pp. 115–94) which tells the epic tale of Will Mariner, the English ship's boy who became a warrior in nineteenth-century Tonga. The story of his part in local battles and intrigues is framed by his voyage to Tonga as a lad of thirteen and by his later orderly life in England. The theme of the poem is provided by the Spanish governor who recounts the tales of Pizarro's conquest of Peru. Admitting that the conquistadores were 'desperate men lured on by greed, lust, gold;/cruel men gripped by a chill thirst for bloodshed', he argues that they were nevertheless justified by their 'greatness of striving', for

. . . man's essence
is not nobility, it is man, unrest,
a rushing of wind, distance . . .
and life's like a long wave breaking, not good or ill,
or right or wong, but action and pressing forward

FitzGerald, *Collected Poems*, p. 123.

This wave is the recurrent image in FitzGerald's poetry of the change that is always the same, where the moment is separated from its results and the unity it achieves is the unity of nothingness, beyond all possible judgement. In this sense, for all its optimism,

FitzGerald's poetry finishes in the nothingness from which it emerges.

FitzGerald returned to these issues in another long poem, 'The Wind at Your Door', [1959] (*Collected Poems*, pp. 236–41). This presents not a long narrative but a vividly realised scene of the flogging of the Irish rebels from Castle Hill. His ancestor takes part as the doctor who was required by law to attend the flogging. A namesake whom he would be proud to claim as kin was one of the men flogged. The poem creates the scene in all its brutality, using the image of the high wind that on that day blew 'splashes of blood and and strips of human hide' at the doctor to blow to the door of the reader the 'old savagery which has built /your world and laws out of the lives it spilt' (p. 237). The conflict is the same as that in 'Between Two Tides', but now made specific to the form European civilisation has taken in Australia. The answer is also the same – acceptance of all that happens.

FitzGerald's robust and active acceptance of the world as it is excludes the existentialist fear that not only are both nature and history empty of meaning, but that there is no point outside them from which we can create our own meaning. He does not resolve the problem, but accepts it. This attitude culminates in the meditative lyric 'Southmost Twelve', which combines time and space in the moment after midnight that is also the southmost, or furthest, stroke of twelve, when time and the world swing to a new dawn that yet may not occur. Nature's laws make dawn

The Uprising at Castle Hill
(*National Library of Australia*)

inevitable, but the marvel of the law is that it could be otherwise. Logically, nature leaves all things possible, 'this thing not least:/a western sun tomorrow'. It is otherwise in the individual, for whom the law is immutable that eventually dawn will not return. Yet in that knowledge is freedom. Because life is finite, the individual is not bound on 'logic's rope, the theme/that step should tie on step' (p. 200). FitzGerald, looking steadily at life from a point after midnight, finds that:

Creature of instinct, I still share the faith
of beast and bird, and call intelligence
knowledge of what I touch — what's bared to sense
as real itself, real in what lies beneath —
and doubt not of tomorrow opening where
the twang of this vibration thins in air.

FitzGerald, *Collected Poems*, p. 201.

The thought of this seems simple, close to the theme of his poems from 'Essay on Memory' onwards. But the words that make the thought concrete point beyond themselves to a solid world which, despite its brutality, justifies a faith in humankind and a joy in life. The emptiness and the harshness of the seas and the Australian continent give room for humans to create a life that fulfils the potential they have brought with them from the furthest stretches of time. We have from his collected prose (*Of Places and Poetry*, University of Queensland Press, St Lucia, 1976, p. 271) the poet's own words for what he has discovered in chasing the Cinderella footsteps of poetry: 'There is in everyday life much that is difficult, much that is sordid. But there is still the wave breaking, and there are still the stars. How good, how good indeed!'.

Katharine Susannah Prichard

The writers and artists of the *Vision* group responded to what they perceived as the sterility of Australian life by trying to create a new world of the spirit, inhabited only by an elite of those capable both of enjoying the momentary purity of delight and of capturing that moment in the eternity of word or line. During the 1920s, another Australian writer, Katharine Susannah Prichard, developed in an opposite direction, trying to change reality by revealing within it the capacity of the ordinary woman or man to realise the extraordinary in her or his own life. Prichard's novels

show the way in which the circumstances of society and environment destroy life, and lead her along the same path of visionary socialism Jack Lindsay was to follow in the 1930s. While Prichard joined the infant Communist Party of Australia in 1920, her work does not become overtly ideological until the eve of the Second World War, when she started publishing her gold-fields trilogy.

Where Lindsay's historical works endeavour to show how individuals are shaped by the historical forces of their time, Prichard's work starts within the romantic tradition. Her earliest book, *The Pioneers* (Hodder & Stoughton, London, 1915, revised edition, Rigby, Adelaide, 1963), describes, as its name suggests, the epic of settlement. She shows how the earliest settlers in south Gippsland attempt to impose their vision on the land, only to see their lives become entwined in the new patterns imposed by the strange environment and its mixed society. The book has much the same ingredients as Boldrewood's *Robbery Under Arms*, with convicts and bushrangers set against the honest squatters who toil for their wealth. These elements, however, are shaped into the popular Australian myth, so that they serve a radical rather than conservative

Katherine Susannah Prichard

purpose. The novel combines images of pioneer, convict and bushman to reinforce the tradition of the egalitarian and independent Australian.

In later novels Prichard presents more realistic portraits of bush people and their lives, but the theme of conflict between ordinary decent people and an evil system remains. The ordinary people are not necessarily heroic, but are plagued by divisions among themselves. In *Black Opal* (Caslon House, Sydney, 1946 [1921]), the divisions are brought to the mining community through the breach of the code of mateship when one of the miners steals another's gemstones and flees the town. In *Working Bullocks* (Angus & Robertson, Sydney, 1956 [1926]) the timberworkers are divided by their different tasks, as millhands, bullockies and tree-fellers, and by the different settlements in which they live and to which they give their primary loyalty. These divisions prevent them from taking effective action against the forces of disruption.

The deepest unity in the novels comes not from the achievement of action but from absorption in nature. In *The Pioneers*, Donald Cameron never becomes part of the land because he seeks to master it. By contrast, his wife, even while conscious of the threat of solitude, recognises that the trees and the hills have brought her her child, and home, and 'a sense of peace and consolation' (p. 19). In *Black Opal* the fiery beauty of the gemstone worked so painfully from the soil is the counterpart of the harsh and usually hostile landscape that comes to beautiful life after the rains, when 'a tapestry of incomparable beauty — a masterpiece of the Immortals — is wrought on the bare earth' (p. 43). In *Working Bullocks*, Red and Debbie have the strength of the trees themselves, and their eventual coming together is as natural a culmination of the forces of nature as the mating of Red's stallion 'The Boss' with his brumby mob.

The ideal of a life lived in harmony with nature and society is disrupted by divisions among the people themselves. It is also affected by the institutionalised forces of business and mechanised industry that separate the individual from nature. One symbol of this is the mining company that, in *Black Opal*, offers the miner security in return for working 'all day at mechanical toil: to use himself or allow anyone to use him like a working bullock' (p. 46). Another is the mill in *Working Bullocks* where Debbie is forced to work. While admiring the skills of the millhands, she recognises the difference between this mechanised

work and the natural relationships workers establish with their environment through labour they themselves control:

> When she went down to the mill for the first time Deb was aghast in that old childish way at what men there were doing with trees. It was fearful and terrible to her.
>
> In the forest the fallers, bullock-drivers and men at the bush landings treated great trees respectfully. They watched trees and logs as though they were animated and at any moment might be expected to crush a man out of existence. In the bush men were reverent of a great tree . . .
>
> But in the mill there was not time for rites to appease dead trees. Deb had never heard of rites to appease the manes of dead trees; but she thought vaguely the men's admiration and reverence for a tree they were going to fall did appease the tree in some way. The trees were not so angry, their vengeance so rapacious and implacable, when they were worshipped as they fell. It was the brutal and callous way great logs were torn up under the steamsaws which dazed and amazed her.

> Prichard, *Working Bullocks*, pp. 183–4.

The kind of mateship suggested in these passages goes beyond the defensive alliance that Lawson's drifters form against failure. Although Prichard's sense of mateship is expressed mainly by men, its source is not so much the male need for company as the feminine drive for unity. Her ideal men, like Red Burke, are symbolised by the dominating stallion 'The Boss'. They see themselves as the masters of creation, taking women as their right. The novels, however, do not allow us to judge the men by their images of themselves. Rather, they provide their own judgement on the men's ability to respond to the sexuality and creative force latent in such women as Debbie Colburn, who contains within herself the strength not of the axeman but of the tree.

The unity implicit in this force is not easily achieved. In *Black Opal* it is achieved in the community by the miners' united resistance to the proposed mining company that asks them to trade their control over their own work and product for the security and dependence of working for a regular wage. In *Working Bullocks* the men have a similar sense of independence arising directly from their relationship with the forests in which they work, but they are already dependent on the mill and its owners. The millhands are already subject to the discipline of machines run in the interests of profit. The strike that temporarily unites them with the fellers and bullockies is defeated because it confronts only immediate grievances and it cannot draw on any wider sense of community. Jean Devanny confronts a similar problem in her novel of the canefields, *Sugar Heaven* (Redback, Melbourne, 1982 [1936]) but with a clearer understanding of the restrictions placed on women.

Prichard brings these themes together in her novel *Coonardoo* (Pacific Books: Angus & Robertson, Sydney, 1971 [1929]). This novel is set largely on a remote cattle station in the north-west of Western Australia, and the outside world impinges only through the agency of the banks, which hold the mortgages and determine the eventual fate of those who work the stations, and the city girls who come to the station for the purpose of matrimony. The station community is, however, itself divided, both between owners and workers, and between white and black. These divisions are for a time overcome by the matriarch who dominates the early part of the novel, Mrs Bessie Watt. The name she is commonly known by, Mumae, is both her son's childish name for his mother and the Aboriginal word for father. It gives her a place in Aboriginal as well as European society, and its associations with both male and female indicate the dual role she plays as master of the station and as sustainer and nurturer of the people on it. The contradictions in her joint role, and in her attempts to maintain the separate integrity of the black and white societies that have become dependent on each other, lead to the tragedy enacted in the novel.

Natural unity is embodied in the novel in the relationship between the Aborigines and the land. Mrs Bessie's respect for this, and her consequent exclusion from her station of both the missionaries who would interfere with the native religion and the white stockmen who would interfere with the women, are responsible for her success in running the station. The natural outcome of this understanding would be for Mumae and the Aborigines to become one, members of a single community. This unity is implied by the attraction between Hugh Watt and Coonardoo, child of the tribe. However, Mrs Bessie is unable to deny her upbringing, and sends Hughie off to school in the south while she trains Coonardoo to succeed her as housekeeper, looking after Hughie's needs and

maintaining him on the station but remaining separate in her Aboriginal identity. Through this scheme Mrs Bessie tries to bind both Hughie and Coonardoo after her own death. Despite her femininity, she expresses the white, masculine demand for control over events which contradicts natural unity. This contradiction provides the source of the tragedy.

The tragedy is worked out in the lives of its victims, Hughie Watt and Coonardoo. Hughie is victim because he cannot overcome the prejudices of his white upbringing enough to recognise Coonardoo as a person or his own desires for her. Coonardoo, on the other hand, is victim because she remains unrecognised and therefore exploited. Hughie exploits her loyalty and the skills with which his mother has endowed her; Sam Geary exploits her sexuality. When Geary takes advantage of the emotional isolation Hughie has imposed on Coonardoo, Hughie is driven to an uncomprehending fury that leads to the final destruction of the station and its people. Mrs Bessie's vision of harmony collapses because her plans to enforce it have defied natural affinities.

The novel is framed by two scenes of Coonardoo alone in the landscape, singing a song to the accompaniment of the clicking of small sticks. The first of these songs embodies the natural unity of human, animal and environment:

> Over and over again, in a thin reedy voice, away at the back of her head, the melody flowed like water running over smooth pebbles in a dry creek bed. Winding and falling, the words rattled together and flew eerily, as if she were whispering to herself, and in awe of the kangaroos who came over the range and made a dance with their little feet in the twilight before they began to feed.
>
> Prichard, *Coonardoo*, p. 1.

The water on the dry pebbles evokes the beauty that can be found in a land by those who come to know it from within, like the kangaroos who come with dance to their feed. Yet this unity is about to be disrupted, as we immediately learn that the singer, Coonardoo, is awaiting the removal by Sam Geary of her childhood companion, Hugh Watt, who is about to leave for school in the south.

The final scene shows the end of the dream. Coonardoo, discarded by Hughie and dying of venereal diseases contracted in her abandonment, has returned home to the site of the homestead, which has been deserted after Hughie's collapse and Sam's eventual purchase of the station. The white cockatoos, symbols of Mumae, are settling to roost in the big gum-tree beside the house as Coonardoo again sings her song. But now the fire falls into ashes, and the sticks lie 'without a spark' until Coonardoo becomes one with them in the unity of death:

> She crooned a moment, and lay back. Her arms and legs, falling apart, looked like those blackened and broken sticks beside the fire.

> Prichard, *Coonardoo*, p. 206.

The tone of this final passage is not of desolation but of elegy. The limitations of Mumae's vision that led to its destruction do not destroy its ultimate truth, which is vindicated by Coonardoo's fealty to her trust. As she reflects just before her death:

> Mumae would see and know that she, Coonardoo, had done as Mumae bade her for Youie. She had looked after and obeyed Youie, although in some way she had displeased him so; brought down the torrent of his anger upon herself.

> Prichard, *Coonardoo*, p. 206.

Her endurance is an assurance that the blindness that has destroyed the vision is not inevitable.

Prichard's later work separates the personal from the political. In *Haxby's Circus* (Angus & Robertson, Sydney, 1979 [1930]) she seeks a purely personal solution in a situation outside the mainstream of society. In her gold-fields trilogy (*The Roaring Nineties*, Cape, London, 1946; *Golden Miles*, Cape, London, 1948; *Winged Seeds*, Cape, London, 1950) she seeks political solutions. However, it is in the earlier novels and in some of her short stories that the personal and the political are integrated. The tragedy of Coonardoo is that in her, to use the words of later debate, the personal is both political and beyond solution. Prichard's insight is that any path towards such a solution must take into account not only the structures of society as embodied both in the family and the economy, but also the total relationship of humans to their environment.

Although Prichard's radicalism represents an advance on Lawson's creed of mateship, being based on positive rather than defensive relationships, it remains backward-looking. Her work opposes the creed of solidarity and the value of human skills and compassion to the sterility of cities and the domination of machines over people. However, the only places where she can find room for these values are on the fringes of settlement or society, where even after two or three generations of settlement the work of the pioneers is still being done. The values created through that work furnished a criticism of the industrial capitalism that was destroying them, but they did not provide an alternative. The political solution Prichard embraced remained external to the world she created in her fiction.

WAR: THE CHANGING RESPONSE

The bugles of England were calling o'er the sea,
As they had called a thousand years, were calling
now to me.

James Burns, 1915.

THE writers of *Vision* sought to create a pure world of imagination as an escape from the ugliness of a world that had produced the devastation of the First World War and its aftermath. Prose writers did not, however, directly confront the war for almost a decade after the armistice. By the time their accounts appeared, the peace already seemed lost through divisions at home and growing discord abroad, and their novels look back at the war through the experience of this post-war disenchantment. Over the next fifty years, the continually changing responses of writers to this war reflect the changes that occurred during this period in Australian society, and in its perceived relationship with the old world.

The war presented a special problem to writers. For the people immediately involved as soldiers in the trenches, the experience was so shattering that at first it seemed possible to confront it only through poetry, which conveyed the situation in its immediacy without any more elaborate framework than that of human emotions and expectations. But for society at large, the war seemed to destroy all the hopes that had been built on science, on socialism, or on

the established order of society. While the historians could provide a chronicle of events, the novelist is bound to supply a pattern to endow events with meaning. This endeavour had to wait until the participants had been able to assimilate their experience and discover a framework that would make it meaningful.

In 1928–32, five major works appeared by English and Australian writers. The English writers Siegfried Sassoon, Robert Graves and Edmund Blunden present their experience in the form of slightly fictionalised memoirs. The fictional mode allows the authors to emphasise character and event as they make sense, rather than as they happened, and brings to their work the benefit of hindsight. However, the first person narrative suggests historical authenticity, and thus concentrates the reader's attention on the way events mould the narrator and his view of the world.

By contrast, the Australians Frederic Manning and Leonard Mann, writing about their experience of the same campaigns in Belgium and northern France, produced documentary novels. Although each novelist presents events particularly as they affect one character, the documentary form places the narrator outside the events. The novelist discovers the pattern or meaning of the events not by experience but by observation. As observers, the Australian writers view events with sardonic rather than bitter irony, and from the point of view of the ordinary infantryman rather than of the officer. This gives their books a distinctively Australian quality.

The isolation of the soldier from the civilians and even from his superior officers provides both the viewpoint and the structure of the war novels. Their narrative shows how the protagonist is taken out of his peaceful pre-war existence and remade, first as a soldier, then as a veteran. In the first stage he learns that his former skills are irrelevant, and his individuality is absorbed into the machine of war. In the second stage, at the actual battlefront, he learns that the machine itself is inadequate and insane. The demand made on him in this situation is not to prove his manliness, but to recreate his individuality within a situation that remains unique, understood only by the actual participants. Finally, if he survives, he must reintegrate this new personality into civilian life.

For the English writers, these problems are essentially individual. Each of their stories is told in the first person by a narrator who has been born a gentleman and therefore joins the British army as an officer. Sassoon's *Memoirs of George Sherston* (1928–36), eventually in three volumes, starts with an idyllic summer of youth that is abruptly ended, with its heroic dreams, by the death of his comrade in Flanders. The remaining two volumes detail a descent into hell, thwarted rebellion and a slow return to sanity, marked by the narrator's decision to return

to the front because his place is irrevocably with his fellow-sufferers. Robert Graves, in *Good-bye to All That* (1929), contrasts the horror and pity of war with the incomprehension of the machine that drives it. Like Sassoon, the narrator concentrates on the way the war changes him. Edmund Blunden, in his *Undertones of War* (1928), shows an Arcadian pastoral world actually being swallowed up and destroyed by the process of war, but again this is focused through the eyes of the narrator, so that the war becomes a personal ordeal. Each book emphasises the ironic contrast of the wartime ideal, where the horrors of constant discomfort, disease and death render absurd the traditional military customs of the regiment and deny the civilised order the war is supposedly being fought to preserve, as symbolised by the golden age of pre-war England. The two Australian writers, Frederic Manning and Leonard Mann, by contrast, write in the third person and concentrate on the experiences of the common infantryman.

Frederic Manning

Frederic Manning was born in Australia, but lived in England from the age of fifteen and served as an ordinary soldier in the British army. The story of his novel, *The Middle Parts of Fortune* (Granada, London, 1977 [1929]), is told from the point of view of a Private Bourne who, like the author, is an educated Australian who has chosen to enlist as an ordinary soldier in the British army. An outsider among the men by birth and education, he uses the war much as an anthropologist might seize the opportunity to visit a strange community, except that Bourne is part of his own study.

The opening of the novel transports the reader into a nightmarish scene after a disastrous attack. Bourne, 'beaten to the wide', loses contact with his fellows and falls into an empty trench and black dugout where only his discovery of a bottle of whisky restores him to sanity. After this dislocation of consciousness, we are gradually led with Bourne back to his regiment and an army world ruled by its own rules. Here the individual's attempt to maintain his reality is fraught with the same difficulties as Bourne's earlier effort to discover his whereabouts. The episode finishes with a description of the troops, utterly exhausted, moving back to their tents and a final pretence of a parade and a smart soldierly dismissal. As they move off, one of the watching camp troops takes his

Help Our Boys
(*Historical Resources Centre*)

pipe out of his mouth and spits. '"They can say what they bloody well like," he said appreciatively, "but we're a . . . fine mob"' The contrast between misery and smartness, horror and pride, is not simply ironic, but is at the heart of the novel, which is written about the theme that war is both an expression and a test of our common humanity. It is not irony but paradox that weariness and suffering still create human pride. The expression of the pride belongs, however, not to the officers who guard tradition to create a military machine, but to the infantrymen who constitute the machine and create its pride.

For Manning's English contemporaries, war was an insanity of civilisation that society must learn to avoid or escape. For Manning, it is a nightmare within which he can learn what he is and what life is. Although he uses an educated man as his narrator, he sets him among the privates and NCOs for whom pre-war life had been no leisurely idyll but a constant struggle. In their company, and amid the horrors of the trenches, Bourne has to discover what can give life value.

One possibility is the sexual love the men pursue while on leave, and recall crudely or lovingly while at the front. Bourne, translating halting letters from an unknown soldier to a girl in a French village, is able to reflect on it as an involved spectator:

> In the shuddering revulsion from death one turns instinctively to love as an act which seems to affirm the completeness of being. In the trenches, the sense of this privation vanished; but it pressed on men whenever they moved back again to the borders of civilized life, which is after all only an organization of man's appetites, for food or for women, the two fundamental necessities of his nature.

> Manning, *Fortune*, p. 50.

Yet love is not enough. War makes man aware of sexual love as a necessity, but he craves more. The comradeship the reality of war creates among the men offers the further affirmation they need. Bourne recognises the strength he draws from it:

> . . . in some ways, you know, good comradeship takes the place of friendship. It is different: it has its own loyalties and affections; and I am not so sure that it does not rise on occasion to an inten-

sity of feeling which friendship never captures. It may be less in itself, I don't know, but its opportunity is greater.

> Manning, *Fortune*, pp. 79–80.

This comradeship is characteristic of working-class and subordinate cultures everywhere. Manning, brought up in the middle classes, finds in it the transcendence of self-interest that enables the men to rely absolutely on each other in difficulty or emergency. This comradeship gives Bourne a sense of his own value, which he affirms by resisting the promotion that is offered to him. Because the war denies him any extrinsic freedom of action, he can affirm his true self by choosing who he will be. This existential view of war anticipates the view David Malouf offers in *Fly Away Peter*.

Bourne discovers the meaning of his life only by allowing life to take everything else from him. This loss occurs in a context — in this case, war — which is apart from everyday reality yet intimately connected to it. As well as giving a documentary view of life at the front the novel enacts a tragedy. This is made clear by the Shakespearian epigraphs to each chapter, which set the action in a universal setting, and by the nightmare opening, which uses the setting of the battlefield to remove the action from considerations of everyday life. Yet other realities keep intruding on the nightmare, in the form of staff officers whose attempts to command the reality of battle are more absurd than the battle itself, of peasants who cling stubbornly to their own livelihood in the face of the absurdity around them, and of recollections of leave in a Britain that remains completely detached from the war across the Channel. These intrusions all serve to maintain the soldiers and their lives in a place set apart.

Bourne's reflections on his experience emphasise the way the special reality of war forces on him a concern with the ultimate meaning of life. In his near-sleep, after the opening scene, he relives the nightmare of the day's action, and tries to understand its significance:

> Power is measured by the amount of resistance which it overcomes, and, in the last resort, the moral power of men was greater than any purely material force, which could be brought to bear on it. It took the chance of death, as one of the chances

it was bound to take; though, paradoxically enough, the function of our moral nature consists solely in the assertion of one's own individual will against anything which may be opposed to it, and death, therefore, would imply its extinction in the particular and individual case. The true inwardness of tragedy lies in the fact that its failure is only apparent, and as in the case of the martyr also, the moral conscience of man has made its own deliberate choice, and asserted the freedom of its being. The sense of wasted effort is only true for meaner and more material natures.

Manning, *Fortune*, p. 10.

But Manning does not allow the reader to forget that the soldier confronts death not only as an absolute, but as a material fact. The novel repeatedly emphasises the appalling nature of death both for the man who suffers it and for those who witness it. Bourne confronts his assertion of tragic power with the horrible actuality as experienced by the soldier:

he has seen one man shot cleanly in his tracks and left face downwards, dead, and he has seen another torn into bloody tatters as by some invisible beast, and these experiences had nothing illusory about them: they were actual facts. Death, of course, like chastity, admits of no degree; a man is dead or not dead, and a man is just as dead by one means as by another; but it is infinitely more horrible and revolting to see a man shattered and eviscerated, than to see him shot.

Manning, *Fortune*, pp. 10–11.

Manning leaves Bourne's past undisclosed. The novel begins with men who have already shed the innocence of civilian life, which exists only as memory or in the sardonic view they have of the replacements who arrive to restore the regiment's strength after the opening attack. Nor does he allow his characters any future. Their only achievement is victory over themselves, not over the enemy. Yet, paradoxically, the book condemns both the war and society by demonstrating the greatness ordinary humans discover in themselves, despite the society and war that disregard it. The conclusion of the novel returns to nightmare, but shot through this time with futility and an overwhelming sense of pity.

Leonard Mann

While Australians appear only peripherally in *The Middle Parts of Fortune*, providing an egalitarian but unruly contrast to the British army, their experience provides the substance of Leonard Mann's *Flesh in Armour* (Unwin Paperbacks, Sydney, 1985 [1932]). This novel is also set in the mud-fields around Ypres and the Somme, and like Manning's novel describes the lives of men set apart from their commanders, their pre-war past, and the civilians who remain at home. Unlike the English troops, however, these Australians are removed from home by distance as well as by circumstance. The England they visit on leave is as strange to them as the towns in France where they are billeted between tours of duty.

The major theme of the novel is the forging of a national fighting force. Mann's portrayal of this force reinforces the mythology established by the official war historian C.E.W. Bean. The troops are careless of appearance, cynical about authority, and superbly disciplined in action. The army is essentially democratic, with easy relations between the men and the officers, most of whom have been promoted from the ranks.

The three stages of the novel trace the development of this army and its spirit. At the beginning we meet the Australians isolated and displaced as they wander around wartime London. In the second part, newcomers and veterans are absorbed into the single fighting unit of the platoon. In the final section, the men of the platoon prove their worth as part of the single Australian army corps. Their final victory, which comes only after they have successfully resisted the attempts of the higher command to break up the battalion that has borne the brunt of the campaign, is an assertion of national pride. They have made themselves into a 'weapon of magnificent cold temper, hammered through the fires of many an engagement and battle, experienced and skilled in warfare more than any others' (p. 161), but they allow their commander to use them only on their own terms. They constitute a people's army that sees itself at once as the representative of its nation and as an elite set apart from its fellows.

The moulding of this military force is, however, contrasted with the disintegration of individuals. The march to victory is accompanied by the deaths of the men who constitute the platoon. Frank Jeffreys, the main character, finds in his love for an English girl a purpose and a future for his life, only to have it destroyed by the jealous taunts of a younger member of the platoon. His companion sacrifices his life to save the others, and Jeffreys himself collapses and is killed. The only two men who have understood the purpose of their common action are destroyed in the moment of its triumph.

The 'Last Fight of the Platoon', the chapter that concludes the action of the novel, presents the breaching of the German lines as the culmination and justification of the whole of Australian history. Moreover, as the novel explicitly presents the final Australian campaign as the correction of British errors and the cause of the eventual allied victory, it implies that Australian society is the final realisation of the ideals of English civilisation. Mann is, however, aware of the cost of the victory in the lives of individuals, and his last paragraph suggests, ambiguously, that the survivors may yet demand their price from the nation to which they return:

> And so the infantry of the AIF laid aside their armour and became, what remains of them, just the sort of fellows you know — or so they seem.

> Mann, *Flesh in Armour*, p. 254.

He seems unable to decide whether the army created a nation or merely set itself apart from its fellows.

Frank Dalby Davison

Manning's novel, although written from an Australian perspective, belongs essentially with British literature. Mann's *Flesh in Armour* does not plumb the existential depths of the soldier's experience of war. Instead, through the author's concern for the revelation of the Australian character in war and the price paid by the individual for the achievement of national identity, Mann creates a separate centre of consciousness by which to judge the world the Australians find themselves engaged in. Although characters in their novels express their resentment for the slackers at home, the conscientious objectors and strikers they regard as benefiting at the expense of the suffering of the troops, neither Mann nor Manning questions the justice of the war itself.

Frank Dalby Davidson

Among Australian writers, such questioning appears only after the Second World War had finally destroyed the illusions that the sacrifices of the first had gained a lasting peace. Frank Dalby Davison in *The Wells of Beersheba* (1933, collected in *The Road to Yesterday*, Angus & Robertson, Sydney, 1968 [1964]) had commemorated the exploits of the men and horses of the Australian Light Horse in Palestine in the world's last great cavalry charge. The narrative is a prose poem in praise of Australia, symbolised by the many and varied districts that bred the horses. The names of Illawarra and the Flinders, Barcaldine, Kosciusko, the Kimberleys, the Darling, Burragorang Valley and Wollondilly, each accompanied by a vignette of the place mentioned, ring out like the roll-call of nobles in a Shakespearian history. The writer describes the hardness of the campaign that leads to the last triumphant charge. The whole scene is focused through the mind of a single man, and then again generalised in the narrative of the preparations for action and the actual charge and battle. Finally, 'Brigade after Brigade, the horses were led in, light horse and gunner, to drink with slackened girth and bitless mouths at the wells of Beersheba' (p. 26). The Australians water their horses at the well God provided in the desert for Abraham and his son. Victory is won by the same qualities of endurance and alliance of man, animal and nature that are shown in Davison's novels *Forever Morning* (1931), *Man-Shy* (1931) and *Dusty* (1946).

The darker side of human nature, the demands of self that lead to conflict and destruction, are absent from Davison's simple tale of the battle for Beersheba. They constitute, however, the central theme of his short story written about the war in France. The emphasis of the story, 'Fathers and Sons' (pp. 209–27) falls not on the courage of the troops but on their betrayal by the greed and lust of the old men who send them to their death. The story tells of an idealistic young volunteer driven to desperation by his father's personal treachery. He dies 'before he had had all the things in life he must have wanted' and after he had been 'tortured in his mind as no young man has a right to be tortured'. This leads the narrator to realise that 'it was our own people, back in Australia, in Canada, in Britain, who really menaced us'. The menace he perceives is not a failure to support the troops, but the lies and deceit that produce the war itself: 'In every case life was in the arms of the older man, not only the anonymous fathers, but also the fathers of the state: for the boys, the kiss of death'. The story goes beyond grief to a fierce contempt for those whose lack of human responsibility causes war.

Martin Boyd

The self-aggrandising deceit, and the accompanying destruction of the human values that are used to justify war, generate the motivating passion of the war novels of Davison's contemporary, Martin Boyd. War, for Boyd, is an integral part of a society that has lost its grasp of human values. His four-part novel *Lucinda Brayford* (Lansdowne, Melbourne, 1969 [1946]) and his Langton tetralogy (1952–62) both trace the history of families torn between England and Australia, but in each case the First World War is the event that reveals the precarious quality of civilisation in both the old world and the new. The structure of both works, with the repeated alternation of the action between England and Australia, represents a search for a society in which human values can be realised. The battles in

Martin Boyd
(*State Library of Victoria*)

France and the parallel mobilisation in England represent the ultimate denial of these values.

Although *Lucinda Brayford* opens and closes in Cambridge, its perspective is that of its central character, who is brought up in Australia and marries into the English aristocracy. Her character is formed in Australia, but her education in values comes from the family in England. The central problem of the novel is the conflict between authority and power, or between a life lived for the pleasure of civilised order and one devoted to personal gain. The novel juxtaposes the golden summers of youth spent by the sea at Flinders and the traditional order of an English great house with the aridity of the outback and the grasping materialism of the new classes of London and Toorak. The rise of these classes causes the collapse of civilised values that culminates in the devastation of the First World War. The last part of the novel traces the aftermath of the war in the crumbling of Europe through to the horrors of Dunkirk, which determine Lucinda's son Stephen to make his fatal stand against the new brutality.

The first scene of the novel is one of disorder and violence, which leads to the flight of victim and persecutor to Australia. The final scene, three generations later, brings the healing balm and hope of King's College chapel, with the voices of the choristers singing the anthem of the resurrection. Yet this joyful conclusion brings to an end the chapter in which the ashes of Lucinda's son Stephen Brayford have been spread on the river, signifying the end of his own futile rebellion and of the hopes of any human regeneration for the failed civilisation that has consigned the young of two generations to evil and death.

The opening scene of the novel shows an England already ruined by money and vice. Following the transformation of society by the Industrial Revolution, the aristocracy have abandoned duty for pleasure, and the middle classes seek the privilege of aristocracy without accepting its responsibilities. The aristocratic Brayford destroys others by the negligence of his self-concern. The mildly religious Aubrey Chapman is too feeble to resist the oafishness that has substituted prejudice for religion. Evensong in King's College chapel, symbol of social and religious order, produces only a chill. The court of Clare College and its graceful bridge, symbols of the order of scholarship, are the scene of drunken debauch and assault. Vane's attempt to cheat at cards marks the grasping mentality of the middle classes, and by its total lack of honour excludes him from even the emaciated values of Brayford. This reversal of values continues to mark the fortunes of the characters in the new world. Vane is exiled to a sheep station that is barren of both charm and comfort, yet yields him a fortune greater than Brayford's own. In the same colony, Chapman continues to lead a life of futile gentility. Thus the new world, rather than redressing the wrongs of the old, intensifies them.

The first generation in Australia virtually repeat the experience of their parents. Chapman's daughter Julie marries Fred Vane, who takes her to the barren station of Noorilla where, like his father, he recovers his fortunes and is able to establish a fashionable home in Melbourne. His daughter Lucinda completes the symbolic cycle by marrying into the Brayford family and returning to England. Although the wealth of the new world repairs the fortunes of the old, the aristocracy remains under siege from the new values it is unable to withstand. The novel ends with the death of Lucinda's son Stephen as a consequence of his attempts to stand against wartime barbarism, and leaves only Lucinda and the bachelor Paul Brayford, thirteenth Earl of Crittenden,

to testify to old values. The final hymn of joy drifting from King's College chapel, and the words Paul reads as he sprinkles Stephen's ashes on the Cam, affirm that the only source of hope for this world lies outside it:

> Of a truth, they have more fantastic dreams than we. They aim at justice, but denying Christ they will end by flooding the earth with blood . . . And that would come to pass were it not for the promise of Christ, that for the sake of the humble and meek the days shall be shortened.

Boyd, Lucinda Brayford, p. 541.

The people flooding the earth with blood are, in this context, the war leaders of all nations, who even as they fight for justice destroy the society and the people they claim to save.

In treating the war as an integral feature of a society that has lost its way, rather than as an aberration or interruption to the normal course of life, Boyd differs absolutely from his predecessors. The innocence of childhood in the novel is already corrupted by images of death and brutality, like the dead trees that rise in 'a hideous arboreal graveyard' behind the grassy slopes and golden beach at Flinders. He shows not the trenches, but the peaceful countryside of Crittenden set apart from the wider world, its defences already penetrated by traitors and barbarians in such persons as an aristocratic gossip-columnist and a recently ennobled brewer. Thus, just as Boyd cannot share the belief in an England lost by war, he is not concerned with war as a way of forming either individual or national character. The movement of Boyd's characters between England and Australia, both in this novel and in the succeeding Langton tetralogy, leaves them at home in neither. They search for a space to build a life that will embody the freedom of the new world and the order of the old without the materialism that has corrupted both.

Although the action of the novel revolves around the wars, the actual fighting is shown only at second hand, from the viewpoint of the civilians. The obscenity of war and its consequences is revealed at Dunkirk, where Stephen recognises a dying man as the choirboy whose magnificent hymns of praise in King's College chapel had filled him with Platonic love. On returning to Cambridge, he finds that even the chapel is dead:

It was filled, instead of with afternoon sunlight filtered into a thousand bright tints, with a grey twilight. The glass had been removed and the vast windows were black and blind . . . on himself, who had last seen it a glorious shell of colour and light, the effect was intensely depressing.

Boyd, *Lucinda Brayford*, p. 510.

The death of the young man, and of colour and beauty are linked in a single process, extinguishing all life and value.

Boyd deals more directly with the First World War, and particularly the experience in France, in *When Blackbirds Sing*, the fourth of the Langton novels (Lansdowne, Melbourne, 1971, [1962]). In this novel, Dominic Langton, the most accomplished yet mysterious of the brothers, returns to England and enlists in the Territorials. The shape of the novel then approximates to the memoirs of English writers, as Dominic undergoes training in the idyllic English countryside of his ancestral home and then moves with the regiment to France, where he and his friend experience a mystical unity with nature as they 'stood naked, restored to innocence in the stillness of the natural world' (p. 79). Their innocence, drawn from the simple worlds of the English and Australian countrysides, starkly contrasts with the experience of the trenches. However, Boyd does not dwell on the physical horrors so much as on the part Dominic finds himself forced to play, not only killing people but also participating in the discipline that forces men into the pattern of brutality. He becomes completely disenchanted with war, and refuses to acquiesce in its processes. The novel concludes with his return to Australia, where he casts his medals into the dam in total repudiation of his part in the war. The novel thus again leads the reader away from the experience of war to a consideration of the moral nature of the society that perpetrates it.

Contemporary Novels of the First World War

Two recent novels that deal with the First World War interpret it by reconstructing the immediacy of experience rather than by putting it into a particular historical context. They nevertheless manage their reconstruction in quite different ways. Roger McDonald, in *1915: a Novel* (University of Queensland Press, St Lucia, 1979) recreates the period with meticulous detail. David Malouf, in *Fly Away Peter* (Penguin, Ringwood, 1983 [1981]), pares away the narrative to a series of stark images.

Roger McDonald

The publishers present McDonald's novel wrapped in a white jacket with the numeric title 1915 in harsh black at the top and the author's name in the same black at the bottom. The red silhouette of an Australian infantryman, with slouch hat and fixed bayonet, is superimposed on the third figure of the date. The explanatory words 'a novel' are in soft grey above the author's name. The effect of the jacket is brutal, with a clear contrast between black and white, good and evil, and the imminent threat of passion and death suggested by the red. Inside, the image is softened and humanised with a photograph of men in the trenches 'taken at Gallipoli in 1915 by Hugo Throssell, VC'. Throssell was the war hero who married Katharine Susannah Prichard, and the use of his photograph links McDonald's novel with both military and literary traditions.

The contrasts of the book's physical form accurately reflect its content. Like the photograph, the novel is documentary in its realism. Its true theme is, however, not life in the trenches but the harsh contrasts and choices presented by life everywhere, and the constant threat of death. The red and white of the cover do not distinguish between war and peace, civilian and soldier, friend and enemy, but between right and wrong. The central characters in the novel, Walter Gilchrist and his neighbour, Billy Mackenzie, represent this contrast, but in the end they are both reduced to the common grey of the photograph. Unlike most war novels, the only major character to die is one of the girls left at home, not one of the men at the front. Yet her death effectively destroys one of the two soldiers whose fortunes provide the story.

The novel opens with the observation that it was 'inconceivable to Walter that a person could be well educated yet morally bad' (p. 3). His problem is focused on Edie Davis, who according to local gossip had tried to drown herself in a dam. In one paragraph we are introduced to a moral question and to the fact of death. In the next few pages, Edie is rebuffed in her advances to Walter, and shortly afterwards is

found dead in an abandoned mineshhaft. The importance of the episode is not narrative but thematic.
Edie raises for Walter the abstract question of moral
responsibility and the practical one of sexuality. In
remaining true to the restrictive morality of his
Presbyterian upbringing and denying Edie he becomes responsible for her death. The novel is about
how he learns from wartime experience that morality
demands the acceptance both of his own needs and
of responsibility.

The moral questions of the first chapter are
immediately entwined with social and class distinctions. Walter is a public schoolboy destined for
comfortable succession to his father's farm. Billy,
who is already earning his own living, comes from a
poor farm and a rough family, and will have to make
his own way in life. As schoolboys they have been
both friends and rivals, Billy the more adept, Walter
with a sense of innate superiority. Walter decides
what they should do, but Billy succeeds in what they
attempt. Sexually, Walter remains inhibited while
Billy enjoys the promiscuous opportunities of a small
town.

These simple distinctions conceal, however, an
ambiguity underlying their relations. Although Billy
appears carefree, he feels trapped in his body, and
envies Walter his apparent certainty. His love affairs
are attempts to escape, and are overshadowed by
the violence by which he expresses his frustration.
Although his father is soaked in whisky and his
mother in unhappiness, their affection provides his
only security, and he is shattered by his mother's
death. He is completely happy only when he is
shooting, whether wallabies at home or Turks at the
front, where he becomes the expert sniper known to
the troops as 'The Murderer'.

Walter is presented as the polar opposite of Billy,
frightened of sex but otherwise secure in himself
and his class. Yet his sexual inhibition matches the
coldness of his family, whose solid worth covers a
failure of feeling. While Billy feels trapped by his
body, Walter is trapped by possessions and a father
who frustrates his wishes. Walter wants to go to
university, to discover art and to make sense of the
world of his feelings, but his father requires him to
take his place on the land. Yet Walter's wishes are
also a desire to stay safely in childhood, to avoid the
demands of sex and love.

The war provides the vehicle by which these

In the Trenches
(*Australian War Memorial*)

polarities are explored. It destroys all the old rhythms
of life, the patterns of seasonal work to which Walter
had clung, and swings 'everyone's life into the
measure of its waltz, breaking up old loyalties and
serenely betraying new ones' (p. 350). But, as
Walter comes to realise, the new life of the trenches
repeats the patterns of the old. Beneath the unity
of the army the old personal rivalries and hatreds
continue to flourish; men continue to bully others
through the power of money and muscle. They
continue to work out their emotional and sexual
problems through the unsatisfactory means of letters
and brothels. Religion no longer offers any meaning,
as the minister who at home had preached that 'as
we are taken and destroyed, so we shall glimpse the
destination' finds nothing to say in the face of the total
and casual destruction of war. But with the future
reduced to the daily routine of survival, Walter
discovers hope in his realisation of the common
experience that underlies even hostile relationships
with his companions, and Billy finds it in the news
of his girlfriend's pregnancy. However, her casual
death by drowning destroys this dream, forcing him
back into his blind rage, so that at the end of the
book he is carried off to the imprisonment of a strait-
jacket and lunatic asylum. The insanity of war is
shown not as the product of an evil system, but as an
instance of the cruelty of life that we can resist only
by endurance and solidarity.

The novel convincingly recreates the details of life in 1915 in the quiet country town and surrounding farms of Forbes, on Sydney's fashionable north shore and in the homestead of a wealthy grazier, and amid the trenches on Gallipoli. The relations of class and power in society are presented as unchanging reality. The quiet natural rhythms of the earlier part of the novel are succeeded by the industrial rhythms of war and the obliterating sweep of rain and flooded river that carries away Billy's girl and her child. This careful construction of a particular time has the effect of detaching the characters from history. They have no awareness of any issues at stake in the war apart from their immediate experience. It is a tide that sweeps them all away with its passion and its reality. It takes them out of the time they had lived in, but nothing seems to hinge on its outcome. War and flood are as one, and the only question is how individuals will make their own lives in the circumstances given them. This perspective belongs to the later history of the twentieth century from which McDonald looks back at a particular war as just one example of the external forces against which humans must contend. The fact that his characters are Australian is important only because they must confront these forces without the protection of established structures and traditions.

David Malouf

Malouf's novel *Fly Away Peter* (Penguin, Ringwood, 1983 [1981]) similarly detaches the war from its immediate history in order to ask the question of the individual response to history. The war in this novel has a similar function to the sentence of death in Camus' *The Outsider*. By taking away from the individual any power over his actions it gives him ultimate freedom to be himself.

The novel works through a series of images rather than through a conventional story. The opening scene shows the main character, Jim Saddler, alone in the swamp with the birds, but troubled by a shadow on his left. The shadow belongs to a biplane which, as a mechanical intrusion on the natural world of the birds, threatens the unity Jim has found there and presents an omen of the global destruction of the war to come. For the moment, however, Jim finds security in a communion he shares with Imogen

Harcourt, a photographer, and Ashley Crowther, the owner of the land, who employs him to record the details of the life of the birds. The three of them share an understanding of the land felt most explicitly by Ashley:

> Ashley saw things differently from his father and grandfather. They had always in mind a picture they had brought from 'home', orderly fields divided by hedgerows, to which the present landscape, by planning and shaping, might one day be made to approximate. But for Ashley this was the first landscape he had known and he did not impose that other, greener one upon it; it was itself.
>
> Malouf, *Fly Away Peter*, p. 11.

Ashley has been educated in Cambridge and can pass as an English gentleman, but on his return to Australia he discovers that here is the 'centre of his being'. This image of space, of a place where nature remains open, where the human can enter but not intrude, acts as the standard against which the other events and images of the book are judged.

The image of the birds in their swamp contrasts with the image that comes to Jim's mind as he encounters the vast industrial toil behind the battle lines in France. This reminds him of a picture from Sunday school, of 'large numbers of men, all roped together . . . hauling blocks of stone up a slope, yoked together in thousands like cattle and hauling the blocks from every point of the compass towards a great cone that was rising slowly out of the sands' (p. 68). Jim is impressed by the magnificent scale of the endeavour and the thought that he is to become a part of it. But as he is absorbed in the business of war its aspect changes from one of purposeful effort to surreal horror:

> the real enemy, the one that challenged them day and night and kept them permanently weary, was the stinking water that seeped endlessly out of the walls and rose up round their boots as if the whole trench system in this part of the country were slowly going under. Occasionally it created cave-ins, bringing old horrors back into the light. The dead seemed close then; they had to stop their noses. Once, in heavy rain, a hand reached out

and touched Jim on the back of the neck. 'Cut it out, Clancy,' he had protested, hunching closer to the wall; and was touched again. It was the earth behind him, quietly moving. Suddenly it collapsed, and a whole corpse lurched out of the wall and hurled itself on him.

Malouf, *Fly Away Peter*, pp. 80–81.

The constant presence in the trenches of the corpses of past battles is a commonplace in war writing, but Malouf converts it from a moment of experience to an image of the central horror of the war that threatens not merely death but annihilation, the denial of every value of life. The touches of commonplace realism in Jim's first thought that it is his companion touching him, and the jokes the other men make of the incident, only highlight the horror.

Ashley comes to realise that the war not only threatens the soldiers, but endangers civilisation itself. The war represents the subjection of the human to the machine. 'Later, what had been learnt on the battlefields would travel back, and industry from now on, maybe all life, would be organised like war. The coming battle would not be the end, even if it was decisive; it was another stage in the process' (p. 112). Against this the human imperative is to resist, as the troops do by asserting their nicknames, hanging on if their luck holds, and going home.

Through these images Malouf, like McDonald, removes the war from its own historical context and places it in our own. We are the heirs of both the process and of those who resisted. One of the ironies of the novel is that the bird sanctuary is in the wetlands that have since been displaced by the burgeoning playground of the Gold Coast. The war, like the pyramids, is a demonstration of the creative potential that remains in the human spirit beside its destructive power.

The assertion of the power of human achievement over time prevents the novel from being a mere retreat from modern life into a romantic unity with nature. Rather, the images of war show the way the human spirit is overcome by the drive for power, which alienates people from nature and from their fellows. The helplessness of the individual appears in the fate of Eric Sawney, whose legs are blown off and who faces the rest of his life with no one to care for him. Yet this image of individual powerlessness is balanced by examples of collective strength. Even Eric's fate is qualified by Jim's practical, although limited, compassion. Then, at the moment of Jim's own death, in a dream sequence he joins with numberless colleagues in digging the fields. This action represents at once the fruitful and collective labour of tending the soil, a return to the nurturing earth, and a journey back to an antipodes where nature is not yet blighted. This symbol of mutually productive labour is matched by the entwined lives of Ashley and Imogen and Jim, who by sharing in the unity of nature give strength to each other. This strength, to stand alone but together, culminates in the closing image of the book, where Imogen watches the lone surfer who attains the freedom of the birds and thereby gives her the strength to mourn Jim and to continue living.

Malouf and McDonald are both concerned to discover the effect of the First World War on Australians' understanding of themselves. This reverses the effort of Mann or Boyd to determine how the war revealed what Australia already was. Yet the novels written over fifty years by Australians about this war are at one in identifying Australia with innocence and Europe with guilt. The war did not defeat the dream of freedom, but made it possible. It revealed to the new world the impossibility of redeeming the old, and so endorsed the validity of the distinctive experience of the new.

9

SYDNEY OR THE BUSH: SAVAGE WILDERNESS

DURING the years between the wars official Australia promoted the notion of a young, clean, white nation free from the vice and disease of older lands. Symbols like the Wattle Day celebrations and life-saving clubs attached the old arcadian dream to local institutions and emphasised service and sacrifice for all. This facile nationalism served to conceal the continuing dependence on overseas capital and to obscure social divisions and conflicts. As the image of the bushman faded into that of the digger and the pioneer, Australian life developed as a provincial counterpart to life in England or the USA. Protected by censorship laws from contamination by the ideas that disturbed more powerful countries, Australians turned their backs on the world and the realities of everyday life, and cultivated instead the idea of the outback as their common and unique property.

Writers were both the propagators and the fiercest critics of this comforting myth. In a long series of popular narratives Ion Idriess confirmed the idea of the outback as the true Australia, and its laconic, capable and somewhat sceptical inhabitants as the successors of diggers, bushmen and Anzacs. Although he portrayed the Aborigines with some sympathy, and in his later *Nemarluk: King of the Wilds* (Angus & Robertson, Sydney, 1941) gave epic dimensions to a black resistance leader, he more generally saw them as rather comic figures who for all their bush skills were fundamentally out of place in the coming

Australia. His sympathies were with the white men and women who brought civilised order to the outback, with the clergymen who ministered to them, and with the police who protected them by bringing the Aborigines within the bounds of the law and inflicting dire punishment on those who rebelled. His values come from Lawson, and the ideals of his honest bushmen provide a contrast to the evils of the city. Although his outback may bring hardship

Ion I. Idriess

and distress, it never holds the horror that Lawson felt, or nourishes the evil that Baynton and Clarke portrayed.

Frank Dalby Davison

Davison writes of the bush with the affection of Idriess but with an understanding of human weakness that takes him beyond the easy optimism of the outback genre. *Man-Shy* (Angus & Robertson, 1936 [1931]) tells the story of a scrub heifer that escapes the muster and lives out its life in the freedom of the ranges. It is set on the edges of closer settlement in Queensland, where the settlers are steadily fencing and clearing the bush for their tamed herds. The opening episode sets the instincts of the wild cattle against the violence and greed of the men trying to capture them. The rest of the novel traces the life of the red heifer as she is forced steadily further back into the ranges, pitting her blind instinct for solitary survival against every effort of men to capture her.

In his story of the red heifer Davison, who had himself been forced off his settlement block, appeals to the dogged sense of survival that was essential in the Depression. But his red heifer is not merely a loner, it is a non-human identity made an isolate, not only by the circumstances of the muster and the escape that separated it from the mob, but by the circumstances of its infancy that denied it the security all young mammals assume, and gave it instead the resilience to force a living from the world. This portrayal exalts the animal over the human, and the individual over society. The bush becomes the last refuge for an existential freedom that dates from before any human society. The struggle to be, to exist, is in Davison's work as old as the land itself, and is animal rather than specifically human.

Davison develops this theme in his later work. Unlike Idriess' account of desert warfare, his *Wells of Beersheba* emphasises the role of the horses and their need for water rather than the actions of the men or the tactics of their leader. *Dusty* (Angus & Robertson, Sydney, 1946) has more human warmth in its portrayal of the relationship between the shepherd, Tom, and Dusty, his half-dingo sheepdog. This is, however, the relationship of two loners. Tom's affinity with nature leads him to take care of the pup after its mother is slain, and Dusty's aptness for herding

the sheep is only an atrophied expression of the instinctive delight of the hunter. As this instinct develops, Tom is forced to take the dog outside the confines of civilisation, and after Tom's death Dusty attains full development as a wild killer. Dusty represents the triumph of the wild over the tame, and an assertion that civilisation, in suppressing the wild, suppresses life.

Davison's attitudes reach their fullest expression in his massive *The White Thorntree* (National Press, Melbourne, 1968), which shows human couples desolate in the wastelands of suburbia. For Davison, civilisation is a wilderness more isolating than the bush. It offers nothing in place of the instincts it denies, so that life becomes a mere groping, in every sense, for a satisfaction that quickly fades. The characters in the novel, however, remain mere ciphers illustrating a thesis.

Davison's short stories, collected in *The Road to Yesterday* (Angus & Robertson, Sydney, 1964) give a more convincing picture of the conflict between instinct and society. In 'Woman at the Mill' the bush that offers freedom to the men isolates and denies the women they use. Even the woman's lover is little more than the tame dog who mates with the dingo bitch in *Dusty*. He provides physical sex but, like her husband, is unable to offer the larger life she needs. In the title story, the narrator returns to the site where the Kentish farmer had found full scope for his creative instincts, only to find that the achievement and the society to which it belonged have alike been swept away by time. The settler has tried to impose his patterns on the bush, not to work with it, and so, despite his lonely toughness, he fails to realise his dream. We can escape isolation and repression, these stories suggest, only when we allow our animal instinct to express itself in the whole of our life and environment.

Other Interpretations of the 'Bush'

Davison's exploration of the bush led him to a wholesale rejection of civilisation and eventually to a complete misanthropy. Two of his contemporaries, however, turned back to the experience of taming the bush to discover lessons for the conduct of contemporary Australian society. Both wrote novels that are pleas for Australian independence, but otherwise their authors drew quite opposite conclusions from their studies of the pioneers. Miles Franklin, first in her 'Brent of Bin Bin' novels and then in *All That Swagger* (Angus & Robertson, Sydney, 1947 [1936]) celebrates a kind of bush idyll that produced qualities since forgotten by an urban society. Brian Penton, in *Landtakers* (Angus & Robertson, Sydney, 1972 [1934]), portrays Australia as a hell of violence and cruelty that must be expiated before its people can emerge from a state of blind dependence.

Both authors use a fictitious but unidentified narrator to emphasise the historical basis of their story. Franklin gives only occasional hints of her narrator's identity, suggesting a family chronicler compiling the story from the records and memories of her forebears rather than an omniscient author creating a self-contained world of fiction. Penton is more specific, telling us that 'very little of this story is imaginative'. He explains that it has been gathered from tales and memoirs of the early settlers, and particularly from the chief character himself, Derek Cabell, when he has become 'a very old and lonely man' (pp. 15–16). These suggestions of factuality place the novels in the actual history of the country, while the anonymity of the narrators excludes them from any direct part in the events they describe. Their comments do not produce a distancing irony, but are invitations to their readers to understand the past so that they can act appropriately in the future.

Miles Franklin

Franklin's *All That Swagger* is the saga of four generations of the Delacy family. It begins with Danny Delacy's settlement near the headwaters of the Murrumbidgee after his elopement with Johanna Cooley from their ancestral County Clare. The story shows the family growing and mingling with its neighbours through the births and deaths, weddings and funerals, picnic races and Christmas parties that are the stuff of country life. Drought, fire, bushrangers, Aborigines and murder provide the drama, and family feuds and alliances the constantly changing substance. Yet behind this elaborate facade the narrator teases us with her elusive presence, reminding us that the

Miles Franklin
(*State Library of Victoria*)

past is something we construct from the hints and traces that remain, a fiction that points to the future we must make for ourselves. By taking the characters of a district history and recreating them as figures of legend, the narrator invites the reader to join her in completing old Danny Delacy's vision of freedom.

Danny dreams of freedom when 'a virgin continent demanded resourcefulness, sharpened wits and ingrained self-reliance in the people'. His dream is, however, doomed from the start, partly because it is incompatible with the grasping qualities required for material success, but more because his grand visions exclude his wife, Johanna. While Danny rides out in search of new pastures, she is left at home in isolation and fear. The land remains hostile, and even in her last hours she is still haunted by memories of 'the bunyip, and the banshee, and the keening of the river oaks', and the little girl she had lost so tragically (p. 269). She has never overcome the alienation she first felt when Danny set her down in his rough bark hut where 'Day or night there was no relief from the Morumbidgee [sic], so lone and dark and far, with the voice of a ravening wind' where she feels she is at 'the furthest extremity of the globe from the placid Shannon in its park-like plain' (p. 18).

If the limitations of prejudice and insensitivity that prevent Danny and Johanna from achieving their dreams are products of the old world they bring with them to the new, so are the dreams themselves a flowering of the old world and its heroic tales of a pagan past

> descended from the *seanachies* and bards of Tara's zenith, and earlier . . . stories of Cormac MacArt, the great king, grandson of Conn of the Hundred Battles, and son of Art the Lonely, whose reign was full of plenty and such honesty that there was no need to guard flocks or lock doors. Stories from Gaelic legendry found fresh voice to the song of the Murrumbidgee [sic] and disclosed a glint of the glories of the Ard-Rights of Eirinn . . .
>
> Franklin, *Swagger*, p. 75.

The tales translated to a new land offer to all the chance to attain a nobility untainted by greed and superstition, but human weakness again defeats the dream. Hope remains alive at the end of the novel in the person of the young aviator, Brian Delacy, symbol of sunlight and soil, heir of old Danny and prophet of the future, but this symbol is too contrived to bear the weight imposed on it. The main action of the novel has ended with the death of old Danny, and the attempt to give his dreams further substance breaks too far from the historic and legendary structure to carry conviction. The meaning of Danny's vision and Johanna's endurance rests within themselves rather than on hopes of national regeneration.

Brian Penton

Penton's *Landtakers* provides neither easy hope nor any spectacles of heroic vision. While Franklin subordinates the treatment of convicts and Aborigines to her larger vision of freedom, Penton shows this brutality as essential to the violent conquest of a savage land which in turn brutalises its conquerors. Only by the acceptance of violence in himself as in others, by the rejection of both gentility and the heroism that dedicates itself to 'deeds as vague and glorious as the Milky Way' does the novel's central character, Derek Cabell, find even a passing peace 'between the ghosts of yesterday and the unborn passions of tomorrow' (p. 360). Yet his acceptance

of violence is also a declaration of independence, of his freedom to be himself.

Penton's novel is about the cost of survival, whereby man makes himself into superman by destroying every human tie of community or obligation. Both work and family are based on power and exploitation, and so produce not fellowship but violent conflict. The isolation of the Australian bush reveals the absolute separateness of each individual in a world where the only mutual bonds are those of hate. The narrator tells Cabell's story in an effort to understand a society that has been created from the suffering and violence of the first settlers:

> If I could piece together the picture of that epoch as I had inherited it from him — the savage deeds, the crude life, the hatred between men and men and men and country, the homesickness, the loneliness, the despair of inescapable exile in the bush; the strange forms of madness and cruelty; the brooding, inturned characters; and, joined with this, an almost fanatical idealism which repudiated the past and the tyranny of the past and looked to the future in a new country for a new heaven and earth, a new justice; on the one hand the social outcasts, men broken by degradation and suffering, on the other the adventurers: blackest pessimism balancing the most radiant optimism — if only I could *see* all this, then I would understand.
>
> Penton, *Landtakers*, p. 16.

The novel opens with a confrontation between the delicate sensitivities of the young Derek Cabell and the brutality of the colony of Moreton Bay. Cabell is forced to surrender a young convict to the flogging yard and is humiliated by the taunts of drunken 'floggers and jailbirds' in a grog shanty. By the end of the novel Cabell has plumbed the same depths of brutality and degradation, and has himself flogged, beaten and killed. He overcomes the natural disasters of drought, flood and fire, and above all the loneliness of a country where 'there are no tigers . . . nothing ever happens' (p. 12). This boredom, the 'heartbreaking indifference, immensity and loneliness' sends men mad, driving them to insane cruelty and the horrors of the drink in which they drown their sensitivities. The country is a purgatory that Cabell endures only by shedding all the feelings of human decency and sympathy that first make him revolt against it. But at the end it makes him its own, and he repudiates his English past in favour of his property in a land where the 'agony of boredom at the monotonous grey of the bush' can give way to days when the 'rain-washed air makes the hills so blue that they lose themselves in the sky' and 'the bush seems to dream on its own beauty' (p. 358).

The novel charts the stages by which Cabell emancipates himself from English gentility. His transformation starts almost by inadvertence as he is swept on by events rather than planning them. By participating in a massacre he knowingly sacrifices in himself 'some fine bright thing that was precious above everything else to him', and is engulfed in an 'uprush of fierce satisfaction' as the killing begins (pp. 124–8). Later, bringing his wool down to the market, he becomes lost and wanders for days in the bush. After being rescued by a selector and taken to a shanty, he finds both company and a wife, Emma Surface. His marriage to her is an acknowledgement that he must take the bush on its own terms. His attempt to repudiate her when he learns of her convict past only makes him more dependent on her abilities to manage his men and property. Finally, her intervention to save him from a fight he has provoked puts him completely in her power, as he realises that she 'taught him really to hate her on the night the homestead burnt down' (p. 356). Emma represents both the degradation and the strength of the land that makes him its own.

In tracing Cabell's destruction, or the creation of his savage strength, Penton does not merely show the cost of settling Australia. He rejects all the myths and ideals by which people had sustained themselves in the face of the hostile or indifferent bush. There is no loyalty between master and men nor among the convicts, who maintain unity against their oppressors only by treating each other with savage inhumanity. The lone bushman does not welcome another to his campfire or share his knowledge of the country with him. Neighbours pursue bitter feuds and married couples torment each other into madness. Even bush skills are merely a means of inflicting cruelty. In this brutal world, only superior brutality succeeds, and the sole achievement is the individual's conquest of his own finer qualities.

The contrast between Cabell and his grasping but effete brothers and contemptuously self-satisfied aunt in England leaves no doubt that the author endorses the savagery of Australia as the true quality of human experience. The source of human ambition is shown as neither greed nor even sexual lust, but the drive to create the self by the exercise of power over others. At the beginning of the novel, this power is concentrated in the convict supervisor McGovern, in the central parts in Cabell, and by the end in Emma. Aborigines and convicts have passed, but the order that has succeeded them still rests on the brute strength and cunning of its beginnings. The only promise offered by Australia is the rawness of a society that allows any individual who recognises its truth to build his life on it, unconstrained by the institutionalised power of older societies. It is an essentially fascist vision.

Xavier Herbert

The characters in Miles Franklin's novels eventually find peace in a country that, as they learn to understand it, offers them nurture. Brian Penton writes of men who, even at the cost of brutalising themselves, force the wilderness to submit to their ambitions. Xavier Herbert, however, portrays a country that remains utterly alien to white civilisation. The land is

Xavier Herbert

unforgiving. Nature, as flood, drought or heat, is elemental, and reduces humans to their elements. The strong do bloody battle against it, destroying whatever stands in their way until they in turn are destroyed in the same way they have lived. The weak, particularly those who bring with them the values of the southern capitals or of England, try to maintain the social veneer that keeps them comfortable, and thus doom themselves to be forever outsiders. Yet the novels are also celebrations of the beauty of the country, and the strength of those who learn to live with its hostility. In an autobiographical essay published in *Overland* (Number 50, Autumn 1972) Herbert wrote that before writing *Capricornia* he had learned that

> . . . Australian cities are not Australian, even much in geography, since spiritually, socially, economically, the people of them live back where their forebears came from, and that even the rural scene is false because of the natural compulsion of the immigrant to extirpate the alien environment. One had to go back to where things were much as they had been when our fathers turned up either dragging their leg-irons or wielding their cat-o'- nine-tails, where you had to look for snakes or black women in your bed before you got into it, could pot your dinner from the kitchen window, or pot a blackfellow and cut off his ears to prove the worth of the notches in the stock of your gun — which is to say, of course, to go back to what used to be called Our Empty North.
>
> Herbert, *Overland*, p. 65.

Herbert's books are written in the spirit of this statement. Their anger is directed at the cruel treatment of the Aborigines, particularly Aboriginal women, and at the exploitation and destruction of the land itself. The destruction comes from the refusal of the exploiters to learn from the people who have lived in the land from time immemorial. Only those characters who learn to submit to the country can achieve any personal integrity, but even they are eventually destroyed. In *Capricornia* Norman is heir to both black and white cultures, but fails crucially in personal responsibility. In *Poor Fellow My Country* (Collins, Sydney, 1975), Jeremy Delacy sees his hopes broken by forces from an outside world too much ripped

apart by greed and hatred for even the most remote of places to provide a sanctuary where restoration might begin.

Herbert's first novel, *Capricornia* (Angus & Robertson, Sydney, 1956 [1938], opens, in a chapter entitled 'The Coming of the Dingoes', with a bitterly ironic history of white settlement in the north. The irony arises from the contrast between the high moral professions of the whites and the brutality of their conduct. They map the country with names that conceal the truth of their actions. The settlement of Treachery Bay, for example, commemorates the massacre of the tribesmen who attempted to defend their own lands. The Aborigines' attempts to live by universal standards of right, and to defend themselves by the means at hand, lead to their death. The whites, on the other hand, are able to massacre the Aborigines without moral compunction because they view them as savages, outside any moral code or any claim to human rights.

This chapter is built around the literary figure of *syllepsis*, the grammatical joining of contraries in a single statement: 'The first white settlement in Capricornia . . . was set up on what was perhaps the most fertile and pleasant part of the coast and the bones of half the Karrapillua tribe' (p. 1). The first part of the figure is the white perception, the lasting Australian dream of settlement; the second the black reality. The opening pages of the chapter present this contrast in a series of incidents narrated as historical chronicle. Then the chronicle changes to the drama of the battle between the trepang-fisher Ned Krater and the Aboriginal leader Kurrinua, headman of the Yarracumbunga tribe. The climax and conclusion of the chapter, as Kurrinua is removed as an impediment to settlement, brings the two modes of thought and action into bitter contrast:

> Kurrinua's heart beat painfully. His eyes grew hot. The pain of his wounds, which he had kept in check for hours by the power he was bred to use, began to throb. But he did not move a hair. He had been trained to look upon death fearlessly. To do so was to prove oneself a warrior worthy of having lived. His mind sang the Death Corroboree — Ee-yah, ee-yah, ee-tullyai — O mungallinni wurrigai — ee-tukkawunni —
> BANG! Kurrinua gasped, heaved out of the sand, writhed, shuddered, died. Ned Krater spat.

In his opinion he had done no wrong. He did not know why the savages had attacked him. He thought only of their treachery, which to such as he was as intolerable as it was natural to such as they.

Herbert, *Capricornia*, p. 6.

The same episode is presented at once as the heroism of fearless death and the proper response to savage treachery. The attitudes are incompatible, but the act of settlement locks them into a bloody unity. Ned Krater's inability to perceive this unity, his blindness to the common humanity he shares with those he destroys, generates his characteristic combination of courage and callousness. While these qualities give him the heroic dimensions of venturer and conqueror, they also isolate him from the land and from the society it produces, so that finally he dies alone and unfriended, a victim of the natural forces he had defied. His brief history inaugurates the action of the novel it prefigures.

The main obstacle to white settlement is not the Aboriginal resistance but the violence of nature. Four settlements are abandoned or swept into the Silver Sea before the foundation of Port Zodiac. This settlement becomes the capital of Capricornia, Herbert's mythical counterpart of the Northern Territory. This land is not merely the setting of the novel but a major protagonist.

The task of settlement is complicated by the guilt implicit in the very fact of white occupation, and maintained not only by the continuing sexual and economic exploitation of the blacks but by the refusal of the whites to recognise this relationship for what it is. In principle they maintain that the divide between black and white is absolute. In practice they cross it continually, and consequently breed a race of half-castes, or 'yeller-fellers', whose own fate is tragic and whose existence poisons their fathers' lives with guilt. The first half of *Capricornia* explores these complications of race, while the second concentrates on the problems as they emerge in the life of one person, Norman Shillingsworth, who is caught between the two races and the two cultures.

The historical and dramatic narrative of the first chapter of *Capricornia* provides the historical framework within which subsequent events are viewed. The second chapter provides a contrast to Ned Krater in the persons of the Shillingsworth brothers, Oscar

and Mark, who arrive in Port Zodiac to take up clerical positions in the administration. They bring with them the effete gentility of the south, but once they don the solar topee of the colonial official they take to themselves the pretensions of the ruling class. Oscar marries upwardly into the landed gentry, but Mark finds the public service too restrictive and moves through beer and fornication into the world of Ned Krater. Oscar becomes possessed of Red Ochre station and legitimate offspring, while Mark fathers a part-Aboriginal child. He at first refuses to accept responsibility for his son, who becomes known as 'No-name', or in pidgin 'Nawnim', later anglicised to 'Norman'. These successive changes of his name symbolise the person who, given no identity by his parents, must find it for himself. His floundering attempts through the novel to find his place represent the confusions and contradictions of a frontier society that rejects its own historical and cultural foundations.

The apparently sprawling pattern of the novel and its violent alternation between calm and upheaval, prosperity and disaster, is the product of the turbulence of life in Capricornia and the guilt at its heart. As in Faulkner's novels of the American south, even the moral possibilities of the individual are determined by external forces that each person must resolve without in any way being able to control. Such societies produce an epic pattern of fiction, in which narrative is determined by history and even domestic affairs are pubilc. The individual can choose either to make his history at the cost of his inner life, to accept the role of victim, or to retreat into the cultivation of inner sensibility. Only the central characters refuse to accept history and try to resolve its contradictions in their own lives.

It is, however, some time before the focus of the novel becomes evident. At first, its structure seems a counterpart of the violent and anarchic nature of the country in which it is set. Of the 108 principal characters listed in the front of the book, at least twenty-one die during the course of the action, mostly by violence or disease. The action alternates between achievement and destruction. Oscar's rise in society is counterpointed by Mark's descent. Yet there is alternation also within their individual histories. Oscar achieves success only to lose his son and be deserted by his wife. Mark is thrown out of the service but finds satisfaction as skipper of a lugger and in fathering a son. His occasions of prosperity are, in traditional Australian style, marked by orgies of booze that lead to remorse, poverty and imprisonment. Nawnim's fate is to be welcomed by his father, then abandoned, briefly fostered by Black Anna and then again abandoned, forgotten in the train and then found by fettlers, and finally reluctantly adopted by Oscar. Underlying these reversals of personal fortunes is the economic cycle of boom and depression and the corresponding seasonal cycle in which the excess of each stage brings about its collapse into its opposite. As Oscar reflects of his adopted environment in a moment of contentment:

> At times he loved it best in Wet Season — when the creeks were running and the swamps were full — when the multi-coloured schisty rocks split golden waterfalls — when the scarlet plains were under water, green with wild rice, swarming with Siberian snipe . . . when cattle wandered a land of plenty, fat and sleek, till the buffalo flies and marsh-flies came and drove them mad, so that they ran and ran to leanness, often to their death . . . when from hour to hour luke-warm showers drenched the steaming earth, till one was sodden to the bone and mildewed to the marrow and moved to pray, as Oscar always was when he had had enough of it, for that which formerly he had cursed — the Dry! the good old Dry! . . . when harsh winds rioted with choking dust and the billabongs became mere muddy holes where cattle pawed for water — when gaunt drought loafed about a desert and exhausted cattle staggered searching dust for food and drink, till they fell down and died and became neat piles of bones for the wind to whistle through and the gaunt-ribbed dingo to mourn — then one prayed for the Wet again, or if one's heart was small, packed up and left this Capricornia that fools down South called the Land of Opportunity, and went back and said that nothing was done by halves up there except the works of puny man.

> Herbert, *Capricornia*, p. 61.

In this single sentence we have the images of excess and failure, drought and plenty, that constitute the central features of the Australian mythology. These images are heightened by the insistent rhythm to an intensity that magnifies at once the despair and the heroism of the pioneers and bushmen whose endurance makes a mockery of the illusions of the cities.

The implication is that, while the bush frontier may destroy humans, it offers the only true test of their worth.

The imagery of this sentence, and the narrative pattern in which aspiration is rooted in violence and culminates in destruction, has led critics to suggest that the fundamental vision of the novel is one in which the brutality of man and nature is answered only by the restless and creative energy of the people who are the authors of the violence. Herbert, like Penton, Lindsay and Slessor, suggests in his work that only an elite of superior beings can redeem the world from its inherent ugliness and brutality. For Lindsay, the artist was the embodiment of this ideal. Herbert found it in the man who has both the strength to survive and the wisdom to understand the bush. In his first novel, none of the characters reaches this understanding, although Norman has started to learn what is required. In his last, Jeremy Delacy finds this truth for himself but does not have the ability to share it fully with others.

Capricornia is a novel of failure. Oscar's attempt to save Norman from society is parallel to the attempts of Peter Differ to provide a safe future for his half-caste daughter and of Tim O'Cannon to construct a multiracial sanctuary for his family. Differ is frustrated by his own alcoholism and Oscar's callous obstinancy. O'Cannon is killed when he is run down by the train while bringing home for Christmas the presents that are the tokens of his love. Because his sanctuary has depended entirely on his own will his death leaves its inhabitants as plunder for the authorities. The irony of their fate rebounds on Norman when he leaves Tocky Differ and his child to horrible deaths while he uses the law to rescue his father from the consequences of murder. The sterile cry of the crow that closes the novel is a reminder of the guilt we share with Norman.

The nationalism of *Capricornia* was, despite its social criticism, in harmony with the spirit of its time. The author's genuine anger at the arrogance and brutality of the whites and their exploitation of the land and its people is balanced by an often lyrical feeling for the country itself, which yields its beauty only to those willing to submit themselves to it. The two-dimensional characters with their descriptive names may border on caricature, but they also represent the reality of people alienated alike from their own past and their immediate environment, and thus deprived of any inner meaning to existence. By contrast, Tocky's tragic death and Norman's responsibility for it forces on us a realisation of the unity of life that alone can overcome the bitterness and brutality the novel has shown.

Herbert's published work for a few years after *Capricornia* was much slighter. A novel on wartime Sydney, *Soldiers' Women* (1961) is a bitter account of the sexual exploitation of lonely men by women rejoicing in freedom from domestic responsibility. The novel *Seven Emus* (1959; written later but published earlier than *Soldiers' Women*) is a slight tale built around the important issue of Aboriginal sacred sites and objects. These were followed by a book of short stories, *Larger Than Life* (1963), many of them very funny and most based loosely on his wanderings and adventures in the outback, and a romanticised autobiography, *Disturbing Element* (1963), in which he creates his chosen self as roisterer and rebel, enemy of the respectable and the intellectual. Both of these books can be seen, however, as preliminary flourishes for the sprawling testament, polemic and story of his last novel, *Poor Fellow My Country* (Collins, Sydney, 1975).

The vast bulk of this work becomes more manageable if we consider it as a trilogy rather than a single novel, but the three parts are nevertheless closely related. They form a continuous narrative of the fortunes of Jeremy Delacy (who shares much of the character and experience that Herbert attributes to himself in his autobiography) and his mixed blood grandson, Prindy. Formally, each volume represents one stage in the life of Prindy. These could be described as infancy, childhood and adolescence, although the boy seems to compress a greater progression of experience into these stages than could be accounted for by the six chronological years they cover. The three volumes also trace Jeremy's affairs with the three women who fall in love with him. Each woman represents a possible solution of the problem of how to live satisfactorily in the country. Thematically, the tone of the work is conveyed in the titles and epigraphs of its three parts: 'Terra Australis: — Blackman's Idyll Despoiled by White Bullies, Thieves and Hypocrites'; 'Australia Felix — Whiteman's Idea Sold Out by Rogues and Fools'; 'Day of Shame — A Rabble Fled the Test of Nationhood'. This tone of bitterness is repeated in much of the book and in Herbert's repeated hectoring of the reader.

Each of the women who falls in love with Jeremy represents both one of the components of the

Australian heritage and one of the possibilities of resolving its contradictions. Lydia Esk stands for the ideal of an embracing commonwealth of nations. This commonwealth would, however, be British, not Australian. Its internationalism rests on the power of British capital maintained by force of arms and manifest in the financial kingdom of the Vaiseys (or Vesteys) that dominates the north. The land itself, shown in the power of Aboriginal paintings by the pool at Catfish, rejects Lydia, and she flees home to England. Aelfreida Candlemas suggests a dream of democracy and community renewed on the basis of a common Anglo-Saxon heritage. Despite her romance with the north, she is a creature of the south, and her dream is a racial fantasy. When Jeremy unwisely follows her south he is cut off from his spiritual source. He eventually recovers his integrity only through a strange dream or encounter with a *Moombook*, or Aboriginal spirit. This experience seems to confirm his oneness with the land, the north that is the only place where he can live effectively, and that Aelfreida has rejected. Both the book and the child she has conceived by Jeremy are destroyed.

Opposed to these predatory women are those who seek not the perfection of domination but completeness — Bridie Cullity, Jeremy's Aboriginal wife Nanango, and the Jewish beauty Rifkah, who dominates the latter part of the novel. These represent the Irish and peasant, the Aboriginal and the ultimate Judaic and sacramental elements of Australia's heritage. Brigid bears Jeremy's baby, Nanango creates at Lily Lagoons a still centre where love spreads from the earth to all living creatures, and Rifkah creates a sacramental wholeness, comprehending Judaic, Christian and Aboriginal symbols in a greater unity.

Jeremy, the 'Scrub Bull' as he likes to be known, is both the disturbing element who provides the focus of the action and the commentator who suggests its meaning. The end to which the action moves is, however, Jeremy's part-Aboriginal grandson, Prindy. Like Jeremy, Prindy becomes the object of contention between people who represent the forces competing for authority in the north. The representatives of the law try to remove him from a natural home into an institution. Ram Babu, the Indian hawker, offers him refuge and oriental wisdom. Jeremy wants to make him the model of a coming society, and the old man Bobwirridirridi hopes to give to him his own store of Aboriginal lore and the power of the magic that threatens white and black orders alike. The contention of Bob and Jeremy for Prindy's adherence provides the central conflict of the novel and leads to Prindy's death. This destroys both Bob's hope of continuing the past and Jeremy's dream of a future that would integrate the land with the major human traditions.

The brutality of the ending seems gratuitous, going beyond the requirements of the dramatic situation to become an indulgence in violence for its own sake. It denies everthing else Herbert has shown us about the integrating power of cultures, including specifically the Aboriginal, that have grown organically as an expression of peoples' relations with each other within a shared land. The intrusion of the whites has broken this organic link, but Prindy seems to offer the hope of restoring it in a new form. The ending is not only a destruction but a denial of this hope. It represents the author's rejection not only of his time or his countrymen, but of humanity itself.

Despite the ending, *Poor Fellow My Country* contains studies of characters like Rifkah and passages of sustained lyricism that maintain the reader's faith in human potential. The opening scheme where Bobwirridirridi comes on Prindy while he is fishing, or the first sight of Lily Lagoons or of the Aboriginal paintings or the Rainbow Pool, or the sustained love idyll when Rifkah goes to Lily Lagoons and offers her mythology and her sabbath fish, play a functional part in revealing the character of the organic culture that sustains a unity of the human and the natural. But Herbert allows himself to become too clearly identified with Jeremy, who becomes his spokesman, rather than a character. He hectors the reader and his countrymen, and eventually turns on his own characters in an orgy of destruction that looks back to the violence of *Capricornia* rather than to the future Jeremy had sought. The novel represents Herbert's response to post-war Australia and its incorporation in international culture, but the frontier past he sets against it inevitably proves inadequate and leads him to despair.

Christina Stead

The opening words of Christina Stead's *Seven Poor Men of Sydney* take us to the 'hideous low scarred yellow horny and barren headland' that 'lies curled like a scorpion in a blinding sea and sky' above the village of Fisherman's Bay by the heads of Sydney Harbour. The rest of the paragraph is crowded with lights and activity as flags flutter on the great mast of the signal tower, gunfire rattles plates and windows, and ships disappear far out at sea. In the last sentence, 'the yellow rim of the great subtropical moon comes up like a lantern from underneath', we are transported to the edge of a world that is at the same time hideous and beautiful, where both the city behind and the sea in front are pregnant with possibilities waiting to be realised. On the next page, one of these possibilities starts to come into existence, as the author tells us 'There was a family there named Baguenault'. The writer has created a place and identified a group of people. Her story can begin.

Christina Stead has said that once she had worked out the characters and setting for her novels, she wrote them down without revision (interview in the *Age* Saturday Extra, 17 July 1982). The stories arise from the characters and their relationships rather than from any imposed plot. Once she identifies her characters, she observes them as they live out the story of their lives. While the author is detached, her characters are not. She understands the passionate

Christina Stead
(*National Library of Australia*)

intensity that lies behind even the most apparently ordinary lives. Her characters wander the cities of the world, where they find as few rules to guide them as did the first explorers in the Australian outback. In *Seven Poor Men of Sydney* (Angus & Robertson, Sydney, 1971 [1934]) she endows Joseph Baguenault's simple quest for knowledge and friendship with the same significance as the lives of the pioneers who hack their lives out of deserts and jungles in Penton's or Herbert's novels. She recognises that the new world of the twentieth century is the city, and that the common citizenship of its inhabitants is more important than any national boundaries. Her first novel is set in Sydney, but from there she travels to the old world of Europe to make it a colony of the imagination of the new.

The title of Christina Stead's first published work, *The Salzburg Tales* (Sun Books, Melbourne, 1966 [1934]), by recalling Chaucer's poem, challenges the established literary traditions and claims them for her own. While Chaucer's pilgrims travel to offer themselves at the shrine of the martyred St Thomas à Beckett to shed their sins at his grave, Stead's have already arrived at the Austrian city of Salzburg to enjoy its August festival and the presentation of the medieval play of Everyman. Their homage is both to a medieval past and to the secular music of Mozart. They come from countries around the globe, and many — lawyer, doctor, translator, schoolteacher, banker — belong to the class of the modern conquistadores who take the whole of the past and present it as their own.

The framework of *The Salzburg Tales* brings together a group of people to exchange stories on successive evenings during the August Festival. This structure produces a tension between the diversity of the individuals in the group and the social obligation to please each other with their stories. There is a similar tension in each story between the attempt to create a narrative that will give meaning to events and the sheer exuberance of the life the narrative contains. This tension is characteristic of Stead's writing, which combines the scientific detachment of the observer with an intense fascination with the people whose lives she describes.

Writing in 1968, Stead recalled an Indian treasury entitled *Ocean of Story*, which, she said, 'is the way I think of the short story and what is part of it, the sketch, anecdote, jokes cunning, philosophical, and biting, legends and fragments. Where do they come from? Who invents them? Everyone perhaps'. She argues that we all have at least one story to tell, 'steeped in our view and emotion' (published in *Ocean of Story; the Uncollected Stories of Christina Stead*, R.G. Geering (ed.), Viking, Ringwood, 1985). During her lifetime Stead published only one collection of stories, yet all her works are extended illustrations of her belief in the story. Each piece of writing seems to be an extended series of tales that unwind from the experiences of the central characters, finding their own shape as they intermingle and complicate each other, reaching further levels of meaning as they reflect on each other.

The stories in *The Salzburg Tales* seem at first merely part of that ocean of story that flows through all of us. The characters are assembled at random to enjoy the festival. They all tell in their turn tales of things that have happened to them or that they have encountered in books or heard from others. The book seems at first sight the least coherent of Stead's works, a mere loose structure framing quite separate tales. Yet this framework merely gives a clearer structure to her characteristic method. The particular characters and tales may be brought together by circumstance, but this chance environment provides the opportunity for exploring the issues that preoccupied her. As one story suggests another, and each teller makes his or her choice of what to tell, the tales impose on life the pattern of art that reveals the choices by which the characters create their own individuality.

By contrast with the loose structure of *The Salzburg Tales*, *Seven Poor Men of Sydney*, the novel written earlier but published after the *Tales*, appears a conventional piece of fiction. It is concerned with character in action in a particular place — with the attempts of a small group of people to survive in the poverty of Sydney in the years leading up to the Depression of the 1930s. Its emphasis falls not so much on their material circumstances and actions as on the stories they tell of themselves in order to survive and make sense of the world around them. The Sydney that sustains and binds them exists with greater reality in their imagination.

The seven poor men of the title are associated with a printery where several of them work. They range from Michael Baguenault, who with his sister Catherine lives a life almost completely detached from reality, to his cousin Joseph, a respectable printer who does his job conscientiously, lives with his widowed mother, and dreams of a life without the constrictions of poverty and ignorance. The others include Baruch Mendelssohn, a socialist intellectual, Tom Withers, a printer whose 'life flowed through his tongue' in scurrilous gossip and fantastic theories, the struggling but shifty owner of the press, an embittered communist, and the crippled Kol Blount, able to live only through words. Michael, who has been detached from society by a childhood illness and a dream of death, as well as by his discovery that he is a bastard, becomes increasingly isolated and eventually suicides. His cousin Joseph listens and records the lives of others as they put them into words. It is Joseph who eventually brings the novel to its conclusion when, many years later, he begins to record their story: 'We were seven friends, at that time, yes, seven poor men . . .' (p. 319).

In contrast to *The Salzburg Tales*, where the storytellers are on vacation and recall episodes from their past at leisure, the tales of the seven poor men are produced under the pressures of work and poverty. They do not use them to give meaning to a past but to shape a possible future. Baruch Mendelssohn, printer, craftsman and scholar, designs through his tales a rational and socialist utopia that will recognise the dignity and creativity of every individual. Withers' cynicism is created by his role as fixer for his employer's shaky enterprise. Chamberlain, owner of the business but as much its captive as his employees, builds fantasies of business success. Joseph Baguenault is the steady journeyman who absorbs and learns, and becomes the historian of the seven.

The other three poor men are excluded by circumstance from the productive process, and their tales differ as a consequence. Karl Blount creates a world of sensuous intellectualism, living in his mind what his body will not allow him to be. Tom Winter, the librarian, compensates for his powerlessness with a reductive and bitter Marxism that remains without roots in experience. Michael Bagenault works only intermittently, and his fantasies suggest alternative possibilities without engaging fully with daily reality.

Michael and his sister Catherine are a pair of doubles, each the *alter ego* of the other. They drift in and out of the lives of the others, disturbing them,

attracting attention, but never fully belonging. Catherine and Baruch Mendelssohn, on the other hand, are complementary and fall in love, each attracted by the other's loneliness, but their personalities are too far apart for the affair ever to prosper. Baruch is, as Joseph sees him, destined to fascinate 'an infinite number of listeners through numberless years of life in other places and other societies' (pp. 159–60). He is an intellectual, living by his intellect, whereas Catherine is 'ruled by her impulsive passions which ever strove with her intellect for mastery' (p. 149).

The whole truth of the novel encompasses both Baruch and Catherine, reason and passion, but in their individual lives they are incompatible. Only Joseph can comprehend the two realities. Catherine despises him as the workman with 'a drained face, full of want, penury and hopelessness, but not despairing . . . beyond salvation'. Baruch recognises in Joseph's 'sombreness and passion' a man who has been suppressed by church and family, who 'does not exist', but 'can come to life', a 'strange, delicate, translucent mind . . . a person confined [but] with so little prejudice' (pp. 152–3). In these phrases Catherine and Baruch create their own independent realities, but Joseph, the listener, uses their phrases to create himself, and in his history records the realities made from their words.

Towards the end of the novel, Karl Blount recounts the story of Australia as a cosmic myth, from 'the dim ante-glacial world' through the geological eras to the arrival of the Aborigines, who populate the continent with their own myths, and then from the arrival of white settlers and their tales of starvation, sorrow and mutiny down to his own time, when 'in the overpopulated metropolis the sad-eyed youth sits glumly in a hare-brained land, and speculates upon the suicide of youth'. The land feeds men's greed with gold, but gives them no water to drink. He concludes that it should never have been won (pp. 305–9). This myth effectively translates imperialism from its European source to an Australian present. If Europe exported its myths to Australia, creating the new world in its own Edenic images, Blount's tale adds European archetypes of guilt and terror, substantiates them in terms of Australian experience, and through them converts European history to merely a part of the prehistory of Australia. The new land becomes not a return to Eden but an advance to the Apocalypse. Thus, when Stead moves in her later work from Sydney to Europe and North America, she is not, like Martin Boyd or Henry James, searching back to a source, but moving forward to assimilate older societies to an understanding nurtured in the world in which their individual histories have reached their culmination.

Christina Stead made the move herself to London in 1928, before writing her first novel, and her work provides a fictional counterpart for her life. *Seven Poor Men of Sydney* describes the world of her youth, *The Salzburg Tales* is the fruit of her first direct encounter with Europe, *The Beauties and the Furies* has the setting of her early life in Paris and *House of All Nations* describes the world of international finance she had known while working in a Paris bank. In her next two novels, *The Man Who Loved Children* and *For Love Alone*, she deals with the personal problems of childhood and family, and her eventual flight to London. In *Letty Fox, Her Luck*, she creates a narrator quite detached from herself, although her concern with the ability of individuals, particularly women, to establish personal independence in a world of financial and emotional dependence, remains the same. Her later novels continue her studies of people's ability to create their own fantasies, imposing and deceiving themselves.

In *House of All Nations* (Angus & Robertson, London and Sydney, 1974 [1938]), Stead takes up the theme of economic collapse that forms the background to *Seven Poor Men of Sydney*. The viewpoint of this book is not, however, that of the victims but of the financiers whose speculations bring about the crash. The bank takes the place of the printery as centre and microcosm and the fantasies of money replace the reality of material production. The tales of the characters become not a product of reality but a substitute for it. The tales themselves change from stories to games as the narrators impose their illusions first on themselves and then on the world.

The comedy of the book gains a darker hue as we realise that behind the games of the bankers lie the more sinister games being played by the communists, Nazis and fascists in the machinations that were to lead up to the Second World War. Despite the crash of the stockmarket and the failure of the bank, the systematic analyses of the left are heeded only by the bankers themselves, who continue to prosper as the world crumbles around them.

The book describes a world in which the products of labour have become, not even commodities, but

counters in a game. The elements in the game include politics and philosophy, friendship and fraud, but all is unreal as the players, without exception, inhabit a world in which the only truth is the success of money, unrelated to the production of actual goods or to the achievement of genuine personal relations. The hero, Alphendery, a supposed communist and an actual genius in the games of the financial markets, maintains his parents, his wife and his children, but lives a life of personal isolation. The glamorous head of the banking house he has named 'The House of All Nations' is a war hero who now lives only for the excitement of the moment. The bank is no more a fraud than its competitors and is essentially hollow. Yet although it fulfils no useful purpose, the bank's eventual fall causes ruin to both employees and customers, while sparing its proprietor and his friends. We have moved a step beyond the world of the *Seven Poor Men of Sydney*, who create their own stories from the elements of life they find around them. In this later novel, the characters live entirely by the stories they tell, so that work itself is transformed into a game. The tragic reality of life appears only in the glimpses we have of the genuine communist, the appropriately named Jean Frere, and in the hints of the catastrophic misery that is producing fascism and communism alike. But for the bankers, these facts are merely counters for their game.

House of All Nations is composed in scenes rather than in chapters. Each scene represents one person's construction of reality, a game that he plays, while the narrative moves in the background. This narrative is the history of the 1930s, but the characters experience it only as detached episodes. In her next novel, *The Man Who Loved Children* (Secker and Warburg, London, 1966 [1940]) Stead goes even further in showing how people turn their own histories into drama. In this novel, for the first time, there is also a genuine antagonist to the drama created by the central character.

Sam Pollitt, the 'man' of the title, must be one of the nastiest characters ever created in fiction. The point of the novel is that he does succeed in imposing, for a time, his own fiction — that is, his own reality — of a loving family on his children. His second wife, Henny, creates the opposing fiction of herself as martyr. Only his daughter Louie effectively resists their tyrannies, telling Sam bluntly that he is teaching his children to hate him, and eventually attempting, with ambiguous success, to poison her stepmother.

Sam, however, overrides all opposition, all failure, with the determined joviality of his personality and his image of himself as the one just and reasonable person in his creation. His proclaimed liberalism epitomises the tyrannical fascism that is conventionally seen as its opposite. The narrator, showing events through Louie's eyes, reveals the full horror of Sam's absorption in his own excellence and Henny's in her own self-pity. Yet the narrator shows also the genuine warmth Sam creates in his curiosity about the world and the genuine sensitivity Sam affronts in Henny until he drives her back into herself.

Sam's failure to comprehend his own family, the gaucherie of his behaviour to his Asian colleagues, which makes even the British seem understanding, the comic and ugly episode where he poisons house and home in his effort to render a marlin into useful commodities, are products of his own imposition of a form of rationality on a world that eludes his patterns of meaning. Similarly, Henny escapes from a world too bizarre for her to comprehend by retreating into the isolated order of the game of solitaire. The younger children accept, although at times reluctantly, the world their parents impose on them. The oldest boy, Ernie, finds escape in the fictional certainties of money. Only Louie, combining reason with imagination, is able to dramatise the alternative world of fiction and thus escape the tyranny of those who would restrict her to their own order.

The Man Who Loved Children appears to be a transposition of Stead's own childhood from Sydney to Washington, Annapolis and Baltimore, although it is a mistake to read it too closely as an autobiography. By transposing elements from her childhood to the USA she distances the novel from incidental experience and reveals the full and tyrannical truth of the family relationships. The American setting, although precisely realised in geographic terms, allows her to concentrate on the individuals rather than their

society. We are presented with the ultimate of new worlds, where each person creates a world in her own life.

In *For Love Alone* (Virago, London, 1978 [1944]) Stead shows a similar situation in an Australian setting. In this novel, however, the desperate oppression of the father provides the motivation for the daughter as she escapes from convention and pursues the life of her own sensibility not as fiction but as exploration. Teresa Hawkins is like the earlier Joseph Baguenault in her determination to seek the meaning of life from those who talk about it, but unlike Joseph her search integrates both intellectual and sensuous discovery. The search takes her to London, but it does not cease there. Rather, when she finds there that she never did really love the man she has followed, she is discovering also that there are no external objects to meet her inner need. As an Australian, she is a seafarer, and by travelling away from her family back to the home of her ancestors, 'a scarcely island up toward the North Pole', she finds her freedom. This freedom is to take love as she finds it, making her life with another but never being owned by him.

The restless visionary, the rational tyrant and the player of games are three types of character that remain constant in Stead's work and indicate her central themes. Through games, particularly with words, people create a world in which they can survive. The tyrants, on the other hand, are impervious to anything outside themselves. They cannot be defeated, but neither can they grow and live. The visionaries occupy the dangerous ground between these two extremes, neither imposing their words on others nor retreating into the world of their own fantasy. Their life is given to the struggle to break out into the new world that Louie and Teresa and even Joseph finally discover for themselves in their different ways.

THE RADICAL NATIONALISTS

AUSTRALIAN nationalism has most often taken the form of a sardonic disdain or resentment of others rather than a particular love of this country or its people. The literary nationalism of the early *Bulletin* expressed a belief in the worth of the common man, particularly the bushman, who became the figure of the true Australian. As the *Bulletin's* nationalism developed into a rural parochialism, the pioneers became the true Australian heroes, and the bushmen and farmers their heirs, a purer race whose virtues at Gallipoli exalted them to the ranks of the immortals. However, the experiences of the First World War strengthened Australian suspicion of British arrogance and European decadence, and this is the basis of the war histories of C.E.W. Bean and the renewed bush nationalism of writers such as Edward Harrington. In the work of Vance Palmer this idea provides the source of a vision of a nation built on freedom and equality.

Vance Palmer

Palmer was far from confident about the prospects for maintaining this ideal, but his life of writing was devoted to making it explicit. In essays, stories and novels he sought to show both the influences that produced the best qualities of Australians and the forces that threatened them. While this commitment gives his work at times a programmatic quality, it also makes it representative of the outlook of the liberal nationalists for whom he wrote. His readers came from the class of professionals and technocrats who produced the post-war reconstruction of Australian industry and society in the 1940s, and the underlying consensus that survived into the bitter years of the Cold War and the conservative freeze of the 1950s.

Palmer's literary career began in London before

Vance and Nettie Palmer
(*National Library of Australia*)

the First World War. For a number of years he sup-
ported himself through journalism and popular fiction,
some of it under the pseudonym of Rann Daly. While
in London he was given the opportunity to turn aside
from the 'forced dramas and snappy endings' required by the magazines and produce instead a series
of sketches based on his 'unique personal experiences'. These were published under the title *The
World of Men* (Cheshire, Melbourne, 1962 [1915]).

The title of this book suggests the aspect of life
that was to concern him throughout his career. The
stories deal not so much with the lives and relationships that people create among themselves, as with
the predicaments that men find themselves in and
the ways they cope with them. A horsebreaker of
charm and skill, who is more at home among horses
than men, turns out to be also a most accomplished
horse thief. A camp cook keeps the men going with
cheerfulness and energy, keeping dissension at bay
with his ability to talk to a grizzler until he's 'got to
find a secluded spot and hide himself till the hair's
grown over the sore place'. The cook also soothes
the men's irritation when the job is not going well
with his observation that it doesn't matter 'whether
we're finished in one month or three', since if 'we're
not working here it will be somewhere else where
there's twelve hours in a shift, only twenty shillings
in a pound, and a long, dusty road between us and
the nearest barrel of doctored beer' (p. 31). This
cynical resignation comes from the tradition of
Lawson's bushmen. Also from Lawson comes the
cook's need to get away for a 'rejuvenating spree'.
As in Lawson's work, the humour and easy mateship
is a defence against an underlying weakness or
sense of failure that every now and then threatens to
destroy the person.

Although Palmer shares Lawson's feeling for
mateship as the refuge of defeated men, his stories
also suggest that it can only mitigate the solitariness
that is the essence of the human lot. In his early
stories, this isolation is particularly the condition of
the Aborigines and mixed bloods who are excluded
from even the compensation of white mateship. In
later stories Palmer's view of life becomes more
complex. Although he still speaks mainly from the
man's viewpoint, a story like 'Greta' (*Let the Birds
Fly*', Angus & Robertson, Sydney, 1955), centres on
the image of a woman battling out her life alone. We
see her through the eyes of the male narrator, but

we are also aware that his sentimental recollections
of his youth obscure her present reality from him,
just as his cowardice or hesitance keeps him from
approaching her and thus facing the truth about himself. Other stories take us into the precarious world
of childhood, with its fears of the incomprehensible
behaviour of adults that can destroy happiness and
visit unimaginable punishment or delight, seemingly
at whim. The Aborigines are portrayed with sympathy, but they still remain apart, the other that cannot be accommodated within the white community.

In this community satisfaction is available for those
prepared to enjoy the simple pleasures of water,
sand and sky, and to meet with stoic courage the
disasters that strike unpredictably but inevitably. Its
highest value is the quiet companionship that comes
from the shared life of family and work, producing a
single harmony of the human and the natural. This
companionship is disrupted by those who lock themselves away from their fellows or fail to trust themselves to the currents of life, and by those who deny
community by attempting to take for themselves
what should belong to all. This simple and honest
creed, which pervades all Palmer's prose writings, is
the basis of his sense of Australian nationalism.

The sense of an achieved harmony of national development, produced from the separate ambitions of
the men who made Australia, gives unity to Palmer's
collection of biographical sketches, *National Portraits*
(Angus & Robertson, Sydney, 1940; enlarged edition,
Melbourne University Press, Melbourne, 1954).
Palmer presents each of his subjects in terms of
his life's work, starting with the landtaker John
Macarthur and the military dictator Lachlan Macquarie,
moving through the nonconformist, the painter,
the judge, the unionist, the prelate, the geologist
and the industrialist, and finishing, in the complete
work, with sketches of Joseph Benedict Chifley, the
Labor leader, John Flynn, the bush missionary, and
Lyndhurst Falkiner Giblin, the economist. The total
of these portraits creates the picture of a nation distinguished by a record of practical progress contribu-
ting to the material welfare of all.

In his historical work, *The Legend of the Nineties*
(Melbourne University Press, Melbourne, 1963
[1954]), Palmer expresses this creed more explicitly,
establishing the legend as he criticises it. The book
argues that the spirit of distinct nationality supposed
to have emerged in the 1890s has more distant ori-

gins — from events such as the Eureka Stockade, the distance that isolated Australia from the rest of the world, and the fear of foreigners. Yet Palmer acknowledges that the national ideal, in both its positive and its negative aspects, reached its height in art and literature 'near the end of the century':

> The forward-looking spirits of those days really did find a stimulus in their isolation; vague, creative impulses germinated in their minds; even in some of their wildest outbursts there was a deep sense of responsibility to the country they were making their own. They were determined that the West should not rebuild its fatal nest here, and the ideas that found expression in their journalism, their politics, and their imaginative writing still give a colouring to the national being.

> Palmer, *Legend*, p. 14.

Palmer concludes that, despite political defeats, the 1890s established the definitive ideal of democratic Australian nationalism and its ideal type:

> . . . a laconic but sociable fellow with his own idiom and his own way of looking at things. He had humour of a dry sardonic kind, a sensitive spirit with a tough covering, initiative and capacity that were qualified by 'near enough' standards of achievement. His mental horizons were comparatively narrow, but his sympathies were broad. What little he had read of Biblical or secular history, he liked to reduce to the homely terms of his experience. In his approach to life he was realistic . . . yet there was a streak of idealism in his nature that expressed itself in his sentiment about mateship and in political movements that made for equality.

> Palmer, *Legend*, pp. 169–70.

This ideal was to inspire not only his own work, but that of the radical nationalists who succeeded him. His emphasis on plain writing about ordinary people became a virtue and eventually an ideological requirement. While Palmer believed the writer should write about the common man, his successors decreed not only who the common man should be but even how he should think.

His own fiction, however, subverts the ideal, either by retreating into a mythical past or by demonstrating the impossibility of political change within the frameworks of the society he admires. *The Passage* is an example of the former, his *Golconda* trilogy of the latter.

The Passage (Cheshire, Melbourne, 1957 [1930]) commences with a vision of the harmony between man and nature as Lew Callinan sits fishing in his 'anchored dinghy rocked gently on the long swell' (p. 3). However, we quickly get intimations of disharmony as he reflects on the way his mother disregards him as she manipulatively promotes the interests of his younger brothers and sisters. The action of the novel arises from this conflict, which drives all the other members of the family away and impels Lew himself into a marriage that ends in tragedy. This action parallels the disintegration of the fishing community itself, which is first relegated to the margins by the promotion of the nearby beach as a holiday resort, and then left nearly destitute when the developers desert their enterprise. Yet this desertion leaves the way open for Lew to come back and, married now to a partner who shares his sense of continuity in the land and people, restore the community on the basis of co-operative enterprise. The concluding paragraphs of the novel return to the harmony and continuity felt in its opening, but now the scene is shown through the eyes of Anna, the mother whose ambitions had led to its first destruction, and whom Lew has now enabled to return to the source of her being:

> She sat brooding on the image of Lew her mind evoked from the night, the dark eyes so like her own, the potency of the slow-moving body, the way he drew power from the earth beneath him. He gave her a sense of her own permanence, satisfied an instinct deeper than affection. All her struggles for her family had been concerned with this: that the life she had brought forth in pain and uncertainty should throw down strong roots and not be blown away by any chance wind.

> Palmer, *The Passage*, p. 271.

The Passage is unusual among Australian novels in using a coastal fishing village rather than a farming or pastoral settlement as its image of an Australian community. It shares with outback novels the ideal that the highest values are created through the conflict with a nature that refuses to be tamed to human purposes, and that these values are in turn destroyed by the intrusion of the materialism and shallow ambitions of the cities. The fishing community remains as vulnerable at the end of the novel as it was at the beginning, both to external forces and to their embodiment among its own people. Lew's actions merely establish an oasis of the past; they do not restore continuity.

In his *Golconda* trilogy, Palmer attempted the more ambitious task of analysing the failure of democratic political leadership in Australia (*Golconda*, University of Queensland Press, St Lucia, 1972 [1948]; *Seedtime*, UQP, 1973 [1957]; *The Big Fellow*, UQP, 1973 [1959]). These three novels follow the life of Macey Donovan from his time as a gouger in western Queensland, through his career as unionist and politician until he becomes Premier of the state and his world falls apart. Donovan has elements in him of both Jack Lang and Ted Theodore, politicians who during the Depression built up enormous popularity only to fail their followers at critical times. While these historical figures owed their political downfall at least partly to outside forces, Donovan's public failure arises from the collapse of his personal life. This in turn reflects the destructive effects of political power. In tracing these effects Palmer reveals the impossibility of belief in politics as a means of transforming society. In the flawed career of Macy Donovan, Palmer diagnoses the necessary qualities of the successful Australian politician. In doing so, he unwittingly reveals the limitations of that decent but unknowing tolerance he saw as the central quality of the Australian character.

The problem at the beginning of the first book of the the trilogy is the same as that in Prichard's *Black Opal*; the leases are in the hands of individual gougers, who are confronted with big companies that want to take them over. Unlike Lightning Ridge, the ore at Golconda, which is presumably Mt Isa, requires capital to exploit it. Unless the individual miners are content to continue scratching the surface, they have only the choice of selling out or forming their own co-operative: 'an independent community. One built on the idea of mateship, which was the true spirit of the country. The pride of free men who owned the tools they lived by and worked for the common good', (p. 54). The words are those of the veteran gouger and political activist Christy Baughan, but his zeal isolates him from the others as much as their way of life keeps them apart from each other and from the wage earners whom Macy Donovan represents.

The gougers form their association, but procrastinate over pledging themselves not to sell out to the company, and thus dissipate the strength they derive from their independence. The battle in the town resolves into one between company and union. Macy draws his strength from the men in the union, but in doing so draws himself away from them. His union becomes a vehicle, not for the co-operative community dreamed of by Christy Baughan, but for the vision of order and prosperity held by the mine manager and engineer, Keighley. In accepting this vision, and his own role as leader, Donovan relegates the ordinary workers to the role of the 'herd', leaving 'their common affairs in the hands of anyone who had the guts to reach out and take charge of them' (p. 79). The first novel of the trilogy concludes with the funeral of Christy Baughan, the old visionary, Donovan's departure from the mining field as its new member of parliament, and the triumph of the mining company, now consolidated and taken over by international capital.

The remaining two volumes deal with Donovan's political career, first as a backbencher and later as Premier. The scope broadens to take in Aborigines, Italian settlers on the cane-fields, political manoeuvering and the morality of strikes, and to show the relation between Donovan's public career and his personal affairs. The story is set against the background of the Depression and the troubled time after the Second World War. Its intent seems to be to explain Labor politics. The task of office takes the leaders away from the masses that have created them. As they accept compromises they develop a contempt for the ideals of their followers. They can no longer accommodate the simple morality of the railway conductor who explains to Donovan his feelings about a forthcoming strike:

'. . . when I've had a bit of sleep you'll find me in my back garden seeing how my tomatoes and cucumbers have been getting on while I was away; they're more important to me than sugar. Sugar!

Maybe it's the stuff that keeps this part of the country white, but I tell you this: when the union declares it black its black as the ace of spades to me, and I won't help in shifting a bag of it'.

Palmer, *Seedtime*, p. 122.

The simple vision of the tomatoes and cucumbers in the back garden is an image of the decent rationalism that inspired both the post-war planners and the leading figures of Palmer's *National Portraits*. The equally simple acceptance of solidarity with other workers as a way of life is the quality that built the Labor movement and underlay the radical nationalist tradition. Donovan's tragedy is that in trying to bring together the two visions and change the world he loses both.

The problem of the *Golconda* trilogy is that, while it starts out to show how a politician betrays his creed, it succeeds in showing how the creed is unable to sustain the politics. The great myth of solidarity offered in the opening chapters peters out not so much on corruption as on its irrelevance to the abstractions of finance. The great ore mountain of Golconda, 'massive and powerfully alive, its roots buried deep in the earth's core, its crest among the stars' whose 'generative heat . . . seemed to smoulder' and which sustained the hopes of its people (*Golconda*, p. 73) succumbs to Keighley's engineering vision of exploitation:

. . . the mountain itself had lost its effect of primeval power. Machines had torn off its crest, and from a flattened base rose a tracery of derricks that looked like the work of mammoth spiders. What remained of the mountain was less impressive than the slag that had been torn from its vitals and now towered in a giant pyramid beside it, blue-black in the afternoon light.

Palmer, *The Big Fellow*, p. 291.

The rough old settlement is replaced by a company town where Donovan and his earlier values have no place. The fulfilment of the rationalist dream gives victory to the companies and the politicians, and the loner Christy Baughan, the mad gouger who dies by his own hand, is the last voice of the true Australia.

The radical nationalist dream that inspired Palmer's work and Donovan's early career remains only as a condemnation of the present.

Rex Ingamells

Rex Ingamells' Jindyworobak movement, born in Adelaide in the 1930s, represents the most passionate and romantic outpouring of Australian literary nationalism. In the fifteen years from 1938, the annual Jindyworobak anthologies and other publications encouraged poets, in particular, to produce a literature that would express Australian reality uncorrupted by alien influences.

The history of the Jindyworobaks, and a selection of their best work, has been compiled by Brian Elliott (*Portable Australian Authors: The Jindyworobaks*, University of Queensland Press, St Lucia, 1979). The name was derived from an Aboriginal word meaning 'to join'. The movement sought to join together Australian literature with its true source, the land, as it was interpreted through its only indigenous tradition, Aboriginal mythology. Rather than finding a source for poetry in foreign myths, Ingamells adopted the Aboriginal creation myth of Alcheringa, the Dreamtime in which the land and its people originated.

Rex Ingamells
(*State Library of Victoria*)

Ingamells set out his creed in the pamphlet 'Conditional Culture' (reprinted in John Barnes (ed.), *The Writer in Australia*, Oxford University Press, Melbourne, 1969 [1938], pp. 245–65). The principles of his argument are that, although the British settlers in Australia have modified the landscape and brought with them a European culture, their life can flourish only insofar as it is lived 'in accord with the laws of natural environment . . . This means that, if Australians are really to appreciate beauty at first hand, they must seek to do so by turning to indigenous nature' (p. 247). To do this, he argues, they must learn to see the environment without the distorting effect of European assumptions and vocabulary, or the larrikinism of unduly aggressive nationalism. At the same time, they must learn to see beyond the relatively unimportant convict heritage and the gloom it engendered in portrayals of the local environment and the society it had bred. In place of these elements of the past, he argues, 'our writers . . . must become hard-working students of Aboriginal culture, something initially far-removed from the engaging and controlling factors of modern European life' (p. 264).

Ingamells derived much of this doctrine from P.R. Stephensen's fiercely argumentative 1935 pamphlet *The Foundations of Culture in Australia* (reprinted in Barnes, *The Writer in Australia*, pp. 204–44), which in turn was provoked by the claim of Professor G.H. Cowling of Melbourne that Australia could have no literature of its own because it lacked suitable history, ruins and trees. Both Stephensen and Ingamells were reacting also against writers like Henry Kendall, an Australian 'writing about Australia in an English way' (Stephensen, p. 214) and poets of the school of Hugh McCrae, who littered the Australian bush with Grecian nymphs and dryads. Ingamells' distinctive contribution to the debate was to recognise that Aboriginal culture offered a unique expression of the natural environment. Ingamells' work demonstrates a regret at the destruction of this culture by the white settlers, but no realisation that it continued to live and change within the surviving Aboriginal peoples. His regret stimulated the urge to save what remained and use it for the purposes of white poetry. His use in practice amounted largely to a futile attempt to replace English nouns and adjectives with Aboriginal words. The result pays its dues neither to the integrity of Aboriginal culture nor to the meaning of the English language. Rather than producing a new synthesis, he succeeded in creating a private mixture of languages that belongs in nobody's world.

In attempting to change the English language to express an Australian landscape, Ingamells makes language a barrier between the reader and any meaning. The Aboriginal words, wrenched into the framework of English syntax, have no denotation except that given by a glossary, and lose any connotations they may have for their original users. The result is that they become mere jingling harmony, trivialising the legends that the poet attempts to keep alive. His verse works only when, in poems like 'Rivers and Mountains', he uses names, whether English or Aboriginal, that have already become signs on a map with all the associations of white settlement attached to them, and with memories of the earlier dwellers behind them, suggested only by shadows

. . .wed with the movement of the water
And the movement of the trees,
And with the sound of the water
With wind-ripples and reed-ripples,
And with the patient sound
Of the wind in the trees.

Elliott, *Jindyworobaks*, p. 8.

When he tries to make the suggestiveness of these vague associations concrete the poem again falls apart, into the banality of the 'coo-ee cry' or the half-recalled legends of the furrow of Ilbumeraka '— Dragged and scooped and tortured from the plains/By the swishing tnatnaja' (p. 9).

Although Ingamells has a genuine respect and sympathy for the Aborigines, his attempt to appropriate their mythology is fundamentally misconceived. At its heart is his concept of Alcheringa, which he translated as the Dreamtime. This implied a mythical past whose creatures of legend could be used to populate the Australian landscape and make it human with their associations, and a way to tame the land by learning its indigenous mythology. The Aboriginal concept is more accurately translated as the Dreaming, a dimension of life that existed in the past but can be continually renewed in the present. It represents the way the world is brought into existence. The humans are the last creatures to be born, and they do not own the world, the world owns them. They are at best its stewards, guarding its truths. These truths cannot be embodied in our lives merely by retelling the legends and preserving the ancient names, so that we see the landscape through them. They become real only as the landscape is incorporated in a way of living as the source of that living. This mode of perception is incompatible with a culture that imposes itself on the landscape in the style of European mythology, where the gods create humans to dominate the world. For good or ill, the European culture of Australia descends from Prometheus and his industrial age incarnation, Faust. We cannot be redeemed by Aboriginal mythology.

Bill Harney

The Aborigines did not in fact depart from Australian society, but they shared their tradition only with those who made themselves part of it. Bill Harney, married to an Aborigine, and Roland Robinson, with a Celtic understanding of the power of story, have both succeeded in marrying the tradition of the Australian yarn to the realities of contemporary Aborigines.

Harney was primarily a raconteur, who obtained his first education in the army, and his most formal education while he was in gaol at Borroloola on the Gulf of Carpentaria awaiting trial on a charge of cattle duffing. The episodes of his life provide the content for his *Content to Lie in the Sun* (Hale, London 1958) and *Grief, Gaiety and the Aborigines* (Hale, London, 1961). These go beyond the normal colourful anecdotes of life in and around the Territory to produce an ideal embodying both Aboriginal and white traditions in a harmony created as they live with the environment. His *Tales from the Aborigines* (Hale, London, 1959) place the Aboriginal tales within the framework of the 'whiteman's yarn'. He opens the book with an account of how he learned the stories from Aborigines who were themselves masters of legend and lore. They told them to him in their English, which he incorporates in his own accounts of the stories in the context in which he heard them. Thus he brings the older culture into the white world without destroying the integrity of either the original tales or their tellers.

Roland Robinson

Robinson spent many years wandering the outback and learning the lore of the bushmen and the Aborigines at first hand. Unlike Harney he was a writer by vocation, and one of the Jindyworobaks. His third collection of stories, *Black-Feller, White-Feller* (Angus & Robertson, Sydney, 1958) is, as its name suggests, divided into two parts. The first part consists of tales drawn from the author's own wanderings around the bush, and the second of tales told to him by Aborigines he has known through his work and travels. In the first part the stories are carefully crafted. In the second they have the apparent formlessness Lawson made familiar. Here the order of the narration seems determined only by the speaker's memories rather than by any imposed pattern of meaning. While Lawson uses this style to reveal a pattern of significance that lies outside the events and the speaker's own comprehension of them, Robinson uses it to leave the stories open to a meaning the speaker possesses but does not choose to share with his listeners. He, like his readers, is listening as an outsider to fragments of a culture that can be fully understood only by those who live within it.

The stories in the first part of this collection, told in his own voice, define this separation of peoples. The theme of the alienation of the white people from the land runs even through those stories that celebrate their attachment. The killing of wild creature — brumbies, rabbits, calves — becomes a symbol of the failure of the whites to create the kind of society symbolised by Aboriginal dance and song. The whites in the stories resist their environment, and only those who give themselves with passive strength to the life around them achieve the completeness they seek. The refusal of this completeness leads to the substitution of violence for sexuality that is at the base of white power over both Aborigines and their land.

The white settlers share with the Aborigines the nomadic life that passes down its lore in casual yarns. The difference is that the Aborigines look back to an integrated society, while the yarns of the whites evoke a sense of fragmentation. They are unable to create harmony in solitude any more than in society. By contrast, the Aboriginal stories give the sense of a harmony disrupted. They are set down in the words of the narrators who told them to Robinson, but this in itself involves a translation into the vernacular — the common speech they share. The translation goes further, however, for the tales themselves are part of the translation of a traditional culture into the context of white settlement. The first of these tales, 'The Battle of Wallaga Lake' told by Percy Mumbulla, is an elegy to a past hero that reaches back to a time when the Aborigines confronted fate directly, not as dependants on a dominant culture. It places the violence of Aboriginal warfare in the context of a culture that linked humans with nature, and thus transcended even defeat. Yet this link is lost with the tribes who lived in the land and the memory of the names they gave it. The refuge used by the old leader, Merriman, in Shoalhaven, has a white name, and his last resting place has gone entirely from human knowledge.

The other tales in the collection are more than elegies: they tell of the survival of Aboriginal beliefs and practices into the present. Their beliefs about spirit women and men, avengers, deathstones, love and marriage continue to give a structure to lives otherwise fragmented by white society. Robinson took this still further in his later work, particularly his long collection *Aboriginal Myths and Legends* (Sun Books, Melbourne, 1966) which starts with stories of the Dreaming and the more recent past and moves to stories in which the same patterns are fitted to contemporary events. He dealt with the same theme in poetic form in the collection *Altjeringa and other Aboriginal Poems* (A.H. & A.W. Reed, Sydney, 1970). In this book he simplifies and orders the rhythms of the storyteller to reveal 'the natural poetry of these spoken narratives' (p. 9). The rhythms and the shape of the lines highlight individual images, shifting the emphasis in the episodes from their narrative shape to their enduring significance, both to the Aborigines and to their supplanters. Stories that go right back to the Dreaming, like Kianoo Tjeemairiee's 'The Water Lubra and the Lotus Bird', acquire the simplicity of the ballads of the English tradition:

O who was that young man who lay
face down upon the ground?
O that was no young man. It was
a girl with long hair bound

Robinson, Altjeringa, p. 48.

The presence behind the poem is not the people and their actions so much as the landscape that contains them and their history.

Although Robinson's own poems deal more directly with the landscape, as seen by the 'white-feller', they show also how the land itself shapes those who give themselves to it. This shaping can be in the Wordsworthian sense of finding in solitude a unity with nature, as in 'The Brolgas', where his sight of five brolgas flying out of the 'pale dark sky' of dawn gives intimations of immortality as he

. . .burned
in ageless youth and, from its mood
renounced the world again, and spurned
all but that fierce proud solitude.

Robinson, Altjeringa, p. 130.

But Robinson is not merely a contemplative. His sense of oneness with the land is earned through hard work in such trades as a fettler, who works

to lay the rails with adze and hammer, shovel and
bar,
to straighten up and find my mates, myself
lost in the spinifex flowing down in waves
. . .and know
myself grown lean and hard again with toil.

Robinson, Altjeringa, p. 127.

Unlike Wordsworth, Robinson realises that nature is not merely waiting to redress human wrongs and ugliness. It does not exist for us until it is brought into being by our wrestling with acts and words. It does not exist for the Balanda, the 'white man all-a-same rubbish', who brings cattle, builds stockyards and homestead, but can never own the country in which the Aborigine can say:

. . .Every waterhole,
plain, river, rock, billabong is our dreaming,
belong to my people right back to Dreamtime.

Robinson, Altjeringa, p. 17.

Robinson achieves the Jindyworobak objective not by appropriating the Aboriginal myth as a basis for a white literature but by learning from it while respecting its integrity and its difference. By bringing it into the white culture as an opposition, he defines the limits and the problems of that culture in becoming a part of the land. The literature cannot overcome the historical fact of subjugation, but it can give a reality within the white culture to those whose identity can only be recognised by a political act.

Flexmore Hudson

Hudson, like Robinson, writes of moments when the land itself seems to capture his being, whether with the ennui of drought or the sudden beauty of galahs flashing crimson home to the creek among the gums. More commonly, however, the land for him offers an escape that is also a condemnation of the foreign world of armaments and wars, and the local betrayals of poverty amid plenty, farmers dispossessed and the young denied both dreams and subsistence. The land of his poems continues to offer to Australians the opportunity to build a society free from these ills. The worlds of natural beauty and human brutality, however, remain merely juxtaposed. This may allow a private resolution to their conflict, but leaves the political hope mere affirmation.

Ian Mudie

Mudie, who like Herbert was associated with the nationalist and potentially fascist Australia First movement of the 1930s, as well as with the Jindyworobaks, also has a sense of the conflict between what Australia could be and what the white settlers have made it. Although at times strident, his nationalism can produce a tender identity with the land and its people. In 'Glory of the Sun' he writes with gentle regret for lost vision, but also with admiration for the qualities the land still gives to its people:

These are my people, each one idle drifts
on his own creek or his own billabong
heading nowhere; the Murray's single flow
points no moral for meandering hearts
nor marches its strong vigour through their verse.
Yet these my people, their dream,
once flowed one instant in a single stream.

Elliott, *Jindyworobaks*, p. 74.

By setting his Alcheringa in the future, Mudie combines the dreaming of the Aborigines and the mateship discovered by the white settlers to suggest a way out of the trap of a people 'caught between blackness and the undreamt dawn'. In the long poem 'The Pioneers' Mudie tries, like Ingamells in *The Great South Land* (1951), to bring both black and white history together in a single epic. The pioneering heroics, however, is foiled by the perpetual betrayal of the Australian dream to foreign money. In the ballad 'They'll Tell You about Me', he condenses the legends of Australians through the generations in the single image of the man who has gone from rumour to legend to the history of tomorrow. In this irrepressible character he creates the endurance that will survive into the future.

William Hart-Smith

At first reading, Hart-Smith's sparse lyrics seem much more like random observations than poetry. Gradually we become aware that, in stripping away irrelevant associations and emotions to make poetry out of the things that constitute experience, he is allowing the land to enter into him and take possession of his consciousness. He is like the subject of his poem 'The Geologist' (William Hart-Smith, *Selected Poems 1936–84*, Brian Dibble (ed.), Angus & Robertson, Sydney, 1955, p. 68) who 'regards rocks as books'. He spends his life interpreting the 'library of neglected books' he finds in the earth, patiently unravelling the magnificent chaos and carelessness with which nature strews her pages, teasing out the puzzles but always looking for the moment of illumination, the revelation of

the clean, undisfigured print there,
especially when the sun, setting,
touches it lovingly
and calls up an echo in his soul
of the same golden glint there.

Hart-Smith, *Selected Poems*, p. 69.

This is not Wordsworth's mystical unity with nature, but external nature becoming a metaphor of the internal nature of the human, with brilliance lying at the heart of each as the reward of patient effort.

In his longest sequence of poems, 'Christopher Columbus' (pp. 17–51) Hart-Smith uses the image of the explorer to contrast the troubled world of political history with the lonely discovery of nature.

The Americas become a symbol of any new world, in which the act of discovery itself brings the human treachery that defiles the uncorrupted splendour the discoverer has revealed.

The poems set in Australia deal more directly with the natural world into which the speaker escapes from the pressures of history. In his search for a lost unity Hart-Smith goes beyond the simpler aim of the Jindyworobaks to establish an identity between the nation and its environment. By avoiding an overt political statement, he shows how this nationalist aim is rooted in a desire to escape from history in order to build a new world grounded only in a mythical past in a land isolated from the rest of the world.

The desire of the Jindyworobaks to restore a lost Alcheringa embodies a double contradiciton. They avoid confronting the history of the settlement that destroyed Alcheringa, and they ignore the origins of their own ideas of landscape and nature in the cultural traditions of the old world. Their work is an attempt to escape not only from history but from the reality of Australia's political and economic dependence on the outside world. The new identity they sought can only be the result of a new synthesis, not a new creation.

Some elements of this synthesis were to be developed in the work of the poets who followed the Jindyworobaks without ever being part of the movement. Others were to be developed by the realist writers who, ignoring intimations of the numinous, the sense of the spiritual, developed that part of the white Australian tradition expressed in Mudie's 'They'll Tell You about Me'. Similarly, a later generation of Aboriginal writers were to take on the task of creating a new identity by resistance to subjugation, bringing their past into the present rather than trying to escape into it.

Kylie Tennant

The realist writers remade the figure of the bushman into the image of the battler. The term goes back to Lawson, but is given its place in literature by Kylie Tennant, who used it as the name of her third novel, *The Battlers* (Macmillan, London, 1954 [1941]). In this novel the battlers are the itinerant workers and the unemployed who drift around the roads of inland New South Wales and northern Victoria during the Depression of the 1930s. They pick up work where

Kylie Tennant

they can, cadging handouts when they must, driven by unsympathetic police sergeants from one dole station to the next. They are the enduring Australians.

The action of the novel occurs along the long country roads, sometimes alive with flowers but more often swept by the bleak winds of winter or the hot dust of summer, and in the country towns where the battlers pause to collect the dole or establish a brief stability in their lives. The story revolves around Snow Grimshaw, quintessential battler, whose reflections provide its philosophic and social framework. Snow regards the inhabitants of the cities as pampered but spiritually strangled, confined by the 'streets of concrete and asphalt, and roaring trams, and people jammed together as though they were gummed to a fly-paper'. He takes comfort from the thought that whatever ills the cities bring on themselves or the world, his kind will endure:

. . .there would always be battlers. The blacks had been driven away from the coast; killed, shot, poisoned like wild beasts; mowed down in thousands; but they were still hanging on. If another sort of people than the white — say, yellow people — landed on the coasts and mopped up the jelly-livers in the cities, they would still have a job on their hands cleaning out the battlers; men and women who could face a desert and live off the country, travelling in small mobs not enough to drink the hidden wells dry. Any invader would have a hard time with the real Australians, who were so dark brown they might as well be black, and so tough they might as well be leather — people who were like the shadows of a cloud going over the fields. They would hold out, as the blacks still held out in the deserts and barrens. . .

Funny how a country shaped people to its ideas more than they shaped the country. The blacks had always travelled about; and now the whites did the same. You saw it even in city people. They were restless at the change of the year, and invented excuses, even if it was only the Melbourne Cup, to trek south . . . And the travellers wandered most of all, because they were closest to what the country was thinking.

Tennant, *Battlers*, pp. 208–8.

The spirit of this passage, which identifies the people with their land, is the same as that sought by the Jindyworobaks, but Tennant shows it arising from the social conditions of their lives rather than from any mystical sense of unity. The phlegmatic and solitary Snow is as far removed as possible from both bush lyricism and romantic ideals of bush mateship. Yet the course of his travels entwines him in both the harsh beauty of the countryside through which he wanders and the lives of those he meets. For all his surly pose as a misanthrope, a hater of his fellows, his necessary creed is the mateship of the road and the solidarity of the union. The travellers survive only as they stand by each other, and the reward of their survival is the vision of beauty.

The most intense vision of beauty comes to the Stray, a refugee waif from the city who attaches herself to Snow at the beginning of the novel and so starts the train of events that changes his life, finally adopting him into full membership of the society from which he has preferred to stand aside. The Stray in her turn learns that, although she has established claims on Snow by standing by him and succouring his child in their need, she must allow him to find his own way, without her if he must. Tramping on around a bend she sees not only the 'curves and swellings of

another hill that soon she must climb', but a vision of beauty amid hardship:

'Strufe!' she said admiringly.

Through the rift in the clouds the sunlight poured down and lit the nearby hills, leaving those behind in a dimness of shadow; and in the flare of that light the hills were a mass of purple flowers, a carpet of them, a brilliant torrent of flowers, pouring down the side of the road in colours of crimson and mauve, violet and opal, opening curious throated bells like snapdragons. . . It was as though the clouds had rained crimson and blue and it had mingled in an indelible dye.

Tennant, *Battlers*, p. 258.

The flowers are Paterson's Curse, 'a bloody weed . . . a plant that's struck it lucky' as Snow remarks later. But they are also an image of the battlers, aliens to the land who nevertheless make it their own and reap its rewards in sudden moments of vision.

Although the battlers keep alive the qualities of the bushman, these qualities are not necessarily limited either to men or to bush dwellers, or even, as Snow eventually realises, to the whites. Tennant accurately portrays the racial and sexual prejudices of the travellers and the roles they force men and women to play, but she does not endorse them. The men, black and white, enjoy their drunken sprees and make the decisions, while the women keep the families together. The Aboriginal matriarch Mrs Sam Little rules her camp, and Mrs Tyrell has established a genuine partnership with her husband Deafy. The white travellers keep apart from the blacks for the same reason the town dwellers exclude the travellers from their society, as a protective strategy to maintain their value in their own eyes by excluding others. In the end, the novel judges people not by their status but by their actions.

The novel is set against the background of the growing threat of the war that symbolises the destruction of the human values that the travellers realise among themselves on the track. The war first enters the novel through the argument between the Dogger and Burning Angus, the two travellers whose fierce political commitments join them in the solidarity of passionate disagreement. The abstract principles of their quarrel over whether workers who support the war against fascism betray their class to imperialism are silenced by their companion, Uncle, who quietly recalls that he was fighting for king and country while his father was buried in a pauper's grave. The sad irony of his words does not so much destroy the validity of the arguments of Burning Angus and the Dogger as reduce them into insignificance in the face of the contrasting human facts of faith and callousness.

The contrasting elements of human nature come into disastrous juxtaposition in the calamitous fire that destroys the travellers' hopes near the end of *The Battlers*. As a symbol, the fire represents the disaster of the war already enveloping the world. As an incident, it is the culmination of the life of a man who has been 'on the track too long', one of those 'madmen who had wandered alone, outcasts from human living, until they developed a vindictive hatred of all men and women', and 'would murder their own mates' (p. 386). The hatred that drives George the Bowerbird, too long outcast from human society, is the same as the hatred that motivates the warmongers who deliberately cut themselves off from humanity. The war, like the fire, is not, in Tennant's fiction, the result of human evil, but of human nature driven into itself until it produces evil. Her answer to it is not the equally violent politics of a Burning Angus, but the human endurance that enables the Stray to battle beyond her catastrophe.

The politics of Tennant's novels are based on a faith in humans even at their most blind, and a distrust of the abstractions into which they try to turn that faith, whether in terms of king and country or of union and party. In her autobiography *The Missing Heir* (Macmillan, Melbourne, 1986) she writes that the disillusion of the failed revolutionary generation of the 1930s all over the world was a part of her, and that the lesson she had learnt was never to give power to evil, never to let tyranny, meanness or cruelty succeed:

> I was not fatally committed to any one set of convictions or ideology, even non-resistance . . . I would argue either side of a question quite happily without being committed. But show me a situation where people were being ill-treated by usurped power and I was into the struggle like some very active, astute little pest.

Tenant, *Missing Heir*, p. 75.

This attitude is expressed in her admiration for the battlers whose human faith enables them to endure both powerlessness and the tragic knowledge of their own failure. These characters appear throughout her fiction, as well as in her memoir of life at Laurieton, *The Man on the Headland* (Angus & Robertson, Sydney, 1971) and her autobiography, *The Missing Heir*. In the latter, she herself becomes the battler as she cocks her snoot at authority, whether of family or state, and pursues her will whither she pleases. She appears not just as an individualist, but as the incarnation of a family of stubborn individualists. While other Australian autobiographies tend to dwell on the golden summers of a youth from which the rest of life can only be a slow decline, Tennant portrays the whole of her life as one of joyous conflict with the forces contending around her. Out of this conflict she creates the still centre that enables her to endure the slow decay and death of her husband, and the even more tragic loss of her son to drugs.

The characters in Tennant's fiction create their own idiosyncratic vigour by their response to people and to the fugitive beauty of the landscapes through which they move. The vastness of the country takes them beyond themselves and lends them the strength to endure its harshness and the cruelties of life. We see it in the Stray's sudden appreciation of the splendours of the purple flowering weeds in the southern tablelands and in the immense sweep of the coast near Diamond Head that opens *The Man on the Headland*:

> The song goes up the cliffs with the quivering heat of grey driftwood, the scent of seaweed and dry grass, up where the track winds higher than the sea-hawk hovering to the ridge-top where the spray gives way to flannel flowers and golden everlastings, pale violets, thick wrinkled banksias holding out honeycombs for the gill-birds. All the froth of flowers splashes over the great dragon-spine slanting inland, rearing up above the sea its crown of glittering quartz.

Tennant, *Headland*, pp. 1-2.

This natural scene is to become a place of conflict where a man battling against the forces of destruction finds not so much himself as a strength he can give to others. The strength comes from the landscape, but it is earned only through his battle. This battle makes real for his time the Australia that also exists outside him, beyond time. In Tennant's work, this Australia awaits all who are prepared to join with their fellows in making it their own. It exists as reality because she has made it true in her words.

Eleanor Dark

The land that shapes Kylie Tennant's battlers becomes in Eleanor Dark's trilogy of historical novels a brooding presence. The Aborigines are linked to it with a law that nourishes and sustains the people in a unity of past and future in 'the everlasting presence which dwells in the heart of man' (*The Timeless Land*, Collins, Sydney, 1941, p. 445). The white men bring to it the institutions and diseases that break this bond, destroying the tribes and leaving the white settlers alienated from the land and divided by laws that lack any unifying centre. The cost of the settlement is embodied in the tragedy of Bennelong. The first volume ends with Bennelong defacing the carving his father had made to celebrate the coming of the first white men with Cook. The trilogy also traces the growth of a new community as the children of the settlers slowly make their farms and roads and buildings in the old land.

The Timeless Land is the first novel of the trilogy, which continues with *Storm of Time* (1948) and *No Barrier* (1953). The first book has as an endpaper a map of the first settlement at Sydney Cove, emphasising the formless state of the colony in the wilderness. The author explains in a preface that, while she aims in the novel 'to give a picture of the first settlement of Sydney, which is always true in broad outline, and often in detail' she makes 'no claim to strict historical accuracy either in my dealings with the white men or the black'. Finally, a glossary of Aboriginal terms and a list of sources brings us to the beginning of the actual novel. This introductory apparatus identifies the work as an imaginative reconstruction of historical beginnings. Its search for an authenticity of experience rather than of fact matched the mood of a nation on the brink of a war that threatened its links with its historic protector and its own survival.

The first section of the novel, entitled '1770–1788', opens with an image of the child Bennelong at home in a timeless order that takes away his momentary sense of trouble, wrapping it in 'a larger contentment

Eleanor Dark
(*National Library of Australia,
Photo: Olive Cotton*)

which included it, and made it trivial'. The novel goes on to present Bennelong as an individual marked by vanity, ambition, passion and sensitivity, but in the beginning these are contained in the wider order he feels around him:

> He was conscious of the world, and conscious of himself as a part of it, fitting into it, belonging in it . . . He was conscious of an order which had never failed him, of an environment which had never startled or betrayed him, of noises such as the chorus of cicadas, less a sound than a vibration on his ear-drums, of scents which he had drawn into his nostrils with his first breath, and of the familiar, scratchy touch against his skin of sand and twig, pebble and armoured leaf.

Dark, *Timeless Land*, p. 19.

The disturbance that has entered this world, the memory of the boat with the white wings that stayed in their world for a few days but that he knows will come back for him and even take him away across the sea with it, remains in his mind, stilled but not destroyed. The novel traces the way this disturbance returns and grows until it shatters not only Bennelong but the whole order of which he and his fellows had been part.

The apprehension at the beginning of the novel is similar to that felt by Australians on the eve of the Japanese attacks, but the novel appeals to a sense of unity with each other and the environment that white Australia has in fact destroyed. Like the Jindyworobaks, Dark was attempting to create a myth that could make her contemporaries feel at home in the land they had usurped, which was now threatened with a new invasion. Although the novel recovers the Aboriginal sense of place, it does not attempt to use it as the base for a new order of white culture. Rather, it seeks to understand the order created from the clash of European society with the new land and its people, and the clashes within that society between convicts and rulers. The Aboriginal experience is presented as something whites should remember and learn from, not as something they can make their own. The only thing they have in common with it is the land.

The white invaders view this land very differently from the Aborigines. For Phillip it is an alien land in which he lacks the resources to bend it to his visions, or even make it sustain a miserable convict settlement, but he knows that the land will make the people its own. He dreams of a future when the shores will be lined with 'streets and lofty buildings, and the homes of a free and happy people . . .' (p. 68). The theme of the novel is how the grounds for this vision are laid both through and despite the sufferings of the people, black and white, free and convict. Dark uses the settlement at Sydney Cove as a metaphor of the way the Australians created themselves as a new people in a new country.

Phillip's vision of the future is, however, no more shared by the other settlers than is his pragmatic commonsense about the business of survival or the Aboriginal sense of unity. For officers like Tench it is an interesting episode in a military career. For wealthy settlers like Stephen Mannion it is an opportunity to build a position for himself in a replica of British society. For the convicts, it is a place of terror. As Ellen Prentice reflects while she is coming ashore for the first time:

It was the place that frightened her. She had never lived so close to trees before. Nor were there proper houses for them to go to . . . And there were blacks. Naked savages, almost certainly cannibals . . . bloodthirsty and ferocious. Having no God and no religion, thought Ellen with simplicity, what was to deter them from wanton slaying?

Dark, *Timeless Land*, p. 81.

Yet Ellen's husband, who shares Ellen's contempt for the savages, nevertheless dreams of escaping from the settlement and learning from the Aborigines how to conquer the country and make it grant him a living as a free man:

His aggressiveness, always aflame against authority, was now turned, too, upon a place which he felt had tried to intimidate him, and he saw escape and survival as a double victory — over his jailer and his jail.

Dark, *Timeless Land*, p. 77.

It is part of the novel's irony that the land creates its people as much from this rebellion and hatred as from Phillip's vision.

Yet, by a further irony, the land makes the convict Prentice its own in a way that it allows to none of the other characters. Governor Phillip returns to England defeated. Bennelong goes with him to England and returns with Hunter, but is by then also a defeated man, unable to establish the harmony of white and black of which he had dreamed. The white settlement is besmirched by the obscene punishments its law inflicts and eventually becomes the property of Major Grose and his New South Wales Corps, who use it for their own profit. But Prentice, escaping at last from the settlement, finds himself possessed by the beauty of the land in its own right:

. . .in front of his sharp, antagonistic eyes an immense serenity of space and colour stretched to the horizon; there the blue mountains were darkening to violet while he watched, and the sun, already half hidden behind, was laying bars of crimson between the saffron clouds. The miles of undulating tree-tops were no longer sombre green, but rosy gold . . . The air was sharp and pure, the silence ancient (pp. 140–41).

Dark, *Timeless Land*, pp. 140–41.

For the moment he realises that his escape is not from something but to something — 'something which he could not but identify with the aloof and uncontaminated splendour upon which his eyes were fixed'.

Prentice undergoes no sudden transformation as a result of this vision. He continues to battle with the land and its people to make them conform to his will, and is at the same time threatened by the expansion of the settlement. Eventually he acknowledges the bonds that hold him and recovers his full humanity when he risks discovery to rescue his wife and child. Breaking from his hiding, he is filled with 'an indescribable sense of conquest, a fierce and reckless joy', and he exults that 'Not until I chose did they find me, and not their cleverness had discovered me, but my own free action!' (p. 408).

Dark reconstructs the story of the early years of the colony with a sense of psychological and circumstantial detail that allows her theme to be worked out through the interplay of character and environment. Phillip and Bennelong stand for the two poles of the racial conflict, Mannion and Prentice for the opposed elements of the class society that replaces the Aboriginal. The horrors of the convict system and the tragic fate of the Aborigines are woven into the account of the slow passage of time as individuals endure and change. The end of this change is to recover freedom of the kind that the Aborigines first enjoyed and that Prentice eventually achieves, but that eludes the others as they attempt to turn Australia to their own purposes.

Despite its elements of tragedy, the novel is basically optimistic. Its realistic narrative presents the chains of the convicts and the obscenity of the gallows as facts of history, social injustices that human reason could overcome, rather than conditions of human existence itself. History would be changed if the reason of a Phillip could be joined with the enterprise of a Mannion. The tragedy of the trilogy is brought about by human weakness rather than by fate. Mannion refuses to heed Phillip's warning that if he regards the land solely as a source of revenue, giving nothing of himself in return, it may end by exploiting him. His eventual death at the hands of Prentice's son destroys both his own ambitions and the hope of a union of black and white understanding. Yet this possibility, having been once created, however briefly, in the lives of Prentice and his son, remains alive for those who succeed them. For all its pity for the past, the novel remains turned hopefully towards a future that humans may build through their own efforts.

Although the trilogy seeks to reconstruct history, the grounds for its optimism lie outside history and in the land itself. The hope is contained in such moments of vision as the one Andrew Prentice has when he succeeds in escaping from the convict settlement, and in the little farm he creates outside the bounds of the military and money. As the trilogy develops, the land accepts some of the white settlers and gives them the kind of freedom and harmony found in Aboriginal society at the beginning of the narrative. This achievement is symbolised in the title of the last book of the trilogy, *No Barrier*, which refers literally to the spread of settlement beyond the Blue Mountains, but metaphorically to the breaking of the bars convictism imposed on the new country. This hope, however, runs contrary to the main story of the novels, which shows the success of power and money rather than the spread of freedom, the promise of which always remains over the next horizon.

Eric Lambert

All wars are brutal, but each is miserable in its own particular way. In Australian novels of the Second World War the misery of the trenches is replaced by a sense of evil that becomes intense in those dealing with the jungle campaigns. The troops could be sustained by the justice of their cause, which transcended nationalism, but the tyranny they fought in the enemy appeared also in their own ranks. Rather than the mass destruction of the First World War, they fought a war of attrition where armies exhausted each other in the siege of Tobruk and jungles of New Guinea. Here the war had a uniquely evil quality that threatened to disintegrate all human values. The digger in these novels embodies earlier images of the larrikin and the battler, but the variety of reactions to his situation is greater and the elements of brutality in the figure are now recognised. Paradoxically, although the novelists recognise the Second World War, unlike the First, as being for Australians both a just war against barbarism and a struggle for national survival, they also see the experience of war in terms of Australians against each other.

These internal conflicts are apparent in Eric Lambert's two war novels, which see the war both as a struggle against imperialism and a continuation of the domestic class conflict. The opening chapter of *The Twenty Thousand Thieves* (Frederick Muller, London, 1980 [1951]) shows the arrival of the Second X Battalion of the Second AIF aboard their troopship in the Suez Canal. Even before they disembark, the author shows the personal hostility between Private Dick Brett and the platoon sergeant, and the general antagonism between Lieutenant Crane, 'of the Cranes of Scobie', and his men. The personal and moral conflicts become more important as they explore the physical pleasures and racial disharmonies of Tel Aviv, but the class issue remains in the background. As the novel follows the battalion through the battles of Tobruk and El Alamein, and through their time in training camps and on leave in Palestine, the personal conflicts become merged in the wider class issue as the men learn to understand each other and are forced to choose sides.

The basic structure of the First World War novels is the rite of passage that moves the characters from the quiet and security of home to the brutality of war. The theme is that of a lost Eden, and the significance of the battlefield is either as a purgatory where the individual discovers himself or an inferno that reveals the moral nature of the society that has produced it. For Lambert, however, the war is a continuation of the struggles of civilian life. The polarity is not between home and the front, or between war and peace, but between those who work and those who command. The attitude of his soldiers to their officers is not an indication of some general Australian character but a product of their experience of authority. The pride the battalion takes in its strength as a unit is like that which Mann's soldiers feel on the eve of their final battle, but in Lambert's novel it comes from the sense of common purpose they draw from each other despite the brutalising discipline their officers attempt to impose. It appears as much in the jack-up or strike they organise when the commander appropriates their Christmas beer ration as it does in the power they take with them into battle. It is, on the other hand, threatened by the abortive jack-up they commence through sheer weariness during their final rehearsals for the battle. Significantly, the protest is not ended by an imposed discipline, but by the shame induced by their platoon commander, who has risen from their ranks and represents their common loyalties.

The novel concentrates our attention on one platoon, and particularly the section of the platoon to which Dick Brett belongs. The characters outside the platoon are largely stereotypes, not unreal but seen from outside, from the point of view of the ordinary soldier whose lives they control. They represent the formal and informal organisation of the battalion, and determine the boundaries of conduct and ultimately the issue of military success or failure. The significant action of the novel occurs in the lives of the platoon members within this ebb and flow of larger events.

The members of the platoon represent the ordinary soldiers who constituted the Second AIF. For the officers, they are 'riff-raff' for whom the war is 'the best thing that could have happened', bringing them the discipline they need. The colonel prides himself on the success of his officers in making soldiers from such unpromising material. 'The other day on battalion parade, as I was looking them over, I thought, "By God, we've done quite a job with you . . . In spite of everything" ' (p. 51). Only their company commander, himself a member of the ruling class, disagrees, but he can offer no alternative for a peacetime future:

> They were certainly more to be pitied than despised. There was no avoiding this fact, he told himself: to the men the officers were a separate and hostile class and he, Henry Gilbertson, was one of that class.
>
> Lambert, *Thieves*, p. 53.

When Crane, the platoon commander, insists that 'we can't compromise too far with the lower classes, in war or peace. If we do, they'll destroy us!', Gilbertson can only reply that 'If they destroy us . . . it will be because we deserve to be destroyed. Because we're no longer necessary' (p. 69). Crane himself is a fascist, in love with his heroic ideal of himself and with 'the dark beauty of violence' (p. 103). The decayed romanticism of his views goes beyond the ideology of a ruling class, to its source in the shame inflicted on him in his youth when he found himself unable to act out the unreal ideals that alone could justify his privileges. For him, the war is not only a defence of his order but a desperate attempt to escape the tortured realisation of his own inadequacy. Through his conflict with Gilbertson and with his men, he brings the wider issues of the war into the battalion itself.

For the men in the platoon, as for the officers, the war is a test of character. However, their standard is not individual achievement but the ideal of solidarity, the extent to which they find a place for themselves within the platoon. Out of this fellowship comes growth. Percy Gribble, the servile bank officer who cannot overcome his fear, becomes an object not of contempt but pity, and is removed from the platoon to attain the just fate of becoming a provost officer. Tommy Collins, cruel and lecherous product of the slums, finds no love through his voracious sexual appetites, but finds trust in the utter dependability of his mate Dooley. Lucas, the sergeant who believes life is a mockery and is concerned only with himself, nevertheless serves the platoon well. Each man becomes what he is.

At the centre of this development are the contrasting characters of Dick Brett, through whose experience we see the events of the novel, and Andy Cain, the tough idealist who educates Dick but eventually betrays himself. Andy breaks down Dick's sensitive aloofness, makes him recognise the others as the products of the conditions of their lives and to see in the war the possibility of changing these conditions. But when his wife rejects him, Andy resolves to become a successful soldier and nothing else. He eventually receives a commission, but in the process becomes embittered, locked in his own loneliness and misery, excluded by his fellow officers and regarded by his men as a 'cranky bastard' (p. 282). By contrast, Dick learns to become one of the men, rejecting his previous images of himself as 'the tragic young poet' and 'the unhappy young soldier with the brazen front and the mourning heart' (p. 212). Yet he keeps the questing mind that forces him to search for a way of life that will give meaning to all he has learnt about his fellows, a society that will give them room.

The closest Dick finds to an ideal among his companions is Chips Prentice, 'the beautiful . . . animal' who represents the generous alternative to Andy's self-enclosed bitterness. 'Tender as a child, terrible as a panther. Everything is thoughtless joy . . . But nothing deep. Go with the tide. Always the next wave'. Chips, hero of both sport and war, is the ultimate development of the Australian male ideal of bushman and digger, but Lambert, through Dick,

recognises that this is not enough. For all his enjoyment of life, Chips is still its subject. Yet at his death, the prose of the novel changes to the first person in words that take the book beyond fiction to the author's lament for all those human beings whose potential is destroyed by war:

> And so Chips died — Chips who was like the laughter and the strength of all his people: who had never feared or spoken a word in anger to even the meanest of them. He in whom had flowered all the splendour and richness of life, lay dead. What had he not had? Strength and beauty — so much more than I. Joy and wisdom and compassion — far, far more than I. Why not I lying dead? . . . I, who halted and feared — I, who could only admire and follow?
>
> Lambert, *Thieves*, pp. 316-17.

In contemplating Chips' death, Lambert transcends the limitations of the historical figure to see only perfection that has not been given the opportunity to fulfil its potential in living.

Lambert finds this potential, present but unfulfilled in the individual, completely realised in the male unity of the battalion, not only in battle but in its pursuit of its human needs in the training camp. The community the troops create from their common efforts and purposes, a body of men that can be purposeful or destructive, is the truth Dick discovers amid the random events of heroism, love, boredom and brutality of the war. The theme of the novel is the harnessing of this force in opposition to the unity of fascism.

The Twenty Thousand Thieves shows the war as a continuation of the conflicts of peacetime. In *The Veterans*, his novel of the war in New Guinea (Frederick Muller, London, 1954) Lambert turns his fierce anger from fascism to the profiteers and idlers of the home front. The novel, written in the first person, opens with the narrator watching his comrades march through Sydney to mark the return of the Ninth Division from the Middle East. He goes home to find his father entertaining an American colonel. 'They've won the war over the dinner-table, I told myself. All that's left is for mugs like me to go and fight it' (p. 29). Instead of the conflict of classes embodied in the conflict of officers and men, we are confronted with the opposition, familiar from the novels of the First World War, of comfortable civilians at home and disregarded soldiers abroad. The Americans play the part of the British High Command in the earlier war. Whereas Lambert's first novel reflected the optimism of a struggle against fascism and for a new freedom, the second embodies the disillusion of the post-war years that seemed to have betrayed all that the war had been fought for.

Lambert's bitterness is directed not only at the racketeers who make fortunes out of the sufferings of the troops, but at the nature of the war itself. The small group of veterans we meet at the beginning of the novel are linked both by immediate bonds of mateship and by their sense of solidarity with the wider group that has been created during the campaign in North Africa. This solidarity sustains them through their encounters with wartime Sydney and their retraining in the skills of jungle warfare, and extends even to those American servicemen who have experienced war rather than benefited from it. The war in New Guinea has a peculiar viciousness that destroys not only the little band of veterans, but also the character of the men involved in it.

This viciousness is seen in the language, where the casual obscenity loses the colour of the earlier novel and becomes merely the protest of numbed minds. It appears in the images of physical horror, of blood splurting and guts spilling, the decapitated corpses and maimed bodies that accompany the deadly struggle in the jungle. It leads to the heroic but suicidal death by which the good man who is the platoon commander frees himself from his personal horror. Lucky, the coward, overcomes his fear not by acknowledging it, as Percy Gribble did in *The Twenty Thousand Thieves*, but by discovering in himself an exultation in killing and power over others, and eventually collapsing into madness. Even Lasher, the tough veteran, is driven into the madness of despair by the death of his mate, and Tully, the 'Rock of Ages' on whom the others depend, dies horribly on a futile patrol. The narrator is sustained amid these horrors by no belief that he is laying the grounds of a just society, and has to remind himself of the necessity of continuing the struggle against an enemy who would bring fascism to his homeland. When even the padre voices a complaint against God, the narrator responds that he knows nothing of God, that 'To me it seems a denial of man' (p. 162).

Yet the novel finally affirms the qualities of courage, goodness and nurture the veterans learn to recognise in each other. This recognition is embodied in the laconic tribute to Silent Lew, the Queensland stockman who utters less than a dozen words in the book, yet has the same dependability as Tully:

'Lew and me were on Billaminka Station together for two years. Best horseman I ever saw.'
'Noisy old bastard,' I observed at length.
'Yair, that was his trouble. Terrible lug-punisher he was.' He smiled at me and for a moment we shared a laconic tribute to Silent Lew.

Lambert, *Veterans*, p. 189.

The ironic reticence points to that tradition of men whose harmony with their land and its people has no need for words. These men have made the country their own by their skills and endurance, and are therefore prepared to fight for what it means to them, rather than for either abstract ideals or the good of the profiteers.

This image of the Australian is contrasted with the image of New Guinea as a place of evil. Returning through the jungle after a spell of illness, the narrator reflects that 'If I were to live in this country for a hundred years, it seemed to me it would always be alien; that I would always hate and fear it' (p. 190). The malaria from which they all suffer becomes an image of the evil of the country and the war. Even Christmas is corrupted into a 'festival of carnage and filth', and during the long and dreary campaign 'the poison that was in our souls ate its way into their very cores. We were men for ever changed' (pp. 194–5).

Yet out of these horrors the human spirit survives, even triumphs. This appears in the pity and the tenderness Lambert makes us feel for the dead. After Tully's death, during that last 'scene in the slow destruction of an army of men' (p. 195), the narrator's sense of loss is still lightened by the memory of the man he buries:

In the filthy place where I now knelt, the journey of a good and gentle man had ended, and it was something for which, at the moment there was nothing I could say or do. Grief or lamentation or rage. What could they mean? Here lay Tully, Tully my friend, at the finish of it all — errors pardoned, all quests ended.

Lambert, Veterans, p. 215.

These words lack the quality of elegy in the lament for Chips Prentice, but they also bring back all that Tully has stood for and taught his mate Bill. When, at the close of this episode and the novel, Bill returns to Australia, he goes with the knowledge that he has a son to whom he can pass on the memory of his mates. His last act in the jungle is to pluck a flower that 'pulsed and glowed with a living flame, like the flame of courage and hope that burned in me' (p. 224). This flower he takes home with him, a gift of life 'from the dim green island'.

Other novels of the New Guinea campaign repeat the theme of life being won from a death that the island and its jungles come to symbolise. In the novels of war in Europe and the Middle East the Australian soldier is shown as taking back to the old world the larrikin incorruption he has acquired in the new. In New Guinea, however, he confronts an enemy that exists outside history, embodied in the damp of the jungle, the precipitous hostility of the hills, and the everpresent leaves that conceal sudden death. The consequence is a war that becomes much more personal, where even the value of mateship is one that has to be earned by the individual and created among particular groups of men rather than one available by the mere fact of membership of the army.

Other novels of the Second World War

Lambert's New Guinea novel emphasises the continuities with the past as well as the differences that change the characters involved, but the crusade against fascism remains central. The war novels of T.A.G. Hungerford and David Forrest, on the other hand, make New Guinea itself central. Because each is focused on a single battle rather than a whole campaign, the emphasis shifts from the strategic objective, the defeat of the enemy, to the struggle of the individual soldiers with their immediate environment. In Hungerford's *The Ridge and the River* (Angus & Robertson, Sydney, 1952) this environment is the inland mountains encountered by a single

patrol in the last days of the war. In Forrest's *The Last Blue Sea* (Heinemann and Australasian Book Society, Melbourne, 1959) it is the successive ranges across which the 83rd militia battalion fights in the battle for Salamaua. In each novel the author concentrates the attention of the reader on the fate of the individual soldier rather than on the outcome of the battle.

Hungerford's novel tells the story of a single patrol. It contains heroes, but the narrative focuses on character rather than action, and on the significance the men find in their lives in the face of sudden death. The achievements of the patrol are themselves heroic and, as the troops themselves recognise, the stuff of which legends are made. 'It's the kind o' thing they put in the papers. You know — "Diggers' courageous fight to save comrade". . .' (p. 138). But the heroism, and the continuity of tradition it implies and which the speaker tries to abrogate, are immediately mocked by his companions. ' "Get off yourself, you big Anzac!" Sweet whispered derisively. "There's only one dirty hide you're working to save, and it's your own. Courageous fight — my foot!" '. The comment is not strictly true, since the soldiers work selflessly to save the life of a man they hate, yet in a wider sense it is accurate. They survive not because of individual heroism but because each can rely on the individual effort of all. These efforts transcend not only personal feelings but even rational calculation. Their heroism lies not in any sense of idealism but in their acceptance of responsibility for each other.

As important in the novel as the moments of danger are the intervals of rest when they talk to each other about their past lives and their hopes for the future. The most extensive of these is the debate between Shearwood and Manetta over whether life continues after death. In the course of their debate, which occurs after the drowning of one of their companions, each in turn reveals the childhood experience that has shaped his adult attitude to life. This discussion shifts the theme of the novel from the war as adventure, or even as a trial that reveals the truth of character, to the war as a part of human life that reveals the truth of the whole. By isolating the combatants from normal life, it reveals them more truly for what they are. The ideals of nationalism are shown not only as quite irrelevant to their sense of self but as contradicting the lessons the war teaches about common humanity.

In *The Last Blue Sea*, David Forrest (David Denholm) similarly shows nationalism as a contradiction of its own premises. Forrest tells the story of a platoon in a militia regiment that was doubly despised, both because of its earlier cowardice in the face of an invasion and because its members were those who, unlike members of the AIF, had declined to enlist for service anywhere in the world, and thus could be employed only in Australia and the adjacent islands. This commitment, for some a matter of necessity and for others of perceived duty, was understood by public patriots as a sign of cowardice or disloyalty. The militiamen thus go into battle not only with the fears of any soldier but with the burden of knowing that the country that sends them simultaneously despises them.

Even more than in the other novels, the main character in *The Last Blue Sea* is the New Guinea jungle. The novel describes the campaign to drive the enemy from the mountains and clear a way to the sea, which becomes a transcendental image as the goal of life, 'somewhere in the future, cool and sparkling and incredibly blue . . . cleansed of all evil . . . when that one had been reached, there was no more war' (p. ix). The novel is an account of how the indi-

David Forrest

viduals in this army cross their personal mountains to gain the goal of the sea. Its longest episode describes the long march of two wounded soldiers over the mountains to the safety of the base camp. The end of their epic climb is not any sudden vision, but an extra helping of food 'for the bone that would be visible when the bandages were removed' (p. 260). This scene places salvation firmly within this world, in a plate of bully beef, and at the same time endows such material comfort with the power of overcoming the physical breakdown of battle and its aftermath. The defeated enemy is not the Japanese, but the weakness of self and the land that wants to absorb everything human.

The paradox of these novels is that it is only in the face of the ultimate destruction that humanity can unleash that the individual finds his central humanity. In Lambert's novels, as in the fiction of the First World War, this humanity is defined against the destructive process of the war itself and the forces that produce it. For Lambert, the enemy embodies fascism, the 'other' against whom the soldiers must battle to define themselves, whereas both Hungerford and Forrest see the enemy too as a product of the fact of war.

For Hungerford, the sight of Japanese soldiers bathing threatens the whole basis of the war, because in their joyful defencelessness they show themselves as men, just like the Australians who watch them and who have frolicked similarly. War creates the unity of the army only by defining it against others, and once this distinction is destroyed the army itself must disintegrate.

Forrest saves himself from the threat of such disintegration only by the distinction he draws between the unity of unthinking loyalty and the unity of men resisting this evil. The young Bren gunner Ron Fisher realises this distinction at the climactic moment when he finally loses doubt and fear in the necessity for action:

At twenty-five feet he saw into the heart of the monstrous parade created in the name of the Emperor: it was human flesh, fallible like his own; and it was, unlike his own, human mind depraved and drilled to the point of sterility.

He could not know that he saw what Colonel Wilson had seen on that day in Greece when the dive bombers came to Larissa, or what other people had discovered in Buchenwald, and others were yet to find on the Burma Railway. He could not know this, and he had no name for it, but his mind repelled it. He saw that it was amenable to force and capable of fear, and fear was what he gave it with the forces streaming from the barrel of the Bren.

Lambert, *Veterans*, p. 162.

In Forrest's novel, as in Hungerford's, the Bren becomes an image of men at war, the horrible parady of sexuality by which the soldier asserts himself in destruction. Significantly, both novelists emphasise the way the gunners sleep with their guns. The sole white casualty in *The Ridge and the River* loses his life when his companion, while crossing a river, lets go of him to try to save the Bren. In the passage quoted, however, the fear and domination symbolised by the Bren is transformed into an instrument of both personal and human liberation, destroying the very forces of domination that it symbolises. This is not the dark romanticism that falls in love with the beauty of violence, but the realism of the dark night of the soul that accepts violence as the price of overcoming evil. In identifying the otherness of the enemy in terms of human identity, the passage also destroys any claim to a superior nationalism on the part of the Australians. The mountains to be crossed are not only those of an alien New Guinea, but also those of individual pride and weariness, and the sea that beckons belongs to the whole of humanity.

In the novels of the First World War, the Australian soldier becomes a judge revealing the rottenness of the old world and the war it has spawned. In the Second World War, however, the reality was closer to home, and the dark otherness of the New Guinea jungles tested and judged the men who fought in them. In the fiction this context becomes more important than the enemy, as the individual has to conquer himself in order to survive. In this battle he comes to depend on others, but in a closer sense than that of the earlier concepts of mateship. The war disintegrates any simple ideals of nationalism or mateship, leaving neither pride nor disgust, but only a sense of a human value discovered through war but in spite of it.

The fiction of the infantry is not the only writing about the Australian experience in the Second World War. Accounts of the war at sea, like the story of the sinking of *The Perth* in Ronald McKie's *Proud Echo* (Angus & Robertson, Sydney, 1953) encapsulate the experience of men isolated in the ship within a wider sweep of history. Accounts of the war in the air, like Don Charlwood's *No Moon Tonight* (Angus & Robertson, Sydney, 1956) or John Beede's *They Hosed Them Out* (Australasian Book Society, Sydney, 1965) have a more surreal quality as they describe the alternation between the routines of life at the base and the long trek and brief inferno of the missions. The Japanese prison camps were places of continous horror where time became merely a sequence of days to be endured while death was resisted. This experience seems to have been captured adequately only in diaries. Some of them, like those of Stan Arneil or Sir Ernest 'Weary' Dunlop, were not published until forty years later. Even in the army, probably not more than one in ten took part in the battles of the infantry. These battlegrounds were, however, the places where history was merged in individual experience.

Ernest 'Weary' Dunlop
(*Artist: Louis Kahan*)

The military expectations and the tradition of the digger the infantrymen took with them into battle were remoulded both by the events and by their re-telling in yarns. The military expectations govern the tactics employed in the battle as it unfolds in narrative, but the novels dramatise the experience in the usually obscene idiom with which the troops meet it and recall it. This colloquial speech carries the experience of generations of resistance to the arrogance of authority and the hostility of the en-vironment. It provides the protective irony that enables the speakers to endure. The narrative in which it is framed shows history from the viewpoint of the troops, as a series of events given pattern only by the immediate objective — the ridge to be taken, the man to be killed, the death and maiming to be avoided. Although the novelists place events in a wider perspective, through the lyrical reflections with which Forrest frames his novel, the image of the flower at the end of *The Veterans*, or the philo-sophic discussions in Hungerford's book, their narra-tives are shaped to present events with simple and shocking immediacy. The chaos that threatens to disintegrate both the individual lives and any pattern of history is kept in check only by strict attention to fact. Like the colloquial dialogue, this narrative style has its source in the Australian tradition of realism, but the authors reshape this tradition so that it deals not just with resistance to the external but with the horror that threatens to destroy all meaning.

SOCIALISM AND REALISM

THE allied victory in the Second World War did not usher in the age of peace and prosperity that had been promised. Australia embarked on an ambitious program of national reconstruction, using the labour of a great wave of immigrants from Europe, many of them refugees from the tyrannies of fascism and communism, to dam its rivers and build new industries. Post-war hopes were, however, dimmed by continuing austerity and by the Cold War that divided the former allies and threatened to erupt into actual war made more terrible by the newly-developed atomic bomb.

Underlying these worries was the more general concern that Australia was both isolated from the centres of power and dependent on them not only for its military and economic survival but also for its ideas. This generated efforts to build economic self-sufficiency and international co-operation, through the United Nations and through military alliances with the USA and Britain. With similarly divided ambition, the generation of writers, artists and intellectuals who had grown up during the Depression and war were determined to establish Australia's cultural maturity, free from both provincialism and dependence. For some, this required the union of the independent national tradition with international movements for peace and socialism. Others rejected the concept of nationalism as itself provincial, and attempted to produce a local tributary to the international mainstream of modernism. Still others fol-

lowed Norman Lindsay in his rejection of modernism as a symptom of European decadence, and tried to return to classical models that would rebuild in Australia the tradition of reason. Despite these great differences, all three groups can be seen as responding to similar feelings of isolation and dependence.

Through the journal *Angry Penguins*, Max Harris and his associates tried to free art and writing from the fetters of a specifically national tradition and bring them into the mainstream of a modernism that owed allegiance only to individual creativity. This attempt foundered when Harris gave an enthusiastic welcome to the poems of Ern Malley, only to discover that Malley and the poems had alike been composed as a hoax by two Sydney poets watching each other carefully to ensure that no sense was allowed to intrude on their empty words. The hoaxers, James McAuley and Harold Stewart, scorned nationalism and modernism alike, and sought to restore both a poetry and a political order based on the classic ideas of reason and order.

Those experimental groups who sought to make an art that would bring light and order to the confused world of experience were opposed to the social realists, who aspired to use their writing directly to lay the foundations of a social order based on equality at home and peace abroad. These writers continued the tradition of democratic nationalism that stretched back to Lawson, and tried to preserve the sense of wartime solidarity that had united them with the

Max Harris
(*Photo: Colin Ballantyne*)

people of Russia in the struggle against Nazism. Many found their natural home in the Communist Party, which offered a vision of peace based on the unity of the common people. They accepted their responsibility as writers for building this unity. They wrote directly for the workers, describing the conditions of ordinary life that denied them freedom, as well as the qualities of decency and solidarity that might liberate them. At the same time, they tried to take their work directly to the workers by publishing in union papers and establishing alternative outlets through the annual anthologies of *Australian New Writing* (1943–46), journals such as *The Realist Writer* and *Overland*, founded during the early 1950s, and through the Australasian Book Society, that arose from the enthusiasm generated by the campaign to publish and distribute Frank Hardy's novel *Power Without Glory* in 1951. Hardy himself had a vision of a mass movement of people's writers and readers, starting with small groups who would publish and discuss their own work and generate a national network that would take the best work to the workers at their doorsteps, docksides and factory gates. The writer was important as a specialist worker in this revolutionary task.

Frank Hardy

At the beginning of Frank Hardy's *Power Without Glory* (Llord O'Neil, Melbourne, 1972 [1950], a

young man and a policeman face each other across a spinning coin. Behind them is the supposed tea-room where the young man, John West, runs a totalisator, an illegal system for gambling on horse-racing. Suddenly the young man spins the coin, a gold sovereign, at the policeman, who takes it. The power of money triumphs over lawful authority to launch John West's career of bribery and corruption.

This opening scene symbolises the theme of the novel. The power West derives from money is contrasted with the blight of the urban landscape through which he travels after his encounter with the policeman:

The shops, many of them shuttered and empty; the old houses, the rows of newer tenements and, sprinkled here and there, incomplete houses on which work had ceased; the TO LET signs; the group of ragged unemployed men standing outside the hotel . . . the spindly children playing listlessly in the gutters; the old man driving the herd of cows home from the river bank where he had grazed them for their owners since morning; the silent boot factory; the carts, buggies, jinkers and hansom cabs; the long queue of despair-haunted people waiting outside the Salvation Army Hall for their daily bowl of soup; the top-hatted, side-whiskered men standing outside the closed bank building, waiting and hoping against hope as they read the notice on the door, CLOSED FOR RECONSTRUCTION.

Hardy, *Power*, pp. 11–12.

The city is blighted by the despair of the 1890s Depression, where life is brought to a standstill by a lack of money. The narrative takes West back into these circumstances, to the occasion when he announced his first scheme to raise himself from poverty by exploiting the desperation of the workers to get their money for himself. In taking us back to the bare shed where half a dozen men divert themselves in their idleness with a desultory game of cards, Hardy establishes the particular historic situation that provides the realistic framework for the novel.

West's first enterprise was to run a book on a crooked pigeon race; this gave him the bank that he used to set himself up as a bookmaker and then to establish his totalisator. The novel then traces his career as he moves from bribing one constable to bribing the Chief Commissioner and a good proportion of his men; from running one gambling shop to operating an empire that extended throughout the worlds of racing, boxing, entertainment and politics, so that through the appointment of his men to select positions of power he operated the state itself. His avarice destroys his family, the condemnation of public moralists deprives him of the glory, but his power is unquestioned.

The opening episodes of the novel contrast the greed embodied in West with the potential power of the workers to free themselves from poverty by solidarity with each other. West decides to escape from his working-class origins by acquiring the wealth that will enable him to join the ruling classes. Most of his family and associates join him, but one, the trade unionist, Eddie Corrigan, maintains a commitment to collective rather than individual action. He believes that the way for workers to escape poverty is to stick together. West's money enables him to gratify his vanity by giving a labourer a few coins to help his wife and kids, earning a grudging admiration for 'a battler who had got on, yet was sympathetic to the poor' (p. 49). Corrigan, however, engaging in the real problem of a woman being evicted from her house, is powerless.

Corrigan represents one alternative to West. He tries to escape poverty by organising the unions, but is defeated by the forces of capital and reduced to powerlessness and penury. The Labor Party politicians who represent the alternative of parliamentary action fare even worse. They are corrupted by the opportunities of power and the ruthlessness of West, who buys them for his own purposes. The few who remain incorruptible are frustrated. Frank Ashton, who tries to keep his ideals while still accepting West's money, becomes a pitiable wreck. Even the Catholic Church, which comforted the poor in their adversity, succumbs to West's influence through a combination of shared purposes and appreciation of his financial support. In raising himself from the working class, West attains the power to destroy the only institutions that give it hope.

Much of the initial fascination of the novel comes from its grounding in history. Most of the characters can be identified with actual figures in the politics of the time, West himself with John Wren, Ashton with Frank Anstey, Blackwell with Maurice Blackburn, Thurgood with Ted Theodore, Treasurer in the ill-fated Scullin government. It has even been alleged that the novel is based on Anstey's lost memoirs, in which, like Ashton in the novel, he tried to redress his political failure by revealing the truth about the corruption he had seen. Yet, finally, this historical basis is also the reason for the book's failure. The quality of its revelations ceases to shock because the reader cannot be sure where historical circumstance merges into imaginative reconstruction, while the factual basis confuses the moral confrontation at the centre of the fiction. Eddie Corrigan, the dramatic alternative to West, fades away and is lost amid the tortuous account of financial and political intrigue.

Rather than being a social document, the novel finishes up as a psychological study of the effects of power on one man. West is destroyed partly because, despite his wealth, the establishment will never accept him as one of its own. This is due not so much to his origins as to his continuing involvement with the sleazier elements of society that those born to an easier inheritance are able to ignore. This involvement in crime and violence cuts him off as well from his family, to whom he becomes increasingly tyrannical and punitive as his isolation increases. At the close of the book, although he has received absolution, West lies alone, locked in impotent rage against a world that continues to defy him, a world that finally denies him the purchase on it that he had thought money would gain for him.

In *Power Without Glory*, Hardy concentrates so much on the details of what happened that he is unable to suggest any plausible alternative to the society he portrays. His historical reconstruction works more effectively in his later novel, *But the Dead Are Many* (Bodley Head, London, 1975) where he deals with the failure of a vision. This novel presents history through the eyes of characters who are realised fully in the fiction, even if they are based on actual people. It addresses urgent and difficult questions of political morality and action rather than offering clear answers. The form of the book, which Hardy calls a fugue, is important not in itself but as a device that frees the narrative from historical time. Events are presented as they come into the minds of the characters, sometimes while they occur, more frequently in recollection. Thus we are given not only the views of the same incident by a number of characters, but different views of the incident by the same person at different times in his life. As in *Power Without Glory*, the most important characters are men, for whom women are a source of occasional physical satisfaction and continual emotional frustration. Political action in

Frank Hardy

the outer world becomes a means of escape from this frustration, an attempt to impose an order on events the participants fail to create in their own lives.

The events of the novel constitute the history of the Communist Party of Australia from the time of the Moscow Trials in the 1930s until the early 1970s. Its background includes the growth of Nazism, the alliance between the Soviet Union and Germany and Hitler's attack on the Soviet Union, Australia's part in the Second World War and the Vietnam War, and the Soviet invasions of Hungary and Czechoslovakia. These events impose the insistent questions of how sane men could accept the constantly changing dogmas and actions of a party that demanded unquestioning loyalty, and of how anyone can go on living in a world whose only hope has been betrayed by the party of the revolution.

These questions are posed through the words of the disillusioned activist Paul Morel, who had witnessed the Moscow trials, and of the writer who has been at once his disciple and his comrade. The novel merges their questions in the wider doubt of whether life has any more reality than the drunken haze of a bar or the idle spill of fortune from a poker machine. In conversation and recollection, words themselves lose their meaning. They become either mere counters used in a futile attempt to recapture the past or interpret the present, or the empty dogma of the bureaucrat who uses the formulations of the party to avoid any encounter with life as it is experienced.

Although Hardy is usually classified as a realist, the most consistent characteristic of his work since *Power Without Glory* is his awareness of the way people use words to construct their own reality to protect themselves against the circumstances of their lives. His own characterisation of himself as battler, as the outsider always trusting that something will turn up to remedy his usual experience of ill-luck, is similar to that of Artie McIntosh in his story 'The Cocky in Bungaree' *(Legends from Benson's Valley,* Werner Laurie, London, 1963): 'good-hearted but unreliable, in debt and often unemployed, taking life as he found it, taking love where he found it; why buy a book when you can join a library?' (p. 33). The words create an image, a public figure rather than the inner man, and the last sardonic remark, a piece of folklore, shrugs off personal responsibility by allotting the speaker a place in popular tradition. Yet the story itself shows the gap between this outer shell and the feelings of the man who lives within it.

The realism of Hardy's work derives from his circumstantial accuracy, but he does not portray this reality for its own sake. *Power Without Glory* is intended to show its readers how life works so that they will try to change it. His comic works and his yarns celebrate the constant inventiveness of the Australian man in adversity, the often grim humour with which he makes the world his own. His novel about the fever of gambling, *The Four-Legged Lottery* (Werner Laurie, London, 1958) shows how this power of creative delusion can lead to tragedy. In exploring a similar obsession in *But the Dead Are Many* he shows the connections between the mania of the gambler and the dogma of the fundamentalist, both of whom flee from the knowledge of present failure into an unshakeable trust in the future. When the basis of this trust is destroyed, life becomes unendurable. Yet the gambler has the advantage that at least he enjoys life until the point of catastrophe. The politician has to live in a world he makes tolerable not by escape but by the iron control he exercises through his words. Hardy's achievement has been to break this control and allow words to play in their own reality, to the destruction of politics but not of humanity.

Alan Marshall

Alan Marshall is another realist writer who created himself as one of his main characters. Like Frank Hardy and Bill Harney he was renowned as much for his yarn telling as for his writing. After losing his job as an accountant when the boot-factory he worked for was closed by the Depression, Marshall embarked on travels about the country, earning a living from freelance journalism. Although never formally a member of a political party, his sympathies were with the common people for whom he wrote. His first book, *These Are My People* (Cheshire, Melbourne, 1942) tells the stories of people he met on a journey by caravan through Victoria. He used the setting of the boot-factory for his first novel, *How Beautiful Are Thy Feet* (Cheshire, Melbourne, 1949), but became best known for his autobiographical *I Can Jump Puddles* (Cheshire, Melbourne, 1955). Throughout his work, autobiography merges with fiction, reportage with story-telling, so that the reality is the truth of experience recreated in the imagination rather than mere historical fact.

In *I Can Jump Puddles* he tells the story of his childhood in a Victorian town, of the polio attack that left him crippled and dependent on crutches for the rest of his life, and of the ways he overcame this handicap to live a normal life with his fellows. The story is remarkable for its lack of self-pity, the simple way in which, unlike adults who looked on him with pity as one who would always be 'different', he so much overcame his condition as to disregard it. It is also remarkable for the picture it gives of a country town and its people, particularly his own family and his mate Joe. In telling of these people, he recreates in their idiom the life of a time still virtually untouched by industrialisation. Their lives are governed by the common sense and respect for others that are epitomised in Alan's father, who is the town's horse-breaker. His remarks when Alan comes home and demonstrates that he has defied expectations and learned to ride characterise his own attitude to life:

> . . . 'A good rider hasn't got to be rip-snorting about like a pup off the chain just to show he can ride. A good rider don't have to prove nothing. He studies his mount. You do that. Take it quietly. You can ride — all right, but don't be a show-off with it. A gallop's all right in a straight track, but the way you're riding, you'll tear the guts out of a horse in no time. A horse is like a man — he's best when he gets a fair deal. Now, walk Starlight back to school and give him a rub down before you let him go'.
>
> He paused, thinking for a moment, then added, 'You're a good bloke, Alan. I like you and I reckon you're a good rider'.

Marshall, *Puddles*, p. 234.

The simple philosophy is not original, but is passed down by generations who confirm it in their experience. It is based on respect for skill and for the world in which he works. The closing remark, by extending this respect to Alan, includes him in his father's world.

This standard informs the two further volumes in the trilogy in which Marshall brings the account of his life up to the eve of the Second World War. In the first of these, *This is the Grass* (Cheshire, Melbourne, 1962), he tells of his early efforts to find work and his experience as he moves from the shelter of home and the ease of the bush into the world of the city

Alan Marshall
(*State Library of Victoria*)

and its harsher values, where he is forced to recognise that his outback values of equality and mateship no longer apply. After the first volume has shown how Alan makes himself fit the world, the other two show how he learns to make the world accept him for what he is. At the same time he learns that his strength as a writer does not come from 'mind-created stories but from his knowledge of people' (p. 35). As these people come to fill his books, he disappears from them and becomes just another character, the person who records the words in which others tell him the stories that constitute their lives. In the final volume, *In Mine Own Heart* (Cheshire, Melbourne, 1963) these lives become burdened by the Depression that is steadily enfolding the world and destroying the opportunity for people to grow into the fullness of life. His account of the facts of the lives he sees around him is deepened by the anger he feels at this unnecessary stifling of human potential.

The narrative in these volumes becomes episodic, losing the unifying drive that the need to assert himself in the world gives to *I Can Jump Puddles*. His own life tends to recede into the background, except when he is forced to make a stand for independence against employers who would exploit or belittle him or acquaintances who try to protect him. For the rest, the places where he works, relaxes or boards are important for the opportunities they provide him to become an observer, entering into other people's lives to discover what makes them as they are.

The crumbling of Marshall's narratives into self-contained anecdotes is not sign of weakness but of strength. He is most at ease in short stories where he concentrates the world of his vision into the unity of a moment. These stories show how his own experience is built up out of his encounters with the others who create his values. By sharing these people with his readers, he shares with them his own love of life.

This love is conveyed through the narrator's description of the way he collects his stories, given as the preamble to 'When a Man Kills, He Runs' *(The Complete Stories of Alan Marshall,* Nelson, Melbourne, 1977). This story is an exploration of the fragile defence mateship provides against madness:

In talking to old men whose experiences I feel would be valuable to me in writing, I am often amazed at the mass of words they use to convey their thoughts, the unnecessary and boring words that obscure personality and knowledge. Listening to them is like washing for gold. As you swirl the water in the dish nothing is revealed but sand. Sometimes in this sand shines a speck of gold. You grasp this glittering speck, the presence of which suddenly gives value to the sand, the revealing mark that illuminates their tale.

Marshall, Complete Stories, p. 363.

The metaphor of washing for gold both associates the writer's method with the tradition of the digger battling to scratch a living and endows the battle with supreme value. The importance of the writer's work is shifted from its worth as literature to the worth it reveals in the lives of the ordinary men and women of whom it tells. This quality in turn meant that Marshall's work appealed to ordinary readers, who found it speaking without apparent artifice to their own everyday experience.

In his last book of stories (*Hammers on the Anvil*, Nelson, Melbourne 1975) Marshall returns to the childhood world of *I Can Jump Puddles*. He now, however, tempers the clear sight of the child with his adult awareness of the costs of the hardship and frustration the child could only glimpse. Joe Carmichael is still the generous friend, but we see also the desperate poverty of his household and hear the dying screams of the pigs that are slaughtered to sustain the family. Jimmy Virtue, the gentle man who never broke an egg or crushed one of the baby parrots he took from their nests to show to Alan, now staggers from the dark in his moment of drunken despair, 'a symbol of all sickness, echoing my own thoughts with his terrible No, no, no, no' (p. 393). In recalling childhood, the narrator faces the knowledge that the adult has no way of hiding from the inevitable grief that life brings or of escaping the destruction that he wreaks himself.

The human failure, both social and individual, that Marshall portrays is, however, enfolded in a wider vision of a natural unity that transforms, although it does not obliterate, the sense of inevitable loss. This natural unity is in turn expressed in the lives and words of those he meets who are prepared to share his life. From them comes the ethic of mateship that he sets against the cruelty and distress of the modern world.

While Marshall's work keeps alive this traditional ethic, it does so by turning aside from the cities and contemporary society to the simpler world of childhood and the bush. The mates he finds in the city are outcasts like himself, the humanity that ameliorates the machine-bound routine of the factory is destroyed by the greater machine of economics. Although Marshall triumphs over distress and misery as he triumphs over his physical affliction, by maintaining the wonder and trust of childhood while acknowledging the inevitable erosions of time, this simple faith sustains him not so much by defeating evil as by turning aside from it.

Judah Waten

Judah Waten

Marshall's contemporary Judah Waten offers a more ideological answer to social evil. Like Hardy and Marshall, he seeks to describe ordinary life, but he shares Hardy's expectation that if people recognise the social causes of distress and oppression they will work to get rid of them by changing society.

Waten's novels tend to be programmatic accounts of how the experience of adversity awakens his characters to the truth of society and the answer of communism. His first novel, *The Unbending* (Australasian Book Society, Melbourne, 1954), traces the fortunes of a family of Russian immigrants to Western Australia in the early years of this century. The family's struggles are set against the background of political struggle in the years around the First World War, as the town and its social groups become a microcosm of the wider society. The forces arrayed against the family, which has no resources except its own labour, appear to leave no alternative to revolutionary change. *Shares in Murder* (ABS, Melbourne, 1957) uses the vehicle of a crime story to uncover the corruptions of power and money beneath the facade of the law. *Time of Conflict* (ABS, Melbourne, 1961) shows how the hardships of the Depression drive the main character, Mick Anderson, into crime and imprisonment. The communism

Anderson eventually discovers is, however, more an ideological shell against the vicissitudes of fortune than the product of a developed awareness of social forces.

In his later novels, Waten develops in more contemporary settings his themes of the clash of cultures in the immigrant experience and the need for revolutionary change in order to escape from poverty and oppression. In all the novels, however, the events seem to lead to a predetermined outcome. This problem is inherent in the conflict between the form and the political doctrine of the novels. Their form implies an individual development towards a defined goal or the discovery of a resolution to conflict. Their doctrine is based on a belief in a truth already known and external to the events of history. By adopting this doctrine, Waten subordinates character and action to an explanation that is not so much discovered as presented as the answer to the problems revealed in the action.

By contrast, the form of the short story provided him with a vehicle within which he could express his most pressing concerns without dissolving them into the abstract patterns of dogma. The short story by its nature focuses on a particular incident or episode. The significance of the episode may derive from the insight it gives us into its wider context, but the problems and conflicts it embodies require no resolution within the narrative. Waten's stories show us characters trapped in their situations, frustrated by their inability to achieve the ideals that nevertheless give their lives substance and meaning. The stories provide no solution to the frustrations.

In his first book, *Alien Son* (Sun Books, Melbourne, [1952] 1965), Waten shows the frustrations that destroy the ideals of a group of Jewish immigrants. They have brought with them from Russia a sense of community, but success in the new land depends on individual achievement that divides the community they try desperately to keep alive by maintaining their traditional practices. They are frustrated by the poverty that defeats personal ambition, and by the imperative need of their children to move out of the enclosed world of their parents into the patterns of the society around them. Unlike *The Unbending*, the stories present these issues through a series of episodes rather than a continuous narrative. The loose sequence is tied together by the single voice of the narrator and the recurring presence of his parents and a few others, but each centres on a different person whose particular experience provides a different perspective on a common situation. At the same time, the chronological ordering enables us to follow the development of the narrator as he grows away from the enclosing security of his family to find his identity in the wider community that will always remain alien to his parents.

Similar themes emerge from the stories written over more than 20 years and collected in *Love and Rebellion* (Macmillan, Melbourne, 1978). The title story, which concludes the collection, shows how the awakening of love can prompt vague feelings of rebellion even in a bureaucrat who has allowed his routine to become his being. 'The Knife', first published in 1957, shows how the ideas associated with the knife by two separate cultures, Australian and Italian, create an impassable barrier of understanding. The knife is both Plinio's sole link with his past and the guarantee of the identity his new environment ignores or threatens. His attempt to assert himself against this threat leads only to deeper isolation. The knife becomes a symbol of the inability of people as individuals to overcome the forces that exclude them from the wider community.

Waten's stories deal with people on the boundaries of society, and particularly with those caught between two cultures. Although he writes during the decades when Australia was being transformed by the immigration that followed the Second World War, many of his stories reach back to those generations of immigrants whose cultural struggles could be ignored by the Anglo-Celtic dominance. They thus not only provide a record of their time, but remake tradition to incorporate not only the struggles and hopes of forgotten and peripheral communities, but the traditions and ideals that they brought with them from two thousand years of resistance and achievement in eastern Europe. Central to these traditions is the Jewish sense of community — alien to the aggressive individualism with which settlers sought to exploit Australia, but harmonious with the other traditions of mateship and freedom that developed during that process of exploitation. This Jewish tradition is also urban, and thus compatible with an industrial, but not with a competitive, economy. Waten shows the divisions the competitive individualism of industrial society creates within the community. He also shows that the ideal of community contains an underlying strength with the potential to overcome these divisions and provide the basis of a just society.

John Morrison

Morrison's story 'Going Through' (*Black Cargo*, Australasian Book Society, Melbourne, 1955) is about the power of the Waterside Workers' Federation and the privilege of getting accepted into its solidarity. After the ordeal of facing the members and being allowed through, the narrator reflects that:

> We feel suddenly rich. And not because of bigger pay envelopes to come. We've got ourselves three thousand mates. We've come through. We're Federation men. We can wear the little blue button with the clasped hands on it. . .

> Morrison, *Black Cargo*, p. 21.

The paragraph celebrates the achievement of solidarity that is the bedrock of John Morrison's values. But a few lines earlier, the narrator has shown how this same sense of solidarity can change the members of the union from 'Warm-hearted men' with 'multitudinous little interests' into 'part of the beast that

John Morrison
(*National Library of Australia*)

rose up and snarled at the man in the black raincoat' who had broken their code. Morrison knows both the value of mateship and the price paid by those it excludes.

Morrison's stories, like Waten's, are ideological, but his ideology determines the perspective of the narrative rather than its outcome. Although he always writes from the point of view of the ordinary working man, he does not suggest any easy answer to his problems. The stories that follow 'Going Through' in the original collection — 'The Compound', 'The Pick-up' and 'The Welcome' — show the conditions in which the watersiders work, the bitter division among them, and the sense of class solidarity that can transcend even the barriers of language and nationality. The stories emphasise the pride of the men both in their work and in their loyalty to each other. This loyalty creates the bitterness of members of the Federation to members of the other union, the scabs who betrayed their mates in the strike of 1926. We are given the picture of an industry with its own structures and its own traditions, symbolised by the Compound, where men are robbed of their power and reduced to supplicants as they scramble desper-

ately for work, and by the waterfront, where they exercise their pride and skill in crossing the boundary between land and sea, between one country and another. The trade in which they assist becomes an image both of the interdependence of free men who create and use the goods being shipped, and of the oppression of a system that has constantly to speed up this trade in the interests of profit and at the expense of the safety, dignity and subsistence of the workers. The ideology is implicit in the experience.

Morrison is one of the few modern writers in any country to understand the significance of work for a complete human life. His stories show how work is deformed by the control of capital, which places authority for the conditions of work, as well as the use of the product, in the hands of the owners. They also show how modern industry by its nature separates work from the other elements of life that it sustains and with which it conflicts. These elements include the gardens the watersiders tend in their spare time and the families their wages have to support. The first is conveyed in the leisurely discussion of the two winchmen while the rest gang are settling a dispute about the length of the ship: 'Now don't forget about them onions, Tom. Over at an angle, and barely cover the roots' ('Nine O'Clock Finish', p. 83). The simple practicality of these words brings into being the whole other world of domesticity where a man produces his own sense of self. The precarious foundations of this world are shown in stories like 'Black Night in Collingwoood (*This Freedom*, Penguin, Ringwood, 1985, pp. 130–40) or 'A Man's World' (*Stories of the Waterfront*, Penguin, Ringwood, 1984, pp. 84–93), where the man's need for the security of his mates or his team comes into direct conflict with his obligations to his family.

While the waterside provides the setting for most of Morrison's stories of class conflict, the home is the context in which he explores the most intense personal antagonisms. These are frequently conflicts between husband and wife, which he usually describes from the man's point of view, but without necessarily endorsing it. This stance reflects not only the convention of the time, but the conditions of work that made the man the provider and confined the woman to the home. The man's problems are bosses, hours and conditions; the woman's are looking after the kids and making ends meet. The inevitable conflict emerges in 'Easy Money' (*Black*

Cargo, pp. 89–99) as the men fill in a break in the work with idle chatter about the subterfuges they resort to conceal their real earnings from their wives. The rough jesting only covers the fact that most of them accept their responsibilities, however irksome.

The family, with its potential for both security and violence, provides a contrasting background to the stories of the waterfront. In later stories the family becomes the microcosm within which the larger conflicts are acted out. In 'The Battle of Flowers' (*North Wind*, Penguin, Ringwood, 1962, pp. 59–86) the narrator's occupation as jobbing gardener involves him in the lethal antagonism of two sisters whose jealousy turns their gardens from places of beauty to wastelands of destruction. In 'Morning Glory' (p. 229–38) the hired man becomes a spectator of events that involve the family in the shooting of a chicken thief, who turns out to be a mere boy. This episode becomes a vehicle to show how the struggle for survival on a small farm separates the family from any wider community. In 'Pioneers' (*North Wind*, pp. 99–127) Morrison examines an even more bitter example of the disintegrating effects of poverty. Years of struggle have turned the farmer from the battler of tradition into a tyrant. His exercise of power over his own family isolates him from humanity and drives him to madness and murder. 'To Margaret' is a similar study of the tyranny of a suburban husband. In the equally bitter 'The Blind Man's Story' (*This Freedom*, pp. 41–58) the tyrant is the childless woman driven by suburban isolation and the need for esteem to destroy her man, until the accident that blinds him puts him completely in her power. Again, in 'North Wind' (*North Wind*, pp. 143–83) the fire that threatens the fragile security of the suburb is not as menacing as the mother-in-law whose detestation of her son-in-law leads her to seek immolation in preference to safety at his hands.

In these stories Morrison goes beyond the socialist realism that determined the subject of his waterfront stories, and explores instead the inner loneliness men seek to escape from in work, mateship and even marriage. The stories are conducted with an art that separates the incidental from the significant, leading us from the details of work or travel into the passions that govern the lives of the individuals involved. This significance is pointed by the oral wisdom embodied in the remarks of the characters as they discuss the issues, or by reference to literary tradition, like the stories of immoral women that introduce the 'Blind Man's Story' with a dark counterpoint to the otherwise genial atmosphere. The common property of these two traditions, oral and written, emphasises the loneliness of the individual in his struggle with the specific circumstances of his own life. They thus give weight to the moral choice everyone is eventually forced to make, whether it is to share a pay packet, side with the bosses in a strike, or admit the truth about a husband.

Money remains an important factor in Morrison's work as a prime cause of the distortion and disintegration of human society. While poverty drives families apart, the pursuit of wealth destroys the capacity for any other relationship. Even more than an economic factor, money becomes a symbol of men's drive for power, just as the home becomes a symbol not of fulfilment but of the woman's drive for power. The mateship of work is not sufficient to contain this, any more than the gardens the old wharfies lovingly tend can shield them from economic reality. Money, the economic basis of society, replaces reality, and thus destroys the possibility of the community within which alone the human can find fulfilment.

The belief in this potential community provides Morrison with a positive element that survives even his most bitter accounts of the destruction of the potential. It is conveyed most strongly in the images of children and young people just entering into the fulness of the world or the hopes and complexities of love, their capacity for wonder and fellowship still undiminished. It remains in adult life in the few moments when men find mateship or women bring their families into a passing unity. The humanism of these images keeps at bay the despair that would otherwise arise from his observations of twisted and defeated lives. The people of the suburbs survive the violence of the bushfire, the marriage survives the malevolence of the mother.

David Martin

Although a realist in style and a socialist by conviction, as a novelist David Martin is essentially a writer of resistance. He is less concerned with any centrally Australian tradition than with the predicaments of race and identity within the Australian situation, and resists any easy generalisations about that tradition or about the contributions brought to it by more recent immigrants. Already an established novelist when he arrived in Australia in 1949, his first novel written in this country, *The Young Wife* (Sun Books, Melbourne, 1966 [1962]), is concerned with the experience of the Greek community in Melbourne in the 1950s. The novel deals with problems and factions within the community, rather than with the divisions between generations as the younger members become assimilated into local ways. At its heart is a vision of the ambiguous nature of love, at once divisive and healing. The plot is an antipodean variation of the tragedy of *Alcestis*, a performance of which also precipitates the events that lead to the tragedy of the novel. In the drama, the wife gives her life that her husband may live. In the novel, the destruction of husband and lover frees the wife, and the closing words speak of pain and joy as she goes into labour for the birth of her first child. Life resists the despair that seeks to overwhelm it.

The plot of the novel concerns thwarted love, but is over-elaborate, a mechanical device to carry events to a predetermined end. The strength of the book depends on the description of particular incidents rather than on the devices that link them together. These incidents represent the contrasting worlds of the novel. The Greek church, with its screen of icons and the soaring ceremony, belongs to the life of the village where every action found its meaning in tradition. These ceremonies still govern the lives of the women, but the men are either hostile or cynical, and the priest just another player in the game of community politics. The further arena of this game is the football ground where the exclusively nationalist Greek team encounters the more cosmopolitan Italians and where his compatriots savage Criton for scoring the winning goal against them. The politics of football reflect those of the community, and are played out in clubroom and committee meeting. These community activities are in turn contrasted with the two Australian entertainments, the one given by the intellectual patrons of Greek culture and the other taking place in the local hall of the township where Criton has sought refuge from his urban problems. The tragedy of the novel is that the values embodied in these different episodes are incompatible with each other. The central incompatibility of the novel is not between cultures, but between the freedom of love and the institutions by which we attempt to channel feeling.

In his next novel, *The Hero of Too* (Cassell Australia, Melbourne, 1965), Martin takes a satirical if affectionate look at a small country town and its people, and in the process demolishes the myth of the bushranger. In his children's books he examines the way particular problems impinge on the task of growing up. The narrator of *The Cabby's Daughter* (1974), for example, is left by her mother's death alone to deal with the problem of a drunken father. *The Man in the Red Turban* (1978) takes a boy in trouble with the police as the result of a rash act, and involves him in the affairs of an Indian hawker, strikes, marriage and death. These problems in turn are woven into stories that bring to life the people of the countryside and small towns of northern Victoria. The consequence is a genial image of the Australian tradition, in which goodwill between individuals overcomes most problems as people learn to take responsibility for themselves. In all these books human responsibility hinges on the choice by the central characters of where they belong. Criton, in *The Young Wife*, fatefully late, decides that he belongs with the girl from the country town rather than in the hothouse life of the city. Bess, the cabbie's daughter, recognises that, whatever the injustice of life, she still has 'the sky and the sun', love and friends, and that her place is with her father even in his troubles. In *The Hero of Too*, this sense of belonging extends to the town itself, which belongs precisely because its impermanence and lack of history make no claim beyond the life created by its people:

Granted that the whole township, for all its casual strength, has this air of impermanence, granted also that it suggests in countless ways that it did not exist the day before yesterday, as time is measured in more venerable societies. You'll find no minsters, no keeps, no winding alleys in which every cat reeks of its crusader ancestry. You may say, if you like, that it is featureless, jumped-up, raw. But would you not agree, looking more deeply, that such vaunted memorials of the past are chiefly memorials of death? The minster was sacked while hapless prisoners were hurled down from the keep, probably to the delight of the alley dwellers. The magnificent gables of Bruges resounded to the echoes of the *carmagnole*; the purple of its tapestries is the colour of human blood. We do not say that Tooramit is attractive because it has no history, but that its own peculiar beauty, such as it is, derives from things that have to do with life and not with mouldering death.

Martin, *Hero of Too*, pp. 7–8.

The novelist, born in a Europe that massacred his family, and himself having experienced two European wars and the massacres that accompanied the birth of a free India, chooses a country that is free from history. The novel goes on to mock the attempts to create a myth from a local history that preferred human fallibility to the heroic dimensions of the would-be myth-makers. Martin's viewpoint is from the seat of the dunny that confers both privacy and equality, and shows people as they are.

In *Where a Man Belongs* (Cassell Australia, Melbourne, 1969) Martin looks critically at the European dimension of Australian experience. The novel is about a journey from Melbourne to Germany, and then back again through Istanbul and Bombay to Melbourne. The journey to Europe is a symbolic return for both the narrator, Max, and his companion Paul Burtle. Max grew up as a Jew in pre-war Germany, fleeing with his father just in time to escape the Holocaust. Paul was a digger at Gallipoli and in France, where he was gassed. Gudrun, whom Paul seeks as a wife, turns out to have been the wife and concubine of Nazis, and herself a Nazi. Max and Gudrun represent the two poles of the European experience, while Paul is the innocent Australian trying to take Europe for his own, both associatively by his visits to galleries and tourist spots, and metaphorically through marriage.

This symbolic pattern is complicated by the personal histories of Max and Paul. Max as a Jew represents the victim of history, but he has also to expiate his own memory of denying the stepmother who had nurtured him as a child. Europe holds no sentimental memories for him, the Berlin of his childhood has been obliterated, and all he wants is to settle the financial affairs left by his father and get back to his work. He is unable to forgive Gudrun for the sufferings inflicted by the Germans on his people, yet through her song she grants him the absolution he needs and thus restores the German landscape to him. As he listens, he is restored to wholeness:

. . . not since setting foot in Germany had I experienced such an intense happiness. This was what I had returned for, these songs and this peaceful stillness, unsullied by a past that tears and blood could not wash clean. I was grateful that a woman was singing them for me, and for the chance that had brought us there. For the first time I believed that I had a right to be where I was, that the world was still one, and that even Germany was still a part of it, even after so much death. It was a surrender, a spaceless depth into which filled an emotion like love.

Martin, *Where a Man Belongs*, p. 170.

The forgiveness he finds is not only for his own betrayal, but for the father who betrayed him by concealing the death of his true mother and for the nation that betrayed the whole Jewish people. It enables him to accept his knowledge that 'there is nothing, literally nothing, that human beings will not do' (p. 169), and that he is his 'own country' (p. 168). He is free from history, and so can return to Australia.

Paul, however, brings nothing from Australia and so can take nothing from Europe. He is incapable of eros, the sexual force that comprehends both land and people. His love for Gudrun is only the release of his fears of impotence, and in spirit he is akin to the the Nazi soldiers with whom he finds easy comradeship. His death from a heart attack, however, releases Max from bondage to responsibility and to Europe. The novel ends as he scatters Paul's ashes near a creek 'flowing deep and clear', and with the sound of a tractor working nearby. These images join nature and work in freedom that has been earned only through expiation of the European past. Paul belongs at last because he can make no further demands. Max belongs because he has made himself his own country by resisting both worlds.

George Johnston

Although David Martin identifies himself as a socialist and has been associated with social realism and socialist causes, his fiction has been concerned with personal rather than social liberation. George Johnston had no public commitment to any ideology, and is concerned in his fiction with the way the individual discovers his own path through the complexities of society. Johnston's own journey, however, began in Australia and led him to Europe before he decided where he belonged. The fictional account of this journey, *My Brother Jack* (Fontana edition, Collins, Melbourne, 1967 [1964]), becomes also a history of Australia's struggles for independence during the two world wars and the years between. But, ambiguously, the growth of the narrator's love for Cressida is also a betrayal of his own past, just as the international scene in which he has learnt to move lacks the simple decencies and certainties symbolised by the brother Jack who has failed to leave the country in the path of his digger forebears.

At the beginning of the novel, the narrator watches in Australia as the troops, including his parents, return at the end of a war. At the end of the novel, and of another war, he has freed himself from Australia and is ready to fulfil himself as an expatriate. In Cressida, who is his first love and is to be his second wife, he has found another 'brother Jack' to accompany him. The real brother, after whom the novel is named and who represents all that is best about Australia, is left behind a broken and defeated man: 'he walked with a limp and the screw turned

George Johnston
(*Garry Kinnane, Ballarat CAE*)

tighter as I realised he had given up' (p. 343). While Jack has failed, the narrator has removed himself from reliance on the dubious interpretations of others, only to discover that the account of reality he has built for himself is equally false.

In the first stage of the novel, Davy's brother Jack shapes his world for him, providing a model of behaviour, explaining to his younger brother, 'the nipper', what is going on, and using his fists and his tongue to force the world to give him his desires. Jack emerges as a character from the miasma of childhood memories of a household dominated by relics and memories of the First World War, and from the dreary wasteland of those south-eastern Melbourne suburbs stranded between affluence and destitution. Then, as Davy becomes an actor in his scene rather than just a receiver of impressions, Jack, with his rejection of authority, his precocious love life, and his strong and effective stand for justice, provides the firm centre of his world. As the mother's circle of authority dissipates, and the father declines into a petty tyrant, Jack maintains the standards of decency and heroism the returning soldiers had brought back from their war.

In the second part, during the Depression years, Jack is defeated economically but establishes a marriage and family of his own. Davy meanwhile finds work first as a graphic artist, then as a writer, and finally as a professional journalist. In each of these situations he uses the lives of others to suit his own purposes, first by using them directly, then by turning their lives into the words through which he constructs a world of language and a career of his own. The cost of his achievement is paid by others. He allows himself to be drawn almost by chance into an affair and then marriage with a woman who ties him to the suburban respectability he despises, joins with her in rebuffing his family, and then turns vindictively against her for being what she is.

In the third stage of the book, Jack seizes the war as the chance to fulfil his destiny by following in his digger father's footsteps. Davy, on the other hand, avoids the call to arms and uses the opportunity to break his suburban bonds. His words turn the exploits of the fighting men into a brilliant fiction of war, while Jack's hopes are thwarted by an accidental injury and his spirit thereafter blunted by the tedium of base camp and headquarters duties. Davy's writings make him a public figure who becomes for his brother the vicarious compensation for his own failure to find a part in the action. Words provide him not only with a substitute for reality but also with the means to escape from its dreary obligations. Finally, words confer on him the glamour that enables him to take a new lover from his close friend, the genuine war hero Gavin Turley, and provide the sophistry that shelters him from recognition of his treachery. They cannot hide from him, however, that his act is a betrayal of his brother Jack, who is given the last words in the novel: 'My brother Davy's not the sort who ever let anyone down, you know . . .' (p. 348). The novel has demonstrated directly the opposite.

Davy's betrayals of his friends and family are a symptom of the emotional sterility of the Australian suburbs, which are unable to nurture a full life. His family looks back to a wartime past that exists in the present only in the figures of the injured and impotent people with whom his mother fills her house. His peacetime job gives his father no satisfaction, so he retreats into drink. Even Jack's resilience and independence is unable to sustain him through the rigours of the Depression, and he is rescued from destitution and death only by his family and his wife. Davy's talents enable him to escape this stultifying environment through the deceptive medium of words. His trade as a journalist becomes an image of the necessary escape from truth into words that is itself at once a betrayal of reader and writer.

The falsity of both the suburbs and their newspapers is set against the reality of the soldiers who created the myth that sustains Jack, and that Davy believes even as he exploits it. Thus, shortly before Davy finally turns his back on his brother, the two of them go together to watch a parade of returned men. The unity and ease of the march represents an achievement that cannot be destroyed by its exploitation:

. . . they marched, not like Guardsmen, but in their big loose straight easy way, the hard brown faces under the tipped-up hats, lean faces with the chin-straps taut and shining on the harsh slanting planes . . . and I thought of Jack when I had seen him at Puckapunyal five long years before, looking just like these men, hard and strong and confident and with his brown legs planted in the Seymour dust as if the whole world was his to conquer, a man

fulfilled in his own rightness, and suddenly and terribly I knew that all the Jacks were marching past me, all the Jacks were still marching.

Johnston, *My Brother Jack*, (pp. 342–3).

Yet, even as he admires, Davy knows that he cannot be a part of this company. His subsequent desertion of Jack merely confirms his earlier realisation in an Italian transit stop that he can become himself only by leaving the Australia whose sustaining myth leads ultimately to the stultifying reality of a household of invalids and a suburb of spiritual death:

. . . I looked closer and I realised that it was not at all the same face as those other faces under my brother Jack's face. A difference had grown into it, or developed out of it. I turned my head this way and that, studying it, and suddenly realised that there was a sort of calculation in it, that this was a face waiting for opportunities, that what was lacking in it was the truth those other faces had for the passionate regard for the adventure in itself, and I knew then that I was not quite one of them, that I never had been, and I never would be.

Johnston, *My Brother Jack*, p. 319.

As Gavin Turley recognises, Davy's weakness is not his ability to falsify, but his inability to conceal from himself his knowledge of the truth. Knowing the truth, he must go away from Australia and his brother Jack who represents the strength he admires, but which leaves Jack, like his parents, with no hope of a future.

The two further novels that complete the trilogy show both the cost of expatriation and the reasons that eventually drive Davy Meredith home, but they leave untouched the discovery that only by freeing himself from the tradition can Meredith find himself. The final novel, *A Cartload of Clay* (Collins, Sydney and London, 1971) was left unfinished by the author's death. In it, the narrator finally frees himself from the tyranny of words when he finds, in the face of death, that reality is as simple and as difficult as a walk along the street. This realisation frees him to enter into his memories, the terrible realisation of his wife's suicide, and the simple attentions of his neighbours. He reconstructs his life in words without falsifying the patterns he has discovered.

Social Realism

Social realism was a response to the fears of the Depression and the hopes of a new society that were generated during the war. Its writers looked at contemporary society to find a continuity of the Australian tradition of mateship that could provide the moral basis of a true democracy. This led not only to an idealisation of the working classes as the heirs of a bush tradition, but also to a narrowing of their interests in the potential of human life for both good and evil. Although love is central to their ideology, their treatment of it remains of the simplest kind. It is most commonly portrayed as a welling up of the natural forces otherwise denied by an unjust society and destroyed by domesticity. The bitterness of the women in John Morrison's stories arises from the lack of any field in which they can exercise a sway outside the family. Even in the work of George Johnston, realist but not socialist, the absence rather than the presence of love is destructive. None explores the idea of love as itself a form of power, with the same potential for destruction as for renewal. Similarly, their attention to the importance of work leads them to see the religious, intellectual and creative aspects of humanity purely in social terms. In their pursuit of new heavens they miss the daimons at home in the human heart.

Martin and Johnston, and to some extent Morrison, took social realism as far as it could go. Their work reveals social tensions too complex to be resolved by the simple ethos of bushman and digger, or by translating mateship into class solidarity. Even the divisions of home and work did not explain the angers, frustrations and satisfactions of common life. The Second World War could not be accommodated within either the imperial or the nationalist sentiments of the First, and in post-war Australia both the bush tradition and the Anglo-Celtic dominance of society were challenged by the post-war immigrants. The newcomers not only built a new industrial base but also brought intellectual, religious and peasant traditions that created their own conflicts in a new urban world. As cities sprawled through the suburbs, work and home became further divided and consumption replaced labour as the measure of value. The individual was forced to resolve these tensions in personal rather than social terms. These changes reduced the literature of conflict and class solidarity to a nostalgic retreat from the present, and writers turned their attention rather to the inner world that gave meaning to experience. Although the work they produced was not always conservative, its effect was to turn attention from social evil to personal and spiritual adjustment.

12

A HEIGHTENED REALITY

THE aim of social realist writers was to describe the experience of the ordinary person and show how this experience is shaped by society. The traditions they drew on, however, had been shaped in the struggles of settlement and war, and lacked the strength to become self-sustaining. The individual had to look either overseas or to a romantic past for fulfilment. Lacking adequate roots in its own land, Australian culture threatened to stifle individuality in the conformity of the suburb and the bush town. The revolutionary dreams of the social realists offered no immediate alternative to the sterility of the present. Other writers sought to expand consciousness more directly to reveal the possibilities excluded by the crass materialism that seemed to dominate commercial and political life alike.

These writers turned in a number of directions in their search for a source of strength to break the bounds of the conformity and parochialism that stunted growth in Australia. A number looked inwards to the individual sensibility rather than society as the source of life. In the same year, 1939, that Kylie Tennant found among the slum-dwellers in *Foveaux* a cheerful courage that sustained them against hardship, Patrick White, in *Happy Valley*, showed a doctor turning his back for ever on the small town that tries to rule everyone's life by its own narrow standards. In a series of novels over the next four decades White developed this concept of the individual who resists

the pressure to conform and instead transforms the conditions of life through an inner vision.

Poets like Douglas Stewart and Judith Wright went beyond the Jindyworobak tradition to create a personal vision based on a harmony drawn by the human from the natural environment. By contrast, Max Harris experimented with a form of modernism that ignored both tradition and national boundaries in order to create an immediate world of symbolic expression. The aim was not to show any external reality, but to reveal how the outer world becomes real only as it is perceived and interpreted by the mind. His novel, *The Vegetative Eye* (Reed & Harris, Adelaide, 1943), expresses this concept both in its title and the structure of its narrative, which is so inward that it becomes completely private. On the other hand, in his later poetry Harris finds authority in the quality of living rather than of imagination, and writes simply of love, or invests his native landscapes with the mythical quality of ordinary people who have lived or suffered in them, from Sturt at Depot Glen to Bert Sassenowsky near Mt Gambier, and workmen in the Alice pub.

Other poets sought to recover an external authority that would both expand Australian consciousness and control the destructive impulses of a society devoted to the individual and the present. Geoffrey Dutton, exploring Europe with the fresh sight of an Australian consciousness, was impressed not by ruins or tradition so much as by a timelessness that brings, if not redress, at least perspective to the horrors of history. The shattered instruments of planes that stand 'amputated of their wings', symbols of the destruction of war, are set against 'harvest time in France' where the 'heavyheaded sheaves/Hang like sunflowers in the heat' (*Antipodes in Shoes*, Edwards & Shaw, Sydney, 1958, p. 19). Finally he returns to Australia, where the land is known, marked by memory, but not made by man, and the wrens still gleam with a brighter blue.

This landscape gives the authority to Robert Clark's poetry, which draws its strength from a classical detachment that arises, not from Europe, but directly from the 'willed aloofness' of a land that will nurture but not be dominated. To attempt to tame it, to impose human will on it, is to breach a natural order and thus to commit suicide. John Bray turns to no particular land, but rather to a Europe of the mind, the world of the classical poets whom he translates and transforms into an Australian present. Their detachment and formal style give him the calm from which to contemplate the foibles of humanity, but also the passion to condemn its barbarities. David Campbell also returns to this Europe of mythology, but he incorporates it in his sense of a wider harmony built by work between human and nature. A.D. Hope also remakes the ancient myths, but with the irony of recognition rather than detachment. James McAuley uses a similar poetic decorum to impose the restraints of his Catholic faith on the disintegrating forces of the modern world. Hal Porter uses language itself as a control, and Rosemary Dobson and Gwen Harwood use the images of art and music to the same purpose.

Much of this writing appeared in the 1950s and 1960s, when Australia was growing rapidly as an urban and industrial society. This society threatened both national and individual identity with the drab conformities of cosmopolitanism, consumerism and bureaucracy. All were manifest in the dead language of governments and the false vitality of advertising and journalism. For all these writers language was a crucial area to fight conformism, to restore the heightened sense of reality through which alone the individuals can recover the sense of their own being. This struggle for language, for the truth of the individual, led the writers at first away from politics, which seemed merely another means by which the mass denied the integrity of the individual. Later, language became itself the basis of a politics of community.

Douglas Stewart

Stewart's work is built on the paradox that the fragile and obscure forms of life, the 'most harmless, most innocent of mankind', are at once the most important and powerful. He celebrates the power of the weak.

This is true even of those works that deal with the famous and the heroic, like the explorers Shackleton and Scott amid the ice, or Rutherford unravelling the mysteries of the universe in his laboratory. These puny human figures are overwhelmed by the vastness of nature, yet at the same time the apparently tiny flicker of mind and spirit is able to make nature its own. The mystery of the universe is the way it lives not only in its immensity, but in its tiniest manifestation. So the Reverend Henry White, finding with the notes of his 'common half-a-crown pitch-pipe' that the village owls hoot to their loves 'Precisely in the measure of B flat' (*Collected Poems*, Angus & Robertson, Sydney, 1967, pp. 7–8) is with his 'crumb of knowledge' as much an emblem of the questing human spirit as the most famous.

Although Stewart's light verse can descend to mere gossip and whimsy, when the image is clearly focused its lightness dissolves the ordinary into a world of adventure where anything is possible. 'Worsley Enchanted' (pp. 175–94), the series of poems on Shackleton's 1914 expedition to the Antarctic, opens with the dream of Commander Worsley that takes him to the office of the expedition in New Burlington Street:

> Commander Worsley supped his porridge,
> 'I have loved the sea, but that took courage,
> To steer a ship through a sky of sleet
> And a mad green sea in Burlington Street.
> Dreams are dreams and waking waking
> Yet still in my mind those waves are racing.'

> Stewart, *Collected Poems*, p. 175.

The four-stressed lines trip on over added light syllables and the word play of rhymes and half-rhymes. Courage becomes as one with porridge, and the skies and seas of the voyagers come home to Burlington Street. Unlike the dense particularity with which Slessor created his sea-captains at home after their voyages, Stewart's Commander exists in the dreams and generalities. As the waves go racing they maintain the determination that takes him from Burlington Street to the wastes of the south, which, in the next poem of the sequence, enter into his mind and shape it:

> White, said Worsley, and glistening, the ridgy plain
> Of sea-water, frozen; being a known substance,
> Though changed. As changes the frozen brain.
> The sky, too, uncertain. At a little distance
> A violet mist arises, fume of the frost,
> Soon turned to gold to hide the killing of the ship,
> The water black in her hold when her timbers
>   burst,
> Her body, black on the ice, raised twisting up
> On the marching floes, then dropped and
>   trampled; crushed.

Stewart, *Collected Poems*, p. 176.

The blank verse of these lines is slowed by the phrasing so that each image stands starkly by itself, yet together they form a symbol of human effort slowed and frozen. The desolate but static beauty of violet, black and gold halts the hurrying lines of the earlier verse, yet the destruction of the last lines is not final. The human voice of Worsley continues in the lines that follow, taking the reader out among the litter of men and dogs on the ice, and beyond into the abstract beauty the mind discovers in the Antarctic night and the moments when they still 'laughed like men'. The human spirit, established in the almost flippant lines of the first poem of the sequence, transforms even the waste that threatens it with oblivion. The sequence follows the crew of the ship in their trek across the ice and then by boat and foot to South Georgia, where three men emerge at the ends of the earth 'Out of the water into the sun'. This final poem is charged with the strength of purpose that has enabled Worsley to survive, and that has endowed Shackleton with almost divine strength.

Hugh McCrae and his fellows in the *Vision* group sought to populate drab human reality with the embellishments of classical mythology, replanting the literary traditions of the old world in the new. Even after Kenneth Slessor turned from this project to the real world of exploration, he still endowed his heroes with more than human qualities. Stewart's

The Doomed Ship, Shackleton Expedition
(*Photo: Frank Hurley*)

heroes, however, remain firmly human while they test their courage, endurance and insight to the ultimate. Their endurance creates for them visions that are products of their minds, and cannot change reality. They represent the universe that comforts with the idea of immortality, but remains aloof from human striving.

> . . . 'I was not alone while I watched
> But if I had fallen asleep he would not have spoken
> Nor laid on mortal flesh the touch of immortal;
> Pity is in their mind, their actions pitiless'.

Stewart, *Collected Poems*, pp. 192–3.

This universe is redeemed by the human action and thought that creates the divine, not by any metaphysical or mythical world breaking into our own.

The speaking voice in 'Worsley Enchanted' is clearly antipodean. Although the characters are English, the poem is not about transplanting a European society into the new world, or even about exploration as such, but about fulfilling a European destiny in a new world. The concept of individual achievement comes from the European Renaissance. The setting of seas and mountains empty of all human life except for the small band of venturers pitting themselves against the forces of nature excludes society and emphasises individuals creating their world by creating themselves. The poem is not just an epic of physical venturing but a celebration of the geographic and scientific endeavour that was born in the Renaissance and has made the universe a human property. This venture quite properly reaches its culmination in the Antarctic wastes at the end of the world.

In choosing this setting, both for this sequence and for his verse play *The Fire on the Snow* (Angus & Robertson, Sydney, 1944), Stewart expresses the island consciousness of a New Zealander rather than the continental consciousness of most Australian writing. The seas and the mountains are ever-present facts, constantly threatening annihilation but granting also moments of beauty and joy when the aurora gleams or the penguins assemble in solemn conclave. The joy of the men on the desolate shore of Elephant Island, and the tenderness of Oates' departure in *The Fire on the Snow*, express a corresponding inner discovery.

In *Rutherford* (Angus & Robertson, Sydney, 1962) the explorer becomes the scientist in his laboratory, 'A haunted place, this tower of knowledge,/Calm with old books but wild with thoughts unknown' (*Collected Poems*, p. 96). In this case, however, the elation of discovery is tempered with reflections on human destiny and the potential for new savagery that is opened as he unravels the mysteries of the atom. These thoughts cannot be contained by the memories of a calm childhood and the productive skills of farmer and craftsman. They are held in check at the end of the poem only by his reflections on the fellowship between scientists that breaks down all national boundaries. The poem cannot, however, reclaim this faith, for when it was published the reader already knew of the consequences of atomic power that had enlisted scientists with everyone else in insane national rivalries. The poem thus becomes a reflection on lost possibilities of co-operation rather than a celebration of particular discoveries. Stewart's concern for the tragic consequences of human division emerges directly in the ballad sequence *Glencoe* (Angus & Robertson, Sydney, 1947). Here he delves back into Scots history for the contrast of hospitality and treachery, cruelty and tenderness that is summed up in his image of a child's hand on the snow.

When Stewart turns from epic to the Australian landscape, he celebrates not so much human achievement as the contradictoriness of life in which delight exists despite our knowledge of suffering and evil. This delight is embodied in such figures as the old

dosser in springtime, with his memories of youth and love, or the mythical bunyip turned playful monster, laughing with the kookaburra even as he 'dragged him down in a hairy hand and ate his thigh-bones after'. They become images of a human spirit that survives age and horror and can still 'catch the moon by her silver hair and dance her around the sky' (*Collected Poems*, p. 228). In images of flowers or fungus he finds both good and evil, 'black secrets of the earth' alongside flowers bursting in a white dream from the grey depths of time. Even when he turns his back on the sea to explore *The Birdsville Track* (Angus & Robertson, Sydney, 1955, pp. 122–41), where the vastness of desert crushes life with drought or heat or the madness of isolation, he finds images of endurance and renewal. The Afghan with his faith, the stockman plaiting his whip, defy death. Golden butterflies mate 'over the ruins/Of the dark house that is nowhere's dead centre'. Drovers exchange jokes on the skulls of dead bullocks. The black stockman is his own hero. The dry bed of the Diamantina still holds memory of floods past and the flood 'not yet born' that 'flows down through time so slowly'. The desert and the track themselves become images of time, which, while it bears all things away, also always brings renewal. This renewal in time, and the surprising joy it brings, constitute the centre of Stewart's work, which in its variety of form and image itself embodies both the pattern and the delight he finds in the world about him.

Judith Wright

Judith Wright's poetry takes its shape from the constant struggle within both nature and history to achieve harmony. The struggle within humans can be resolved through love and in the birth of new life. While she celebrates this in 'Woman to Man', 'Woman's Song' and 'Woman to Child' (*Collected Poems 1942–1970*, Angus & Robertson, Sydney, 1971, pp. 29–31), Wright knows also that the resolution is only momentary. While the mother remains inescapably the link that joins the child to the night of her generation and unbeing, the child must find its own way into 'Pain and dark . . . passion and the day'. The unity of love leads only to further division. In 'For My Daughter' (pp. 204–5) she speaks of the time when to fulfil their humanity parent and child must walk their separate paths, each to fight the lion of her needs on her own. Nor is this inner lion any more real than the snake she finds at the heart of nature, at the very brink of the 'live water' the speaker comes to in 'The Killer' (p. 53). The snake represents death, the obverse of the new life of the child, yet its coming is also a birth: 'Black horror sprang from the dark/in a violent birth'. Rather than nurture it, she beats and strikes it till it dies, only to find it 'has slipped from . . . death aside/and vanished into my mind'. The act of killing the snake is a fact of the speaker's personal history, but the violence cannot be obliterated. It remains in her mind, a part of nature. The poem, like so much of her work, is an attempt to redeem the moment of history from time and the death it brings.

In 'The Cycads' (p. 41) Wright presents an image of the apparent defeat of death by these strange plants that have survived past their time while around them 'the rising forests of the years . . . silt with leaves the strata of first birth' (p. 41). Their unchanging survival in the midst of constant change seems a form of living death as 'cursed by age, through each chill century/they watch the shrunken moon, but never die'. Their 'cold seed' enables us to reach back into the unfathomable depths of time, but it contrasts with the warmth of the life around them, 'the brilliant birds/that cry in air one moment, and are gone' (p. 42). Attempts to evade death deny the life that exists in the moment.

Judith Wright's poetry captures living moments

Judith Wright
(*Herald & Weekly Times*)

from the past and enables them to live on in the present. The New England poems preserve the lives of the people, right back to the Aborigines, who were moulded by the country until they became part of it. The brother and sisters whose thoughts now flit between their rooms like moths, the madwoman hiding behind her hawthorn hedge, still in their age bear testimony to the strength of the life of their youth that has now leaked away through lost years. In 'South of My Days' (pp. 20–22), all this history is gathered together in the memories of old Dan, serving him as a blanket or a hive of honey as age lurches in around him in his cottage. The winter that makes the bony slopes of the tableland wince is also his age, but that age carries the life of his years and so gives promise of the renewal of further summers in their wave of rambler roses and the lives of those who hear even if they do not listen. For them, the country and its stories will still go walking in their sleep.

While these memories of the past make the country their own for the white inhabitants, the Aborigines remain outside this new consciousness. Like little Josie in 'Half-Caste Girl' (p. 19), 'buried under the bright moon', they are shut out of the present by the stone walls of a history that denies them even succession. In 'Nigger's Leap' (p. 166) the Aborigines remain as a slightly guilty memory hidden by 'the night that tided up the cliffs'. That night may have carried the same question for the whites as for the Aborigines, but their death has denied the opportunity to answer it. At the heart of Australian history the Aborigines remain a dark absence:

Never from earth again the coolamon
or thin black children dancing like the shadows
of saplings in the wind. Night lips the harsh
scarp of the tableland and cools its granite.
Night floods us suddenly as history
that has sunk many islands in its good time.

Wright, *Collected Poems*, p. 166.

The quiet rhythm of the lines is of mourning, not harmony. By their death they separate 'us' from nature, from the land that gave them life and that their memory still holds. Until this breach is redeemed, the whites cannot make history and are threatened by the same flooding of darkness and oblivion, leaving not so much as a bora ring to keep their possession of the land.

Wright's concern with this guilt at the heart of Australian history is a continuing theme in her work. In *Generations of Men* (Oxford University Press, Melbourne, 1959) she tells the epic story of her family's struggle over three generations to establish themselves in Australia, first in the Hunter Valley, then in Queensland, and finally in New England. It is a story of achievement, from the early solidity of the 'great house of cool stone corridors and high-ceilinged rooms . . . summer-roses, lemon-hedge, lavender and sage and queer herbs for *tissanes* . . .' (p. 2) to the house where Grandmother May Wright at the end of the book recreates the comfort of her own grandparents. Between these points, it takes us through the years of Albert Wright's lonely toil, his marriage and hardships in Queensland, and the uncertainties of his work to establish himself in the sheep country of the tableland. Despite the title, the figure at the centre of the story is the grandmother. May Wright. The book tells of the transplantation of European style to a new country, the harsh testing of that style against the realities of the environment, and the way the Wrights slowly learnt to adjust to the nature of the country until they could use it again to support the elegance of the old order. Yet, at the end, May Wright remains insecure, threatened by the encroachments of new settlers, needing to jeopardise her achievements to purchase still more land. She is sure in her own achievement, but it still remains infirmly rooted in the land.

In establishing a replica of European society, the Wrights learnt to use the land, but they still did not belong to it. The Aborigines had played no part in their story except as occasional helpers or problems to the people displacing them from their lands. The Wrights treat them compassionately, but to May Wright they remain incomprehensible. She feels repulsed by them with 'the kind of fear that had prompted the white men to kill and kill, not because of the little damage the blacks could do them materially, but because of a threatened deeper damage, the undermining of a precarious way of life that existed by denying what the aboriginals took for granted', (p. 89). Although the land belongs to May and her people, they cannot belong to the land.

Twenty years later, in *Cry for the Dead* (Oxford University Press, Melbourne, 1981), Wright sought to overcome this dispossession by retelling the story of settlement as it must have seemed to the Aborigines. Because the Aborigines left no documents, she has to use the records of the white settlers. Wright uses these writings to reverse her earlier picture of steady progress. She shows a society founded on crime and punishment, gaining its wealth by the exploitation and destruction of the land and its people.

Cry for the Dead opens with a description of a country supporting a rich Aboriginal life of song and ceremony, trade and social innovation. This life is torn apart, first by the diseases and social disorder spread from districts already subjected to European settlement, and then by the white settlers themselves and their brutal weaponry. Judith Wright tells the story both of the resistance of the Aborigines to the destruction of their economy and society, and of the consequent extermination of the tribes who stood in the way of the white advance. In the end, not even their languages can be traced. The tragedy was not so much an act of deliberate genocide as the inevitable consequence of cultural arrogance and incomprehension, driven by the greed that disrupts all natural harmony.

Judith Wright grew up between the wars. Her early work, published in the post-war years, reflects the growing consciousness of the specifically Australian environment and the history of its human occupation. In her later work, this interest is first localised in the specific relations of woman, man and child as they create new life that then enters its own history, and then generalised into the whole interaction between the human and the environment. In 'Eve to her Daughters' (*Collected Poems*, pp. 236) the root of the tragic incompatibility is seen in the determination of Adam to create himself as master of the universe. First he determines to control it mechanically to serve his ends, and so 'he has turned himself into God,/who is faultless, and doesn't exist'. The tragic breach arises from the self-certainty that closes itself from nature, the other. In much of her most recent poetry the refusal to accept this other is the source of the disaster. The answer does not lie merely in a retreat to nature, which itself contains the violence that man employs against it, but in the love that knows the world without illusion yet still has the courage to give without demanding. In contemporary society Wright finds this detachment and unity only in isolated moments and images. Bureaucracy excludes the wholeness of human response from its neat vision of the world. In 'The City' (p. 278), the poet finds herself excluded:

> No doubt this explains why all my applications
> seem to remain unanswered.
> All I get from the man behind the grille
> is the same old rhyme, 'Your case isn't covered by
>   our regulations,
> but we'll consider your representations.'
> Nothing comes in the post.

Wright, Collected Poems, p. 278.

The destruction of language leaves humanity with neither nature nor history. Until the alienation between humanity and nature is healed, human nature will continue to be divided and suppressed. In the new world of Australia, the whites will continue to be strangers to the land and themselves.

David Campbell

Campbell also writes of the life created by man in encounters with nature, whether in the form of woman or of land. Rather than reducing woman to an object for man's use, Campbell's poetry shows how both the land and woman demand man's surrender of self as the price of yielding their bounty and completing his self. His work, both stories and poetry, deals with the tension between the urge to get out and explore new territories and the need for the comfort of a home. A grazier and athlete himself, Campbell was a member of one of the pastoral families whose history was an attempt to satisfy these two needs. His poetry carries their work of settlement further as he creates his life in the image of the land.

In Campbell's war poems, the remembered security of home and its extensions gives measure to the perils of battle and stability within it. 'Soldier's Song' (*Selected Poems*, Angus & Robertson, Sydney, 1978, p. 10) revolves around the image the soldier clings to of the Murray as home. It remains 'in the mind/And at a word it flows', sustaining life in deserts and in tropics. In 'Men in Green' (pp. 11–12), on the

other hand, the contrast is between the safety of the speaker's plane, in which he ferries the soldiers to the front, and the incommunicable experience of the jungle they have kept back with their 'fifteen spitting tommy-guns'. Their going out from the bright world of the summer sun into the dark where 'Nature had met them in the night/And stalked them in the day' is the price paid for the speaker's security, which is undermined by the remembered men in green.

These poems are, however, atypical. His work at this time is more concerned with rural Australia, with the tasks of working with sheep and dogs and the creation of the home. 'The End of Exploring' (p. 14) opens with a call to the world, and closes with the end of the journey, both finish and purpose, as the traveller returns with 'love to dog-bark, gate, and sweet cock-crow'. The homely images of achieved domestic comfort contrast with the breadth of the world in the opening stanza, where the language sprawls wide and easy like the gate and the road running from it:

> See! down the road by the brown tree
> The gate leans wide like morning. Here's winter's
>   green;
> Here the summer's bleached affairs; and here
>   between
> Rain work and wind work, the road winds free.

Campbell, Selected Poems, p. 14.

The freedom of the opening lines is, however, quickly caught by the tight phrase of the winter green, and the summer leads into the reminder of the hard 'Rain work and wind work' that stand between the call of the road and the affluence of the shed and the dog, the grain and the sheep of the next stanzas. The work is both that done by wind and rain, and that of the farmer to check their ravages. The achievement is both a human and a natural product. While the road calls, the work waits, and the time that allows both choices still brings the explorer to the same end.

The poems of the land capture the regular round of the seasons, bringing their different work but also the moments of rest when the land enters into the hearts of those who work her. 'Night Sowing' (p. 27) brings together the images of cultivation and love, and the poems 'Droving' (p. 58) and 'On the Birth of a Son' (p. 54) extend this image to embrace not only the unity in time of love but also the unity through time of the renewing family. The boy's birth is marked by the fall of the fence his father has so carefully constructed, but this fall also lets in the view, the landscape becoming the image of life that follows a 'line/Not of our choice at all'. The line runs free, yet leads to the same cycle as 'My tall son' who

> Droves with his girl the white-faced steers
> From the high country, as we would years
> Ago beneath a daylight moon . . .
> And it seems in spite of death and war
> Time's not so desperate after all.

> Campbell, *Selected Poems*, p. 58.

Work and love unite the human and natural in a cycle that goes beyond history.

Campbell senses the past as a cycle of continuity rather than as a history of change. The individual makes a life rather than a society. Appropriately, he named one of his sequences of country poems 'Cocky's Calendar' (pp. 37–42) and another 'Works And Days' (pp. 74–78). Both titles refer to earlier works of pastoral, but the poems locate the sentiments firmly in the present.

The first sequence provides an antipodean and unsolemn counterpart of Edmund Spenser's sixteenth-century English *The Shepheardes Calendar* of love-sick swains. While Spenser's Colin complains of love that leads him astray and consumes his fire, Campbell more robustly sees it as leading to children who may

> . . . grow up strong,
> Got while the thrush drew out his song,
> And love like you and I when we
> Lie beneath the wattle tree.

> Campbell, *Selected Poems*, p. 41.

His song ends, not with the drear of winter, but with the hawk who 'rides at peace in hurrying air', holding songs and tempests and 'all of time in his still stare.'

'Works and Days' (pp. 74–78) is an antipodean counterpart of the classical work in which the Greek poet Hesiod places the practical lore of farming in the framework of the mythology of the five ages of the world, from which he derives his belief in the moral value and necessity of work. Campbell's work

is not, however, didactic, but a matter-of-fact account of the joys and tribulations of the farmer's lot. These include the bitter times of lambing, when

> Some poor bastard's copping the crows. Then it blows
> A blizzard — lambs hunched in cat-humps behind each stump
> And boulder; and next day it's like a fall of snow.
> There's nothing flatter than a dead lamb.

> Campbell, *Selected Poems*, p. 76.

They also, however, offer moments of 'loafing', when the world offers itself as a reward for work, and 'instead of crows, the high larks are singing'. The morality, like the reward, is implicit.

Campbell is not merely a pastoral poet, although, as he says, even his dream poems have their link with the country. His sequence 'Starting from Central Station' (pp. 105–111) is a reflective account of the history that brought his family from Scotland to Australia. Although like 'The End of Exploring' the chronicle finishes with images of the settled estate, the achievement is troubled by his sense of having failed his father. The last poem, like an epilogue, brings the author back with only his memories to protect him from the suburban reality that has succeeded his father's achievements, 'a brick veneer, a bungalow,/In the drive like a biscuit box instead of a house'. In 'Branch of Dodona' (pp. 97–103) he offers an irreverent retelling of the story of Jason and the Golden Fleece in which the timeless cycle belongs as much in a contemporary present as the romantic past. In 'Hotel Marine' (p. 90) an urban present dissolves into an illusion that is at one with dreams. The final sequence of the collection 'Deaths and Pretty Cousins' (pp. 131–54) takes us behind the respectable surfaces into the affectionate scandals of a country family. All these poems, like his short stories, are marked by delight at the manifold ways in which life manifests itself, its own patterns mocking the forms in which we try to confine it. But the writing remains alert to the work that lies behind the delight.

Campbell writes of a settled Australia in which the European tradition has become fully assimilated. The tradition is, however, essentially one of the free landholder able to choose the terms of his own work.

Like Marshall's bushmen and women, the tradition belongs to the past, even though the work of the countryman may renew it constantly through the returning seasons. The work of renewal demands attention to the environment, but it offers no engagement with the wider social forces that first brought the settlers to their country, nor with those that isolate them from urban society and threaten to dislodge them from the world of their creation. The poetry renews a myth as old as Hesiod and as new as the age of the squatters, but the myth speaks for only a small part of the Australian experience.

John Blight

Like David Campbell, John Blight has been characterised too narrowly on the basis of the content of his early work. Although he had published earlier work set in Queensland, his two books of sea-sonnets published in 1963 and 1968, and the description of the speaking voice as 'beachcomber' established him as a kind of hermit poet writing from his solitude by the sea. Although the poems are written from the refuge the shore and the sea offer him from society, they have none of the mystic or meditative qualities their location might suggest. Rather, they dramatise the conflict the speaker wages with society to retain his integrity and independence.

This conflict begins as resistance to the demand to become one with the mass 'for the common good', to be 'lined up with the crass, the crude,/garbed in the tunic of nationhood . . . drilled, ruled with an iron rod . . . stood up for country and for good' (*My Beachcombing Days*, Angus & Robertson, Sydney, 1968, p. 15).

Resistance requires first the clear sight to see the other as it is, for 'if we cannot see/anything but the shoal, we, in our world, must swim/and swerve with the turn of the shoal, live lives akin to them' (p. 14). The speaker identifies not with the shoal but with the shark, 'the sea's international crook', and admires the creatures that follow the distinctive law of their own nature. The cunjevoi clings to the rocks and makes its whole being a squirt. The sea-birds keep their distance, refuse to 'own us' or 'sing our music'. While the sea and its creatures remain outside us, it offers material for metaphor and fancy. Through fancy and metaphor, the mind makes even

the sea its own, as the beachcomber makes himself from his seashore gatherings.

The individual lives, however, not only by mind but by pleasure. His image is the rotund sailor who opens this collection and who has become wholly his laughter. He is also the gourmand who enjoys the fish recipes of the second poem, where the delight of taste is joined to the practical lore of cooking. Eating, cooking and laughter become images of Blight's own use of language as a way of mastering and consuming the world as well as of presenting it to others. Through language he both makes and gains control of his experience. These elements are brought together in the poem 'The Turtle' (p. 58). The rhymes trip on in a playful sequence of five, four, three and two to fill the statutory fourteen of the sonnet form, thus making the form itself a kind of play. Within this form, the turtle becomes an image of both gustatory pleasure and the chef's skill as he

> . . . garnishes dishes to make lip on lip
> smack with a gourmand's ambition to tip
> down all of the flavours which the tide's rip
> stirs in an oyster, or a creature like this.

> Blight, *Beachcombing Days*, p. 58.

These riches provide the standard by which to measure the human indecencies that try to capture the sea, pollute its harbours and deface its bays with 'their customary tendencies of glass and gilt' (p. 71). The attempt to fasten Australian coasts, towns and islands down under English names and to impose on them European ways of seeing is merely another form of this denial of the intrinsic quality of their existence. Eating, cooking and poetry establish control through the play that establishes the self by entering into dialogue with the other. The denial of the other is not a form of control but a denial of ourselves.

This denial becomes a more important theme in Blight's later work. In his sequence of 'New City Poems' (*Hart*, Nelson, Melbourne, 1975, pp. 11–18) the city itself and the bricks it is built from become the image of denial. The result of the denial of life is symbolised by the figure of the title poem, 'Hart', which is itself like a novel, condensed into the two pages of the moment of the speaker's death. Hart's death disturbs the city crowd, and costs his partner money, but they draw back from the spot and avoid the fact. Denying Hart's death, they deny his life, and therefore their own.

The title poem of Blight's next collection, *Pageant for a Lost Empire* (Nelson, Melbourne, 1977) expresses the same theme through the life of a man who, like Hart, defines himself by his achievements, only to find they have isolated him from the living. The speaker is one or both of an imperial governor and a business tycoon. In either role he manipulates others, eventually to lose any touch with reality. The speaker lost in his mansion or eyrie becomes Australia, and his blue shirt the symbol of the toil that has built the present only to be dispossessed. This last symbol makes the whole poem an elegy for the European civilisation that has made the world its own but loses itself. In 'A Ball Game' (pp. 102–3) this loss is in turn generalised into the ultimate decay and death of the world itself, which the speaker contemplates with equanimity as merely part of a glorious cosmic ball game. However, this perception of the otherness of the universe and cosmic time no longer brings the affirmation of self, but merely resignation.

The collection does not close on this note, but on the sequence 'Emily — a poem of remorse' (pp. 135–44) in which the speaker looks back on a marriage that ended in the failure of divorce and, possibly, murder. In the end, as the speaker awaits death in a prison that may also be his own self, he reflects on the achievement of his partner's life. He has been her sacrificial beast — at once victim and killer — but now his thoughts free her from time and give her life permanency. His final thought of her is that 'Like a tempest or/a fire, she compassed all'. As he has reflected on her absence

> . . . She shall
> be always above (after
> the smoke has cleared), over deserts,
> over the ice, or the widest
> tropic sea.

Blight, *Pageant*, p. 142.

This is not the romantic fallacy of beauty outlasting time, but the recognition of the power of language to create the other that establishes our own meaning.

It is the reverse of the mindless action that elsewhere Blight finds as the central characteristic of contemporary Australia.

A.D. Hope

A.D. Hope, born in 1907, has lived through two world wars and seen the collapse of revolutionary hopes into tyranny and civilisation into barbarism. His poetry seeks to contain the destructive forces of human nature within the recurring order of myth and the controlling forms of language. Douglas Stewart and Judith Wright find an ultimate source of harmony in the created world. Hope, however, depicts a world in which the power of human reason barely serves to contain the passions that maintain life but constantly threaten to tear it apart. At the centre of his poetry lie the figures of imperial Adam and mother Eve in their many guises, creating in joy only to see the sexual lightning stroke produce the monstrous life of the murderer. Those who accept the paradox can control it with laughter and reason. Those who turn away from it become part of 'the chatter of cultured apes' a decadent civilisation has substituted for life.

The language of Hope's poetry is most commonly controlled in discursive modes employing the five-syllabled iambic line in a variety of rhyming schemes. Unlike the eighteenth-century writers who provide his models, he rarely uses rhyme to accentuate the thought pattern, but rather to underpin the flow of narrative or discourse. His poems move not as a series of propositions but as unfolding narratives that tie the individual images within the total pattern of the argument. The poetry convinces by logic rather than surprising by the force of experience suddenly wrenching language into new patterns. The formal pattern of the language becomes the moral framework of order through which we are able to contemplate new and often horrifying dimensions of experience. The alternative, modernism's surrender to the experience, is in Hope's eyes a descent into a barbarism of poetry equivalent to the barbarisms of the world it confronts.

In 'The Dinner' (*Collected Poems*, 1930–1965, Angus & Robertson, Sydney, 1966, pp. 49–50) Hope reveals the disintegrating possibilities implicit in the most ordinary of events. The poem, written in the most conventional rhymed couplets, opens with a stanza in which the order of the verse invokes an order of civilisation that rises to the divine. The first line mentions angels, the evening brings 'a new heaven and a new earth', the dressing of linen, silver and crystal of the table brings a grace to the food and the wine. Then one gesture transforms the scene from order to savagery:

> Delicate, young and cradled in delight,
> You take your seat and bare your teeth to bite —

The reality of the carnivore appears behind the forms of ceremony and beauty. By the end of the poem, the speaker has become absorbed in a vision of total savagery:

> Hollow with rage and fear, I crouch and stare,
> And hear their great jaws strip and crush and
>   chew,
> And know the flesh they rend and tear is you.

Hope, Collected Poems, pp. 49–50.

The visions of horror do not cancel the scene of the gracious dinner that they succeed, but express possibilities that constantly threaten our veneer of civilisation.

A poem such as 'Imperial Adam' (pp. 83–94) combines the same iambic pentameters in the four-lined rhyming stanza of lyrical verse. Rather than the flow of narrative of 'The Dinner', this form presents a sequence of images, each with room to expand into a complete thought. The first stanza presents a complete picture of Adam, his puzzlement and the footmarks of Jahweh, of God. It is not merely an image, but a dramatic moment in the context of its place. The successive stanzas build a sequence of such scenes, through which the poet is able to create abrupt switches of mood as he views the episode from new perspectives. The first three stanzas suggest mystery, first of the advent of God and then the presence of woman. The next four move from the sensuous generosity all nature brings to the occasion to the ridiculous delight of the act of sex itself. Then, in the climactic moment, joy turns to terror and triumph, to dissolve again immediately into the tender fecundity of the whole of creation that stands waiting around. Just as terror awakes

in the moment of conception, so birth lays the first murderer on earth.

The following poem, 'Pasiphae' (pp. 84–5), is a pagan counterpart of 'Imperial Adam'. In this poem, the union of woman and beast fills her with monstrous life and with triumph. This establishes a general pattern that goes beyond the specifically Judaic connotations of the story of Adam and Eve. The poems are not concerned with notions of sin and disobedience, but with the act of conception itself that unites not only male and female, but the animal and divine elements of humanity. It is, in the strict sense, a moment of awe in which the human attains both its highest and its lowest potential. Hope returns constantly to the theme that the renewal of life is at once fulfilment and terror, as each new life both contains our power and escapes our control. This, for him, is the original sin to which all humans are heirs, and from which no saviour can free us. Each generation is doomed to live out the same pattern.

Another element of this pattern is shown in 'The Wandering Islands' (pp. 26–7). This poem is also written in the four-lined stanzas that provide a sequence of episodes rather than the logic of argument. The islands represent both individual humans and the mind, 'the shipwrecked sailor' that inhabits each of them. The only contact one ever makes with another is when they clash in the moment of love, a 'casual thunder' that nevertheless hurts, an 'instant of fury' that leaves 'the crash of ruined cliffs, the smother/And swirl of foam' as they fall apart. Although the poem finishes with renewed loneliness and despair as the sailor realises there is no rescue, nothing outside himself to turn to, the moment of love remains as a fact that has broken 'the long isolation of the heart'. The poem expresses the dilemma that we are only ourselves and alone, and yet the only meaning we have comes from others. The whole of Hope's work explores the means we use — passion, reason, violence — in an attempt to escape from this dilemma.

Hope depicts another aspect of duality in 'The Martyrdom of St Teresa' (pp. 63–4). In this poem he shortens his line to four feet, giving the verse a musical rather than a discursive quality:

> There was a sudden croon of lilies
> Drifting like music through the shop;

The bright knives flashed with heavenly malice,
The choppers lay in wait to chop . . .

Hope, *Collected Poems*, pp. 63–4.

The suggestion of devotion in the first half of the verse is contradicted by the second part with the same kind of *oxymoron*, the deliberate contradiction we find in the phrase 'heavenly malice'. The poem goes on to disclose that the occasion is in fact devotional as the 'little nuns of her foundation/arrived on foot, by mule or cart' to get pieces of their Mother Superior as relics for their worship. The play of poetry and knives masks the fact of butchery, and a passion for the divine becomes a thirst for blood. The desire for the eternal life of divine love becomes, in effect, a longing for death. Yet the triviality of the posthumous butchery of Teresa's body is irrelevant to the achievement of her life, in which this 'so small a saint' nevertheless had made kings fear and popes hate without herself knowing fear or hate.

The comedy of 'The Martyrdom of St Teresa' comes from the disproportion between the nuns busily carting away bits of the body and the true significance of her life. The language of bureaucracy, which the poem ridicules as the antithesis of life, conceals from them what they are really doing. Yet the true martyrdom of Teresa was to be forced to become a member of the bureaucracy, tied down by its language as she channelled her vision into running a chain of convents. Bureaucracy represents those everyday duties and ties of existence that finally deny life until, as in 'Crossing the Frontier' (pp. 200–2), it can be recovered only by willing the death contemporary society seeks to deny. Love and art are both deadly because they break the fetters with which we seek to bind life.

Australia, far from being a new land free from the wrongs and guilts of Europe, is in Hope's poetry a home only for bureaucracy, where the emotions and superstitions that give meaning to life elsewhere are drowned in the sands of stupidity ('Australia', p. 13). In this early poem, Australia becomes a metaphor of the contemporary world, even its colours an image of the impersonal 'drab' uniforms of modern war. The succeeding stanzas develop the argument through images of the emptiness at the centre, the living water drowned in the sand of stupidity, the monotonous tribes surviving without life, the five cities like teeming sores. The whole is summed up in the culminating image of a

. . . vast parasite robber-state
Where second-hand Europeans pullulate
Timidly on the edge of alien shores.

Hope, *Collected Poems*, p. 13.

The poem then turns around in two stanzas that transform the desert from a wasteland of mind to a source of spirit, the 'Arabian desert of the human mind' and set the savage scarlet and green of the land, colours that suggest the force of primitive life, as a spring bringing life denied in the learned chatter of older lands.

The hopeful conclusion of 'Australia' is not a trust in the land itself, but a hope that its remoteness will enable its inhabitants to observe the older world with eyes unclouded by the miasma emitted by the decay of history. Through his life's work Hope uses his antipodean vantage not as a point of departure of explorations into new territories, but as a place in which he can reclaim the mythology of Europe for the present. From the cold plains of Canberra he converses with the muses of the warm Mediterranean and, like Borges, relives the passions inscribed in bitter nordic runes. His life's project is described in his 'Letter from Rome' (pp. 129–48). This poem, which among much else describes the joys and endurance of a victim of the modern tourist industry, explains the reason for his absurd pilgrimage to find the European roots of the tree of life which, in 'dumb continents below the Line' takes on such 'a different pattern and design'. He finds the answer at Nemi, oldest of holy places, where a knowledge of the self transcends all the absurdity and conflict of reason and passion, mind and body:

I was possessed, and what possessed me there
Was Europe's oldest ritual of prayer.

Hope, *Collected Poems*, p. 144.

The moment brings him an apprehension of the spiritual qualities that evade the confines of any creed or doctrine, as body prays without 'intention' and 'mind by the bare force of its assent'. The moment is one out of time that nevertheless gives time meaning.

Yet Hope's letter does not leave the reader with this elevated view of Europe. The poem finishes with a commination or denunciation of the modern image of hell, 'accenti d'ira, orribili favelle', the noise of motor bikes that

> . . . fill with hideous and inhuman noise
> All your once pleasant cities of the plain.
> It is the curse of Hell that it destroys
> Good of the intellect;

Hope, Collected Poems, p. 146.

His unshielded antipodean awareness is able to find the source of its spirit in Europe, but is not deceived by its betrayal in modern reality. In his later work Hope plunders the Europe of myth for its beauty, returning Europe's compliment, but he never loses the detachment of his antipodean standpoint.

Finally, Hope's poetry celebrates the human achievement that transcends the duality of life to create from it, like Teresa, lasting works of the mind and spirit. His 'Ode on the Death of Pius the Twelfth' (pp. 209–11) uses the splendour of the Massachusetts woods in the fall as an image of old age transfigured by an epiphany of light flooding the heart with strange illumination. His book *The Age of Reason* (Melbourne University Press, Melbourne, 1985) recaptures from history inconspicuous moments of achievement over suffering and death. His poem 'On an Engraving by Casserius' (*New Poems 1965–1969*, Angus & Robertson, Sydney, 1969, pp. 12–16) shows the literal transcendence of death by the skill of the engraver and the science of the dissectors whose work he depicted. The work of these pioneering anatomists combines art and science to produce a knowledge that, unlike the science of today, embodies general truth without dissolving the singularity of the individual:

> Bodied in this one woman, he makes us see
> The shadow of his anatomical laws.
> An artist's vision animates the whole,
> Shines through the scientist's detailed scrutiny
> And links the person and the abstract cause.

Hope, New Poems, p. 13.

This image of the general in the particular might well describe Hope's own achievement. The steadiness of his line governs, with reason and laughter, the disintegrating passion with which humans seek to escape their duality. This duality in turn is embodied in the myths that are constantly enacted but must be remade in words in each generation so that we can escape from their disintegrating force into understanding. Through reason and myth, passion is controlled to create the works of art, intellect and spirit that produce our harmony. Through recognising 'the cannibal longings in the blood' we can avoid the descent into barbarism until, like the bird on its last migration, we give the earth the tiny burden of our death.

Although Hope's poetry shows the ancient dualities being constantly re-enacted through time, it is modern in its confrontation with the contemporary manifestation of horror in the mass, of which bureaucracy is an expression. It belongs, however, to no place. While Australia is home to the poet it is merely one more part of a world united by a common fear and oppression.

He eventually overcomes the duality between the self and the world that threatens it with annihilation, by withdrawing, like Pius, into contemplation where all is resolved into an original harmony of being. The passion is not spent, but takes its place in the greater harmony reason creates from nature.

James McAuley

McAuley sang of a universe of honeycomb and laurel, where the poet's bay leaves of praise would match the sweetness of the life around. At the centre of the sweetness, however, he found a canker of evil constantly threatening destruction and disintegration. As he could find nothing in the universe or in the human mind with the power to destroy or contain it, he turned in despair to the God whose grace continually renewed a celebration of innocence. He is a lyricist rather than discursive like Hope. The formal metres of his verse serve not to control the violence of passion within the order of reason, but to show the everchanging but always secure order of God. Yet the poet's need for the security of faith was not always met by the event. Jarring lines in the political argument of 'A Letter to John Dryden' or the didactic

James McAuley
(*Angus & Robertson*)

narration of *Captain Quiros* betray the will to believe rather than the achievement of faith.

McAuley's earlier poetry moves between the poles of love and fear. 'Monologue', a love lyric, becomes in its second part a poem of tender eroticism in which lust, far from being evil, fulfils the promise made by love (*Collected Poems 1936–1970*, Angus & Robertson, Sydney, 1971, pp. 3–4). At the end of the poem the speaker finds not the death of extinction, but the loss of the solitary self in the wider brightness of the beloved.

Yet human love in McAuley's work offers only momentary fulfilment. The country itself disturbs him, its familiarity speaking to him only of unease and sterility:

> There the blue-green gums are a fringe of remote
>   disorder
> And the brown sheep poke at my dreams along
>   the hillsides;
> And there in the soil, in the season, in the shifting
>   airs,
> Comes the faint sterility that disheartens and
>   derides.

>   McAuley, 'Envoi', *Collected Poems*, p. 6.

The land becomes the image of its people, 'hard-eyed, kindly, with nothing inside them . . . independent but you could not call them free'. He finds himself fitted to the land, finding in it at times even beauty and order, and the life-bringing gush of artesian waters. These, however, bring not the fulness of life but only the 'fretful seed', a promise of trouble as much as of hope.

Just as the land resents the promise of the seed, so in 'Gnostic Prelude' (pp. 6–7) the awakening of individual sexuality betrays the 'gnosis of the womb', the instinctive spiritual wholeness of the child. Sexuality brings the adult's awareness of division, and is described in images of a 'monstrous light . . . red and streaked with pain' that destroys the 'Dark Eden' of innocence. The search for love becomes a flight from the 'mad and malevolent eyes' of consciousness in vain search of the sweet comfort of the womb. Love is not the loss of self in a greater unity, but extinction.

The personal unease with sexuality expands into despair at the failure and disintegration of modern civilisation in the two major poems of McAuley's first collection, 'The Blue Horses' (pp. 7–9) and 'The Incarnation of Sirius' (pp. 23–4). The first, suggested by paintings of the German painter Franz Marc, sets the image of fierce blue horses against the industrial structure of the city. The mysterious sound of horses' hooves comes at night to the sleeping city. The horses bring from the hills the promise to 'open and expand' the city to the infinite spaces and light of the world. The city, however, denies them. Its own creative potential, shown as 'delicate cranes manoeuvre/Like giant birds above their load', is, however, contradicted by their function, to 'furnish supplies of war', and by the division at the heart of the city between those who work and those who possess. The visionary hooves of the horses cannot break through with their dance of life. As the mills weave their universe of decay, love is denied and the city becomes only a slum culture shaken by the scream of the Blue Horses but unable to hear their message.

In 'The Incarnation of Sirius', McAuley describes the actual destruction of the doomed world of 'The Blue Horses'. The 'great anagram of God', the Dog Star Sirius, which is the 'monstrous form of God's antagonist', destroys the laws holding the universe together and flares out as a blazing candelabrum bearing anarchy. A cyclic event, it is both outside our control and a testimony to the order of time that will bear it away just as it brings it. The winking star at the close of the poem is a threat, but also an assurance that even the worst destruction finds a place in a greater order.

In McAuley's later books, published after he had embraced Catholicism, this order becomes the immediate subject. The nature of this order is suggested by the title of McAuley's second collection, *A Vision of Ceremony* (Angus & Robertson, Sydney, 1956), and explored in the major poem in the collection, 'Celebration of Divine Love' (*Collected Poems*, pp. 73–6).

This is a sequence of fifteen-line stanzas, each with a different pattern of rhymes, tantalisingly suggesting a formal order that never settles. This pattern suggests the underlying concept of the poem, which traces the universal history of humankind in the life of the individual. Each stage is both new and an incarnation of unchanging creative love. In the deliberation of this art McAuley, like Hope, simultaneously rejects the romantic belief in the unmediated outpouring of inspiration and the modernist attempt to allow form to grow out of content. Instead, the carefully crafted form provides the vehicle for the meaning that becomes embodied in it.

Each separate stanza of the 'Celebration' presents a stage of the history of the soul in a static form like a medieval illumination, where each detail both contributes to the total design and refers to a further level of allegorical meaning. The first seven stanzas represent the seven ages of man, and the eighth forms a kind of coda from the perspective of the saints in eternity. This final stanza turns from description to invocation, calling on the souls of the contemplative to keep their faith that wanderers may still find their way to the truth.

The poem does not argue for God, but shows life without Him and then demonstrates the effect of His coming, setting everything into its place in His divine order. The poem justifies the troubles of history and personal existence by catching them all up into a single timeless pattern. Yet this consummation, taking part outside time, sitll leaves unresolved the problem of how we live with our history within time.

McAuley tackles this question in his verse epistle, 'A Letter to John Dryden' (*Collected Poems*, pp. 85–95). This poem starts from the observation that the worst Dryden feared has now come to pass in the mind of an age that is 'loud, indistinct, moronic'. The epistle demonstrates this collapse of standards in every part of life. The tenets of Christianity have been forgotten, secular schools and universities impart knowledge without wisdom, political passions keep alive the fires of hate once kindled by Protestant enthusiasts; believers are hopelessly confused; the only consistent principle is the rejection of the spirit in favour of materialism. The consequences of this spiritual indifference and moral relativism include the tyranny of an uninstructed majority, divorce, crime, suicide and abortion. The moral vacuum is such that even communists are allowed to teach! The public spurns the only alternative, a society built on the vision of the incarnate word. Yet the vision of this society is kept alive by the few who see with the eyes of faith the map of an undistorted and unsimplified world:

> . . . tranquil, vast, created mystery,
> In all its courts of being laid awake,
> Flooded with uncreated light for mercy's sake.

> McAuley, *Collected Poems*, p. 95.

The confrontation with the actual world leads, therefore, like the 'Celebration of Divine Love', into a timeless vision.

For us to accept this vision as a practical basis for living requires that we accept McAuley's characterisation of our times as being true historically and logically as well as metaphorically. The poem requires too many leaps of faith to allow this acceptance. The easy image of the abortionist as a symbol of modern hostility to life becomes an argument against the social acceptance of divorce. The condition of the modern world is attributed to a lack of true knowledge, but uninstructed 'Humility' and 'Serene content that does not ask for more' are put as sufficient answers. Since the poet has framed his poem as an argument, he must be judged not just by the power of his vision but by his logic and evidence. He fails the latter test.

Like Hope, McAuley seeks to renew ancient

myths. He does not trace them to their European source, but seeks to plant them in an Australia free of the taints of the old world. His epic poem, *Captain Quiros* (*Collected Poems*, pp. 111–76) is an attempt to renew the vision of Australia as *La Austrialia del Espiritu Santu*, the Great South Land of the Holy Spirit of Spanish imagination. Yet, for all the life he brings to the visionary Quiros, the abiding impression of the poem is the impossibility of sustaining his unworldly vision in the actual world of human passion, fear and ambition. The renaissance of which Quiros and his voyage were a part destroyed the possibilities of a world populated by 'simple toilers of the plain'. The material conditions of the voyage, which McAuley preferred to despise, were as incompatible with the leader's hopes as was McAuley's vision with the realities of modern life. Both sought escape rather than transformation.

While McAuley's most ambitious projects fall short of their ambition, or at best fail to engage with the modern world, his lyrics realise his vision. The pastoral 'In the Huon Valley' (*Collected Poems*, p. 200) finds a celebration of fulness in the world of modern commercial activity:

> Something is gathered in,
> Worth the lifting and stacking;
> Apples roll through graders,
> The sheds are noisy with packing.

McAuley, Collected Poems, p. 200.

The vision is contained in the 'something' that, surrounded by busy labour, still offers testament of the existential value of the apples that are the cause of the activity. Similarly, in 'Pieta' (*Collected Poems*, pp. 178–9) the pared lines of the lyric, which exclude anything except the essential facts and gestures, embody the faith that enables the speaker to face one of the most terrible of experiences, the loss of a new-born child.

Hal Porter

Porter represents the Australian as tourist, never happier than when about to embark on a ship or train to leave his country, embarrassed by his compatriots abroad and sustained in foreign parts by the

Hal Porter

knowledge that he will eventually return home.

In Porter's 'Answers to the Funny, Kind Man' he describes his main preoccupation as being with the 'Many wonders, and none of them more wonderful than man', which he explains means 'men, women, and children, and their cats and cattle and catastrophes, superb slums and bashed-up abbeys, gardens and bomb-droppings, off-moments and on-moments, glamorous vices and threadbare virtues, blood-chilling nobilities and heart-warming blunders, their charm and wickedness, their unending variety and fatiguing sameness, their alarming depth and their more alarming shallowness' (Mary Lord (ed.), *Portable Australian Authors: Hal Porter*, University of Queensland Press, St Lucia, 1980, p. 386.). He claims to lack imagination, so that his stories are all taken direct from life, transmuted 'from personal experience, or the witnessed experience of others, direct into what reads . . . like true-to-life fiction'. His immediate preoccupation at the time of writing was 'with Australians themselves . . . getting them down on paper with unequivocal distinctness, warts and haloes, faults and powers'. These negative disclaimers themselves suggest the tourist of life, the Watcher, to use the figure of his autobiograpy, who observes others, getting them down on paper to satisfy himself by keeping them at a distance. His prose transmutes life into a fiction of style and colour, but static. The figures in his work are objects in a museum, assembled in brilliant tableaux encased in the commentary of the collector.

These qualities are evident in his first novel, *A Handful of Pennies* (*Portable Australian Authors: Hal Porter* [1958]). The tourists in this novel are Australians attached to the occupation forces in Japan after the Second World War. The novel is in the third person, but the tone suggests an observer rather than an impersonal author behind the narration. Near the end of the book, this observer invites the reader to become part of it, as he presents the action to us as an example of the way we all behave: 'One of us did that; let us look; let us steal or buy a relic; one of *us* did that!' (p. 162). Any judgement we make on the actions and characters we have just been shown will, therefore, be a judgement on ourselves.

The action of the novel takes a small group of Australians, 'a handful of pennies', and shows each of them in the foreign setting of Japan that tests and judges them. Within this setting we see also a few Japanese whose lives become caught up with the Australians. Most of the Japanese men are hurt but remain unaffected at their core. The women, on the other hand, are scarred for life. By contrast, the Australians are not so much changed as revealed for what they are — people from a nation too young, too raw, too provincial to understand the world they find themselves in. Rather than allowing this world to affect them, they take refuge in booze and insensitivity.

The insensitivity of the world and the need to find a secure refuge from it form a constant theme in Porter's work. One of his earliest published stories, 'Revenge', written when he was twenty, shows a schoolboy subjected to emotional assault on the train on which he is journeying home to Gippsland (Leonie Kramer (ed.), *Hal Porter, Selected Stories*, Angus & Robertson, Sydney, 1971). The boy takes refuge in his book of de Maupassant's short stories. The book physically shields him from the need to talk with the blowsy woman who tries to intrude on his privacy.

The stories in the book give him refuge in a world of the mind from which she, whose 'literary Everest' is Barbara Cartland, is excluded by her own inadequacies. The train journey, another recurring image in Porter's work, represents the impermanency of life, in which we travel constantly in search of a security that always eludes us. The only weapons left to the boy, or the author, are those of the mind that provides a refuge wherein wit can construct its own weapons. The devastating salutation with which the boy ends the encounter is of the same order as the authorial comment on the woman's 'mental Everest'. Both serve to keep an intrusive world at bay, to pin it down by definition. This is the function of Porter's art.

In *A Handful of Pennies* the Australians encounter a whole society devoted to controlling a threatening world in this way. The events of the novel reveal the inability of the Australians to penetrate this culture and find within it the humanity they share with the Japanese. The relationship between Truscott and Imiko promises to transcend the national barriers, but is ended when Truscott is transferred back to Australia. Imiko, who has represented the stillness at the heart of the traditional Japan, is left to the alternatives of poverty or prostitution. Even at its strongest, the tradition she embodies proves unable either to transform the Westerner or to resist the fatal allure of modernism.

Imiko's brother, Kazuo, recognises that the invasion of the Americans and their allies leaves him no alternative but corruption. His past has been taken from him, and he cannot believe in the future. The West has driven him into the same predicament Porter feels himself born to as an Australian, heir to a culture that gives him freedom but nothing with which to sustain it. His art, which provides a refuge from the hostility of the philistines, is also an attempt to fill the emptiness.

Porter rejects the institutions of modern democracy and education because they embody materialism, hedonism and individualism. He believed these were the source of the destruction of human standards and the corruption of modern life. His rejection represents not only an aesthetic distaste for vulgarity, but a distrust amounting to a fear of people. For example, writing in the second volume of his auto-biography of his pre-war experience as a teacher in Williamstown, he describes the children as a mob, a 'juggernaut capable of bulldozing itself down' and containing 'a quality of danger and a fuel of frenzy'. The successful teachers are not those who encourage learning, but those who contain the mob, who are

. . . adequately equipped to smother the danger and transform the frenzy. The equipment is the diamond-cut-diamond one of intimidating a more dangerous danger and a more skilled frenzy. In this, each teacher to his own technique: steel-lined sweetness, bullocky shoutings, fishwife screechings, Shakespearian denunciations, but mainly the iron control in the velvet manner, the suggestion that just beneath the patient mask of the Archangel Gabriel are the lineaments and fangs of Attila the Hun.

> Porter, *The Paper Chase*,
> Angus & Robertson, Sydney,
> 1966, p. 9.

In the abandonment of these forms of discipline he finds 'not only an irresponsible giving-away of the tribal rights of adulthood and the powers due to experience, but a gesture of great impropriety and greater danger' that eventually produces the hordes of tattooed barbarians he later finds infesting Trafalgar Square (pp. 9–10). This distrust of people in general forces him to keep his distance, rejecting any commitment to the wondrous variety of human experience other than that of the collector assembling it for the purpose of his own baroque carnival.

Porter traces the source of this distrust in the first volume of his autobiography, *The Watcher on the Cast-Iron Balcony* (Faber & Faber, London, 1963). This book opens and closes with the death of his mother. Remembering this scene from the later time of writing, he recalls looking 'through a lens of tears' at her corpse 'hearing, beyond the useless hullabaloo of my debut in grief, its unbelievable silence prophesying unbelievable silence for me'. He travels back in memory to his earliest consciousness and then traces the eighteen years of his life until he comes back to the scene at the bedside and the mourning that followed. He portrays himself as a watcher who, like all children, is never innocent, but uses others for his own purposes. Porter, however, retains this quality into adulthood. In making him an artist it also disables him from being absorbed in the life of others, whether of his family, the country

town or the suburban school. The writing creates the only world in which he need not distrust himself or others.

The common experience of the book is in part just the experience of the environment of bayside suburb and country town in which he grows up and which he learns to love even as he knows he must escape it. It is the exciting possibilities of Bairnsdale, first seen as pure light that 'gushes and surges and soars away from my minuteness in every direction, upwards and ever upwards, . . . outwards and southwards over the river-mouths, the swan-haunted lakes, the very South itself, and the world's felloe' (p. 53). It is the sense of danger he finds in river flats and town common, and the delightful dirt of the neighbouring children. It is the regular household routine by which his mother gives order to the promises of the world. It is the experience of belonging to a family, particularly the exuberant cousins of his mother's family, the Ruffs. This exuberant love of teeming life is expressed in the 'old-fashioned garden and farmyard' of his grandparents:

with something of everything . . . a child's paradise: bantams, turkeys, geese, ducks, Guinea fowl, Rhode Island Reds, beehives, cows, lambs, dogs, cats, a parrot, a cockatoo, a tame one-legged magpie, currants, fruit-trees, a sunflower-paddock, a maize-paddock, currants, gooseberries, raspberries, strawberries, clumps of bamboo, lavender, guelder rose, a row of elders, primroses, peonies, snail-flower creeper, bleeding heart, and ten kinds of violets.

> Porter, *Watcher*, p. 106.

The profusion of this catalogue is an evocation of a natural plenty that now flourishes in Australia. It is also the source of his mother's 'delight in growing things' which she has passed to him and his sisters so that 'if there be a dimension after death in which grieving for the senses is possible, I shall grieve for no person however once agonisingly desired and passionately beloved . . . for nothing half so much as I shall grieve for the loss of the earth itself, the soil, the seeds, the plants, the very weeds' (p. 106). Like Porter's description of the country town, this catalogue excludes people in favour of things. By taking this life into himself, extending himself through words to comprehend the world, he can hold at bay any immediate involvement in human ties that could jeopardise his control.

His rejection of commitment arises also, however, from the awareness of the comedy of human relations that comes to him as he is watching the funeral of one of his school students, shortly before the death of his own mother. As the funeral procession comes to the school, a ripple of laughter runs through the ranks of the assembled children as a little fox-terrier falls in front of the band and performs a kind of parody of the solemn march. This spectacle of laughter at the heart of grief, of the absurdity of the human tragedy, moves him to tears. It is a further step in the isolation he pays as the price for his sense of wonder. The attempt to escape from this isolation into the world was to keep him on the move throughout his work.

Porter does eventually reach a resolution to the conflict he sees between human institutions and the forms of life they destroy in seeking to embody them. The story 'Fredo Fuss Loves Life' (*Fredo Fuss Loves Life*, Angus & Robertson, Sydney, 1974. pp. 107–216) is built around the affirmation of the title, which appears as a graffito on the wall of a Mediterranean village, presumably in Malta. The anonymous narrator's speculations on the author of the message lead him to describe a week in the life of the village from the perspective of its bars. Through this discussion we see the set of glitterati, rich and cynical, despised by the village they scorn but tolerated while they bring money to it. They are contrasted with the poorly genteel English eking out their retirement, and with the villagers themselves, secretive, self-possessed, but opening their homes and their lives for the day of the Festa. The Festa and the parrot Mabel, as well as the enduring bar-owners, represent the life that eludes the glitterati, but that even the retirees can glimpse, and that finds its expression in the mysterious author of the graffito. His slogan is an affirmation of the human spirit that creates the art that resists the distortions imposed on life by society.

The poems collected in *In an Australian Country Graveyard* (Nelson, Melbourne, 1974) make a similar affirmation, in this case over history rather than merely the superficialities of contemporary life. In these poems Porter comes back to the Gippsland of his youth to consider the lives of its white settlers.

The opening poem of the title sequence starts by placing their far southern graves in the context of the Britain from which they came with their clutter of possessions and concepts. The graveyard is a monument to this clutter, where 'anachronism's rife:/the landscape plays at Constable and Gray' (p. 3). Their dreams have puttered out in this environment where 'Hay-wain or hansom . . . will never come', but their tombs still present a chronicle of achievement. The second poem in the sequence, 'The First-comers' (pp. 5–14), which describes the earlier voyages, presents the Australian destination as an 'inviolate Arcadia', where the hardships of the voyage made necessary the realisation of the dream. The other poems deal with individuals, some successful, some, like the spinster, going to their grave still waiting for the prince to rescue them from the nightmares of their isolation. Yet these individual griefs and failures are brought into harmony by time, which has made them one with the landscape. This is expressed as much in Porter's drawings as in his words. These emphasise form rather than line, merging all details in a complex pattern of light and shade. The work does not celebrate so much the pioneers themselves, but time that has brought the Australian landscape into the wondrous flood of history. The individual failures disappear in this greater miracle.

Rosemary Dobson

If Hal Porter displays his characters in the showcases of a museum, Rosemary Dobson illuminates them on the canvasses of art. This gives her poetry a quality of stillness, akin to the paintings of the Dutch masters that often provide the starting point for a poem. 'In a Convex Mirror', the opening poem of her *Selected Poems* (Australian Poets Series, Angus & Robertson, Sydney, 1963 p. 1), for example, identifies the speaker and her companions with the mirror in which they see themselves and the painting that captures the moment:

See, in the circle how we stand,
As pictured angels touching wings
Inflame a Dutch interior
Bespeaking birth, foretelling kings.

Dobson, *Selected Poems*, p. 1.

The likeness established between figures in the painting and the place from which the speaker watches continues through the poem. Thus 'the room' of the second verse may be either the room in the painting or the room where 'we stand' looking at a mirror or a painting. The speakers may be people in the present looking at a painting of the past, or the imagined onlookers whom the original painter captured in his oils as they gazed into a mirror. Past and present, observer and actor, are caught in a single complex of relationships, at once active and still.

Dobson is concerned with such relationships throughout her work. A painting, like a mirror, is wholly a surface, yet on that surface the arrangement of light and colour, line and shape, indicates depths that we interpret as we look. The world of the painting finally exists, not on canvas, but in our minds. In the same way, the words of Dobson's poetry select and arrange images from an experience. Like her seeker at the oracle of Trophonios, she bathes these images in the rivers of forgetfulness and memory so that she may 'recall the sacred message' unclouded by unnecessary detail (*Over the Frontier*, Angus & Robertson, Sydney, 1978, p. 33). The poems record the surface details that survive in memory or history or art, but in reading their careful relations we reconstruct the passions and endurance, the despair and the agony that lie behind the surface. Each poem comes, to use another of her titles, like 'The Message in the Bottle' to the reader who can

. . . recognize in what I say
the voice that speaks to me alone
and he the predetermined; he
the listener, finder, watcher of
the wrack that's washed in from the sea.

Dobson, *Frontier*, p. 46.

The messages in her bottles are drawn from the Pierian spring of the muses, and speak of love, poetry and oblivion, 'the three things that draw me on' (p. 29): love, the force in her work that transcends and redeems the individual; poetry, the art with which she makes sense of life; and oblivion, which is not only death but the unknowingness against which poetry and all the arts speak.

The images of Dobson's poetry are the commonplaces of life: leaves fallen from a grape-vine, but caught on a Greek vase; a girl at a window; the slogans on the railway hoardings of her youth; Mrs Potts, the flat-iron put out to cool by the peppercorn trees. From these simple forms we build in our minds the patterns that constitute the miracle of life itself. These are shown in painting, in the precious shape of the bone flute that creates music, in the wonder of science that reconstitutes the world of the past from an analysis of pollen. Yet she is aware also of how each such construction also leaves out much of the truth. 'Drowned Person' (p. 19) is both an elegy for 'a young woman, gracile,/delicate' who died by water, and a discussion of how little we can know of another. The pollen analysis can provide a 'limited history', but tells nothing of 'the dark side of the mind/. . . the heart's deviousness,/the body's wilfulness'. The poem, however, like the Dutch interior, does allow us to see these things, not directly, but by implication. The careful description of 'existing data' is framed by the opening lament for the fire that after death must consume all we know of the body, and the closing list of 'such *weedy trophies*/ as willow, nettles, crow-flowers and daisies' as she carried with her to death. The flowers, with their associations of grief, poverty and love, answer the

Rosemary Dobson
(*National Library of Australia*)

opening description of oblivion. The bare recital of fact thus becomes charged not merely with a sense of loss but with a sense of the fulness and potency, for good and ill, of the life that has been lost. The last line, shortened to four syllables and rhyming the humble daisies with the eloquent trophies, emphasises the tragedy that ends anguish and hope alike with such simple accompaniment.

Although Dobson takes the whole of time as her province, this makes her no less contemporary or Australian. She argues in an introduction to her 1963 *Selected Poems*, that 'every artist should have complete freedom of choice in his ideas. It should not matter if he ranges back in time, provided . . . he tries to use the equipment of thought and technique that is available to him in his own time with which to shape his work' (p. viii). Dobson's poetry belongs to our time, with its emphasis on both the power and the inadequacy of the human mind, on the recovery and analysis rather than on direct re-creation of experience and expression of emotion. We are aware always of the distance between observer and action, word and reality, in a world where mind and observation are the only realities.

This is nowhere clearer than in her sequence of 'Poems from Pausanias' (*Over the Frontier*, pp. 27–46). In these she meditates on episodes from the work of the Greek traveller of the second century after Christ. She writes of the rivers and springs, statues and sanctuaries that he saw, and on the beliefs and customs that clustered around them and that they sustained. She prizes his details in their separateness, rejoicing in the life they reveal between their fragments:

I store the pieces that he found. Am loath
to bring together all to make a whole.
I *like* the broken pieces in my mind.

Dobson, 'Phigalia', *Frontier*, p. 35.

Such pieces — the hens pecking, the grass between the paving stones, the 'little pipe of polished bone' found in Attica, a miraculous gift of sight — convey the sense of life continuing unchanging beneath the vicissitudes of history. This idea is concentrated in her images of springs, always changing and always the same, containing 'the cool cupping of water' that is symbol at once of life and its counterpart, poetry.

If the central fact of life is death, its most important manifestation is birth. In several poems in *Cock Crow* (Angus & Robertson, Sydney, 1965), Dobson poses these facts against each other in terms of the mother's experience. She tells of going 'Three times to the world's end' and three times returning like Lazarus with 'Tidings of life beyond the dark' (p. 7). Each birth is also a death both in the pain and threat to the mother and in the child's necessary and inevitable movement — 'As stars move to their destined place' — away from the life that gives it birth.

The birth of the child involves the writer in the continuing life of the world. Yet the involvement is also painful, threatening the mother's life by absorbing it in the life of others. The title poem of the volume, 'Cock Crow' (p. 13), embodies this dilemma, as the speaker flees from her sleeping mother and daughter in her desperate need to be herself, 'Wanting to be myself, alone'. The moment of relief enables her to create the symmetry of art from her own being and the dark trees and night that close her round. For a moment she knows herself,

. . . separate and alone,
Cut off from human cries, from pain,
And love that grows about the bone.

Dobson, *Cock Crow*, p. 13.

The separation allows the love, cries and pain to come together in their proper shape. Yet this moment, a metaphor for art, is broken by the sound of 'the cock crow on the hill', a reminder of Peter's realisation of his betrayal of Christ and of the continuing demands of life. Art and self-possession become betrayal, and the speaker returns home. Although the moment is described as 'brief illusion', it remains and gives the poem its value. The detachment of art is not the alternative to life, but a necessary part of it.

Dobson writes as one who delights in this ambiguity, which reveals at once the wonder and fragility of the world. The wonder is humanity itself, which invests the world with the love, art, ceremony and science that fill her poems. But humanity, which realises the wonder of the world, also threatens it. Both wonder and threat are captured in the poem 'Into Winter' (p. 10), in which the two are poised against each other both in the 'spinning crystal of the world' and in the child born 'to be the man/To save the world at the last hour'. The speaker of the poem knows the 'double doom' of the woman who bears a child into a world where darkness is gathering, where humanity's achievements are being steadily obliterated:

> In Europe, Asia, Africa
> The camp-fire lights that man has struck
> Between his hands fade one by one;
> The prowling beasts draw nearer stll.

Against the threat, the speaker, both poet and mother, can only

> . . . Hive my summer days
> And keep their honey in my heart
> As clear as spring-water, unstained
> By speck or stir of what's to come.

Dobson, Cock Crow, p. 10.

The action seems trivial when compared with the threat, yet the riches of the hive can 'feed the promise in the womb' of the child who will save us from the doom. The stillness of the artist and the hope of the mother together ensure the future. The spring and the honey represent, in their material substance and nurturing significance, the unity of nature and culture that alone stands against destruction.

Gwen Harwood

Harwood's poems also speak of art and love, but rather as a measure of anguish or of the unattainable than an achievement of meaning. In the moment of love after physical passion, as in 'Triste Triste' (*Selected Poems*, Angus & Robertson, Sydney, 1975, pp. 24–5), the heart calls from the prison of the body to the spirit in its promised paradise. The only peace it finds, however, is the 'paradise of sleep'. Similarly, in 'The Old Wife's Tale' (p. 10), the woman recalls the dance of youth, the transcendence of love and the reward of children, but with the sense of something always missing:

> . . . 'Grant me more
> than this bare subsistence, I crave
> some combat worthy of my sword'.

Harwood, Selected Poems, p. 10.

Gwen Harwood
(*Graeme Kinross-Smith*)

Time, however, breaks the moulds of her hopes, gives her children back as strangers, and leaves her in old age still seeking, but now for 'the hidden seminal springs of peace' rather than further battle. The only truth she finds is in the parable of her 'winter-landscape face', a sign of the ending of life in inevitable death. Again, a postcard with the painting of a winter's scene familiar from her childhood brings not order but regret for the irrecoverable security of the past, and awareness of a present empty of passion but imprisoned in 'stiff gestures' as she hears 'the lonely/voice call "I hunger" through the snow-bright air' (p. 14).

This is poetry of engagement, not the search for order but the struggle to discover moments of meaning. At best, order comes as a safeguard against enveloping pain and disintegration. The child's jar will not hold the light, but it comes back to it in the morning to banish the phantoms of the nights, even though we know that they will come again in their turn. The stones worn by the sea are a reminder of past happiness and a talisman against the fear and pain of the hospital, a symbol that trouble creates its own beauty. While these moments of order are achieved, they remain moments, fragments as easily destroyed as restored by the constantly changing sea of time. The consciousness that reveals nature

to the human also separates her from it in unbridgeable grief:

'What is truth? cries the heart, as the gull
rocks in changeless estate, and I turn
to my kingdom of sorrowing change.

Harwood, Selected Poems, p. 6.

The calm order of the lines serves only to hold in
check the constant threat of chaos.

The symbols of the searching mind and disintegrating
life are brought together in the sequence of poems
about Professor Eisenbart. Eisenbart is a physicist
whose mind ponders the formula that will at once
explain the world and destroy it. His own life is,
however, ruled by tides of passion, which first entrap
him with the music of Mozart 'in a copper web of
hair' on the schoolgirl who becomes his mistress. He
tires of this passion, and dreams of blowing up the
moon that symbolises the feminine principle of
change against his masculine ambition of order and
destruction. The pictured phallus that hangs above
his bed is, however, on a dead hunter. Eisenbart's
mind is dead, and only his disordering passions keep
him alive. In the final poem of the sequence, he finds
his cultivated 'indifference to love and luck' pierced
by the sight of a woman meeting her lover and his
children. The moment of greeting is a prize gathered
from the 'cloud-sliding watery drift/of winter' that
symbolises the loss of earlier loves. Eisenbart
understands the moment, but for him it can mean
only the anguish of one who knows he is 'Too old to
love, too young to die'. Life is not to be understood,
but endured. Yet while this is Eisenbart's conclusion,
the poem denies it. The images of the man and
woman meeting and the children playing provide an
answer as well as a measure to Eisenbart's despair.

The sense of an established order gradually grows
stronger in Harwood's later poetry. In her second
collection Professor Kröte, a musician, takes the
place of Eisenbart. Kröte endures his exile from the
European culture of his youth only through drink and
his memories and dreams of a music greater than
he is now able to play or his audiences to appreciate.
The idea of this music, however poorly it is realised,
nevertheless gives meaning to his life. Although
vicious children torment him, destroying his peace,
his dream children bring him the beauty and harmony
of his music, and while he is in hospital an admiring

student even pierces the nightmares of his fever
with the quick brush of a kiss.

The music that brings elusive moments of vision
to Professor Kröte becomes total reality in the
'Impromptus' dedicated to the musician Rex Hobcroft.
Words and music become one as 'thought moves/in
visions' and

clear as a landscape filled with sun
issues this theme, a drift of air
brought into form by mind and hand.
Let heart put off its cloudy care,

rejoice to learn how in the plain
texture of truth its peace is found,
and rest in elemental joy
under this firmament of sound.

Harwood, Selected Poems, p. 58.

The form of the words contains both the landscape
and the mind and hand that shape it into harmony.
In Harwood's third collection, this harmony is
extended to include all of time, as she moves in
memory to youth in Brisbane and the power of love
and music, and the nurturing care of her parents, to
survive not only their own death but the speaker's
awareness of the death waiting to claim her own
voice. Remembering her father's care, she is able to
assert that even when death rolls her 'in one grinding
race/of dreams, pain, memories, love and grief' from
which no hand can save her,

the peace of this day will shine
like light on the face of the waters
that bear me away for ever.

Harwood, Selected Poems, p. 97.

Grief and pain are absorbed in the greater unity
created by the human mind and human responsibility,
and by the simple gift of water through which two
friends are able to share 'the wholeness of this day'.

The two European professors in Harwood's work
renew the theme of exile in Australian poetry.
However, they are figures the writer describes, not
expressions of her own consciousness. Their loneliness and alienation are real, but their conflict is not
so much with a peculiarly Australian provincialism
as with the loss of the tradition of high culture that

is characteristic of the later part of the twentieth century. Importantly, however, the tradition Kröte brings with him is worked in Harwood's poetry into the principle of art that produces harmony between the human and its Australian environment. The conflicts that remain within the pattern are those individual and universal ones of creation and destruction, time and death.

Patrick White

White's return to Australia after the Second World War induced in him a sense of panic at the exaltation of the average. He determined to discover, in place of the dun-coloured realism prevailing in fiction, the 'extraordinary behind the ordinary, the mystery and the poetry which alone could make bearable' the lives of ordinary people ('The Prodigal Son', in Geoffrey Dutton and Max Harris (eds.), *The Vital Decade*, Sun Books, Melbourne, 1968, p. 157).

White's first novel closes with its main character turning his back on the country town that represents Australian provincialism. His second is set in London against the background of growing tumult in Europe, and his third, *The Aunt's Story* (Penguin, Ringwood, 1963 [1948]) traces the pilgrimage of Theodora Goodman from Australia through Europe to America. The three books thus take us steadily further away from Australia into a realm of existential freedom.

Patrick White
(*The Age*)

Theodora Goodman's journey begins in Meroë the Australian sheep station with the romantic name given it by her exiled father. Here she kills the hawk that represents the freedom of spirit denied her by her bondage to her mother and convention. By killing the bird, she asserts her right to its freedom. Released by her mother's death, she travels first to the *Jardin Exotique*, a hotel somewhere in Europe, and finally to America. The *Jardin Exotique* is populated by eccentrics and obsessives washed up with their delusions intact from half a century of wars and revolutions and intrigues. They live inside their minds, and their company releases Theodora from her dependence on any objective external world. In the final section, among hard-headed but kindly people who do not seek to control her, she finally discovers release from time, reason and self: 'In the house above the disintegrating world, light and silence ate into the hard, resisting barriers of reason, hinting at some ultimate moment of clear vision' (p. 286). Here she meets Holstius, from whom she learns to accept the irreconcilable duality of life, 'joy and sorrow . . . flesh and marble, or illusion and reality, or life and death' (p. 289). In this acceptance, she learns also to recognise the reality of each of the different lives she has led, and thus is able to submit to being taken into the care of an asylum. Her inner reality can no longer be touched.

These three books would seem to farewell Australia in favour of a pure world of the spirit that contradicts both the harsh necessities of the land and the narrowness of the people these have bred. Yet Theodora finds her eventual peace in a similar environment to that of her Australian youth. In his next novel, *The Tree of Man* (Eyre & Spottiswoode, London, 1956 [1955]), White devotes himself to a detailed exploration of two lives that are not only representative but symbolise the history of Australian settlement, from bush pioneering to urban sprawl. These lives in turn come to symbolise, as the title of the novel suggests, the whole life of humankind.

The opening scene of the novel is an archetype of human settlement:

A cart drove between the two big stringybarks and stopped. These were the dominant trees in that part of the bush, rising above the involved scrub with the simplicity of true grandeur. So the cart stopped, grazing the hairy side of a tree, and the horse, shaggy and stolid as the tree, sighed and took root.

The man who sat in the cart got down . . . Birds looked from twigs, and the eyes of animals were drawn to what was happening. The man lifting a bundle from a cart. A dog lifting his leg on an anthill. The lip drooping on the sweaty horse.

Then the man took an axe and struck at the side of a hairy tree, more to hear the sound than for any other reason. And the sound was cold and loud . . . The silence was immense. It was the first time anything like this had happened in that part of the bush.

White, *Tree of Man*, p. 3.

These lines suggest not merely the coming of human-kind to Australia, but the coming of humankind to purposive settlement anywhere.

The detail of the stringybark bushland in this opening scene is specific, but the import of the man coming, stopping and getting down, the horse taking root, and the dog lifting its leg, is general. The blows of the axe, at first casually, then with purpose, represent the work of domination. The silence we hear for the first time by contrast to the sound of the axe represents what until this moment has always been but is now forever destroyed. It is not just the silence that possessed the south land before the coming of the whites, but the silence of the human generations before the first agriculturalists stepped out from their past of hunting and gathering and began the making of history.

The action of *The Tree of Man* expands from this point. First, it gives the man a name, Stan Parker, and then, once he has cleared his land, he obtains a wife. Their lives together then follow a sequence of spring, summer, autumn and winter, as they pass from the intense excitements of establishing their lives together, the coming of a family, the separations and infidelities of maturity and the excisions and abdications of old age. This cycle is punctuated by the classic Australian events of flood, drought and fire, and accompanied by the development of a small community, its expansion into a local town, and its eventual absorption within the spreading suburbs. The raw bush youth of the opening chapter is transformed into the querulous old man sitting in the sun on a patch of suburban lawn at the end. Behind this cycle of change, however, the constants remain — the dog following at his feet, the gob of spittle on the path, and the ants in the cracks of the paving. Beyond these, the trees remain, and the grandchild who, unlike Stan's own children, sees them and becomes one with them.

In *The Tree of Man*, the problems of the world — war, crime, depression — are seen as they impinge on the lives of one man and one woman. These two live out the Australian dream, establishing settlement, family and community, only to see it all taken from them by time and human weakness. The only lasting achievements of their lives are those that come from outside the material history, in such forms as the holy simplicity of Bub Quigley, the paintings of Mr Gage, or the vision of God that Stan finally is given in a gob of spittle. By the end of the novel, all other promises of life seem destroyed by its transience, and all that remains is the continuity sensed behind the material events and symbolised by the trees. The hope of Australia becomes not the creation of the new world suggested by the opening scene, but the recovery of old verities. The novel shows how the attempt to create a life based on dominance, characteristic of the European expansion, destroys the truths it seeks to establish. Stan's search succeeds when he has ceased to try.

The destructive and creative aspects of this search for meaning continue to occupy White through the substantial sequence of works he has since published. Although it is outside the scope of this study to examine them individually, even a brief glance will indicate the complexities of his achievement. The comedy of manners in his plays and short stories is given its edge by his awareness of the conflict between human hopes for beauty and vision and the equally human fears that constrain it. The novels study different manifestations of the vision.

In *Voss* (Eyre & Spottiswoode, London, 1957) the figure of the explorer becomes an image of the megalomaniac vision that both opens a new world and destroys it. Voss's own vision, which confounds the petty businessmen of Sydney who seek to use it for their own glory, is contrasted with the self-effacing Christian resignation of Palfreyman, the ardour of Judd, and the nurturing gift of Laura, who alone is able to incorporate his vision in her life. *Riders in the Chariot* (Eyre & Spottiswoode, London, 1961) brings together four people who see different forms of the vision but are brought together in a common surrender to its truth. Mrs Godbold, the survivor, has some aspects of Theodora and some of Laura, while the painter, Alf Dubbo, anticipates Hurtle Duffield in *The Vivisector* (Jonathan Cape, London, 1970). As the title suggests, Duffield destroys others in his drive to realise his vision in paint. Dubbo is a victim who destroys only himself. In *The Solid Mandala* (Eyre & Spottiswoode, London, 1966), the vision is divided between the twin brothers, Arthur and Waldo Brown. Waldo is the would-be intellectual in whom the search for the vision turns into a hatred of life that eventually kills him. Arthur, the simpleton, gives himself naturally to the search, and finds his vision in the mandala that is at the centre of his glass marble and that gives him the pattern of his dance under the blossoms of the wheel-tree 'sizzling with fire, burning its way back through time' (p. 288). In the mandala, and in Arthur, the twin possibilities of life, Adam and his three brides, Christ and Tiresias, become one, giving him a strength that sustains others, even Waldo. In *The Eye of the Storm* (Jonathan Cape, London, 1973), by contrast, the vision and capacity for life are concentrated in the single person of an old woman who sustains herself by taking from others. Yet the moment of vision Elizabeth has in the quiet eye of the cyclone off the Queensland coast gives her an understanding of the unity of all life. This lifts her beyond the self-centred and self-consuming lives of her children, the ageing princess and the ageing Lear who are destroyed by their own narcissism. Elizabeth Hunter is her own work of art, offering a vision of truth to those capable of learning.

White's most recent novels, *The Twyborn Affair* (Jonathan Cape, London, 1979) and *Memoirs of Many in One* (Jonathan Cape, London, 1986), like his self-portrait, *Flaws in the Glass* (Jonathan Cape, London, 1981) deal not so much with the search for a unifying vision as with the manifold possibilities contained in a single life. Like the search for a vision, this has been implicit in his work from the earliest books. In *Happy Valley* (Harrap, London, 1939), the schoolteacher Moriarty is destroyed because the town imposes on him only a single life, and the doctor, Oliver Halliday, flees the town to escape this fate through the development of his other possibilities. Theodora Goodman leads several lives. Stan Parker is freed from the constraints of his life because he observes possibilities in others even if he cannot fulfil them in himself, while Amy is destroyed because she shuts out the stories of the salesman and refuses to accept any reality outside her own experience. The illuminates of the later novels are those who not only pursue their own visions but can accept the visions of others, either to nurture them, like Mrs Godbold, or to capture them in paint, like Hurtle Duffield. In the latest novels, however, the characters completely live out the different possibilities they contain. The central character of *The Twyborn Affair* is at different times catamite, mistress, war hero, stockman and madam. The novelist in *Flaws in the Glass* is his own creation. In *Memoirs of Many in One* he presents himself as merely editor of the memoirs of a woman who 'acquired names as other women encrust themselves with jewels and bowerbirds collect fragments of coloured glass' (p. 9). With the names go not only personalities, but whole lives. The book is partly about growing old, but more about the tragedy of life that never allows us to express more than a tithe of our potential and the comedy that never allows us a single being.

A Fringe of Leaves (Penguin, Harmondsworth, 1977 [1976]) brings together the two themes of vision and personality. It tells the story of Ellen Roxburgh, who by the time the narrative opens in the Sydney of the 1830s has already changed from the Cornish farm girl Ellen Gluyas to the wife of the gentlemanly Austin Roxburgh. Wrecked on the Queensland coast, she undergoes several other transformations, including literally taking into herself the substance of others, before reaching the comparative safety of Moreton Bay. Behind all her wanderings, however, lies a vision of the truth she once associated with the bay of Tintagel, redolent of Arthurian legend, and savoured in her immersion in the well of St Hya, near her Cornish home.

Unlike its successors, *A Fringe of Leaves* is embedded in Australian history. Austin's brother, Garnet, has prospered in Van Diemen's Land after leaving England in suspicious circumstances. The visit of his brother and sister-in-law brings English gentility into conflict with the exploitation on which it rests. Ellen's first image of the colony is of a place that hides its moral infection beneath the form of a neat English town. This town is built on the labour of convicts dragging and braking at carts of freshly quarried stone, 'teeth bared in sobbing mouths . . .

skin streaming with light and sweat . . . all but removed from the life around them', reduced to the condition of 'human beasts' (pp. 73–5).

Throughout Ellen's experiences in Van Diemen's Land, the promises of order and civilisation are contradicted by the reminders of unsubdued nature in glimpses of convicts and wilderness. This implicit savagery erupts in Ellen's rape by Garnet, which both violates her security and rouses an answering lust in her person. Her subsequent sufferings in Queensland, her period as a virtual chattel of the Aborigines and her escape through the good grace of a convict, constitute a journey into the depths of both the country and her own self through which she is able to reconcile the opposition of culture and nature, of desire and order. The fringe of leaves she wears to preserve some modesty is also the fringe of leaves the continent wears to conceal its savagery. Only as it is penetrated, in all senses of the word, is truth discovered and a true establishment of Australia made possible.

Through her marriage and visit to the colonies Ellen Roxburgh becomes a part of the history of the colonisers. After the wreck she lives the history of the victims. Through this experience she returns to the sources of human life. The Aborigines are neither idealised nor condemned, but live the life imposed on them by their environment and transcend it in the rituals of the corroboree that Ellen shares. After immersion in this well of mysticism she finds in the convict Jack Chance the godlike lover of Tintagel. Her escape with him is also a re-enactment in the Australian bush of the wanderings of Tristan and Iseult on their journey to the Tintagel Ellen had been fated never to see. Like Voss, she celebrates the unity she discovers in a mystic communion in which the roots of the water-lilies become a natural counterpart of the water and wine of the Christian mass (p. 285). This act of communion brings Ellen to-

gether with the land and her lover in a common joy. By accepting his captivity and guilt as her own, she expiates the oppression of the society to which she had migrated by marriage, and becomes instead free in a new world of her own. Unlike the visionaries and artists of earlier novels, who free themselves by escaping history, Ellen Gluyas finds freedom by taking history into her own life. In the last scene of the book, on the boat returning her to Sydney, she is able to accept again her role in society, but is no longer controlled by those who surround her.

White's fiction recreates the history of Australia in forms that unite European myth with the identity shaped between the Aborigines and the land. The vision of his central characters is given its urgency by their awareness of the social forces that seek to constrain and destroy. At the same time, their experiences undermine the validity of the myths as ways of interpreting reality. Stan Parker's pioneering dreams and Norbert Hare's Xanadu alike fall beneath the blight of suburbia, and suburban respectability culminates in a re-enaction of the Holocaust. Ellen Gluyas undergoes each of the succeeding myths of culture and nature, and finds all wanting except reliance on herself.

In the earlier novels, the visionaries can preserve themselves only by finding an escape from society. Ellen Gluyas during her wanderings discovers the strength that enables her to endure within history and society. The characters of White's three latest books have the freedom literally to write their own histories. This freedom goes beyond that of either the pioneer shaping the land to his own purposes or the artist consuming life to make his own vision. It frees the individual from confinement in either nationality, gender or social role. Each individual is left free to create himself or herself from the ultimate realities of ageing and death.

—13—

ORIGINS

———

THE changes in Australian society as a result of post-war immigration and industrial development, and the cultural shock caused by the fall of Singapore and the consequent change of military dependence from Britain to the USA, threatened established ideas of national identity. One response to this uncertainty was the assertion of an indigenous Australian tradition by the realist writers discussed earlier. Another was the re-assertion of British and imperialist associations. Martin Boyd, in both *Lucinda Brayford* and the Langton novels, did this critically, contrasting the ideals of the tradition with the reality of its destruction by contemporary materialism. Ethel Anderson, in the sequence of stories published as *At Parramatta* (Cheshire, Melbourne, 1956), recalls the tradition rather as a colonial past. Within the firm security provided by this social order she is able to examine both the human foibles society condemns and the real evil it condones but contains. Writers of the newer generation, however, were not able to rest easily in either of these traditions, and strove rather to create for themselves an order from the various and fragmentary traditions confronting them.

Thea Astley

The task of creating a new order required that writers first go back to the origins of the traditions they found around them. Thea Astley's work shows one aspect of this search for origins. Her novels are set in the present, but they range over the separate traditions of Catholicism and the bush, the life and bigotry of small towns and the isolation of the cities. Her first novel, *Girl with a Monkey* (Penguin, Ringwood, 1987 [1958]) examines a north Queensland town through the critical eyes of a young teacher who is about to leave it forever after the failure of her love affair and her disillusion with the school and her colleagues. Her most recent, *Beachmasters* (Penguin, Ringwood, 1985), examines one of the last vestiges of colonial society, a small Pacific island state involved in a rebellion on the eve of independence. An odd assortment of British, French and Australian expatriates try to maintain a traditional European order that crumbles in the face of the unchanging elements of restless sea and vegetable fertility that govern the patterns of life on the island. The teeming jungle and the outbreak of a revolt reveal European law and culture as irrelevant or treacherous. In the end, only personal loyalties matter.

In her collection of stories, *Hunting the Wild Pineapple* (Penguin, Ringwood, 1981 [1979]), Astley looks at a similar white society in north Queensland. The characters in these stories, however, are alone in their encounter with the luxuriant jungle around them. In their huddle of settlements they construct an elementary society from the fragmentary European traditions of anarchy and domination they bring with them. The language and plots of the stories duck and

Thea Asley
(*National Library of Australia*)

weave with the same intense irrationality as the tropical seasons and jungles, and the lives of the stragglers and misfits who inhabit them.

The opening story, 'North: Some Compass Readings: Eden', seems to provide a map for the collection. In fact it tells the reader some details of the past of the one-legged narrator and a strange love affair of his ageing neighbour. The story is an apparently random sequence of memories, without any neat pattern of beginning, middle and end. The narrator gives it meaning only as he remakes his history in the language of the present. The people in other stories are gathered from all sorts of pasts and traditions by the search for work or the need to escape it. They make their own meanings as they choose their own patterns of acceptances and rejections. Their semi-hippy culture is no passing fashion, but a way of life as old as human settlement in the tropical jungle that mocks human pretensions. Queensland, on Australia's last frontier, is also mentally the oldest remaining colony, where tradition is always new. Unlike the Pacific island where Western order decays, or the barren city that empties it of meaning, the northern rainforest still offers people a chance to be their absurd, tasteless, extravagant selves. Their way of life becomes a parable of the new world

making its own patterns from the scraps of the old. In returning to the jungle, they find they have returned to their origins, although they still keep with them in their disillusion a scatter of hopes and artefacts as promise of a future.

Manning Clark

The writer who has been most influential in constructing a new Australian tradition is not either a poet or a novelist, but the historian Manning Clark. His histories go back to the sources that have moulded Australians' identity as both transplanted Europeans and a new people. They will be judged elsewhere as history, but their importance as literature should be recognised. His major work (*A History of Australia*, six volumes, Melbourne University Press, Melbourne, 1962–87) from the start embodies the tragic theme of the failure of those most passionately committed to realising their hopes. He sees the eventual Australian society as a product of the conflicting forces of the rationalist enlightenment, Protestant piety and Catholic devotion. Each of these intellectual and religious forces is entangled in its own culture and in colonial struggles for power and prestige, so that the visions of even the greatest become soiled by politics and defeated by personal weakness. As Clark's work unfolds, he gives more emphasis both to the nature of the land in which this struggle occurs, and which it shapes, and to the Aboriginal inhabitants who alone had developed a culture that understood the environment. The greatness of his work as literature lies not merely in the ambition of the theme or even the vision that encompasses space and time in telling the story, but in the succession of portraits of the flawed men and women whose ambitions created Australian society despite their own hopes. Some of his portraits, such as that of Henry Lawson, bend the record to mould the character to the shape of its author's own preoccupations. Together, however, they constitute a galaxy of characters who embody in their contradictions a hope for a future that will value the weak, the stubborn and the perverse as much as the triumphant. Clark's vision floods the deserts of Australia's failure with a visionary hope that springs from the Judaeo-Christian prophetic tradition of the West like the brief rains that maintain life on the furthest borders of extinction. This hope enlightens even the briefest and grimmest of his anecdotes:

> In March 1877 a young black girl of fifteen who had been disowned by her own people for granting her favours liberally to the white men in return for food, tobacco and alcohol, wandered round the streets of Echuca, quite unprotected and friendless. A white man befriended her and took her to the police station, hoping the sergeant would be moved with compassion for her and by what was likely to happen to her if she was cast again on the world to pursue her evil course unchecked and unrestrained. The sergeant took the stern line that she had worked her way to Echuca and would be able to get back 'by her own line of business'. In the eyes of the few who viewed such events with pity and the dread felt by men who were powerless to stop what they believed ought to be stopped, another young life was wrecked.

> Clark, *History*, vol. IV, pp. 213–14.

The hope of the future lies not in the tale, but in the way the author shapes it to reveal not only the horror, but also the compassion, and the few who realised the truth at the time. With such tales, with the weaknesses and achievements of Robert O'Hara Burke and Caroline Chisholm, John Curtin and Robert Menzies, Clark creates a past that gives some hope of a future uniquely suited to the Australian condition.

Vincent Buckley

Clark's feeling for an order that has been lost and broken in its transition to Australia, and for the struggle to recreate it, is also evident in the work of Vincent Buckley. The whole of his writing — poetry, criticism and autobiography — represents an attempt to incarnate a tradition in the present. The elements of this tradition come from his Catholic faith, the literature of the past, and the lives of his forebears in Ireland. His work combines these in a present comprising the landscapes of Australia and Ireland, the lives of his family, and the ceremonies of love and religion that stand against the cycle of death and disintegration. These ceremonies provide the universal framework within which he places the daily experience of work and society.

Vincent Buckley
(*Graeme Kinross-Smith*)

Buckley's critical writings emerge from the principles of F.R. Leavis, with their emphasis on the function of literature as an expression and shaping of the values created by the community through its everyday experience. The words of the writer enact the 'struggle to define oneself and one's values at the heart of the issues one feels most deeply' (*Poetry and Morality*, Chatto & Windus, London, 1959, p. 183). In this process of definition the work of art goes further and 'creates new values in the face of life' (p. 200). Buckley's own work is clearly a product of such a struggle. However, he parts from Leavis by refusing to accept the work of art as the 'guarantee of the truth of its own world' (p. 211). The work of art demands from the reader a response to the values it creates and enacts. This reponse can take the form of modifying, qualifying, completing or even rejecting the values of the work. For the reader to respond in any of these ways is to

> recognise the fact that art is not its own sanction; its sanction is reality; and we respond to works of art according to our prior response to reality, though they can modify or enrich our response to

reality by the manner in which they elicit our response to themselves.

Buckley, Poetry and Morality, p. 211.

Buckley does not argue that we should judge a work of literature by moral or religious values external to it, but that our final response to it must be in terms of our own values. In his poetry he discovers in his daily experience of the world the lives and values of those who have gone before him and shaped his consciousness. In his criticism he responds not to the imposed or asserted values of a particular tradition, but to the lived experience he finds within the works themselves. This leads Buckley both to revalue the Australian tradition and to incorporate it within the wider history of the expansion of western Europe. This history becomes the story of both the expansion of faith and the destruction of the traditional patterns and practices that nourished it. His criticism traces the continuing elements of what he terms the *numinous*, the sense of indwelling spirit, that writers have discovered in this secular and rootless world. His poetry discovers the same moments of apprehension in daily life.

Buckley argues that what has frequently been identified as democratic and nationalist in the Australian tradition is in fact a kind of 'utopian humanism or insistence on the soul's radical innocence'. Australian writing is an expression not of guilt but of frustration. Rather than a belief in ordinary people, writers emphasise the importance of living fully. Richard Mahony is frustrated because he can find no outlet for his energies in the society around him, while Herbert rejoices in the destructive violence that destroys the crass and the mediocre. Buckley identifies this tradition as 'vitalism', the insistence on the will or on the joyous importance of the moment ('Utopianism and Vitalism' in Grahame Johnson (ed.), *Australian Literary Criticism*, Oxford University Press, Melbourne, 1962, p. 17). At its most intense, this moment leads to the kind of divine revelation he traces in the work of British and American writers in his book *Poetry and the Sacred* (Chatto & Windus, London, 1963). His own poetry is, in the words he uses in this book about George Herbert, a way of 'extending and completing in language a contact with the world which is religious in its nature' (p. 18). It is not concerned with what is specific to Australia, but with the universal that can be grasped through an understanding of Australia and the traditions it contains. By going back to his origins, Buckley overcomes the twin frustrations of a colonialism that separates him from his past and that denied his ancestors their own fulfilment. The contact with the divine renews human energies by bringing them back to their source. It occurs when for a moment there is a break in the continuity of the profane life around us. This may occur in the administration of the sacrament, but in Buckley's work it is equally likely to come as he contemplates the urban cycle of destruction and creation, or walks through the bitter country of his Irish ancestors and feels them living in his present. In these moments, themselves precisely located, he escapes from the frustration of the present into a unity that goes beyond both time and place.

Although Buckley seeks contact with the sense of the divine, he avoids the confessional. The reader always has a sense of the speaking voice of the poem, the personal experience lying behind the pattern of the language, but, at least in his later work, the voice is controlled by the form. Even in as personal a poem as 'Parents' (*Selected Poems*, Angus & Robertson, Sydney, 1981, pp. 77–8), the speaker turns a conversation with his parents into a meditation on the inevitable separation of generations who are still held in a unity of concern:

> It's their needs, not mine, that flutter here
> In the questions and the anecdotes. I stare
> At the rust encroaching on the walnut branches
> Or the pile of litter where the biggest pine-tree
> Used to stand, before my absence killed it.

Buckley, Selected Poems, pp. 77–8.

The first of these lines aligns the reader with the speaker as an observer of the situation. The fluttering needs suggest all the unresolved questions that surround any relationship, any life. Then the rust and the trees and the litter bring us back to the situation only to remind us again of what is lost. The speaker's guilt does not arise from any failure, but from the inevitable passage of time. The remainder of the poem unites its three characters in inconsequential gossip of local events that converts the 'least important man' into legend both 'Menacing and remarkable'. Yet in this welter of facts and dates 'the deepest bonds are lost', and as the speaker departs he leaves his parents 'barely/visible in the window's copper sheen'. The light on the window, like the form of the poem itself, gives a pattern that both preserves and loses the individual.

The theme of 'Parents' is the loss time brings and the breaking of the single world of childhood, now only remembered, as we assume responsibility for the individual and public worlds of adult life. The poetry does not express emotion directly, but uses situation and feeling to detach speaker and reader from the immediate experience and enable us to contemplate its meaning.

The opposite to the detachment of art is the irresponsibility of political involvement that denies the reality of division by imposing a deceptive unity of action. The evils that follow from this abdication of responsibility form the theme of Buckley's 'Eleven Political Poems' (pp. 85–9). These evils are not just the ranting syllables of political speeches or the death and terror that stalk the modern world, but the reversal of truth that creates this nightmare world. Buckley examines this evil in its totalitarian forms of the secret police and the state that replaces private life with a ludicrous public parody. He also looks closer to home, at the atrophied and unaware public figure, at fools rewarded, goodness disregarded and virtue steeped in blood. His greatest condemnation is reserved for the 'Christian Gentlemen' who abdicate public responsibility in the name of private morals. Failing to see the evil around them

They struggle to remember which they chose,
A scorched earth policy or
The laying-on of hands.

Buckley, *Selected Poems*, p. 86.

The blasphemy of this confusion between the ultimate symbol of human destruction and a central symbol of Christian humanity can be answered only by the personal surrender described in the last of the poems in this sequence, 'Day with its Dry Persistence'. In this poem, which has no overt political reference, the speaker gives himself simply to the world that surrounds him and the possibility it offers of revealing God. Implicitly, a true politics can follow only from this surrender of self, which offers escape from the divisions the politicians seek to heal by imposing their own unity.

In his major sequence, 'Golden Builders' (pp. 111–36), Buckley creates unity from the cycle of destruction. The opening poem provides the two poles of the sequence, the builders' tools destroying the streets and buildings of Carlton and the inscription on the threatened Sabbath School: 'Feed my Lambs'. Yet the hammers and saws are also musical. They glow in the light of sunset, 'the hammers are molten, they flow with quick light'. They destroy shops and churches, but they also carry the promise of building a new city of God to replace the present carnal city, a place of machines where rats die 'screaming at my knees' and the skill of the engineer guides the abortionist to the 'child like a bolt in her womb'.

In 'Golden Builders' Buckley brings us the whole life of an inner city as he has experienced and seen it — student lodgings, cafes, streets, churches, the university and the cemetery, noises and smells, friends and their tragedies of pride and chance. The verse forms he uses are as varied and opened as the life he describes. While the poles are destruction and creation, the centre is his perception of human fate:

And man is born through grieving skin
And warps his limbs in misery.
Of earth-mould, but high within,
His brain glitters like an eye.

Buckley, *Selected Poems*, p. 126.

This verse comes from the end of a poem in ballad metre that contrasts the doubt and faith, grief and joy that constitute human life. Its last two lines break this rhythm, forcing our attention on the paradox of the brain and eye that grow from the earth mould of which we are constituted. This paradox at large provides the substance of 'Golden Builders', the poem celebrating the city that is at once the place of hope and despair.

Despite its manifold potential, the city provides no sanction for the triumph of good over evil, no way of healing its own divisions. In his latest work, Buckley seeks this sanction both in the past that remains alive in him and in the love that produces the 'late winter child' who unites past and future in herself. In his volume of autobiography, *Cutting Green Hay* (Penguin, Ringwood, 1983), he traces the past back to where he emerges into consciousness as an Australian. The opening sentence states the problem: 'What is clear is the typicalness and the anonymity of my ancestors at the point where they migrate from Ireland' (p. 3). His families are all Irish and

Catholic, but they have little sense of this past and the stories he grows up with are of Australia, lacking any mythological dimension. He does not know his grandparents, yet his father's stories carry with them a sense of lost generations still living through them. This vague sense of continuity has, however, been broken in the reality of everyday life in the new country.

Buckley's autobiography reveals none of the anguished guilt often associated with tales of Catholic boyhood. Its characteristic is rather a sense of incompleteness that he strives to heal by faith, words and actions. In *The Pattern* (Oxford University Press, Melbourne, 1979) the healing comes as he moves through the land of his ancestors. The wholeness he finds in the prose and verse sequence 'Gaeltacht' (pp. 10–15) or in 'Rousings of Munster' (pp. 16–17) is religious but not particularly Christian. Rather, it is the spirit Catholicism shares with paganism, an emanation of the land itself that still carries the memories of the people who suffered and left:

> . . . we

> saw the pan of the valley reeking with mist.
> If you followed them, you might have thought
> it was a hag's country
> because of the gaps in the land's
> contours, houses built with gaps
> inside them . . .
> Each house fits, a stone,
> into the stone jumble; black
> smoke wavers on its surfaces

> Buckley, *Selected Poems*, p. 36.

Like the land, the verse is worn down to the barest images that speak directly to our consciousness. Only in this way, by selection and listening, can the past emerge into the present.

The bringing together of past and present prepares the way for the coming of the daughter, the late winter's child, who grows in Ireland between husband and wife as confirmation and enlargement of their love until the poet at last is able to address her directly: 'rally/your own body into the world' and 'fight your way home' (p. 24). The world, made home for her, receives her as the sanction of wholeness.

Les A. Murray

Murray has sought in his poetry to bring together the various traditions he has inherited. Like Buckley, he has returned to the land of his ancestors, even to the extent of spending a winter in a Scottish crofter's hut. Whereas Buckley is aware of the discontinuity of forgetfulness, the loss of a family and national past, Murray is more concerned with cultural discontinuity. His Scottish and Cornish forebears broke with their own past by immigrating, but they also brought with them a Protestant belief that excluded them from the tradition and communion of European Catholicism. As they cleared the bush for their farms they made the land their own, but at the same time they displaced the Aborigines and destroyed the unity of land and people. Their failure to communicate with the Aborigines left their own identity incomplete. Murray's work attempts to complete the journey of migration by restoring a unity of faith, land and tradition.

The nature of this unity is expressed in the title of his collection *Selected Poems: The Vernacular Republic* (Angus & Robertson, Sydney, 1976). 'Vernacular Republic' stands for a people brought together by a sense of place enshrined in the common language they share. The origin of the term vernacular in the Roman word for a house-slave also suggests a people who, in order to stand in their own right,

Les A. Murray
(*Graeme Kinross-Smith*)

need to cast off the slave status symbolised by subjection to a crown and foreign flag. It represents too the common people, who are kept outside the action of politicians and intellectuals but nevertheless shape the fundamental attitudes of the community.

Murray opposes the vernacular culture to the values of the educated elite. In an essay on 'The Australian Republic' (reprinted in *The Peasant Mandarin*, University of Queensland Press, St Lucia, 1978) he argues that this elite is 'the natural upper class of a socialist world order, and has come into existence as it were in anticipation of that order' (p. 148). Its values are formed by the formal education and high culture that, Murray believes, 'in Australia, as in any other colonial territory, are systems of foreign ideas imposed from above whose usual effect is to estrange people from their own culture and injure their rapport with their own people' (p. 150). The vernacular cultures comprise the Aboriginal, immigrant and folk cultures that are transmitted by word of mouth or, to a limited extent, through books not recognised by the guardians of official culture.

Murray elaborates these themes in 'The Human-Hair Thread' (*Persistence in Folly*, Angus & Robertson, Sydney, 1984). In this essay he shows how in his poetry he has tried to enlarge white Australians' understanding of the land with the older Aboriginal traditions ignored by his forebears. His empathy with rural dwellers makes him suspicious of the urban left that has made Aborigines a political issue. The 'sunny, self-righteous, generalising confidence of urban commentators' has shifted guilt from 'feckless, primitive . . . Doomed, inferior' Aborigines onto 'the white rural population', which it considers 'bigoted, conservative, ignorant, despoilers of the environment, a doomed, obsolete group' (p. 6).

Yet Murray's idealisation of rural values and his feeling for the battlers who, like his own family, have made a place for themselves in the bush, conflicts with a sense of alienation he shares with city-dwellers. In part, this is because he cannot fully share the past of the Aborigines his own ancestors have displaced. Further, he himself is a city-dweller, knowing that cities are 'debris driven by explosions' that nevertheless are the place from which we must start if we are to earn the land's forgiveness for the crimes of our own twentieth century and the deeds of the ancestors who spread the guilt of Europe across the globe ('Toward the Imminent Days', pp. 40–7).

Murray tries to repair the alienation through the constant return, characteristic of urban Australians, to the country and their origins. In 'The Buladelah-Taree Holiday Song-Cycle' (*The Vernacular Republic: Poems 1961–1981*, Angus and Robertson, Sydney, 1982, pp. 159–70) he describes the 'Long Narrow City' of cars that snakes north in 'the season when children return with their children/to the place of Bingham's ghost, of the Old Timber Wharf, of the Big Flood That Time'. They return to a country where the past lives in the names of places and the settled lives of the people who have remained and who welcome their relatives with the hospitality of fresh sheets and childhood rooms. The incantation of the place names for a moment restores the people to their land as they watch from their caravans the 'Cross . . . rising on his elbow, above the glow of the horizon;/carrying a small star in his pocket'. The homeliness of the imagery bridges the gulf between human and nature, but the poem ends on the word 'Holiday', reminding us that the moment may be holy but it is also transitory, aside from daily life.

Behind the desire for return in Murray's work is a deeper hurt he feels for an irrevocable exclusion not merely from his ancestral lands but from the continuity of life. This exclusion could be traced back to his Celtic forebears, driven by their harsh religion from the unity of Christendom and by enclosures from their highland crofts. The story was repeated in Australia when Murray's father, who had worked his father's land, was excluded from his will and driven off the ancestral property (*Persistence in Folly*, p. 17). The human-hair thread has been broken too often to be easily mended. In 'The Steel' (*The People's Otherworld*, Angus & Robertson, Sydney, 1983), the sense of a break with the past becomes absolute in his feelings that his birth by Caesarian section has both separated him from a natural succession himself and been responsible for his mother's later death. The closing lines of the poem associate this separation with his father's continuing hurt at exclusion from his land. The resolution to the poem is not reconciliation, but the conclusion that death and justice are incompatible in this world, where an act of grace can bring destruction. The people's otherworld is the justice they seek and are denied by death, the truth of this world. The ultimate source of exclusion is implicitly not any fact of history, but the beginning of history in the fall of Adam and the expulsion from Paradise. The restoration of continuity, unity and justice can come about only through the return of God to the people in an otherworld that will overcome death.

In his long verse novel, *The Boys Who Stole the Funeral: A Novel Sequence* (Angus & Robertson, Sydney, 1980), Murray attempts to recover this unity through an epic journey that takes its hero back from the city to his rural past and beyond it to rebirth from an Aboriginal Dreaming. Through the journey Cameron Reeby and Kevin Forbutt, the young men who steal old Clarrie Dunn from the undertaker to give him a proper funeral, encounter the dichotomies of displaced Europeans and dispossessed Aborigines, city and country, birth and death, tradition and modernity.

As the boys travel off to the country in their old Morris, Murray contrasts their idealism with the tired indifference of their elders and the casual thuggery of hoods in a wayside cafe. The story is not only a search for meaning, but a parable of modern life. At its heart is the old digger, Clarrie Dunn, who shed his blood in the war as the price of his life. The boys who steal him feel that, brought up in the city without the rituals of war or genuine labour on the land, they are shut out from the reality of life. When they take his body back for burial in the country from which he came, they in their turn are taken into the life of the country.

The country folk preserve the past, but do not have the power to renew it. The economic threat to their livelihood is also a threat to the values they represent. They in turn accept Kevin into their fellowship when he brings their kinsman back to them, but only Kevin can acquire the strength to renew their community. He does this by undergoing rites of expiation for the city and his own immediate family and past.

Clarrie Dunn, the old digger the boys return to his home, is a warrior, a type Murray describes in Section 9 of 'The Buladelah-Taree Song-Cycle' and which he has said is characteristic of the New World ('Human-Hair Thread', p. 25). The warriors have the words of power that come from knowing the rituals of settlement and war. They constitute the basis of the vernacular republic for which Murray

speaks, in opposition to the high culture of colonial servility. Clarrie Dunn has shared this power in a youth spent working the land and then in the male fellowship of the platoon at war. However, the war has halted his further development and, driven from the land, he has spent his further life vainly seeking for the security of the platoon. His achievement has been to hand on his sense of continuity to his nephew Kevin, who responds to it by giving him a proper funeral, and thus earning his own place in the tradition. In Murray's economy, however, although the place can be earned by human response, it can be finally secured only by human sacrifice. This is provided through the shooting of Kevin's mate Cameron, the ritual scalding of Noeline Kampff, the city harpie who has stolen his father and threatens the balance of sexual relationships, and Kevin's mystic initiation into the landscape at the hands of figures representing respectively the Celtic and the Aboriginal past.

After he has been released through this expiation from his city ties, Kevin is free to work with his newly-discovered relatives on the land that had been intended for Clarrie Dunn, and to anticipate in his turn marriage and the continuation of the tradition. However, this resolution depends on the reader accepting the mystic significance of Kevin's final initiation. In this the Celtic Berrigan and the Aboriginal Njimbin cut him to reveal the crystal of truth that joins him with time. They then teach him the 'blood history of the continent', according to which the original rites of the Aborigines have been displaced, first by farmers waging war with their ancestors, and then by 'consumers of landscapes' who deny death and so kill their children. He is then allowed to eat of the bowl that sets him apart from others and from easy satisfactions, but reveals to him 'the depths of your happiness' and commits him to give up the childhood of illusion, to share his dreams as he cuts down his 'childhood forest to feed your children' (p. 66). Finally, they take the whole of the landscape and its history and fold it into a stone they massage against his stomach until, 'Warm, particulate, it enters him' as 'a mate for your crystal, to help you with civilization' (p. 67).

The resolution of Murray's sequence is in effect the product of a meditation on the place of sacrifice in a godless world. The modern world has lost any sense of the spiritual in the landscape as it had been experienced in both Aboriginal and Celtic traditions.

It has also lost its sense of the sacramental. The mass the priest celebrates for Clarrie Dunn is shared by the congregation as a social practice confirming the solidarity of their community. For the moment

> humans are stilled, the worlds are linked
> and the centred Mass-bell rings.

> Murray, *Funeral*, p. 35.

Immediately afterwards, however, the police, agents of the state, are at the gate seeking to arrest the boys who have made this moment possible. They finally escape only through the death of one and the rebirth of the other.

The problem with this rebirth, however, is that the poem promises mysticism but offers mystification. The death that has preceded it seems arbitrary, the ceremony itself remains irrelevant to the problems of continuity and economic survival the poem has raised. Kevin may find his own solution through marriage, but Cameron is dead and his Jeanette can never return home. The re-enactment of the past cannot give it back to the present.

Murray's language itself enacts his attempt to renew the past in the actualities of the present. His rhythms loosen the traditional poetic forms in the laconics of Australian speech. In the 'Song-Cycle', the vernacular is strengthened by its marriage to the rhythms of Aboriginal song-cycles, which with their repetitions and rhythms accenting the first syllable of phrase and line obtain a similar incantational effect to some of the celebratory passages of the Elizabethan prayer-book or the King James version of the scriptures. In *The Boys Who Stole the Funeral* Murray adapts the rhythms of common speech to the form of the sonnet. While this works well for the main part of the narrative, it fails to achieve the desired resolution of incarnating the other in the ordinary at its mystical conclusion.

The effect of the sequence of sonnets is that of a succession of snapshots, of a family album arranged to tell a tale. Each is self-contained, but contributes to shaping an emerging totality. As the boys and Clarrie Dunn's people prepare for his funeral, we overhear talk that also takes us to the heart of Murray's concern about the fate of his country:

> Nothing that the west has done to the tribes of the
> world

exceeds the wickedness we have done to our own. And now every year we are slowly withdrawing
> from this continent
from all the hope and work, shrinking back into
> the cities . . .

> Murray, *Funeral*, p. 18.

The complaint in these first two lines is given substance with the metaphor of the long withdrawal, the shrinkage, with its connotations of a reduction of humanity. But it draws its strength from what we have already seen of the country life, that combines practicality with a living sense of what is proper. It can cope with death, and therefore with life, with a sense of humour that is at the same time a respect for the decencies of living.

At the end of the work, however, this incarnation of the formal in the everyday is lacking. The Berrigan and the Njimbin, with the various spellings of their names indicating their lack of specific ambience, are given a certain disreputable reality by their sardonic comments to each other, but their offering to Kevin exists only as the rhetoric of words:

> This is the grit that sparks the pearl, chants the
> Birroogum,
> crystal in the sheaths of the coloured coatings,
> crystal,
> light stone of light, stone that heals, touch of
> visions.

> This is the fraction we heal in light, chants like
> Njimbin,
> the craze and the crush, the stains we wash, the
> facets
> we uncover and plane, the crystal in the crystal.

> Murray, *Funeral*, p. 63.

The metaphor exists only as metaphor, without relation to the world it is supposed to redeem. The language professes to refer to the outside world, or to a reality beyond the outside world, but finally refers to nothing, not even itself. It fails to achieve the reconciliation Murray seeks.

This conflict is at the heart of Murray's poetry. He is no Luddite, breaking machines and turning his face against the modern world. Rather, he seeks to bring modernity back into touch with its sources. In poems

E' (*The Vernacular Republic: Poems 1961–* pp. 54–59) or 'The Powerline Incarnation', 141–3), he shows how the works of science ...d technology are both instruments and products of humankind's marvellous fertility of invention, and can be the means of sudden, if sometimes puzzling, revelation. But the source of this revelation is finally outside this world. It is no longer contained within its culture and therefore can be shared only by initiates. Thus the poetry cannot bring to the vernacular republic the unity Murray perceives as both its need and its promise. The human-hair thread unites past and present only in a common predicament.

Yet it would be wrong to leave Murray's work on a negative note. If he has not shown how salvation can be brought to the vernacular republic, he has at least made us aware of the republic's existence. The rural or 'Boeotian' world of his poetry is more than a corrective to the intellectual cruelties represented by the abstractions of the city. It is a community in which the values of sense and decency are created through the intercourse of people going about everyday work that is sanctioned not by profit but by the usefulness of the food and clothing it produces. This conception of work shows a way beyond the dichotomies of the elite and the people he finds at the heart of the intellectual and cultural life of the cities. The sharing that occurs in the 'Buladelah-Taree Holiday Song-Cycle' suggests the basis for a community of the future built on these values, just as its form, recalling the Aboriginal traditions, creates a link with an older past. Murray may not have created a unity, but he has at least restored some of the links.

Geoffrey Lehmann

Lehmann shares with Les Murray, with whom he was associated both at Sydney University and in their first collections of poems (*The Ilex Tree*, Australian National University Press, Canberra, 1965), a concern to redress the disintegration of contemporary society by bringing to it the unity that country people construct with nature through their everyday work. Lehmann is not, however, so much concerned as Murray with preserving a tradition from the past. Indeed when he writes about classical Europe it is with an interest in it as an example of a civilisation in decay rather than with any desire for emulation. Yet

the ordered country life he describes is as much a constructed ideal as was the nineteenth century's view of classical Greece.

This ideal is developed most fully in his *Ross' Poems* (Angus & Robertson, Sydney, 1978). This book comprises seventy-five monologues by a man reflecting on his life as a farmer in central western New South Wales. Through these reflections he recreates not only his own life but also the world of his parents and neighbours, brother and children, a world made from the interaction of human work and uncontrollable chance:

Every year the weather's unusual.
Stepping from my bed in the dark
I tread on the stem of my pipe
and break it.
Directing milk jets into a plastic bucket
I'm distracted for a second
And a hoof of polished ebony shifts stance
and tips the white foam on the earth.

Lehmann, *Ross' Poems*, p. 60.

The free verse counterpoints the succession of images and the grammar without imposing any further structures of rhyme or rhythm. The effect of this is to make the reader immediately aware of the things from which the speaker makes his life, with only the occasional line marking a moment of decisive action. The verbs and prepositions work below this structure to build a syntax of actions that creates in the poetry the unity the speaker makes from the otherwise random details of his life. The form thus mimes the nature of rural life itself, a succession of seasons and tasks that demand the work of attention rather than action. Yet this unobtrusive attention still gives the whole the only structure, the only meaning it has. The farmer makes his farm and his landscape from the raw materials of nature, just as the poet, attending to the farmer's words and work, builds from them a series of poems that encapsulate a life in its context of a time that extends back to the first dawning of life.

Lehmann's poetry is conservative and backward-looking in its invocation of this way of life that machines have made obsolete, and that even in its time was dependent on the forces of the market and manufacturing it preferred to ignore. Ross recognises the world of commerce and chemicals and bursting populations that threatens his own, but he can rest secure in a continuity reaching back into the depths of human history, a place where 'Man's tools' are still 'the last stronghold/of something ancient' (p. 18). This continuity is, however, in jeopardy in an economy that converts the products of the farm into goods for sale and thus determines its conditions of existence, just as the farmer ignores the world of the Aborigines that this economy has displaced, and who appear in the poems only in a glimpse through a hotel window or as wild blacks in the memories of an old man.

In exploring the depths and limits of Ross' life, Lehmann demonstrates an understanding of the environment as something we construct from the data of nature rather than as something given and elemental. He returns our attention from the economic value of the farmer's work to the world he makes by this work.

Ross, the practical farmer, has no illusions about beneficent nature. Instead, he uses the skills he has learnt from his forebears to continue their work of creating from the environment a harmony that sustains the human values represented by parents, wife, children and neighbours. By learning to understand the land, he makes a possible future for a European civilisation transplanted to this far verge of the world. Yet he is not able to give this future even to his children, who are 'stolen by that Evening Star' (p. 61) and leave the country for cities and lovers. The potential future continues to exist only in isolated rural pockets and in the metaphysical inner world Lehmann explores elsewhere.

Randolph Stow

What Stow seeks in his writing is to be found in the future rather than recovered from the past. The landscape of his work is itself alienating, demanding not understanding but surrender. Characteristically, his poem 'The Singing Bones' carries an epigraph from Barcroft Boake and is a rewriting of Boake's ballad, 'Where the Dead Men Lie' (Hall (ed.), *Collins Book of Australian Poetry*, 1981, pp. 47–9; 285). The past is the memory of the pioneers who 'died of landscape', but for whom no holy days are kept. 'The

Ruins of the City of Hay' (pp. 287–8) recalls the city in the field of childhood. This city is an image of all the fabled cities that offered safe refuges from death only to be blown away by the winds of time. Fulfilment comes only when, as in Stow's poem 'Dust' (pp. 288–9), the settler abandons the effort of resistance and allows 'Jungles, deserts, stars — the six days of creation' to come 'floating in'. The woman who so surrenders, however, does not herself see the miracle of August for which she has opened the doors, and her neighbours continue unaware, sleeping 'behind sealed doors, with feather/dusters beside their beds'. Life bears its truth only to those who no longer seek it.

Stow's early novel, *To the Islands* (revised edition, Collins/Picador, Sydney, 1983 [1958]) opens with a scene of the Garden of Eden. The snake is already in the garden. He lives in Heriot, the missionary who is both the god whose will has created the garden, and the Adam who is compelled to earn his daily bread in it by the sweat of his brow. He appears also in the form of Heriot's antagonist, the Aboriginal Rex, who is responsible for the death of Esther, Heriot's daughter in God, and the corruption of Stephen, his son in God.

Randolph Stow
(*Photo: Mark Gerson*)

The main action of the novel deals with Heriot's realisation that he no longer has any faith, and possibly never has had. He believes he has killed Rex with the blow of Cain, and abandons the mission to wander in the wilderness. He is followed by the Aboriginal Justin, who saves him both from suicide and from starvation, and leads him to the coast. During the journey Heriot gives up all remaining ambition, even for self-justification. Like Lear, Heriot realises his common humanity only as he comes to appear mad in the eyes of others. He accepts his guilt, but cannot begin to free himself from it until he recognises the pride at its roots. This he does when he meets a fellow-murderer, and realises that neither can offer the other anything except understanding. His final human encounters, with the crazed survivor of an abandoned mission and with the mouthless gods painted by generations of Aborigines, release him from his past. At the end of the novel he waits alone on the beach, gazing at the sunset for the vision of the islands that promise release from all time.

Heriot finds his release only when he learns from the old Aborigine, Justin, to listen to the land. Listening remains the central theme in Stow's work. At the start of *Tourmaline* (Macdonald, London, 1963), the whole township is listening for the coming of hope, for a return of the water and the gold that can renew its life and its connections with the world. The story of the novel is narrated by the policeman, the Law, who represents both the memory and the order of the town but cannot sustain its life. The diviner, Michael, who comes from the desert to the town, represents not the old Law but the new life of material and spiritual renewal. The material hope comes from Michael's discovery of a gold reef, the spiritual from his establishment of a new church combining both Christian and Aboriginal beliefs in a wild nocturnal ritual. The Law is subverted, and the townsfolk desert the storekeeper and the publican who have maintained their material existence, and follow their new prophet to his promised riches.

The novel is a complex parable of true and false spirituality. Michael, the water diviner, creates a unity based on delusion and cruelty. He defeats even the natural love that Deborah opposes to his power. The Law remains suspicious of him, but is powerless to resist. Only Tom Spring, the storekeeper, and old Dave Speed, a prospector who remains outside the town's society, keep their integrity, but they lack the words to convince their fellows. Even when

Michael himself is exposed and disappears into the desert, the publican Kestrel inherits his power. The voices of the possessed fill the ears of their fellows and so prevent them from listening to the slow movement of the sand or waiting for the natural return of the rains that alone promise life.

The life-giving waters and the gardens they can sustain represent a continuing human hope, but the desert reveals the truth. As Dave Speed puts it to Tom Spring:

'. . . You and me can remember when that pub veranda was covered all round with passion-vines, and bloody good it was, too, to sit out there at this time of day, with a schooner, in the cool . . . But the place is better now than it ever was then. We've got to the bare bones of the country, and I reckon we're getting to the bones of ourselves. If the water comes, it'll be when we've stopped needing it. We're coming true, mate'.

Stow, *Tourmaline*, p. 86.

Speed's words offer the explorers' myth of truth through hardship as an alternative to the easy dream of a wasteland subdued and blossoming.

Stow confronts the issues of community and the individual more directly in his partly autobiographical *The Merry-Go-Round in the Sea* (Penguin, Harmondsworth, 1968 [1965]). This is the story of a boy, Rob Coram, growing up around Geraldton in Western Australia during the Second World War and post-war years. His life is equally involved with his schoolfriends in the township and with his close family of cousins and aunts and uncles from four generations and as many properties. The family offers the certainty symbolised by the merry-go-round that always returns to the same point. But his experience shows this security as an illusion. The merry-go-rounds are successively broken, and even the merry-go-round in the sea is revealed as a rusting shipwreck, no more than a 'crude promise of another merry-go-round most perilously rooted in the sea' (p. 276). This unattainable vision is the only security that survives.

If there is no security, however, Stow nevertheless shows that the world into which Rob grows is rich with possibility. His family brings together the traditions of Europe in an Australia shaped by the deeds of the pioneers, the words of the poets and the facts of the environment. Rob's aunts give him the rebel traditions of the Celts and Eureka, his grandfather brings the heritage of the squattocracy, and his uncle by marriage offers the romantic past of Malta. Rob's consciousness is fired by British and Australian poets and nourished by exultation in the senses that bring him the sounds and scents and seasons of the town, the fragrances of his aunts' exotic gardens and the delicate beauties of the countryside. At home he shares the life of the gentry, at school the rough mateship of the town. Yet the security of this warm community is jeopardised both by conflicts within and threats without. Only as he faces these does Rob discover his own identity.

The conflict within the community arises from the contradictions between the British traditions, themselves split between English conformity and Celtic rebellion, and the Australian environment. The external threat comes from the war with Japan. This provides a central image of the bloodshed on which the apparent security of the community is based. Killing is a constant part of the life and history of Australia to which Rob feels himself heir. He participates in the trapping and shooting on which farming depends. This killing merely continues the history of Europeans in Australia, which begins on the west coast when the bloody deeds of the Dutch on the Abrolhos Islands contradict the brave name of Costa Branca, White Coast, supposedly bestowed on their landfall by first comers. The islands are just over the horizon beyond Rob's sight, but they remain part of his consciousness:

> Darkness and fires and massacre. The staid Dutch merchants and their wives from the wrecked *Batavia*, camping as best they could on the barren islands, must have settled down grumbling on that night. And then, the torches and swords, the blood on rock and sea, the mutineers prancing, in the richest clothes from the rifled chests, round their crazy peacock of a Captain-General.
>
> Stow, *Merry-Go-Round*, p. 113.

The combination of greed and death, riches and madness, remains a constant in the history of Australia that Rick describes sardonically as 'First, half-starved abos', then marooned mutineers, then lead-mining convicts. And at last, respectable folks like us Maplesteads, kid' (p. 238). Even this apparent stability is

precarious, as Rob senses when he watches his town succumb to the bulldozers and realises that 'a world so congruent, so close-knit by history and blood and old acquaintance, had become fragmented into a mere municipality' (p. 215).

In coming to terms with the bloodshed of history, Rob has also had to recognise the existence of the Aborigines at the borders of his consciousness. His elders despise them as 'blackniggers', but their disturbing presence qualifies his security in his country. Black schoolfellows share his classroom and the bunyip haunts the waterholes of his childhood. His Celtic imagination finds a sympathy with the painted hands on the rock walls of a cave he visits on a picnic with his aunts, but he is unable to resolve the relationship between these relics of the past and the miserable creatures he knows in the present. The aunts dismiss his questions, leaving him with only a disturbing awareness of a reality outside the certainties of the comfortable society he knows:

> He felt the cold rock under his hand, where a dead boy's hand had once rested. Time and change had removed this child from his country, and his world was not one world, but had in it camps of the dispossessed. Above the monument of the dead black people, the sheoaks sounded cold, sounded colder than rock.
>
> Stow, *Merry-Go-Round*, p. 56.

This awareness points to the central contradiction of the novel, between the achievements of the society within which the boy grows to consciousness and the precarious foundations it has within this new country at the end of the world. By the end of the novel, the security of family and community have crumbled, and Rob knows he must face both inner and outer coldness on his own. Stow's later works leave Australia to explore this mystery of the individual in the strange jungles of Papua and the cosiness of England's home counties.

Poets of the Suburbs

For many poets of the post-war generation the art of poetry was not so much a search for unity as an attempt to capture the fleeting moment in the constant dance of forms and words. Much of their work is set in cities and suburbs, with their inherent theme of the individual life disjoined by isolation from both society and history. Bruce Dawe and Bruce Beaver capture this society in the laconic rhythms of its speech. Evan Jones and Chris Wallace-Crabbe write a more formal, even courtly, verse, which sets the commonplace in a framework of tradition and myth.

Chris Wallace-Crabbe

Wallace-Crabbe's work claims the whole past for the present. In one of his earliest poems he writes of his attempt to find 'accents that ring true' in the present to retell the ageless truth that

> Time without end, the living soul
> Creates and conquers some new hell.

> Wallace-Crabbe, *The Music of Division*, Angus & Robertson, Sydney, 1959, p. 3.

The bleak vision of the a life of unchanging fate is answered by the strong verbs of creation and conquest, which give form to the cityscape he sees around him and the painful struggle he envisages through it. The formal structure of the poem, with its tight rhyming scheme and repeated couplet ending each stanza, suggests the pattern each life is fated to endure. This concept becomes concrete in the next poem in this collection, where the railway station becomes an image of both the loneliness of the individual and of the arteries that run through it and create a 'tangled unity/of man with man and man with part' (p. 5).

In later work, Wallace-Crabbe develops this awareness into a specific commentary on Australia, which stands apart from the world and yet shares its dilemmas. Speaking for his readers and contemporaries in his poem on 'Melbourne' (*In Light and Darkness*, Angus & Robertson, Sydney, 1964), he reflects that

> . . . like the bay, our blood flows easily,
> Not warm, not cold (in all things moderate),
> Following our familiar tides. Elsewhere
> Victims are bleeding, sun is beating down
> On patriot, guerrilla, refugee.
> We see the newsreels when we dine in town.

> Wallace-Crabbe, *In Light and Darkness*, p. 4.

Wallace-Crabbe is ambivalent about his people. He recognises that the Australian dream ends with the gardener tending his own back yard while cars strangle his city and ideas grow elsewhere, but he also finds a certain comfort in a country where 'much has died . . . Little has been born'. As he says in 'Terra Australis', this leaves Australians as

> . . . the final children of the earth
> Whom knowledge has not scarred,
> Delighting still in sunlight and green grass
> Back in our own backyard.

> Wallace-Crabbe, *Selected Poems*, Angus & Robertson, Sydney, 1973, p. 40.

Wickedness belongs elsewhere, with adulthood.

Innocence, however, is complicated as it becomes involved in history. Wallace-Crabbe, like Buckley, wanders far from Australia in his work, taking the pilgrimage to Asia, Europe and the 'damp Antipodes' of London with its 'tinny gas meters' and thoughts of mythical forebears who nevertheless continue to rumble with a very Australian 'bloody great thunderous laughter' (*The Emotions Are Not Skilled Workers*, Angus & Robertson, Sydney, 1980, p. 69). The journey through time leads him also into more complex emotions and looser forms that allow the free play of words around the constant variety and beauty that redeems the pain in his work. As he says in his 'Pagan Song',

> . . . the sun is new every day:
> spring always returns.

> Wallace-Crabbe, *Emotions*, p. 53.

His optimism is severely tested when he contemplates the futile battlefields of Gallipoli in a long sequence that creates a montage from the classical associations of the Aegean, the ironic reflections of the troops and prose extracts from their actual letters and diaries. The poem closes with memories of 'the spasmodic fire of ghostly riflemen' alongside 'the funeral rites of Hector, tamer of horses' (p. 24). It thus moves us back from history to myth, leaving us to find its meaning in our own time.

He again brings myth and history together in 'Star Quality' (pp. 67–75) which searches for traces of God in moments of joy and epics of endurance and loss. After examining attempts to create a god through art, science, religion, knowledge, exploration, he concludes:

> Listen, God, whoever you are,
> The debt is paid in blood;
> Slow, gold, the sandstone rises
> And seedless apples plump Apollo's tree.

Wallace-Crabbe, *Emotions*, p. 75.

Despite the ambivalent lack of seed, the promise of apples and gold remains. The conclusion has an Australian innocence and courage.

Evan Jones

Wallace-Crabbe walks us through cities and countries and history in search of meaning. His contemporary Evan Jones instead stands aside as a wry observer of the action. Even in the delicate love poems to wife and family we are conscious as we read of the watcher in the wings still aware of his separateness in the most intimate moments. Watching his infant daughter he reflects on the time to come when she will want of him only 'room and board, no questions'. The only comfort for the parents is in the knowledge that 'always, somewhere, still' they will 'stand between you and the darkest night' (*Recognitions*, Australian National University Press, Canberra, 1978). The bond of the family is real, the only defence against despair, but it is only that. The individual remains alone.

Friends, places, ceremonies in Jones' poetry serve the purpose of keeping loneliness at bay, of allowing the speaker to find a secure place in the world. The form of the poems serves the same purpose, disclosing order in the random play of words and feelings. So the poem 'Snapshots for Margot' (p. 11) opens with three lines that seem related only by approximately similar length and metre, and the casual associations of a Carlton party. These are then answered by another three that unfold a pattern of rhyme, beginning with repetition of the third line and ending with a return to the first in the line 'You moved across the threshold and stood near it'. Just as the action of the woman completes the moment, the light phrase 'near it' lightly answers the 'claret' of the

first line. The same pattern in the final verse leads us to the image of the speaker sitting:

> . . . reading, brooding, seeing you as
>   my love, my bride, my wife, and still my love.

Jones, *Recognitions*, p. 11.

In rounding the circle of completeness, these lines enclose the speaker in the house without cancelling the image of him sitting apart, observing the love that is at the same time his fulfilment.

Geoff Page

The name of Geoff Page's collection, *Smalltown Memorials* (University of Queensland Press, St Lucia, 1975) seems to sum up the achievement and ambitions of this group of domestic poets. The title poem suggests one episode of excitement recalled amid countrytown drowsiness. Yet the poem reaches a concluding image of hard stone that both corrects the more fashionable social concerns of the present age and reminds the reader of an underlying strength in the otherwise insignificant community. Page seeks this strength in lines pared to the barest sequence of images. By apparently skating over the surface of things without comment he reveals the depths of joy and despair beneath the appearances of everyday existence. In his 'Poem of the Eye' (*Clairvoyant in Autumn*, Angus & Robertson, Sydney, 1983, pp. 74–6), he traces the associations of the eye from the trivial and everyday to the terrible. The opening image of the widow with her husband's glasses carries its overtones of grief. These are developed through the speaker's observation both of the vulnerability that lies in the eyes of cattle and the wonder of the eye in the pattern of evolution. The poem then swerves horrifyingly to a final image of our time, the blinding of Indian thieves with 'cycle spokes and acid' that produce the screams that 'will break always/what sleep is left in us'. The simplicity of the concluding line, 'The eye is our most human part', thus takes us to the centre of our human predicament, the wonders we can see and the grief and terror we cannot avoid.

R.A. Simpson

Page shows less interest in form than in image. By contrast, R.A. Simpson's poems are formally elegant reflections on the problems of faith and commitment. The form provides the detachment that enables him to view the emotion, the sense of loss, the reminders of crime and betrayal that haunt the suburban existence and make even childhood drawings the furnishings of a prison. Against the loneliness he can place only the task of the artist, the Michelangelo, to make a 'conquest of this hour' (*This Real Pompeii*, Jacaranda, Brisbane, 1964).

Peter Porter

Porter similarly takes refuge in form from the human predicament that 'Man is social and should live alone' (*Collected Poems*, Oxford University Press, Oxford, 1983). In his case the poetry does not so much unravel this puzzle as convert it into a pure dance of words. The self is lost in the recurring and absurd patterns of art and history, which nevertheless still plant enduring seeds:

> Backwards went the barefoot sage: he chanted
> to the hedge birds and fell over the cliff,
> the chronicles showed what could be done with an
>   'if',
> winds still storm the trees he planted.

> Porter, *Collected Poems*, p. 145.

Both comedy and tragedy are, however, encompassed by Porter's ironic awareness of the ultimate absurdity produced in our lives by the unbridgeable gap between our consciousness and the outer world. He defines his own condition in 'In the Giving Vein' (pp. 173–4):

> We're in a fire, singing; I'm the one
> Whose voice you can't hear; perhaps my round
> O is agony, I shall insist it's praise.

> Porter, *Collected Poems*, p. 174.

The existence of any listener is as problematic as the existence of the speaker, but the speaker still insists on defining his own action.

Andrew Taylor

In Taylor's work, a similar impulse to find the permanent in a world of change leads not so much to the play of form as to the relaxation of the self into the comforts of domesticity. His suburban lover never comes to the girl who waits, but even in her waiting love still dwells, 'muttering and immense over the roofs' ('The Lover' in *The Cool Change*, University of Queensland Press, St Lucia, 1971, p. 70). Her expectations create their own satisfaction, so that

> Later she will go inside, out of the rain,
> disappointed, yet she will form a prayer
> of thanks to him who came to terrifyingly near.

> Taylor, *Cool Change*, p. 70.

It is little, but what life has to offer.

David Rowbotham

Rowbotham has followed a different path to a similar end. In his poem 'Pen of Feathers' (*Selected Poems*, University of Queensland Press, St Lucia, 1975, p. 144) he describes his progression from 'mountains to the sea and more —/And to the shoreless from the sea-made shore'; that is, from romantic poetry of nature to urban and philosophical themes. This he attributes not to any attempt to follow fashion, but to following his own path towards 'the theme of growing old'. The resulting poems range from recollections of boyhood in Toowoomba through reflections on the country towns and their people to accounts of Brisbane and the wider world of his overseas travels. A constant theme is the person or place caught between two worlds. These include men like Pepper, the mixed-blood stockman from Camooweal who is accepted by the whites only to find his dark ancestry seeping back into him; Brisbane, a city avoiding its future by denying its past, and the poet himself in America, trying to bring together his antipodean youth, the San Francisco of Francis Drake and the Golden Gate, and a Europe that holds both the origins of contemporary Australia and the shadows of war. For the most part, he meditates on these themes in restrained and lyrical verse. When, however, he contemplates the tragic triumph of the Manhattan project that gave the world the atomic bomb, he turns to a free verse that uses the rhythms of speech to bring together both the high hopes and their subsequent betrayal by 'thirty years of president-commanders/ Stockpiling pure research despoiled by selling' (pp. 160–1). The events provide an imagery that makes any complexity of form redundant.

All of these post-war poets understand the pain and terror as well as the joy of life. Their work, however, circumscribes these feelings, transmuting them into art and thus making it possible for us to contemplate and bear them. The ordinariness of the life they show is not an avoidance of reality, but a refuge from which we can look at the world without being destroyed by it. In this they very much represent the Australia of their time, when Australians had ceased to be worried about their identity but still felt secure behind the protection of tariffs and Western allies. They remained onlookers in a world where the media brought news of wars and horror came to them through the media, but in which they participated only vicariously through their expeditionary armies. Even the atomic bomb seemed to most a promise of safety rather than a threat of extinction. Page's 'Poem of the Eye' is in a sense a farewell to this period, as he recognises that Australians can no longer keep their eyes shut to painful truth. Yet even this poem shares with the others a stance of remoteness. In both tone and form the work implies an audience of the select few who choose a suburban life but remain above it, communicating with the noble past and the cultural centres of the present. The poets draw their materials from their Australian experience in order to construct a universal country of the mind. The inhabitants of this country are, however, few.

Two other poets of the suburbs speak for their community rather than from it. Both Bruce Beaver and Bruce Dawe have used the vernacular not to construct a private world but to disclose the world this vernacular culture creates. Rather than seeking escape in form or image, they use the rhythms of common speech to portray at once the sleep and the terror of the everyday experience they share with their suburban neighbours.

Bruce Beaver

Beaver's poetry is the more immediately personal and terrifying. The first of his 'Letters to Live Poets' (*Selected Poems*, Angus & Robertson, Sydney, 1979, p. 35) opens in an apparent void:

God knows what was done to you.
I may never find out fully.
The truth reaches us slowly here,

is delayed in the mail continually
or censored in the tabloids . . .

Beaver, *Selected Poems*, p. 35.

The lines speak of a desolation into which news of terrible happenings elsewhere drops inexplicably. Only as the poem proceeds does it reveal time and place as the period of the war in Vietnam and the suburb of Manly. This latter piece of information is conveyed to the reader only as the writer stops thinking of the poet to whom the letter is ostensibly addressed and remembers that

near by our home there's an aquarium
that people pay admission to,
watching sharks at feeding time:
the white, jagged rictus in the grey
sliding anonymity,
faint blur of red through green,
the continually spreading stain.

I have to live near this, if not quite with it.

Beaver, *Selected Poems*, p. 37.

Manly's tourist attraction becomes a nightmare image not just of Vietnam but of the contemporary world.

These lines do not convert nightmare into art so that we can contemplate it in safety but use art to remind us both of the reality of the horror, of the machines of private and public bureaucracy that sustain it, and of the human life that it threatens, the 'poet still living at this address'. Poetry, the art of truthful speech, becomes a means of maintaining humanity and, literally, sanity. It enables us to remember what lies outside the prisons we build for ourselves. As Beaver reminds us in Letter IV, there are

Above the roof television aerials, certainly,
But also clouds.

Beaver, *Selected Poems*, p. 38.

The clouds represent not just nature, but a natural world that we call into being as we observe and enter it. Our ability to survive depends on our ability to observe and record such apparently mundane facts, from which springs the exultation that answers the destruction we make around us. Nature, with its apparently wasteful and random delight in life, offers the alternative to sterility and death in the suburbs:

> . . . Is it waste to ripen fully and truly in season?
> To fall like some strange and feathered fruitage
> out of a sky all sunset and first stars?
> Is it worse than our unique way of falling
> out of a wastage of breath into an earth soured
> by the blood and tears of each ravaged generation?

> Beaver, Letter IX, *Selected Poems*, pp. 45–6.

In later poems in this sequence the writer collapses the distinctions between internal and external, human and natural. He enters his own hell of mental illness where only 'Three depressants and one diuretic a day' save him 'from the pit'. He becomes one with the outcasts of life, the metho drinkers in the park, Nebuchadnezzar on his knees and the monsters in the menagerie (Letter XII, pp. 49–50), and eventually comes to understand 'only the man who is at war within himself' (Letter XV, p. 53). The letters chart the sway of his mood between depression and elation, between 'self-destroying anger and inner violence' on the one hand and calming memories of days by the sea or at his grandparents' house in the country on the other, culminating in visions of the denizens of hell that grow the faces of angels. As the oppositions of calm and violence, sanity and madness, good and evil dissolve into each other, the poetry reaches a balance in the still moment created by 'the gift of the living word' (Letter XXXIV, Hall (ed.), *Collins Book of Australian Poetry*, pp. 303–4). By refraining from imposing form, and instead allowing the rhythms to speak themselves, the poet is able to speak the truth of his conflicts, and so escape them without denying them. Yet, revealingly, he does not reprint his final poem in his *Selected Poems*, ending the sequence instead with a vision of maggots and angels (p. 73).

After his *Letters*, Beaver reverted to an apparently looser but in fact more tightly controlled form in which punctuation and grammar are relaxed to enable the verse to work more through the associations and placements of the words on the page. In this work the rhythms are subordinated to the images, but Beaver continues to speak of people and places he has known. With the autobiographical *As It Was* (University of Queensland Press, St Lucia, 1979) he

returns to the looser rhythms of the vernacular, and alternates longer reflective poems with passages of prose in a discontinuous narrative of his life from his earliest memories through attempts at suicide and his mental breakdown, and a long section entitled 'bucolics' in which he recalls his stays on his uncle's dairy farm. At the centre of the book a long section called 'The Poems' (p. 57–66) talks of how his poems grow out of the streets, beach and rubbish of Manly, from 'everywhere else/than within me'. The more clearly autobiographical passages extend this concept by showing how he himself is created from and by his surroundings, taking into himself the conflicts and anxieties that surround him, as well as the moments of joy that provide the ground of his meaning. The discontinuity of the form reflects the discontinuity he finds in life, just as the act of setting it down gives stability to its ebb and flow. The words of the narrative in turn counterpoint the sepia photographs of the author and his family. These snapshots, while lacking the depth and inwardness of the words, nevertheless fix the elements of his life in the precise moments of time in which they are located, and thus serve to make the link between outer event and inner experience. They give the book the grounding in a world of reality that country-dwellers gain from the fixed routine of their work, but that is lacking in the disjointed rhythms of Beaver's city.

Bruce Dawe

In Dawe's work the pain is hidden by the wit and rhythm of his forms and the variety of his subjects. He tends to use either the third person or dramatic monologue, thus concealing the person of the poet behind the voice of the speaker. Dawe's command of ordinary speech is matched only by Barry Breen or Leon Slade at their best, and his tone is unmistakable. It suggests the best of Australian black-and-white art, the sardonic drawl of understatement found in the cartoons of Alex Gurney or Stan Cross, the idea of the battler drawn by Jim Bancks or Emile Mercier, but also the depth and compassion of George Finey. All these elements appear in a poem like 'Drifters' (*Sometimes Gladness: Collected Poems 1954–1978*, Longman Cheshire, Melbourne, 1978, p. 101). The long loose lines of the poem slouch over the page like the the drawl of the people themselves, each encapsulating the reaction of one part of the family to

Bruce Dawe
(*Longman Cheshire*)

their next departure, until the final quatrain of four short lines which, in the single image of the bright berries held out by the wife to her husband, combine both the promise of her life and its continual thwarting.

The tone and style of 'Drifters' are exactly the same as his justly famous 'Life-Cycle' (p. 180–1), which uses Victorian football as an image of humankind's need for pattern and ceremony. The poem works simultaneously in two directions. It satirises the obsession of modern society with spectator sport, which it has made its religion. Yet, like all satire, the poem works only because it takes its subject seriously. The speaker does not mock; he shares the faith that Chicken Smallhorn, champion player and commentator, returns like the corn-god who renews life, and that the 'six-foot recruit from Eaglehawk' provides the 'hope of salvation'. The poem shows how humanity's needs remain constant behind the everchanging forms we find to satisfy them.

At the heart of Dawe's poetry is the realisation of the chasm between our needs and our experience. In 'Life-Cycle' this appears only in the inadequacy of the vehicle of football for the weight of expectation we put upon it. In 'Drifters' the wife's ability to bridge

the gap with the gift of berries only makes her recurring disappointment the more wounding. In 'Homecoming' (p. 90) the chasm between need and possibility is made greater by the technological resources that enable the bodies to be brought home from Vietnam while leaving unchanged the 'bitter geometry' that makes the whole exercise 'too late, too early'. The subdivisions society provides to contain our lives are unable to contain our feelings. In this lies both the comedy and the tragedy of Dawe's poetry, which is a protest against this condition of modern humanity.

This protest is expressed in terms as varied as the bitter 'A Victorian Hangman Tells His Love' (p. 171) and the quieter but equally intense 'At Shagger's Funeral' (p. 117). The first, a poem of protest against capital punishment, nevertheless shows the hangman as also a victim of a time hideously deformed by puritanical zeal. The hangman, unable to accept the grossness of life, takes his victim as the bride who will lead him to sanctity. Shagger, on the other hand, is a social being whose life is too large to be wound up by the mere decencies of a funeral. Both poems are animated by the urgency of the speaking voice, which in the one case gives its own form to the free verse, and in the other over-rides the formalities of rhyme with the sense of indignation at the rude interruption of a life lived with such gusto. The poetry in both cases comes as a surprise, emerging from the speaking voice rather than being imposed on it. Dawe achieves this effect even in a poem spoken by as unsympathetic a character as the drill sergeant in 'Weapons Training' (p. 87), where the speaker despite himself concludes his crude monologue with his discovery of the truth that 'you're dead dead dead' — the end of militarism. The tone of this speaker becomes in turn the voice of the Roman centurion affixing the nails in the much more solemn 'And a Good Friday Was Had by All' (p. 192). In this poem, however, the voice subsides in awe as the cross rises and transfigures the human it carries, leaving below only 'a blind man in tears'.

Dawe's poetry conveys the suburbs not merely in its incidents and locale but in its tone. The men who serve in the armies and are brought home in their black bags are the children of the suburbs, and the values they learn produce the wars as much as they create the mysterious stone throwers threatening the foundations of their security. But they also create the rituals that assuage their pain. Dawe conveys simultaneously the pain of our existence and the hope that makes it endurable. His Australians, far from being bystanders of the global drama, are its creatures and its actors. Unlike Beaver, he does not finally withdraw from the community into the moment of self, but through his poetry enters into its activities so that they speak for themselves. He is, however, like Beaver in that the divisions he finds are not merely between human and landscape, or the individual and society, but at the core of the human self created by modern society.

Alone with God
Francis Webb

The central theme of Francis Webb's poetry is pain. Even in an early poem such as 'Morgan's Country' (*Collected Poems*, Angus & Robertson, Sydney, 1977, pp. 46–7) the emphasis falls not on the conflict between bushranger and police, or even on the moment of killing, but on the country itself, which with the 'Cave, his mother' and the 'stone Look-out, his towering father . . . looks grey, hunted and murderous'.

The Australian landscape in Webb's work is not so much an environment that the white settlers must come to terms with, a landscape of the soul that threatens madness, but an environment that offers salvation. In the early sequences *A Drum for Ben Boyd* (Angus & Robertson, Sydney, 1948) and *Leichhardt in Theatre* (Angus & Robertson, Sydney, 1952) Webb deals with men who vainly try to conquer the country, but in both cases their failure is held at bay by the dramatic mode that, ironically, dissipates the tension into action and reflection. In 'Eyre All Alone' (*Collected Poems*, [1961], pp. 181–92), however, the emphasis has shifted from the man as actor to man as sufferer, and the journey of exploration, precisely based as it is on the historical record, becomes a metaphor of the soul's journey into the hell of loneliness and back.

Eyre, an explorer of Australia, becomes the modern Everyman, the European summoned by death and with only his black companion, Wylie, to accompany him in the role of Good Deeds, 'the huddled works/Of my soul, in motion'. The poem completes that episode of the European imagination that began with Columbus perceiving the New World as a Garden of Eden, and continued through Defoe's epic of colonisation in *Robinson Crusoe*, where the white settler takes the black man from the hell of a fallen world into the new heaven of mercantile wealth. The experience of Australia from the first contradicted this myth, rewriting it as the descent into hell. Webb's explorer takes the myth a stage further, as the physical dependence of the white man on his black companion becomes also a moral dependence. Wylie does not, however, share Eyre's dreams, but is led by more social hopes. He links Eyre to the society and stability for which he offers his pilgrimage as sacrifice:

Hurrah for the catlike mile,
The gin of your vision,
And your boomerang-shaped smile.
Sons and daughters germinate in your eyes,
Through their territory I grovel on hands and
    knees.

Webb, *Collected Poems*, p. 184.

While Wylie represents Eyre's social hopes, a pagan Virgil who accompanies the seeker through Purgatory until he can recover heaven, as a black man he is still merely an instrument of the white man's purposes. The myth cannot be complete until Aborigines become the actors of their own destiny, taking back the European world for their own. This force drives the work of Colin Johnson, but meanwhile Webb's work remains tied to its European source.

Although Eyre comes from the wastes of the deserts to the town of Albany like the Israelites coming from Sinai to the Promised Land, he himself is, like Moses, excluded at the last moment. Wylie is gathered in by his tribesmen and 'taken back to earth', becoming one with the 'unbound geometries of the good soil'. Eyre himself remains 'truly alone'. As he approaches the town, 'all doors are closed and stilled the merrymaking'. Even when the doors open to disclose golden faces, his appearance keeps him apart:

. . . My torn stinking shirt, my boots,
And hair a tangle of scrub; the long knotted absurd
    beard
That is my conscience grown in the desert
    country.

Webb, *Collected Poems*, p. 192.

Captain Rossiter Comes to Eyre's Aid
(*State Library of Victoria*)

While the poem finishes with the sound of something moving on the main road, of life going on beyond him, Eyre remains outside in the desert that has become his conscience, his knowledge of truth. This knowledge is not something that can be shared.

The source of Eyre's hopes and Webb's vision is not merely the culture but quite specifically the religion of Europe. Between the earlier poems of exploration and the Eyre sequence lies 'The Canticle' (*Collected Poems*, [1953], pp. 69–84), in which Webb explores the impact of St Francis of Assisi on his time.

'The Canticle' opens with the precise date and place of AD 1210 and a 'brawny Umbrian moon' as travellers awake to continue their journey to Assisi. The following stanzas are dense with details of the journey and the travellers, but as they near Assisi the tone changes and the lines shorten to describe a traveller coming towards them. He seems

For a solitary
Moment of dim
Morning to carry
Assisi with him.

Webb, *Collected Poems*, p. 70.

Although the speaker rejects the challenge of this approaching man, his appearance changes the direction of the sequence. The following poems provide equally dense circumstantial detail, but place now becomes subordinated to purpose. The leper, the father, the wolf, the jongleur, the serf and the knight are each seeking within the conditions of their lives to find a sure base, but each is constrained. The wolf, the animal, has freedom in the 'final repletion of doing'. Each of the others can work and sing and fight, but finally can 'speak only as a man'. But then the coming of the saint redeems creation, first in the form of Brother Ass, then in the life of each of the others, extending to them forgiveness and light, until he himself achieves the stigmata, the signs of the Christ in whom God is incarnate and suffering. Only this mystical vision can give meaning to the wretched and deluded lives of the other people, and even to the blind hunger and dumb suffering of wolf and ass. In the saint's achievement the others, and nature itself, receive freedom. This freedom beyond time and space, the prize Eyre painfully brings back from the wilderness, is the constant aim of Webb's search.

By the later sequence 'Ward Two' (*Collected Poems*, [1964], pp. 223–32), Webb's pilgrimage has become wholly inwards, into the anguish registered by the pneumo-encephalograph or the world of Harry, the moron who finds grace by laboriously trying to shape the word he cannot write, or of the homosexual on whom there is 'no judgement, . . ./And the object becomes simply ourselves'. The truth Eyre brought from the desert is known to those who have never left it and to those who have painfully made their way back to it. The four walls of the asylum provide a path to God by excluding society. But God also comes directly into the asylum in the grace brought by dawn and the laugh of a kookaburra:

> This lumbering giant ghost of laughter while the
>   dregs
> Of planets are drained, the cup shakes:
> His guffaw like some coup of megatons past belief
> Shivers our gold and copper grief:
> History's bowels roll for breakfast as history
>   wakes.

Webb, Collected Poems, p. 227.

The moment of revelation shakes the universe as the copper and gold of the sunrise change from grief to joy. Yet if the inhabitants of the asylum for a moment feel themselves restored to history, and munch at their porridge with gusto, their feeling is illusory. The poetry establishes order in the careful pattern of rhyme that contains its revelation, but it does not release them from the asylum that keeps them from participating in history. Webb finds his truth in the moments of quiet, of birth, of accepted death, in reaching the end of a journey, rather than in any pattern that can give meaning to continuing activity. The density of the language takes the poet out of

history as it charges each moment with the weight of eternity.

Thomas Keneally

Keneally's novels are about guilt and pain projected from the consciousness of the individual onto the stage of history. The results of this projection vary from gothic distortion and myth to plain narrative that professes merely to offer events as they happened. Behind the apparent variety of this work lies a constant concern with the ambiguous human choice between good and evil.

In Keneally's first published novel, *The Place at Whitton* (Cassell, London, 1964), history is transmuted into a gothic tale of murder and mystery in a seminary. The seminary represents a retreat from the world of events into a realm of faith, but is invaded by forces of evil that have their origins in involvement in the history and passion of the outside world. In his second novel, *The Fear* (Cassell Australia, Melbourne, 1965), Keneally confronts Australian fears of communism and Japanese militarism, which threaten the secure and Catholic world of the narrator with their images of disease and destruction. Later works go further back in history. *Bring Larks and Heroes* (Cassell Australia, Melbourne, 1967) is set in an unnamed convict colony 'at the world's worst end', and *The Chant of Jimmy Blacksmith* (Angus & Robertson, Sydney, 1972) is set in the time of Federation and retells the tale derived from the life of the Aboriginal killer, Jimmy Governor. Several of his more recent novels look at the issue of violence in the particular context of war. *Gossip from the Forest* (Collins, London and Sydney, 1975) uses the discussions that led to the Armistice in 1918 as a frame through which to view both the causes and effects of war. *Confederates* (Collins, London, 1979) examines the nature of mass warfare from the viewpoint of the participants. *The Cut-Rate Kingdom* (Allan Lane/ Penguin, Ringwood, 1980) looks at the effect of the Second World War on Australia and its leaders. *Schindler's Ark* (Hodder & Stoughton, Sydney, 1982) is a direct reconstruction of the life of an historical character, and in *A Family Madness* (Hodder & Stoughton, Sydney, 1985) he examines the nature of fascism and the power of the individual to resist evil.

In *Bring Larks and Heroes*, Keneally deals directly with the moral dilemmas of colonialism. These are indicated in the first chapter, where the central character of Corporal Phelim Halloran is disclosed on 'the edge of the forest . . . without any idea that he's caught in a mesh of sunlight and shade' (p. 1). The forest is the primitive frontier, the physical environment within which the action occurs. The mesh of sunlight and shade represents the timeless dilemma of fate in which Halloran, with all other humans, is caught. In the novel this dilemma takes the form of the convict system that binds soldiers, officials and felons alike. More generally, however, the mesh represents the fate against which the individual struggles to maintain an illusion of freedom. The narrator comments that Halloran 'has the illusion of knowing where he's going', but adds that 'if any of his ideas on this subject were *not* illusion, there would be no story' (p. 1). History is not the record of action, but of the tension we produce in our efforts to bend fate to our will. The novel traces the history of Halloran and his 'bride in Christ' to the tragic end when fate reveals the trap in which they have been held.

The novel exposes the bases of power and morality that constitute the political realities of the colony and the elements of Halloran's dilemma. The people are intruders in a hostile land characterised by the heat of the 'alien forest' where 'the sunlight burrows like a worm in both eye-balls'. In this desolate environment authority, in such persons as Mr Commissary Blythe and his wife, maintains its defences in the form of a 'futile vegetable garden', 'pretentious mahogany . . . furniture' and disappointed hopes of 'a volume of industry within the new colony that would make a Commissary a substantial figure, doing substantial work' (p. 3). Lacking any work, Blythe falls back on the assertion of duty with which he attempts to starve his wife, while she redresses a blighted life by imposing the tenets of her costive piety on the love she sees dawning between Ann and Phelim. Phelim rejects the tyranny of the their law in the name of moral theology, Ann by spontaneous feeling, but the law retains the power to control their lives and eventually crushes them.

The tragedy of the novel is implicit from its first pages, when the sunshine and shadows that signify Halloran's love also symbolise the prison that holds him. He and Ann are made vulnerable by the love

that elsewhere would be a source of strength. Ann can remain his bride in Christ only for so long as their marriage can remain apart from society. However, Ann's pregnancy betrays their secret, and Halloran's humanity involves them in society and subjects them to the power of Mrs Blythe and the officers. Neither the child Ann carries nor the religion and poetry Halloran bears within him survives to bring grace and humanity to the new land. The promise of the grandchildren who might have been born to them, bringing 'larks and heroes to our hedge' (p. 225), is cut off by the noose that symbolises the law of the colony. By denying life, tyranny ensures that the land remains alien to its white invaders. It remains stubbornly outside human comprehension, as Halloran realises at the moment of his death when, as 'Every prayer, curse and snatch of song unleashed itself up the vent of his body', he is left with the awful question, 'Am I perhaps *God*?' (p. 247). The colony has denied him every other possibility of life.

Halloran is destroyed by the intrusion on an alien land of a European society, based on the domination of powerful men over women, workers and the environment. The insecurity of power produces tyranny that excludes the alternative possibilities of life offered by art, religion and love. The artist Ewers is unable to paint the riverscape because the result would be a lie, so that those who saw it would think 'that this river led to a kingly town, that Eden lay at the headwaters', instead of realising that 'it serves to connect the world's worst town to the world's worst village, tyranny to tyranny, slave to slave' (p. 33). Halloran feels that in his love for Ann he is 'living in a legend' with 'all the fervours set down in legends and poetry' (p. 17), but the legends of his past have already been denied by the power that is destroying the peasantry of Britain and Ireland and that sent its sons as convicts or soldiers to the new land. Similarly, neither his own theological learning nor the bleak Protestant zeal of Hearn nor the pious platitudes of the Anglican parson, Calverley, can compensate for his forced separation from his own church and its priests. Nor can Hearn's revolt against the system offer real hope. Hearn offers only another form of power, and can find a future for himself only by escaping to the USA, where the people have already succeeded in establishing a free society. The love between Halloran and Ann challenges the basis of power and thus arouses the envy and malice that eventually destroys them.

The heavy mahogany furniture of the Blythes, the social pretensions of the officers and their wives, the hollow rituals of the law that fail to disguise the brutal basis of power, all demonstrate the lack of any human basis for society in the new land. The outward marks of civilisation are denied not only by the brutalities of the penal system on which it rests, but by such scenes of depraved humanity as the excremental smell, leering faces and sordid couplings that make Surgeon Dakin's hospital an image of ugliness and vice rather than of the healing we might expect (pp. 46–7).

In *The Chant of Jimmy Blacksmith*, Keneally looks at the continuing forms of colonialism. The novel confronts the pretensions of white Australia at the time of Federation with the reality of the exclusion on which it is based. The story of Blacksmith's campaign becomes a corrective counterpoint to the hollow celebrations of the new Commonwealth, which has conferred on its people a state of grace that enables them to laugh at 'the old crimes done, all convict chains a rusted fable in the brazen Arcady'. The 'other viciousness, the rape of primitives' remains outside their consciousness (p. 177). Blacksmith's life is an

attempt to accept colonisation by taking its values within himself, followed by a bloody campaign of revenge when the colonists still insist on excluding him from their society and refusing him identity as a person. His rampage arouses all the guilty fear the white community has endeavoured to suppress. His execution is an attempt to bring these fears again under the control of the white law, and thus avoid the necessity of examining cause or conscience.

In his most recent works Keneally has chosen to seek the origins of evil in the Western experience by recreating episodes of war and savagery in their harshest detail in order to strip illusion from history. While Phelim Halloran finds that the fervours of his legend and poetry cannot survive the rigours of the antipodes, Keneally seems to be saying that neither myth nor legend can explain the horrors of the modern world. These later works allow no symbolic overlays to person or action, but select these to confront readers with the need to find their own meaning in the world they construct. *Bring Larks and Heroes* remains as the novelist's symbolic creation of this world at the point of its origin in the subjection of the last continent to the mechanical logic of a West that believes only in its own destiny.

14

OTHERWORLDS

AUSTRALIAN writers from Buckley to Keneally have been preoccupied with seeking the origins of the guilts and conflicts they find in the society around them. Another group of writers have, however, sought to escape from a world they have found enclosing, denying individuals the right to fulfil the powers and dreams they find within them. They have sought an escape to another world, beyond the borders not only of Australia but even of the Europe from which Australia's confining institutions have been transplanted. For some, this other world has taken the concrete form of Asia, either as the source of a wisdom more in tune with the spirit than that offered by the monotheistic religions that come from Judaea, or as the site of a politics that can absolve us from the guilty basis of Western materialism and exploitation. For others, it has been a dream world of myth and magic, embodied in art but reaching back to our pagan roots. For others again, it has been a world of the future, where scientific process has resolved the bonds of our present ignorance. For all, however, the search for the otherworld is prompted by a rejection of the mechanical rationalism of contemporary society, which they see as a fundamentally insane denial of human potential. Yet most often their search itself proves futile, discovering only greater horror or even more insane rationality. The power of mechanical thought controls even our dreams.

Christopher Koch

Christopher Koch is driven by a particularly intense need to escape. He grew up not only in Australia, but in Tasmania, the most remote of settlements and scene of Australia's bloodiest history of convictism and near genocide. The speakers in his novels find themselves exiles from birth, growing up 'in an island of hills, a fragment separated from the parent continent by a wide stretch of sea. It is different from the hot Australian mainland; it has a different weather and a different soul, knowing as it does the sharp breath of the south, facing the Antarctic' (*The Boys in the Island*, Angus & Robertson, Sydney, 1979 [1958], p. 6). This island state is politically 'part of the Commonwealth of Australia; physically, it is not . . . In the upside-down frame of the Antipodes, it duplicates the Atlantic coast of Europe' (*The Doubleman*, Chatto & Windus: The Hogarth Press, London, 1985, p. 23). Neither European nor Australian, its people are at once at home and alienated in its landscapes. Koch's fiction revolves around the double image of this antipodean reality, which seems at once to be the image of a comfortable England and its savage opposite.

This duality means that his characters constantly carry with them a sense of exile from the true centre of their being. They are condemned to lifelong attempts to escape, at first into books and into the

Christopher Koch
(*National Library of Australia*)

faery worlds of northern myth, later to the mainland or overseas. The island from which he seeks to escape is itself haunted by the memory of the deeds of its early white settlers: 'Half-seen shapes of lust and fear lurked in the sulking green bush . . . and at times I caught the land looking at me out of the corner of its eye'. The guilt of settlement remains as a reproach to the living:

Then I would remember that we were in Van Diemen's Land, where crimes and monotonous misery had made their indelible traces a hundred years ago; where transported pickpockets from the rookeries and thieves' kitchens of St Giles and Camden Town had yearned for a London they would never see again; where the sealers and shepherds and convicts, out of reach of the Government in Hobart, had made slaves and victims of the doomed Aborigines, hanging the heads of the husbands about the necks of their wives, using the amputated fingers to tamp their pipes. And I wondered at times if the spirits that vanished race

had believed in, as well as their own reproachful spirits, still lingered here in the gullies or among the dunes.

Koch, *The Doubleman*, p. 62.

These memories hang over the youth of Koch's characters. Although they flee to the mainland, Europe and Asia to escape them, his fiction constantly returns to this origin. Even *The Year of Living Dangerously* (Nelson, Melbourne, 1970), set wholly in Jakarta in the last year of President Soekarno's rule, when Indonesia was involved in an uneasy alliance with China and confrontation with Malaysia, has as its theme the need to shed guilt in order to discover the authentic person.

The story of this novel is told by a nearly anonymous narrator, known only as 'Cookey' or by his initials R.J.C. It revolves around the Wayang Bar in the Hotel Indonesia, where Western correspondents escape from the troubles they have come to report. The bar provides gloom and alcoholic company as a relief from the poverty of the city and the ugly brawling of its politics. The life of Indonesia, however, comes into the bar through its name, Wayang, the name of the Indonesian shadow-puppet show that portrays, often with contemporary detail, the unending struggle between light and darkness, good and evil. In the outer world, this drama takes the form of the struggle between Muslims and Communists for power under the dayan, the puppet-master Soekarno himself. Inside the bar, it is repeated in the reactions of the journalists to this conflict in which they unwillingly find themselves caught, and in the turmoil of their inner lives as they attempt to avoid responsibility.

The plot of the novel follows this inner turmoil in the experience of the Australian journalist, Guy Hamilton. The Australian-Chinese dwarf, Billy Kwan, whom he employs as his cameraman, becomes his eyes and his conscience, and forces him to become involved in the life of the country he reports. Billy makes Guy his partner in the battle for the light, for good, but Hamilton doubly betrays him. Yet eventually Billy's death forces Hamilton to make his own choice, to decide for himself which place to occupy among the Wayang people — the place of light or the place of darkness. Kwan and Hamilton are alike in choosing for themselves the roles they will play, instead of remaining puppets playing the roles allotted to them by others. By choosing involvement in history, they paradoxically free themselves from it and unite the personal with the public.

Koch portrays the Indonesian world of poverty and corruption, spirituality and carnality, with an affection that does not ignore the realities of either power or suffering. Although Billy Kwan suggests that the ineffectiveness of the Europeans is a mark of the decadence of their own societies, and although the wayang plays represent a timeless reality outside the European concern for action and control, the novel does not oppose a mystic Asia to secular Europe. The orderliness of the British embassy or the Dutch airlines represents a safety absent from the crowded slums and villages of Java, but, like the Wayang bar, it is only an order of momentary escape. Jakarta is not merely an Asian city, but the scene of a confrontation of power politics in a post-colonial world. The matters at stake are not merely diplomatic success, but the survival of people like Billy Kwan and Hamilton's other assistant, Kumar. These issues are dramatised through Billy's vain attempts to sustain the slum dwellers Ibu and her child Udin, or in Kumar's passionate question: 'Then why should I live like a poor man all my life, while stupid people in your country live well?' (p. 289). The only answer the novel can offer to this questioning is the implicitly Christian response of personal humility and acceptance of responsibility for one's own actions.

A constant theme of Koch's novels is the need for a truth outside the self that will nevertheless sustain our real natures. Guy finds this truth by accepting responsibility for others. Billy Kwan seeks it in the hero-figures of Soekarno and of Guy Hamilton, and among the people of the bazaars and kampongs. For Francis Cullen in *The Boys in the Island* it is only to be found elsewhere, in the Otherland of the city of night he had glimpsed from Mr Mooney's 'jumping-off place', where he sensed 'a life lived inside a high, far melody, out in the wide-spread air' (p. 15). He seeks this world in Lutana Rise, in his love for Heather Miles, in the pubs along the Hobart waterfront, and eventually on the mainland, but each time is disappointed. The narrator of *Across the Sea Wall* (Heinemann, London, 1965) seeks it first in a general idea of overseas, then in his Latvian earth-mother, and then in India. Finally, in *The Doubleman* the narrator, Dick Miller, seeks it explicitly in Elfland. In a world of mysticism made concrete in the form of

music and art he seeks the conditions of an existence that will transcend the circumstances of his present.

The 'Doubleman' of the title is explained in the book's epigraph as the 'Co-Walker, every way like the Man, as a Twin-brother and Companion, haunting him as his shadow . . .' Immediately, this would seem to be Darcy Burr, the man who communicates with the dead and entraps Brian Brady, and through him the narrator, in his fantasies and in the band he constructs as the vehicle of his power. Behind Darcy, however, is Brod, Clive Broderick, who first appears to the narrator as a mysterious figure in an alleyway, who later materialises to teach Darcy and Brian the guitar, and who continues to exercise his power over Darcy from beyond the grave. But the theme of doubleness runs throughout the novel. It is the mysterious world outside the ordinary, that Dick Miller senses in the figures of his toy theatre, and that has reached out to him in his childhood to strike him with paralysis. This world has itself a double nature, both as the enchanted Elfland whose inhabitants alone know the truth, and as a hell where its victims wander in the solitude of damnation. It represents a rebirth at the furthest edge of the new world of the old world of northern mythology and the Gnostic heresy. According to the Gnostics, all matter is evil. The human must therefore escape from the material world into a realm of pure spirit. Dick Miller follows this path of escape only to find that it leads to destruction.

The elements of the pattern are the same as in the earlier novels — the two friends, as close and as different as brothers, and the woman who beckons away to the Otherworld. In this case the idea of the woman is embodied in two characters. One, Deidre, is Aphrodite or the Elf-queen, the spirit who teaches of love but also destroys. The other, Katrin, is Artemis, the earth-mother, representing the power and attraction of Europe. Both women, however, remain fixed in their childhood roles, refusing to accept responsibility for their adult choices. They therefore easily become instruments of the baleful purposes of Darcy Burr, who uses the professional name of Thomas the Rymer, the man taken as her own by the Queen of Elfland. Obsessed with his own occult power, he seeks to use his band to build Europe's 'places of power' in Australia, 'here, among these pagan rocks' (p. 293). His power is broken only when Dick and Katrin choose the freedom and risk of rationality. Their choice destroys the attractive possibility of a paganism that would unite both northern and Aboriginal mythology, and leaves the narrator alone in his mushroom hallucination beside the clean waters of the Pacific.

The resolution, as in Koch's earlier novels, remains unsatisfactory. Billy Kwan is unable to escape from pragmatism, Dick Miller is unable to escape into mysticism. Like Guy Hamilton or Francis Cullen, Dick escapes from illusion, but the reality that now confronts him is left unexplored. The novels take their characters to the point of maturity as their central characters accept responsibility for their future and their marriage, but the picture they leave us of failed relationships offers no suggestion of what a mature relationship could be. The implication is that love and hope are themselves merely illusions of adolescence. Neither in Australia nor in Europe or Asia does there seem to be any tradition, other than the obliquely suggested possibility of Christian grace, that might sustain a unity of the individual and culture.

The Year of Living Dangerously is one of several novels published at this time that deal with the theme of Australia's ambivalent relationships with postcolonial Asia. These novels, set in South-East Asia, differ from works about the alternate threat and promise offered to Australia by a more remote Japan. Hal Porter and T.A.G. Hungerford, writing of the earlier post-war period, portray an occupied Japan caught between pride and emulation, an older spirituality corrupted by power, and a newer materialism building on the corruption. Their Australian characters are gross but still claim the power of their European origins. Harold Stewart, on the other hand, went to Japan as a pilgrim. His Australian background, which had always been subordinate to his deeper interests in mythology, becomes as irrelevant as the modern world he rigorously excludes from his poetry. His latest work, *By the Old Walls of Kyoto* (Weatherhill, New York and Tokyo, 1980), is a series of poems with a scholarly prose commentary. The poems, which follow the cycle of the seasons, provide for the reader a continuing meditation on Buddhism, while their physical world is a Japan that preceded any European contact. The work represents not a loss of faith by the Westerner in his own culture, but a complete rejection of the modern world.

On the other hand, the novelists who set their tales amid the political turmoil of South-East Asia are very much concerned with the present. Their characters represent a range of responses of Australians to the disturbing situation they find themselves in after the collapse of their British and US protectors.

Blanche d' Alpuget

Blanche d' Alpuget's *Monkeys in the Dark* (Penguin, Ringwood, 1982 [1980]) is set in Indonesia a year later than Koch's. It is after the defeat of the attempted communist coup, and the consequent massacre of some half million people suspected or accused of communist sympathies, but before President Soekarno's final loss of power. Even the Wayang Bar of the Hotel Indonesia appears as the Ramayana Bar. This is the site for the corruption by the Australian agent of the Indonesian idealist whose information precipitates the novel's conclusion. Whereas the political scene forms the background for Koch's novel (the challenge that forces his characters to decide who they are), in d'Alpuget's work the political manoeuvres and conspiracies provide the substance of the plot.

Although this plot revolves around the sexual behaviour of her characters, their fate is finally determined by their place in the political game. The portrayal of Indonesian politics in this novel does not polarise East and West, or even progressive and conservative, but rather shows it as a ruthless

Blanche d'Alpuget
(*National Library of Australia*)

struggle for power in which Australian diplomats are as deeply implicated as any others, and in which deception, torture and massacre are normal practices. The European expatriates, isolated by distance from home in an artifical world of promiscuous sex, behave neither better nor worse than the Indonesian pimps, generals and businessmen. The beauty the land offers as a promise is denied by the stink of its canals, the corruption of its rulers, and the casual cruelty of its inhabitants. Even the idealists are themselves led by circumstances to betray their ideals. Alex is as powerless to help her lover as she is to save the horse from the torture that contradicts her hope in humanity. The sexual politics at the surface are shown as merely a manifestation of the politics of greed and power that control society. In accepting the fate of marriage to the cousin who has destroyed her lover, Alex acknowledges her lack of power over anything except a sexuality she can use to exploit but not to change the world.

A similar political interest informs d'Alpuget's later novel, *Turtle Beach* (Penguin, Ringwood, 1981). This novel is told from the point of view of Judith Wilkes, an Australian journalist sent to Malaysia to report on the plight of the boat people fleeing from Vietnam. Through her involvement with the refugees, with an Indian lecturer, and with the life of Minou, the former Saigon bar-girl now married to the Australian ambassador in Kuala Lumpur, she is able to free herself from the shackles of a barren marriage.

The violence and distress Judith encounters in Malaysia act both as a judgement on the shallowness of her life and ambitions in Australia and as an image of the twentieth century for which all are responsible. The anger they evoke becomes itself a further cause of personal and social disintegration. The cultural mixture of Malaysia offers no solutions, but merely demonstrates unbridgeable barriers, even between people locked in the same situation. Although Judith frees herself from her marriage, she is forced to recognise that she is unalterably separate from Malaysia and its problems. Leaving both her lover and the refugees, she returns to the safety of Australia.

The only person, Australian or Malaysian, who escapes the constraints of her situation is the former bar-girl Minou, who in a final act of *Satyagraha* (non-violent resistance), unites traditional belief with the needs of the present. While her need to survive has given her an anarchic contempt for convention, her unswerving loyalty to family has preserved her integrity. She is therefore free to sacrifice her life to save her compatriots, although ironically not her family. The novel thus leads us ultimately to an area of personal responsibility beyond politics. Its central concern remains, however, the search for a moral response to the disintegration inflicted on the contemporary world by its politics. Both public and sexual politics represent a despairing search for a primeval unity, an attempt to escape responsibility for the lonely self.

Robert Drewe

The lonely self is the central subject of Robert Drewe's *A Cry in the Jungle Bar*, (Collins, Sydney, 1979), which describes the travels and troubles in Asia of an Australian rugby footballer and agricultural scientist working for the United Nations in Manila. The Asia of the novel comprises the international hotels, seedy nightclubs, meeting tables and suburban enclaves of the professional expatriate. The novel's central character, Dick Cullen, moves through these with rituals of drinking, jogging and flirtation that give the appearance of meaning to his barren life.

Although Cullen is officially concerned with raising standards of living by improving the care and breeding of buffalo, his direct encounters with poverty are limited to street touts and the faces of beggars seen through restaurant windows. His knowledge of this world is circumscribed by statistics and scientific fact, and his comprehension of his own emotions is as limited as his understanding of the wife who finally leaves him. In short, Cullen combines mid-life, mid-century and mid-world crises in a single figure of insensitivity. Like the gauche tourists who greet him in the Jungle Bar of the Eden Hotel, he is the Australian abroad who carries his country with him, unable to rid himself of its habits or understand the otherness of the cultures and people among whom he moves.

Asia exists in the novel not as a place in its own right, but as a background that enables the author to examine more clearly the characteristics of the contemporary urban Australian. The protected enclave Cullen and his wife share with other international public servants and shysters (but not with their children) and the shallow sexual affairs which preoccupy them, signify lives lacking any dimension beyond the everyday. Asia is merely a more corrupt extension of Sydney, its real problems and possibilities shut outside by barbed-wire fences and guarded gates.

Nevertheless, another world of suffering and violence exists at the boundaries of the novel as a threat to the security of its characters. The book opens with Cullen's fear of being knifed in his sleep, and ends with him facing death at the hands of a guerrilla patrol. The political reality of Asia thus becomes a symbol of the threat we try to shut out by our suburban rituals. The self is lonely because it has become detached from the conditions of its existence. Asia warns us of this detachment without offering a solution. Drewe's next book, the collection of stories in *The Bodysurfers* (James Fraser, Sydney, 1983) brings the Australians back home, where they use the images of sea and sound to represent the hedonism they adopt as a distraction from the disintegration at the core of their lives.

Tony Maniaty

Asia offers yet another image of reality in Maniaty's *The Children Must Dance* (Penguin, Ringwood, 1984). The island of Inhumas, which generally resembles East Timor after the departure of the Portuguese, is the setting for a novel based on the quest of Nick Ranse, an Australian botanist in search of the truth of the apparent suicide of his uncle, Sam Goddard. Goddard had left a safe university position to come to the island. He has built in the jungle above the capital a replica of his house by the Brisbane River where Nick had been brought up after the death of his parents. In searching for the clue to his uncle's choice of exile and death, Nick is also trying to discover and come to terms with the truth of his own childhood and identity. His uncle had desperately sought completeness, fleeing an Australia that denied him tranquility, but building in Portuguese Asia the house that was a 'false reserve of this replicate past' (p. 34). Here Nick finds the diaries that reveal Goddard's struggle between the desire to distil 'his immense knowledge into finer and finer detail; and all the while miniaturising his world to the size of a forgotten transistor' and the conflicting desire 'to spread out and see the nature of things' (p. 93). Science promises to shut out the threat of the human disorder into which, despite himself,

Goddard is dragged by his affair with Teppy Zervos and his thwarted desire to construct his nephew in his own image. Nick Ranse breaks his bondage to his uncle's memory in part by making violent love to Teppy, but finds himself instead brought under the sway of the island and its complicated affairs. He is eventually able to liberate himself only by choosing involvement.

Far from being a refuge from the world, the island of Inhumas brings together the decay of both the old cultures of Europe and Asia, and the new, rootless culture of Australia. They are locked together in a single pointless struggle for survival and order. This struggle culminates in the futile war, waged in the name of ideals but destructive of all value. The war is characterised by the scene in the town of Maracacume after its capture by the enemy, whom Ranse sees 'cooling their scorched bodies in the pool, playing mercenary polo with the priest's head' (p. 167). The scene marks not only the cruelty of war, but also the destruction of the relition and education the priest had given as the offering of the West to its colonies. The pretensions of empire, the hopes of revolution and delusions of intellectual control that have given them birth reach their common end on this island as its society disintegrates through the remaining scenes of the novel. Yet out of this disintegration a few rebels and their Western sympathisers find a truth beyond survival in the continuing determination to resist. The past has nothing to offer them, and they have no hope of a future, but they can control their present. Nick, however, discovers this truth too late to give it to the children in whose dance lies a hope beyond the individual.

David Malouf

Malouf's writing may be seen as a search for the positive within the material circumstances of life. Like Koch, he is fascinated by doubling, by the possibility of an alternative reality, and like Patrick White he is seeking a way of transcending reality. Unlike either of these writers he is never satisfied with gestures to the infinite. His characters work out their destiny in a densely realised world of their here and now, while still recognising that this temporal reality exists only as they transform it into their own subjectivity.

Malouf's work shows how we transform the ex-

David Malouf
(*National Library of Australia*)

ternal world and make it our own through every part of our daily activity. The transformation takes place in the language his characters use to define themselves, in conversation and fantasy, and in the narrative of the novels. It occurs also through their work and play: the art with which Frank Harland puts his landscapes onto canvas (*Harland's Half Acre*, Penguin, Harmondsworth, 1985 [1984]), the observations Jim Saddler records of the life of the swamp (*Fly Away Peter*, Chatto & Windus, London, 1982), and, in *12 Edmonstone Street* (Penguin, Harmondsworth, 1986 [1985]), Malouf's recent autobiography, chosen objects: the objects his mother surrounds herself with, the shop his grandfather arranges as a theatre where he holds court to his compatriots while his wife toils her sixteen-hour day behind the counter, and the garden this same Arabic-speaking grandfather so carefully tends in his retirement. Reality in Malouf's work is neither an external world that is given nor an inner life of pure subjectivity, but is the product we build from the constant dialogue between these two realms.

In his first novel, *Johnno,* (University of Queensland Press, St Lucia, 1975), Malouf writes of Dante and Johnno, two boys growing up in wartime Brisbane. The story is told in retrospect by Dante, who tries to understand why Johnno, the hero and rebel of schooldays and university, loses his way, drops out of society, and finally drowns himself. The story reveals the precarious and contingent nature of our lives and the alternative identities we create for ourselves. Johnno rejects any imposed identity and asserts for himself the right to live outside the conventions and expectations of others. However, by bestowing on him an ironic nickname, he ascribes to Dante both function and personality. It is only late in the novel that Dante, and the reader, learn that, for Johnno, Dante has always represented the exotic, the higher reality towards which he has aspired (p. 154). By this time, however, Johnno's life has proved to be a fraud, an illusion that has passed with youth.

Johnno's defiance of Brisbane drives him to Africa, then to Europe and Asia is search of the place where he might lead a life to match his dreams, but the dreams lack substance. As they fail, he is driven home, sinking steadily from romantic hero to defeated if still defiant drunk. He ends his life by drowning in the Condamine, the river that suggests both the romance of the Australian overlanders and the reality of a muddy river that starts with a fine flow to the north only to turn right around and trickle through a series of waterholes to its destiny in the Southern Ocean.

The novel does not end with Johnno's death but with the narrator remembering the dream that sustained his own father through the years of Depression and poverty. Dante's grandfather had come from Lebanon, his mother's family was Jewish, escaping the Holocaust by only a generation. Dante has to construct his own identity from their dreams and from the streets, buildings and backyards of the Brisbane in which he grows up and to which his parents and Johnno act as his guides. Each person remains locked in his separate dream, but the novel closes with the narrator's reflection that 'Maybe, in the end, even the lies we tell define us. And better, some of them, than our most earnest attempts at the truth' (p. 170). The dream Johnno created thus remains as a possibility, even if it has been eventually defeated in his own life.

The multiple possibilities of every life, including the possibility that we may actually be living more than one of these alternatives, together with the contradictory truth that our lives and identities are arbitrarily determined, constitute a continuing theme in Malouf's work. Dante, in *Johnno*, creates one identity from his wanderings with his friend through the streets of Brisbane, makes another for himself through his poetry, and realises years later in Europe that any identity he has depends on the chance decision of his mother's family to immigrate from Europe (p. 120). Returning to the same subject in his autobiography, *12 Edmonstone Street*, Malouf reflects on the arbitrary choice that brought his grandfather to Australia rather than South or North America, as well as on the peculiar twists of political history that make his father an Australian while leaving his grandfather an enemy alien even after 70 years of residence (pp. 132–3). In the same passage, however, he points out how his father used his fists to make his offical definition his own, just as he has earlier shown how he himself resisted his mother's attempts to impose on him a mode of English gentility and chose instead to be an aggressively larrikin Australian (p. 33).

Malouf shows how consciousness itself comes into being from the dialogue between the body and its surroundings. His autobiography traces this dialogue back in memory until he comes to its centre:

And so at last we come down to it, the body — that small hot engine at the centre of all these records and recollections; gravely preoccupied, as it hoovers about the house and yard, with its own business of breathing, pumping blood, processing the fruits of the earth, but in every sense meeting reality head on — as dirt that stains, sunshine that warms or burns, berries that delight the eye but when tasted catch fire in the mouth. And is that smell lemon-blossom or some passing woman's scent?

Malouf, *12 Edmonstone Street*, p. 53.

Reality exists, but only as it calls the perceiver into existence.

It is just because we are made by circumstances before we can start to shape our own identity from them that our existence has so many possibilities. We cannot change the circumstances, but we can choose from among them. Several of Malouf's novellas and stories explore this idea of choice and its conse-

quences. In 'Eustace' (*Child's Play*, Chatto & Windus, London, 1982) the prowler meets one particular girl by chance and discovers just one of the ten possibilities offered by the girls in the dormitory. He and the girl then choose to accept the particular possibility that has been offered to them, and that remains dormant but alive in the existence of each of the other girls, just as their pet hamster retains its private reality for them even after it has been removed to the sanitised public sphere of the science laboratory. In 'The Prowler', the story Malouf has chosen to pair with 'Eustace', he shows the other side of the phenomenon. Instead of watching the prowler and his victim moving into a sequence of events, the narrator presents a sequence of events that create the roles of prowler and victim, until everyone in the suburb fits the part. In 'Child's Play', the novella that precedes these stories, Malouf uses the preparation and execution of a terrorist assassination attempt to demonstrate how, even in choosing to make this dramatic intervention in history, the perpetrator becomes merely a cipher of the plot he has chosen and the accidental events that follow.

History is important to Malouf both as an account of the circumstances that create the individual and as a challenge to action. The first poem of his collection *Neighbours in a Thicket* (University of Queensland Press, St Lucia, 1974) refers to the sense of alienation he feels towards a Brisbane changed from the world of his childhood, and his sense of relief as he discovers lily-ponds now made safe for him. Other poems refer directly to the intimations brought from the war into the schoolground, just as in *Johnno* the violence and excitement of war contributes to the boys' daring and unease. With its threat and opportunity, the world demands a response that will change it.

The changes of history provide the subject of two major novels. *An Imaginary Life* (Chatto & Windus, London, 1978) is set in Thrace at the edge of the Roman Empire in the time of Tiberius, who has exiled the poet Ovid to a grubby village on the Danube. Here Ovid meets a wild child, a dumb youth from the vast steppes that stretch beyond the river, holding in their immensity the barbarians who will overthrow the empire. Ovid also is dumb, for he no longer has an audience for his Latin poetry and must learn a new tongue — Gothic — to speak with his neighbours. He has lost one world, but in teaching the wild boy to speak he gains another, and thus participates in a history still to come.

Harland's Half Acre (Penguin, Harmondsworth, 1985 [1984]) is set a hemisphere and 2000 years apart from *An Imaginary Life*. It deals with a similarly formless world, that of the artist Frank Harland in twentieth-century Australia: 'It has not been discovered . . . The people for it have not yet come into existence' (p. 116). Harland's own life is brought into existence partly by his art and partly by the efforts of the narrator, Phil Vernon, to comprehend the art and to tell the story of the painter. Harland's country comprises poverty, violent death and betrayal, as well as love and nurturing. Harland makes it his own by acquiring a parcel of land, but more importantly by painting half an acre of canvases that give to the world the imagined reality he has created from his life. Through these paintings he makes a unity of his history, realising as one the many possibilities he has known.

Malouf is concerned with the polarity of the life we lead and the life we may lead. This appears in many guises — the secret life of the body and our public social role, our view of ourselves and the view others have of us, the life we choose and the life we desire. Australia itself represents a historical version of this polarity, being at once the imagined counterpart, the antipodes, of Europe, and a new world still to be discovered.

This contrast runs through his collection of stories, *Antipodes* (Penguin, Ringwood, 1986 [1985]). These stories literally move between Europe and Australia, but the two worlds also exist within individual stories as images of the possible alternatives open to their characters. The world of the stories is neither one pole nor the other, but the globe that swings between.

In the first story, 'Southern Skies', the two worlds are both literal and metaphoric. They are brought together in the figures of the Professor, a refugee from the Europe where he belongs, and the narrator, a sixteen-year-old just discovering the vastness of the world beyond himself. The world of the Professor is represented by 'a formal courtliness, a clicking of heels and kissing of plump fingers that was the extreme set of manners that our parents clung to

because it belonged, along with much else, to the Old Country' (p. 7). This Old Country is, however, also 'far in the past and another country' which the young people 'found it imperative to reject' for the same reasons that their parents clung to it. The two poles, therefore, come to represent both two cultures, and the opposition of youth and age.

The story brings the two generations and their worlds together in the common fulfilment of separate needs. The Professor, caught in a job that provides a position but no opportunity to extend himself in scholarship, to use the wealth of his learning, finds in the narrator a way back to vicarious youth and a person to whom he can pass on his frustrated learning, particularly his passion for astronomy. The boy finds in him an admirer, an audience before whom he can practise the roles of his developing adolescence. The Professor's life is effectively over, but reveals to the boy both the lightness and the seriousness the universe holds.

The issue of the real world is raised most clearly in the story 'A Traveller's Tale'. This is set somewhere north of Brisbane, in country that is a world of its own. It is separated not only from the rest of Australia but from the culture the narrator, a travelling lecturer, is employed to bring to it:

Poor white country. Little makeshift settlements, their tin roofs extinguished with paint or still rawly flashing, huddle round a weatherboard spire. Spindly windmills stir the air. There are watertanks in the yards, half-smothered under bougainvillea; sheds painted a rusty blood-colour, all their timbers awry but the old nails strongly holding, slide sideways at an alarming angle; and everywhere, scattered about on burnt-off slopes and in naked paddocks, the parts of Holdens, Chevvies, Vanguards, Pontiacs, and the engines of heavy transports, spring up like bits of industrial sculpture or the remains of highway accidents awaiting a poor man's resurrection. A tin lizzie only recently taken off the road suddenly explodes and takes wings as half a dozen chooks come squarking and flapping from the sprung interior.

Nothing is ever finished here, but nothing is done with either. Everything is in process of being dismantled, reconstructed, recycled, and turned by the spirit of improvisation into something else. A place of transformations.

Malouf, *Antipodes*, pp. 130–1.

The picture painted is of a world of struggle and decay, but also implicit with possibility. It is the debris of the old world set down in the new world to find a new life that will belong to it, not just the rehash of old culture the lecturer offers. He is out of place only because he is unable to establish any connection with this world, not because the world itself excludes the transforming possibilities of art.

In this unfinished world the narrator encounters a further life that is alien, drawn from a European past that may itself never have existed. He meets a woman who claims to be the daughter of a famous singer. This woman and her husband are characteristic north-coast battlers, yet each is sustained by belief in an exotic past of courts and courtiers, intrigue and revolution, flight and survival over two continents. Their tale is fiction within fiction within fiction — the woman's story of European splendours within the man's story of domestic love within a traveller's tale of the northern canelands where everything is constantly transformed. The antipodes of man and woman, Australia and Europe, are transformed from polar opposites into worlds enclosing each other. Europe is enclosed in the poor shack in Australia, but at the same time the woman in the shack is enclosed within the story of Europe that contained and magnified her supposed mother. Man and woman create themselves in their stories.

In moving between the two worlds of Europe and Australia, Malouf demonstrates that Europe itself is a creation of the new world that has sprung from it but that now defines it. History provides these antipodean realities, scattering the people at random between them, but the people then make their own choices of who they will be. Their choices may bring violence and disintegration, death and madness, but they can also produce wholeness of being. The otherworld of his imagination proves to be the world of our own time.

David Ireland

To turn from the work of David Malouf to the novels of David Ireland, Walter Adamson and Peter Mathers is to turn from a world that is ultimately

David Ireland
(*National Library of Australia*)

comprehensible to one that remains stubbornly alien. Ireland gives us images of a world of artefacts constructed by our intelligence but outside our control, where the best that we can hope for is a small asylum within which we may endure our ineffectiveness in peace. Mathers' world allows its people no peace, but involves them constantly in its own destructiveness. Unable to remain passive, their only resort is to make the anarchic tide of history their own.

A constant current of menace runs through Ireland's work. His early novel *The Chantic Bird* (Heinemann, London, 1968) is ostensibly narrated by a young psychopath to a sympathetic writer, but when the writer becomes intrusive the narrator knocks him off as casually as he has told of getting even with all the others who have offended him. The recorder of events in *The Glass Canoe* (Macmillan, Melbourne, 1976) starts asking incautious questions and disappears from the scene, apparently embalmed in an ornamental barrel. In *The Unknown Industrial Prisoner* (Angus & Robertson, Sydney, 1971) and *The Flesheaters* (Angus & Robertson, Sydney, 1972) the violence is institutionalised in a social structure that generates violence in the individuals by the strength with which it contains and controls them.

Violence, both public and private, is the animating principle of the fiction.

In each of his three institutional novels, Ireland uses a particular institution — an oil refinery, a home for those needing care, and a pub — as microcosms or *metonyms* of the wider society that builds them to serve its needs. Between them, they represent the three major aspects of industrial capitalism. In the oil refinery, production has become process, the task so divided among the workers that each man's duties have been robbed of meaning, and the product itself is irrelevant to any perceived activity among the workers. The unknown industrial prisoner of the title is every one of the workers, including the management and unions who feed off each other but ultimately are powerless to affect decisions made for the plant by its foreign controllers. Merry Lands, the mysterious asylum of *The Flesheaters*, is the refuge for those who no longer fit into the industrial system. Like the refinery it operates by a set of rules and hierarchies that relate neither to the subjective desires of the inmates nor to any evident objective purpose. Finally, in *The Glass Canoe*, the bar of the Southern Cross provides a semblance of autonomous life for the workers who find there a boozy companionship apart from both work and home.

The conditions of work and play make home irrelevant, and Ireland offers us few scenes of domestic life. These few scenes mainly concern the Samurai, a character in *The Unknown Industrial Prisoner* who for a time suffers from the illusion that he can control his life by persuading his fellow workers to join in cooperative action. Samurai is, however, unable to sustain his vision in the face of the impenetrability of company and union. The workers find sufficient satisfaction in the 'Home Beautiful', the sanctuary of delight that the Great White Father organises in the mangrove swamps that surround the refinery. When the structure of work is disjointed, the potential of the individual is reduced to the search for immediate gratification. Neither individual nor collective fulfilment is any longer possible.

The same truth applies to the workers' leisure hours, as shown in *The Glass Canoe*. The Southern Cross Hotel both represents the society from which the drinkers come, and offers a complicated metaphor of their lives. The 'glass canoe' of the title is slang for a schooner of beer, but it is also an image of the precarious voyage into oblivion it provides for each of the drinkers. This voyage is itself a relic of the hunting rites that once gave structure and meaning to human life. In the pub, the drinkers are able to retrace the steps that have led them from the free state of primitive man, known in boyhood but lost under the demands of work, and an adult world in which they are powerless:

> In their own bodies they had travelled man's road from primitive hunter, through herder of flocks, to our present settled-city civilization. Where *they* were the sheep, the hunted.
>
> And yet these sheep were something more when they were drinking. The golden drops stirred something inside that wasn't human.
>
> Ireland, *Glass Canoe*, p. 12.

Through drink they recover the illusion of primitive power, but at the same time drink reduces them to something less than human. The narrator reflects that perhaps the violence and aggression that govern their life in the pub are in fact the essence of humanity:

> Maybe it was all too human. Maybe it was the hunter and destroyer of life inside them that had never made the transition to a settled life husbanding plants and animals.
>
> Ireland, *Glass Canoe*, p. 12.

Yet again, Ireland goes on to suggest that the violence is not primitive, but the result of a life which denies expression to human energies:

> Once upon a time they were decent men, unaggressive, hard-working, tired at the day's end. They drank to erase the ache and the tiredness.
>
> Now there's only a few of us do a hard day's work, even though we're as poor, relatively, as our grandfathers.
>
> We drink to erase everything.
>
> Ireland, *Glass Canoe*, p. 12.

In the last line the hope that the pub offers of restored strength is revealed as illusion. The condition of the drinkers is the result not just of the loss of power, but the loss of work itself. The tribal rituals they re-enact remain meaningless, the sexual exploits they recount destroy the possibility of human relationship, the only female figure to come into their lives as a person is Sharon, the bar manager, who sets the limits but remains outside them.

The structure of the novel, with its solitary attempt to break out of the pattern and its defeated return to the pub, suggests that the final cell Meat Man will occupy on this path to the grave will be the refuge of alcoholic philosophy already inhabited by Alky Jack. The words in which he tries to record his experience are as powerless to avoid fate as is the attempt of the sociology student Sibley to tame the tribes with science.

The tribes of Ireland's fiction are lost in a world in which the logic of science and humanism has provided the alternatives of refinery, asylum and pub to meet the irrational needs of human desire. The books show these institutions alternately as the denial of humanity or its supreme achievement. When Ernie lies writhing on the ground in paroxysms of grief, his companions turn away. Only the disregarded Blackie comments, 'They're only humans, they don't understand' (p. 91). The implication of the novel is that the dispossession of the tribes that has created our civilisation has left us with only those human instincts that are incapable of human relations. Ireland's later novels suggest his despair at humanity by taking as their themes a woman who turns into a panther, a world that has destroyed humankind, and a world seen from the perspective of animals. Yet the imagination that can conceive these worlds, and the sardonic humour with which the author portrays them, keep despair at bay.

Walter Adamson

Ireland's view of the structures that divide society and destroy the possibility of community is shared by Walter Adamson. In *The Institution* (Outback Press, Melbourne, 1976), he gives a chilling picture of an asylum that resembles the Merry Lands of Ireland's *The Flesheaters*. Adamson's work was, however, originally written in German, and shares more of the political scope of Kafka, from whom the genre derives.

Adamson's asylum seems to exist in a place without a location, outside a society in a vague state of insurrection against its equally vague but sinister government. Schiller, the main character, is taken there by anonymous attendants who remain speechless, except to verify his name and require him to lie on the stretcher. Within the asylum, authority is direct. Schiller challenges it by playing soundless music, the equivalent of the words Scotty and Lee Mallory use to try to win some personal space inside Merry Lands. In this asylum even this freedom threatens the structure and is denied. The only alternatives the novel offers are complete anarchy and complete control. The vision is that of Orwell, who in *1984* recognised that authority can only be absolute, and must extend to the individual's least thought. The inmates of the institution are denied watches and mirrors, because when everything is taken care of they need neither time nor identity. Human logic creates its own contradiction by making a world that denies the place of the human. In Ireland's world this structure is still external, leaving a place for anarchic if brutalised humanity within. In Adamson's fiction, the control has become absolute, with even the absurdity of silent art being forbidden. His asylum is a literary equivalent of Edvard Munch's *Silent Scream*.

Adamson takes the reader beyond Orwell's logic of power into a world of metaphysical denial, where destruction begins within the individual. Our source of identity is the mirror in which we see ourselves, and which thus enables us to give ourselves a role in the world. Denied our mirrors, denied any reality or power we can contradict, the dialectic with others that creates individuality vanishes. The double becomes one, our world becomes also the otherworld, the asylum and the fortress are the same. Schiller's ultimate art, the music of silence, denies humanity, because when the discourse of art, the only guarantee of humanity, can mean anything it also means nothing. The circle ends where it begins, inscribing an empty zero as the sum of our meaning.

Peter Mathers

Mathers' fiction is an attempt to restore the otherworld of contradiction, to refuse the denial that robs us of self. Jack Trap, the hero of *Trap* (Cassell Australia, Melbourne, 1966), is a part-Aboriginal who refuses to accept any of the expectations society attempts to enforce on him. His expedition into the centre of Australia is both a rejection of urban, white

society and a confrontation with it. Trap is determined to remake Australia in his own image. As a
start, he remakes the chronicler of his activities,
David David, whom he jolts out of his conformity and
turns into a disciple. David's consequent recording
of the history of Trap and his forebears rewrites
Australian history.

Mathers carries this project further in *The Wort
Papers* (Cassell Australia, Melbourne, 1972). This
novel includes complete histories of the colonisation
of Tierra del Fuego, the abduction of its inhabitants
and the deforestation of the rainforests of eastern
Australia. These episodes become constituent parts
of the continuous history of European expansion and
destruction. The destructive forces they manifest
are, however, aspects of the same force that enables
such individual figures as Jack Trap to survive. Trap,
descendant of both colonisers and the colonised, is a
citizen of the otherworld that Europe has created
and that continues to resist its dominion.

Gerard Murnane

Murnane, by contrast, writes of people completely
dominated by the world of circumstance in their daily
lives, and able to escape only into the otherworlds of
fantasy, until the distinction between fantasy and
reality becomes obliterated. The historical world his
characters inhabit is itself distorted by their fantasies
of true Australian bushmen redeeming the servile
decadence of Europe, and of the true inheritors of
Irish Catholicism redressing the wrongs of English
Protestant overlords. In Murnane's earliest novel,
Tamarisk Row (Heinemann, Melbourne, 1974),
Clement's father explains to him the relationships
between Europe and Australia:

> While the pale peak-faced Europeans went on
> copying their ancestors' methods of farming,
> tipping their caps to the local baron or grand-duke
> as he rode away from his turretted castle to spend
> the winter in Venice or Rome, and marrying their
> first cousins from the same village so that their
> stupidity and lassitude become thoroughly bred
> into their children, the bushmen of Australia were
> choosing great tracts of a land that had never been
> touched by a plough and crumbled like rich fruit-
> cake when they drove the corner posts of their
> boundary fences into it, droving overland the

> mobs of sturdy sheep and cattle that bred with
> zest under the proud gaze of their owners and filled
> the enormous properties with meaty full-blooded
> progeny, and devising for themselves, with only
> their native intelligence to guide them in a country
> that was hindered by no senseless traditions or
> customs, those farming methods that would make
> Australia the world's greatest producer of wheat
> wool beef and milk . . . the Europeans call them-
> selves Catholics but know little of the mortification
> and self-discipline and resistance to persecution
> that are the marks of a true Catholic.

Murnane, *Tamarisk Row*, pp. 55–6.

This passage encapsulates the comfortable
Australian dream, and distances the new world from
the horrors of overseas. Clement can rest in his
knowledge that the little churches and comfortable
homes built by the devout in Australia remain safe.
But the dream itself lies outside daily experience,
which is filled with the cruelties of school and frustrations of home. The land is not safe for the dreams
of a Catholic boy. His father explains that their forebears got here

> too late to see the country as it had been for thou-
> sands of years when only scattered tribes of
> Aborigines wandered through it scarcely disturb-
> ing the parrots and dingoes in remote gullies
> where they did as they pleased, and too late to
> make Australia a Catholic country, so that now the
> lands of Australia would always be covered by
> roads and farms and suburbs of cities in patterns
> that bigoted Protestants and Masons had laid out.

Murnane, *Tamarisk Row*, p. 118.

Young Clement therefore has to spend much of
his time devising in his backyard, under the Tamarisk
tree, a city of his own, with the mysteries and abandoned hallows and neglected enclosures that a Catholic
could claim as his own, and the racecourses and farm
houses where his dreams of prosperity and sexuality
could be fulfilled. His father similarly lives in the
fantasy land of the addicted gambler, and Clement
himself finds alternative fantasies in the splendours
of the church, the modelled landscapes of his neighbour's aviary, the lives of the saints, and the mysterious bodies of the neighbourhood girls.

Murnane's fantasy world is related to the other-world of Koch's novels only insofar as it offers an escape from the frustrations of the everyday. It is not a world ruled by dark powers, but by a projection of hopes. It is built on the image of an Australia so flat that it allows room for any future. The problem is, as becomes more evident with each of his books, that the characters find it difficult to know which landscape they inhabit.

While Clement built his landscape under the tamarisk tree, the protagonists in the later books spend their time searching for a reality they know exists outside their everyday experience. In *A Lifetime on Clouds* (Heinemann, Melbourne, 1976) this reality lies in sexual fantasy, and in *The Plains* (Norstrilia, Melbourne, 1982) in the centre of a true Australia that may not exist. These histories and geographies constitute the true land of Murnane's dreaming. Their identity constitutes the subject of the six stories that form the circular novel of *Landscape with Landscape* (Penguin, Ringwood, 1987 [1985]). Each of these stories appears to be an episode from the life of a single narrator, yet they are consistent only in that each tells of an attempt to escape to a reality. The place of this dreaming will provide the opportunity to write the work that alone will make its landscape real. This landscape sometimes seems to be Melbourne, sometimes Queensland, sometimes Paraguay, and often sexual fantasy. When he despairs of finding it, the narrator seeks escape into alcohol. The closest the author comes to defining this landscape is the remark that it is 'the space between myself and the nearest man or women who seemed real to me'. (p. 25). Murnane fills this space not only with fantasy but with his observations of people's comic attempts to evade reality by dramatising their own fictions, and the tragedy of massacre and individual death that can be contained and endured, but not denied.

Other contemporary Australian writers have explored the otherworlds of fantasy in various forms of speculative or science fiction. George Turner, after chronicling the affairs of a provincial town, turned to science fiction as a means of discussing more global problems of the modern world. In *Beloved Son* (Faber & Faber, London, 1978) he tries to 'tell the truth about history' by bringing back to earth a crew of spacemen who have been hurled into outer space before the final holocaust convinced the nations that they must abandon war. The novel both portrays the continuing tensions of nationalism and the bleak side of an international bureaucracy of peacelovers, that alarms by its boredom rather than by the kind of horror portrayed by Adamson. Lee Harding uses the notion of intersecting dimensions to explore psychological problems. Damian Broderick, in *The Dreaming Dragons: a Time Opera* (Penguin, Ringwood, 1981 [1980]) creates a myth of the Australian landscape that unites Aboriginal lore, scientific learning, and traditional metaphysical speculation in a novel that raises the issue of our responsibility for our own actions, only to be side-tracked into intellectual games about possible evolutionary alternatives. In *Valencies*, written with Rory Barnes (University of Queensland Press, St Lucia, 1983) the authors play with the juxtaposition of complete technical and biological control and unchanged human emotions. The language accentuates the shock of the new by its combination of esoteric scientific jargon with contemporary colloquial. Once the language is penetrated, however, the plot resolves itself into the dilemmas of personal and social politics. For all its esoteric ambience, it belongs in the twentieth-century world of Western dominance, made starker by being removed from any specific location.

The insistent concern with the otherworld among these authors is a response to the same disintegration and alienation of the modern world embodied in the work of Koch or Ireland. The fascination with science and its technological offshoots represents intellectual enchantment, yet science is continually presented as something 'out there', alien, not as a human product. The obsessed scientists are similar to Koch's Darcy Burr, playing with powers beyond their control. The plots of the novels are concerned with redeeming science, bringing this power back under human control. For all the authors' delight in its intricacies, they are unable to envisage a science that is anything other than a further instrument of domination, another prison of the human soul. By remaining stubbornly alien, their otherworlds are extraordinarily contemporary.

15

BREAKING THE BOUNDARIES

I N the 1960s the Western world was swept by a new spirit of freedom in the arts. During this period, which lasted for the ten years from the rise of the Beatles in 1963 to the first oil crisis in 1973, booming consumer economies ensured full employment and the welfare state provided a safety net for the intervals between jobs. These conditions provided for the young a security that enabled them to believe that such continuing imperfections as slums, inequalities and institutionalised warfare were purely the fault of the old who clung to the machinery of power. Students called on workers to join them in campus revolts to initiate the millenium by abolishing war and exploitation. New technologies enabled ideas to be transmitted around the globe in an instant, and gave local groups the capacity to produce and distribute their songs and words to new audiences in the streets, the pubs and the lecture theatres. The collapse of the modes of mass production seemed to usher in an age of Aquarius when the unmediated production of the arts would meet the needs of the people. The insistent rhythms of rock battered the old citadels of rational discourse with the new message of sensual gratification. It seemed the consumers of the world had only to unite the cast off the chains of the past and enter a world of personal freedom.

This movement reached Australia in the late 1960s, when Australia's involvement as junior partner in the war in Vietnam was making political subservience irksome. The new ideas of dissent and liberation

generated an impatience with all established traditions, and opposition to the war provided a focus for agitation. In a spirit of independence, Australian writers plunged into the international turmoil, joyfully embracing US models to express their opposition to the new imperialism. When, in 1975, Saigon fell to the North Vietnamese, the defeat of the Americans was celebrated as the culmination of a decade of

Vietnam Protesters
(*Mirror Newspapers Ltd*)

struggle. The fall of the Whitlam Labor government in Canberra six months later, and the consequent discrediting of its vision of national renewal, demonstrated that there was a price to be paid for internationalism. Nevertheless, the writers who had commenced publishing in the previous decade continued as a major force in Australian writing in the bitter years after. Their work has ensured that Australians remain aware of what they have in common with the rest of the world, as well as what makes them distinct.

Frank Moorhouse

With the title of his first collection of stories, *Futility and Other Animals* (Gareth Powell Associates, Sydney, 1969), Frank Moorhouse challenged the orthodoxy of Australia writing. A prefatory note by the author explains that the stories constitute a 'discontinuous narrative', and its characters a tribe, linked by their sharing the same external and internal landscape. This landscape is indicated in the first story of the collection, 'The Story of the Knife', which moves by a series of flashbacks from the setting in a beach cabin to tell the story of the ending of a love affair. The episodes alternate between the external landscape of the cabin and an inner Sydney party. Instead of details of the physical setting and the background of the lovers, the author details the music, drugs and physical sex. The conversations are about emotional honesty. The inner landscape is filled with the politics of sex, symbolised by the knife that intensifies their lovemaking and signifies the end of the affair. But then a twist of circumstance makes their feelings irrelevant. There is no plot, only the immediacy of the moment.

The story challenges expectations by its episodic quality, by the absence of clear development of plot or character, and by the explicitness of its language. Moorhouse writes of people whose first responsibility is honesty to themselves, and all else follows from this, including an apparent lack of responsibility to others, even their lovers. Anne explains her feelings, Roger observes and calculates, even exploits her, but both are emotionally honest. The demands they make of their partners are physical.

In the title story Perry, the owner of the cabin, has to accept that he is alone in the jungle of despair before he can accept the child who has been left dependent on him. The gun he carries is a symbol of his despair, but he is forced to explain it in more ideologically correct terms.

'Having a gun isn't being militaristic or aggressive, Or being a thug. Having a gun is like having a vote. Or a say in things. A vote is for times of social stability and a gun for times of social disruption or upheaval. A man defends himself with an argument when confronted with an argument and with a gun when confronted with a gun.' He said it like a part in a play.

Moorhouse, *Futility*, p. 136.

These words are like the script of a play; they tell the listener what he wants to hear, not the true reason the speaker has purchased the gun, to take his own life. He admits the truth to his new wife, Robyn, when she refuses to accept his rationalisations. She is not, however, able to persuade him to get rid of the gun, to overcome the sense of futility that creates his need for it. Only when he prevaricates to the child about its purpose does his script impose itself on him, the words making their own truth. The gun becomes not the instrument of despair but a means to frighten it away. His acceptance of responsibility for the child enables him to accept responsibility for himself.

Moorhouse portrays a world whose people live, as one of them puts it, on the border of two countries, futility and hope. They are academics, salesmen, writers, artists, drifters and dole drawers. They are concerned with the environment, health, drink, drugs, food, politics and their bodies. They live in Sydney or drop out in bush shacks, or they travel the world. Vaguely left in their politics, they are libertarians or anarchists rather than committed to any party. They represent the new class of an affluent society, not necessarily wealthy but able to get by, living not by producing goods or services but by exchanging words and images. The environment is something for them to be concerned about, not something they have built with their labour. Their lives, like their work, are made up of fragments, each moment lived for itself, finding no place in traditional structures of church or nation. These lives are their most important real product. They are citizens of a global metropolis, finding their freedom within, rather than as part of, the structures of politics and economics that operate by an autonomous logic indifferent to human purpose.

In *Days of Wine and Rage* (Penguin, Ringwood, 1980), a collection of writings from the 1970s linked by later commentary, Moorhouse describes both the random beginnings of the movement that coalesced around the student newspaper *Tharunka* and similar journals, and its steady development towards a conscious program of liberation. The starting of this program was the ambition to free language from the legal restrictions and social taboos that had kept writers within approved limits. The writers involved saw this linguistic revolution as a part of an attempted 'renegotiation of the relationships between men and women, adults and children, and a rethinking of the sexual and emotional relationships between people of the same sex' (pp. 7–8). By recreating their own lives, they would build a new basis for society. Their work did produce a new basis for sensibility, but their failure to engage with other economic issues left this sensibility vulnerable to changes in the economic climate and the rise of a new conservatism, personally libertarian but socially repressive.

Moorhouse's own work provides an index for this retreat from the optimism of the Whitlam decade. The stories in his early volumes describe the dilemmas faced by members of a generation trying to create their lives solely on the basis of their own experience, unsupported by either productive work or traditional structure. Then, in *The Electric Experience* (Angus & Robertson, Sydney, 1974) and in the script for Michael Thornhill's film *Between the Wars*, he takes a step back to examine the experience of his father's generation.

Both the film and book are set in a fictitious town on the coast south of Sydney, in the district where Moorhouse grew up and where D.H. Lawrence had set his novel *Kangaroo*. In writing of this area Moorhouse is not only seeking out the truth of the generation against whose values he has rebelled, but is also examining the myth of the independent Australian that Lawrence had found concealed a hollow at the centre. Moorhouse does describe the narrowness and emptiness of small-town life, but he also understands the satisfactions it offers. Dr Trenbow, the town doctor, who makes a brief appearance in the novel and has a more central role in the film, shows that it is possible to live within the town's limits without being bound by them.

The book comprises two intertwined parts, labelled narratives and fragments, which taken together build a picture of the life of George McDowell, soft-drink manufacturer and Rotarian. His life has had two highlights — his visit to the St Louis Rotary convention of 1923, and his introduction of electricity to his home town. The first defined his aspirations, the second symbolises his achievement. In bringing his town into the modern world, George unconsciously undermines the solid country values for which he stands, and prepares the way for his rejection by the succeeding generation. This rejection is the subject of the story 'Filming the Hatted Australian', an episode in *The Electric Experience* that seems at first reading like an afterthought, an episode from another novel. Instead of dealing with the world of George McDowell, it describes a film crew at work on a documentary. The subject of the film is, however, a contemporary of McDowell, a man who worked for him at one time. The crew, who include McDowell's daughter, supposedly are recording their interview with him in order to document his life's experience; actually, they treat him with ignorance and cruel contempt. The story demonstrates an unbridgeable gap between the world of McDowell and the hatted Australian and that of the young filmmakers. Yet, like the book as a whole, it also shows that Moorhouse is able to bridge the gap, using the people in each world as a commentary on the other.

Moorhouse's 'discontinous narratives' weave back and forth around the same cast of characters as he builds the story of his times. Later stories, like the last episode in *The Electric Experience*, take up characters or incidents from earlier ones, extending our perception of the complex pattern of events we weave and in which we are woven. Deliberately, fact and fiction are mixed, the true narrative of his involvement with the underground press or his speculations about sex or the Labor government with fiction of the liberated woman, the academic lecture or the Jack Kerouac wake. His work does, however, seem marked by an increasing sense of disillusion. The people in the earlier stories maintain the hope that they will in some way defeat futility, find the true relationship, build a new society. In the later ones the sense of despair and breakdown becomes stronger. As the narrator, speaking as the author at a conference, remarks in one story, 'Anything I'm *for* is likely to be defeated'. The forces ranged against the individual seem too strong, and the attempt to create authentic life on the basis of honesty to experience degenerates into mere narcissism.

Moorhouse began his career as a journalist, and his work occupies the borderline between reporting, which recreates experience, and fiction, which produces it. The author is an active figure in his writing as he comments, questions, prods the readers and jostles his characters. It is the style of a writer who is confident, like his character T. George McDowell, that he can make the world his own.

This is very much the mood of the 1970s, when everything seemed possible for those with the courage to be themselves. This spirit flowed also into the journalism of the time, particularly in the irreverent *Nation Review* (1972–81), where such writers as Mungo MacCallum, Bob Ellis and John Hepworth jostled for space with irreverent black-and-white artists like Nicholson, Roberts, Cook and Leunig. *John Hepworth: His Book*, with illustrations by Michael Leunig (Angus & Robertson, Sydney, 1978) gives the flavour of the time. Hepworth constructs the fiction of his own life in a series of reminiscences, reports and fantasies that take the mickey out of stuffy respectability in favour of anarchist abandonment to the pleasures of the flesh and the spirit. Two election diaries chronicle the disillusion that succeeded this time of hope. Mungo MacCallum's *Mungo on the Zoo Train*, with drawings by Patrick Cook (University of Queensland Press, St Lucia, 1979) collects articles about the federal elections between 1972 and 1977, when Whitlam suffered his last defeat. Bob Ellis's *The Things We Did Last Summer* (Collins, Melbourne, 1983) starts with the small hopes rekindled with the return of Labor in 1983, and moves backwards to the tumultuous events around the dismissal of Whitlam and the dreary years that followed. In both books the writers are as much actors as recorders. MacCallum revels in the high drama, and Ellis converts the often tedious days of campaigning into a film that rolls past and present, hope and despair, into a single montage of grief for a country determined to betray its promise.

Australian Drama

Moorhouse's stories capture the excitement of a decade, its feeling of liberation and expectation, and then the closing in of restriction and disillusion, some of it imposed, some merely the product of time. These feelings were expressed in the life and death of the weekly *Nation Review*, in the explosion of little poetry magazines and poetry readings, and in the new drama that came to birth around Sydney's Nimrod and Melbourne's La Mama and Pram Factory theatres.

Australian drama had been tied to the model of the well-shaped play. Its major achievements had been Ray Lawler's *Summer of the Seventeenth Doll* (1955), Richard Beynon's *The Shifting Heart* (1957), Peter Kenna's *The Slaughter of St Teresa's Day* (1959) and Alan Seymour's *The One Day of the Year*, which was barred from the Adelaide Festival on patriotic grounds in 1960. Although these were essentially realist plays of the kind pioneered by Louis Esson and Vance Palmer with the Pioneer Players between the wars, they had the advantage of professional production and demonstrated that there was an audience for Australian work in the theatre. Nevertheless, apart from the plays of Patrick White, little fresh Australian drama appeared until Jack Hibberd's *White with Wire Wheels* (1966) and *Dimboola* (1969), Alexander Buzo's *Norm and Ahmed* (1968) and David Williamson's *The Removalists* and *Don's Party* (1971).

In 1970 the musical *The Legend of King O'Malley* by Michael Boddy and Bob Ellis established a new

David Williamson
(*Herald & Weekly Times*)

mould with its mixture of music hall comedy and historical chronicle. This kind of episodic narrative has been further developed by Barry Oakley in *The Feet of Daniel Mannix* (1975), and by Dorothy Hewett in her turbulent chronicles of youth and love. David Williamson has used more traditional forms as a vehicle for his social satire. Jack Hibberd, in *Dimboola*, takes apart the illusions of a country town in comedy that reveals the darkness within. In his *A Stretch of the Imagination* (1973) the monologue gradually takes on a poetic force that deepens to tragedy as the old derelict recreates his life for the audience. John Romeril, in *The Floating World* (1975) develops a similar intensity as he strips his characters down through their personal posturing to the deep hurts that history has imposed on them.

These plays all extend the bounds of drama to encompass the colloquial Australian. Later playwrights such as Stephen Sewell and Louis Nowra have abandoned the naturalistic starting point to develop surreal works embodying wider political and existential problems. Bill Reed has made poetic drama from the travails of exploration, Phil Motherwell and Barry Dickins have shown the poetic potentials of suburbia, and Jack Davis has used drama as a means of revealing both the solidarity and the exclusion of the Aborigines.

New Australian Poetry

At the same time as the dramatists were working to extend the language and form available in the theatre, poets were breaking the bonds of traditional prosody and syntax to enable verse to express the struggle for a new sensibility. Unlike the modernists of the earlier part of the century, they were not trying to rebuild tradition so much as to discard it. They did not take their inspiration or models from a revival of classicism, but from the endeavours of US poets to devise rhythms and forms that discarded all authority except that of vernacular experience. Thomas Shapcott's anthology, *Contemporary American and Australian Poetry*, (University of Queensland Press, St Lucia, 1976) demonstrates the affinity between US poets and the Australians who used them as a model. The book starts by juxtaposing the ordered forms of A.D. Hope and Judith Wright with the fractured syntax and open forms of John Berryman and the disembodied imagism of George

Oppen. Rather than using the language of control, Berryman opens his words to the logic of dream, wrenching the details of Beethoven's life and work into the 'ground zero' of the present, while Oppen lets the words themselves become the images, opening the mind of the reader to them as individual signs. These mark the two paths Australian poets were to follow, although the anthology also reveals how such writers as Francis Webb had anticipated these courses and how many remained aloof from the influence.

Thomas Shapcott

Shapcott's own work demonstrates the liberating influence of US models. His earliest poems play with song and structure, but tend to tight form and precise image in the manner of Melbourne domestic. *Inwards to the Sun* (University of Queensland Press, St Lucia, 1969) opens with a page containing only the title, 'This Blank Page', starting a sentence that continues on the next page:

> is where I exist. See, and already you
> begin to know me, an insistence somewhere
> that your eyes transmute into Voice —

Shapcott, *Inwards*, pp. 10–11.

The reader calls the poet into being by attending to the language that constitutes that being.

This uncertainty, not only about the external world but about his own existence, and his awareness that all he has is the language with which he makes everything, separates Shapcott from his predecessors who clearly saw themselves writing in a tradition and using their art to record, transform and transcend a world they knew through their experience. In Shapcott's poetry the certainties of traditional structures are undermined by his awareness of a material universe constituted from blind forces, a culture shaped by illusion and a language debased by propaganda. The poet, having nothing but words, must use them to build the world afresh. His new world is not an Australia already shaped by tradition, but a reality to be brought into being.

Although subsequent poems in this volume are controlled by traditional forms, the imagery works to subvert and overturn the certainty they imply. In 'Schoolgirls Playing' (p. 18), the dance that patterns their experience becomes a snare, 'a web that binds them in their play/to all the truths they practise to unsay'. The truths must be unsaid before they can be renewed. In the sequence, 'Five Days Lost' (pp. 49–54), the speaker's language gradually breaks down from coherent statements that preserve his identity to an absorption into the unpatterned unpunctuated wilderness around him

> of voices earning loving things
> no not dying alone and no one needing
> no one being voices
> and yellow dazzling voices
> until the syntax collapses as voices and light fade into

> union
> and
> I am

Shapcott, Inwards, p. 54.

In later poems in the volume, the visual structure itself provides meaning that cannot be tied down by the syntax and metre. 'Ceremony for Cedar: 1' (p. 79) is written in a rectangle divided by a diagonal space that splits both the poem and all but its first and last lines into two. We can therefore read it as any one of three poems — the whole, or either half. The words, instead of tying down meanings, allow readers to construct their own experiences of the house and the people in it.

In his long sequence, *Shabbytown Calender* (University of Queensland Press, St Lucia, 1975), Shapcott allows the whole life of his provincial Queensland home town to spread across the pages. Within the cyclical structure of the year, history produces its own linear structure as particular people and places come to the poet's attention. The sequence is held together by the monthly fugues that provide the catchline on which he builds each succeeding section. The individual poems are open, producing meaning from the interaction of particular scenes and images, but together weaving the pattern not only of the town but of the life of its observer. History exists in the town in its buildings, the memories and attitudes of its inhabitants, the impact of floods and pollution, but is in turn subordinate to the seasons and the renewing cycle of the generations. It is all held in the 'Shabbytown Fugue' of May (p. 46):

> Boys like young unbroken animals
> the little oxfaced girls
> morning dance with shadows
> blown away with morning
> let them trample over
> let them be rough with affection
> they shake the flowers of their heads
> they break the oleander
> and every street is home
> they are not lost
> where the world spins
> our children laugh full and defenceless
> they will not believe they shall be cursed
> they shall be cursed

Shapcott, Calendar, p. 46.

The last two lines embody the poles of repetition and renewal between which the poem moves. The preceding images can be read horizontally as answering each to each, vertically as a bunch of images of the town. Together they provide the lattice within which we make our lives and our meanings.

Michael Dransfield

While Shapcott's work sprawls and opens into new structures, Dransfield's existential uncertainty condenses and concentrates, upwrapping meaning from minimal words and images. Even a relatively spacious sequence like 'Geography' (*The Inspector of Tides*, University of Queensland Press, St Lucia, 1970), which piles image on image and expands into the feedom of prose as he names the elements of his life, concludes with the void of self imprisoned in history. More characteristic are the poems where he allows image to follow image down the page and out of the world into the self-contained world of true self-consciousness, as does mad King Ludwig in his dream of swans, or dream as a swan:

> at the edge of the palace
> mountains

> at their dim border
> the world mutters worn curses
> their armies do not come
> they fear the flowers
> above and

below us
discovery freshens the pre-world
the ancient gleams, in light
as for the first time

Dransfield, *Drug Poems*, Sun
Books, Melbourne, 1972, p. 68.

With the world shut out, the world can begin again.

John Tranter

Dransfield takes us to the furthest point of consciousness, beyond which we are in the territory where nothing can be said. Tranter, by contrast, takes us away from any particular consciousness into a world filled with images and events, but without any apparent patterns. While Shapcott opens himself to experience, Tranter is overwhelmed by it. The experience is not, however, so much of an objective world, but rather of a world the poet experiences only through the constant noise it makes. Its words are charged with a multitude of meanings and significance, but lead us to no single reality beyond them.

In 'Red Movie' (*Red Movie*, Angus & Robertson, Sydney, 1972; reprinted in John Tranter (ed.), *The New Australian Poetry*, Makar Press, St Lucia, 1979, pp. 148–58) Tranter provides an epigraph that gives a clue to his method: 'That which can be studied is the pattern of processes which characterise the interaction of personalities in particular recurrent situations or fields which "include" the observer'. As modern physicists declare, any process is changed by being observed. The observer becomes part of the process. Thus in Tranter's poetry we cannot distinguish the observer from the objective world or his dreams. The patterns of arrival and departure, invasion and desertion, recur through the sequence. Sometimes they form an 'experiment which succeeds' and therefore must be left in search of new images drenching with 'the gust of life' (p. 150). At other times they constitute an experiment that offers promise of nothing. In both cases, the experiment having been made, the words having been said, it ceases to be an experiment. We must move on. The movement of the poems takes us through some episodes, such as the new husband leaving his wife or the search for a suitable madhouse, which seem to occur in an objec-

John Tranter
(*National Library of Australia*)

tive world. Others, like the departure of the dreadful sailor with his knowledge of our buried life, seem part of a nightmare. Even a sequence like 'The Failure of Sentiment and the Evasion of Love' (pp. 154–7), which seems to be a series of images or episodes of failed love, is interrupted by historical images of the Mongolian Khan and Egyptian traits that seem irrelevant except to open windows into further worlds of experience. The readers must make their own connections.

The affirmation of the way we live in language is characteristic of the 'generation of 68', as Tranter names his contemporaries with reference to the student revolts of that year. Language was the key to their assault on the barriers of convention, tradition and official mendacity. As Nigel Roberts wrote in John Tranter's anthology, *The New Australian Poetry* (p. 48):

Poetry is not an escape/but
    an appreciation
        of reality.

Tranter, *The New Australian Poetry*, p. 40.

Tranter's work produces its reality by the formal

freedom that combines the visual appeal of shape on the page with the tones and elisions of colloquial speech. The occasional obscenity reminds us of the power of language to shock and open as well as to control and shut down. John Forbes uses language more to point to a world outside him, but as he reminds us in his sequence on three drawings of heads, we bring this world into existence in words or art, and can as easily erase it again. Richard Tipping's poems, on the other hand, use highly visual and formal devices to remind us of how the world creates its own forms to impose their meaning on us. The world lies in wait for us to open our eyes and find its poetry.

The new poetry found its voice not only through public reading and the pages of little magazines, but also through the series of Paperback Poets published by the University of Queensland Press and through anthologies. Much of this work was collected in *The First Paperback Poets Anthology*, edited by Roger McDonald (University of Queensland Press, St Lucia, 1974). This includes the dreams of Dransfield, more conventional discursive work by David Malouf, suburban images of Leon Slade and Geoff Page, the disjointed narratives and dialogues of Richard Packer, and Judith Rodriquez's bold visual challenges. Another anthology of the time, Robert Kenny and Colin Talbot's *Applestealers* (Outback Press, North Fitzroy, 1974) is designed to provide a continuing dialogue between the contributors. The poems, with their clash of images and speech rhythms, are encompassed in a sequence of graphics, notes, photographs and an episodic introduction that together invite readers to move around them in their own fashion and build them into their own structures. The book does not itself produce meaning, but provides the materials for readers to undertake the task themselves.

John Tranter's anthology, *The New Australian Poetry*, on the other hand, is a more ordered survey of a completed body of work, fitting each poet into an intellectual structure defined by the polemical introduction. In his introduction, Tranter argues that behind the variety of styles adopted by the poets of his generation lies a common belief in the importance of poetry 'as an integral part of a wider struggle for freedom' (p. xvii). The new poetics that resulted is based on the tenet that 'the mental landscape can be displayed as being more variable, complex and

humanly meaningful than the external, because it includes the "real world" as one of its attributes' (p. xxiii). This is analogous to our experience of films or television, where we are embraced in a world constituted solely from images that sweep us into their own life. The cuts and swings characteristic of Tranter and others in his collection are comparable to the cutting, panning and montage of television narratives and advertisements. A mood is created from a sequence of images that are their own message.

The one hundred sonnets in Tranter's *Crying in Early Infancy* (Makar Press, St Lucia, 1977) have a tighter form and seem to make more explicit statements than his earlier work. Between them they provide a kind of mental autobiography, starting in the aftermath of a party from which he travels back into memories of Brazilian jungles, Balinese holidays, karma dreams and nightmares of war to the 'town where I was born', where he wonders 'who gives a . . . about a "good start" ' (p. 41). The sonnets include memories of dreams, people glimpsed in passing, conversations. At the end he has reached where he started, ready to begin again on the poem or the journey, to take again the risk of destroying himself by the act of writing that involves him in a world where destruction is more likely than creation.

Other Poets

Other poets collected in these anthologies have moved in the same direction towards a poetry of more explicit statement. Robert Adamson, who is represented in Tranter's collection by the surrealist sequence 'The Rumour', and the meditative if bitter 'Sonnets to be Written from Prison', has since written more conventionally lyrical poems set along the Hawkesbury where he lived. In a series of lyrical poems in *Applestealers* (pp. 203–11), Robert Kenny traces the process by which his life is written through memory, dialogue, the landscape itself, where 'imagination geography/are indivisible/ — are existence'. The world itself creates him, making each moment of waking a choice as he contemplates the 'lovely intelligence/that seduces the rigmarole of the hours'. In *The New Australian Poetry*, however, he is represented by a series of prose statements in which the great detectives of fiction supposedly explain how they interrogate the world (pp. 189–95). The controlling metaphor, extended in his later novel *The Last Adventures of Christian Doom: Private I* (Rigmarole, Clifton Hill, 1982), is that life itself is a detective story in which the observing intelligence creates the facts as it interrogates its experience. With his colleague Kris Hemensley, Kenny has worked as publisher, editor and writer to create an autonomous reality from words exchanged by writers around the world. In practice, this world is very much a projection of intellectuals in countries of the Pacific rim and central Europe, who seek to escape from material struggles into a Zen universe of word, silence and gesture. The vehicle for this project was Hemensley's journal, *The Ear in the Wheatfield,* and its results are collected in Hemensley's anthology *The Best of the Ear* (Rigmarole, Clifton Hill, Melbourne, 1985).

From experiments with the ultimate freedom of language, several poets have been forced back to recognise the final limits of circumstance. Tranter had quoted with approval Nietzche's proposition that 'the apparent world is the only true one' (*The New Australian Poetry*, p. xxiii). The experience of the later decade was to show that this apparent world could not be abolished by the freedom of language. The poems of Alan Wearne and Laurie Duggan in Tranter's anthology already show a concern for political and historical circumstance. Wearne's sequence from 'Out There' (pp. 286–300) creates the circumstances of an attempt at suicide from the meditations of three individuals about the event. Although the event itself remains outside these poems, the speakers produce its context by their own attempts to define themselves in relation to the boy whose attempt on his life has forced them to question their own. Duggan, in 'Elegy: Melbourne 1940–71' (pp. 274–7) attempts to construct a picture of the past from an assemblage of notebooks and memories and his own later comments. His writers include a painter and a poet, deliberately using their environment to construct their own images, which Duggan then uses to build his own understanding of a past age. Significantly, the poem is much denser in detail than 'Sydney Notes' (pp. 277–9), which records in a random scatter of images the speaker's

displacement to a new environment and the consequent attempt to build a new identity. The mode of the writing is, however, closely related to the historical situation of the speaker.

Alan Wearne and Laurie Duggan have both since published book-length poems. One constitutes a novel about the fall of the Whitlam government and subsequent disillusion, the other builds a history of Gippsland from fragments, observations and meditations. In *The Ash Range* (Pan, Sydney, 1987), as in his Melbourne elegy, Duggan allows a past world to return through letters, diaries and reports, as a history that provides the language of the present. Several characters from Wearne's *The Nightmarkets* (Penguin, Ringwood, 1986) appeared in extracts in *The New Australian Poetry*. The completed poem shows them living the lives and politics they construct, like the speakers in 'Out There', from the words with which they constantly tell their stories. For Wearne, however, language is not a self-contained reality but the product of *dialectic*, the dialogue with the other, with the people and and the environment who make Australia's history. His characters talk conversationally about their own experiences and their attempts to make sense of their lives. Their lives interweave as they become involved with each other or in the same public activities, but each story remains separate. They are made by the same history, but they make different stories, different lives, from it. Although they achieve some success in their lives, none of them find their hopes fulfilled. At the end, the narrator can only retreat from another experience of hope postponed, and prepare more words for phases still to come, for another 'story based on tomorrow starting tomorrow' (p. 292).

Wearne and Duggan have moved beyond the modernism that made language the subject of the poetry to work that allows language to find its own way to defining a world. Duggan inherits his world from the scraps of language left by history and Wearne from the tales people tell to give unity to their disrupted lives. Brian Matthews, in *Louisa* (McPhee Gribble, Melbourne, 1987), uses a similar method to recreate the life of Louisa Lawson from a mixture of historical narrative, commentary, reflection and fiction. All these works, paradoxically, make the lives they record more real by their recognition of the impossibility of fully knowing even ourselves, let alone the history from which we are made. They have moved away from the assertion of the 1960s that we could make the world by imposing on it the image of our own freedom, into a readiness to enter into a dialogue with the world and allow it to impose its patterns and names on us.

Other writers during this period have endeavoured to pass from dialogue to a monologue in which existence speaks directly through the language of their work. Mark O'Connor's poems of the North Queensland coast or the Mediterranean use simple forms of verse to bring the reader into direct contact with the forms of nature and history that the poet observes. These forms slide as easily through his verse as the islands of Greece eroded through the stomachs of goats into the waters of the Mediterranean. Alan Gould's poems use a complexity of forms to pin down the precise moment of experience. This varies from the intricacies of travel and domesticity to the old Norse world stripped down to essentials of place and action. Robert Gray and Kevin Hart both pare their poetry down to sequences of images that create the sense of time suspended. Even Gray's poem 'The Meat Works' with its images of blood, flies and stench, finishes on a moment of contemplation (*Creek Water Journal*, University of Queensland Press, St Lucia, 1974, pp. 52–3). Other poems become themselves meditations where the self escapes through the precisely described reality of things into a timeless world beyond them where the individual is both intensely the self and nothing. The karma of Buddha reduces the business of Australia to insignificance.

Contemporary Women Writers

While one element of the new writings of the angry decade was a concern with language for itself, the world reduced to words, other writers felt there was more to be said, particularly about the circumstances that, like Dransfield's 'affectionate concrete', pressed and oppressed their consciousness. These included not only traditions and forms, the dead hand of the past operating to control them through language, but also the social structures of a patriarchal society.

Women have always played a major role in Australian literature. Catherine Spence affirmed the right of women to independence, the moralists of the later nineteenth century asserted the values of continence and temperance. Richardson was concerned with the division of the complementary parts of personality into conflicting roles. Contemporary women writers have continued to show a concern for these matters, but like their male counterparts they have also felt that liberation must begin by freeing the self in the body. For women, this often meant freeing themselves from bondage to a male world that sought to use them only as instruments of its own purposes. Moorhouse and Wearne are among the male writers who have shown a particular sensitivity to the need of women to define themselves. For many women writers, however, the first step towards freedom was to find their own words to express their condition. Whereas their male contemporaries found their place by accepting the city as their natural habitat, opposing it to the restriction of the small town, the women found themselves equally marginal even in the metropolis. Their first need was to claim space for their own emotional life.

In their anthology, *Australian Women Poets* (Penguin, Ringwood, 1986), Susan Hampton and Kate Llewellyn have not only given room to women bending the language to establish their space, but have shown how their efforts rest on a tradition of women's poetry going back to Ada Cambridge and Mary Gilmore, and earlier, to the time of the convicts. For these earlier poets it was sufficient to state the female dilemma, but contemporary women writers have found it necessary to go further and alter the language and literary forms. The freedom established by modernist approaches to language enables them to use it not just as a way of placing and controlling experience, separating subject from object, but as an expression of the prelinguistic rhythms that embrace our lives and are normally more part of musical than linguistic expression.

Vicky Viidikas

The poems of Vicky Viidikas, in particular, break through the controlling functions of language to allow it directly to express, not just her feelings, but the patterns of life that generate both thought and feeling.

Her words do not merely express her condition but free her to make the world her own. The two photographs of her in *Applestealers* show the doubleness of this endeavour. In one, she is a child cuddling a koala; in the other, she is an adult, standing outside a wooden dunny, naked except for her hat. These pictures suggest her approach to life. He poetry is warm and giving, but also defiant of convention, presenting the author naked in her feelings. Her sequence of prose poems, 'Four Poems on a Theme', in *Australian Women Poets* (pp. 200–2) shows both aspects of her work. They describe, or appear to describe, the progress of a love, from the feeling of being inside paradise, through enclosure in structures to the verge of break-up. At first the 'risk is gold'; then, even amid the library that controls, love can take them away from 'structures . . . tired defences'. Then, as the man seeks another woman without breaking from the first, the speaker finds language just empty structure, unable to replace him or to support her. Finally, finding reason inadequate, but refusing to be any 'virgin sock-washer' for a man seeking to have both adoration and the surrounds of care, she accepts that the 'alternative to restrictions' is 'Going down. With no permanence . . . Without end'. The language that reveals the situation cannot control it. The sentences are flung at the reader, or the lover, without conventional syntactical structure, as both weapons and signposts. Through them the speaker accepts without yielding.

In the *First Paperback Poets Anthology* (Roger McDonald (ed.), University of Queensland Press, St Lucia, 1974), Viidikas is represented by poems that approach a jazz idiom. 'Loaded Hearts' (p. 181) is a series of one-line statements or exclamations without any punctuation. Each line is a sign pointing to one of the self-absorbing games of the counter-culture. The whole is held together not primarily by syntax but by a driving rhythm that is more like a rock drumbeat than any pattern of conversation. The poem starts with the two symbols of music and drugs:

> Oh boy Ken the smiling mountain is playing his
>   guitar
>
> The beautiful Irene is taking another pill.

It continues through the gesture of:

> Oh boy to the phallic teashirt
> Oh sigh to the Baba breadknife
> Oh gee to the landlord's prayer

to the comic pathetic ending or summary:

> They're playing darts with hypodermics
>
> The fools are recording pain
>
> We're making weapons from our dreams

> Viidikas, *Paperback Poets Anthology*, p. 181.

The last line, with the shift from third to first person to include speaker and reader in the whole scene, has a characteristic ambivalence. The pain is real, but the apparently random acts of escape made by the players also turn it into a weapon.

Dorothy Hewett

The decade of the 1970s also saw Dorothy Hewett emerge with a new and clearer voice in both poetry and drama. Like other women writers, she uses language as a weapon to free the passionate force of love from the fetters of society. These fetters are seen as the instruments of the fathers, and of the society that listens to their voices of conscience and conformity rather than to its own heart. Money and the state become metaphors for this power. These concerns have been present in Hewett's work from its beginning, but her latest books serve to identify and clarify them. Although her earlier work is written within the social realist forms of the radical tradition of Australian nationalism, its energies attempt to subvert the forms even there.

Hewett's novel, *Bobbin' Up* (Australasian Book Society, Melbourne, 1959), is a tale of the human bondage of a textile factory. However, the solidarity the women find in resisting management is also a solidarity of sisterhood. Their strike forces them to choose between their fellow workers and their lovers as surely as John Morrison's wharfies are torn between loyalty to union and to family. The choice the women make, however, enhances rather than divides them as individuals. They discover their own worth, the necessary condition of love itself.

Similarly, although the language of her earlier poetry is controlled by conventional forms, these are subverted by the assertion of the drive and need for a

Dorothy Hewett
(*Graeme Kinross-Smith*)

of freedom as the hooves of their horses beat into the ground the mutterings of her ancestors, the 'dour and sardonic Quaker men' and the

> . . .women with hooked noses, baking bread,
> Breeding, hymning, sewing, fencing off the stony
>   earth
> That salts their bones for thanksgiving when
>   they're dead.

Against this dour struggle for control, rewarded only by the ambiguous salt that may be savour but may also be sterility, the speaker lauds her escape with Clancy as

> . . . the old men rose muttering and cursed from
>   the graveyard
> When they saw our wild white hoofs go flashing by,
> For I ride with landless Clancy and their prayers
>   are at my back,
> They can shout out strings of curses on the sky.

Hewett, *Windmill Country*, p. 16.

Yet the speaker, even in the joy of escape, knows also that the dour struggle of the Quaker men and women still produced value, and that her freedom has its price, paid in the part of her left behind in 'that moonlit dust outside the Kunjin pub'. True freedom demands the unity of the two lives celebrated in this poem, the joyous energy of the landless Clancy and the productive work of the dour settlers.

Other poems in this collection deal with the sadness of love, with desertion, with loneliness. The best known, 'Go Down, Red Roses' (pp. 21–2), is a lament for all the men whose work produces our well-being at the cost of their own. It is, nevertheless, a woman's poem — not the poem of the woman as comforter of others without comfort for herself, but of the woman who knows she is one half of an equation that separation will never allow to be completed. Man and woman are equally victims, but while the man has the gift of constant endeavouring, the woman is superior in her gift of knowing.

In her later work Hewett abandons much of the control of form, instead reworking timeless myths of creation and fall into the circumstances of the present. She opens her collection, *Greenhouse* (Big Smoke Books, Sydney, 1979), with a poem (p. 15) that is at once an invocation and a summary:

freedom that finds its furthest expression in love. The end of the poetry is not the freedom of the woman from the man, but the love that embraces both in the single anarchic freedom that is all that stands against solitude and death. The search for this freedom is the motive force of her politics, her remaking of mythology, the questing of her plays and the celebration and lamentation of her poetry.

The opening poem of *Windmill Country* (Overland, Melbourne, 1968) is a tale of age and the evil that destroys love. The setting is the fairy-tale world of 'an evil Chinese princess' and 'diseased prince' rotting in 'our turret of courtesans'. The turret is the tower of the traditional story, a symbol both of phallic male power and of imprisonment by female jealousy from which the maiden will be released by the handsome prince. But these lovers have chosen imprisonment in the tower and, using wealth to isolate themselves from life, have turned love to disease. They have shut out the world, and therefore no prince can come to their rescue. Their diseased love becomes a symbol of the envy that imposes it fetters of wealth on the world for its own gratification.

By contrast, in 'Once I Rode with Clancy' (pp. 16–17), Hewett takes the traditional ballad form and images of a traditional Australia to create an image

In this romantic house each storey's peeled
for rapists   randy poets   their lovers
young men in jeans play out seductive ballets
    partner my naked girls
scripts by Polansky   Russell   Nabokov

The speaker is at once pander and observer, but also a player:

I wrinkle waiting for a Prince

Hewett, *Greenhouse*, p. 15.

The open language invites experience, but the speaker waits on it to fill her with meaning.

The recasting of myths and fairy tales in this volume — the Snow Queen, Cupid and Psyche, Lancelot and the Lady in the Tower, to name some — gives the paradoxical effect of an eternal recurrence in a present that we remake every moment. Facing the monster of destruction and oblivion, her uncompleted self goes on

accumulating the world . . .
I face the Minotaur   the moon turns on
    my forehead
I stand in a planetarium whirling with stars.

Hewett, *Greenhouse*, p. 104.

The female consciousness heals by comprehending all. This all, however, continues to move out into particular moments of love and politics.

While women's writing expanded the consciousness by opening the language of poetry, women were also active in developing the forms and concerns of fiction. Anna Gibbs and Alison Tilson have collected a wide variety in *Frictions* (Sybylla Press, Melbourne, 1982). They range from stories by Georgia Savage and Elizabeth Jolley, who use traditional forms to reveal the shifts with which people cope with the absurdities of life, through the revelation of tragedy beneath the slick surface in Dorothy Johnson's anecdote of a massage parlour, to the non-narrative fictions of Sneja Gunew or Kate Llewellyn. Gunew disrupts continuity to reveal the random and contingent way in which an identity is constructed. Llewellyn places a stream of consciousness against the objective gaze of the narrator's daughter to construct both desperation and a structure to contain it.

Helen Garner

The need to build a structure to contain our freedom, and the way the structure itself becomes a prison, provide the themes of Helen Garner's fiction. Her work moves around the scenes of the Melbourne counter-culture, and like Moorhouse's writings can be mistaken for a simple transcription of reality. Unlike Moorhouse, however, Garner makes her points not by apparently random juxtaposition but by a careful drafting of form. Far from being discontinuous, her narratives select people in a particular situation and follow its development to a conclusion. The people are identified against the ideology that rules their lives, and the development discovers the limitations of the ideology.

Garner's first novel, *Monkey Grip* (McPhee Gribble, Melbourne, 1977), starts in a communal house in Fitzroy, where, despite such limitations as an insufficiency of chairs, life is ordered and the members of the household, adults and children, 'ate bacon for breakfast every morning of our lives'. Nature appears to impose its own order on the human chaos: 'It was hunger and sheer function: the noise, and clashing of plates, and people chewing with their mouths open, and talking, and laughing. Oh, I was happy then. At night our back yard smelt like the country' (p. 1). The careful selection of details, the shaped sentences, the precise punctuation, combine to produce the effect of orderliness as nature. But then the action of the novel erupts, throwing into doubt not only the proclaimed happiness but also the possibility of natural order. Far from ordering life, nature becomes a disruptive energy in the person of Javo, who bursts into the narrator's life, disturbing her comfortable relationship with Martin beyond the possibility of recovery, even through the healing balm of loving. Javo, 'the bludger, just back from getting off dope in Hobart', with his 'burnt skin and scarred nose and violently blue eyes' exacts a commitment he does not return. The narrator has to make her own discoveries, her own choices, and ultimately impose her will on the disruptive forces of nature. The careful plotting of the streets of Melbourne, the details of the journeys to the coast, Tasmania, the aptly named Disaster Bay, support the working out of the plot, but the events take their own way until they exhaust their own energy. Then Nora, the narrator, has to resume her own life, return to a home that can never again be taken for granted as natural.

Garner's second novel, *The Children's Bach* (McPhee Gribble/Penguin, Ringwood, 1985 [1984]), uses a similar structure to set the security of a more conventional household and marriage against the insecurities of adolescence on the one hand and the attractiveness of irresponsibility on the other. Rather than posing nature and order as opposites, this book opposes routine to daring, reaching a conclusion without resolution. The *Children's Bach* of the title, the name of an instructional manual, functions as a symbol of art as the only order we can extract from the turbulence of life. In *Postcards from Surfers* (McPhee Gribble/Penguin, Ringwood, 1985), Garner approaches closer to the style of discontinous narrative, but again each story is carefully shaped to reveal the exact extent of its dilemmas. Rather than miming the incoherence of the life she portrays, Garner provides a series of exact prisms through which we view it separated into an order not apparent to the participants

Garner views the world from the point of view of the woman who is stifled by the order she is required to provide. The children tie their mothers to responsibility, but also, as with Vicky in *The Children's Bach*, act as a reminder of lost freedom. For Jean Bedford, in the stories in *Country Girl Again* (McPhee Gribble/ Penguin, Ringwood, 1985 [1979]), as in her historical novel about Ned Kelly's sister, *Sister Kate* (Penguin, Ringwood, 1982), it is social forces that distort life, forcing women into roles that deny life or condemning them when they take their own way. In Beverley Farmer's work, by contrast, the very fact of being a woman is a denial of freedom. Two of her stories in *Home Time* (McPhee Gribble/Penguin, Ringwood, 1985) show rape and harrassment as instruments of male power, exercised in one case by the rapist and in the other by the husband who holds his wife responsible. In 'Place of Birth', family, relatives, pregnancy and even the weather conspire against the woman. Her only freedom is to use the camera to make a record of her world, but this ensures that she will always be absent from the record. In 'Home Time', even the act of recording increases the writer's vulnerability. Her husband finds in her writing a threat to his own identity, and in an act analogous to the very violence she has recorded he destroys her work. Both work and family are circumscribed and threatened by a male world, and even in fantasy the woman is stalked by dreams of terror. Yet, in the

rhythms of life of which she is a part, there is a freedom. In the end, the Greek blessing speaks the truth: '*kali eleftheria . . .* it means *good freedom . . . good* (easy) *birth*' (p. 200).

Carmel Bird

The narrator of 'Home Time', like the characters in the other works of these writers, achieves her freedom by telling her story. Bird, in *The Woodpecker Toy Fact* (McPhee Gribble/Penguin, Ringwood, 1987), uses the fact of female narration and linguistic invention as the starting point for her collection of stories. The title story of the book opens with the sentence, 'my mother was a magger', and a footnote explains that the verb is derived from the magpie, 'the scandalmonger of the woods' (p. 3). By gossip over the back fence, the women weave the narration of their lives. They make language serve their purposes: 'One of the most hypnotic habits of the maggers was the constant use of possessive pronouns and parentheses. They constructed sentences that could go on all day in dizzy convolutions as one relative clause after another was added' (p. 4). The example that follows shows a particular incident being embedded into the social history of the community. The language is not merely local, however, but takes its vocabulary from the whole culture. The narrator herself adds the term 'woodpecker facts' from her attempt to join in the discussion by offering some fabulous facts derived from the local toymaker, whose factory has lost the last three letters of its name and so changed into an established event — changed, the grammarian in Carmel Bird might wish to say, from present continuous to perfect tense.

In the same way, the subsequent stories in the volume present the completed facts of the tragic, precarious, frightening and quite fortuitous life of the Tasmanian town of Woodpecker Point. A falling quince leads to the death of a hated bully of a grandfather. A woman is cruelly raped by a man whose parting gift is the threat of his unavoidable return. Marriages teeter on the edge of disaster. A man shoots his children. Muriel Plum communicates with the dead by way of the well at the bottom of her garden, and doctor, vicar and council conspire to fill it in for her own safety. Words cannot alter facts, but narrative can hold fact, fiction and fantasy in a single net of safety. The telling allows life to go on, bringing the destructive male element under the control of the constructive female.

Kate Grenville

Kate Grenville's work emphasises not so much the constructive as the vital qualities of the feminine. In her stories, *Bearded Ladies* (University of Queensland Press, St Lucia, 1985) this vitality expresses itself in strategies for survival. Her novel, *Lilian's Story* (Allen & Unwin, Sydney, 1985), takes these strategies much further in the life of a woman who completely breaks with her father's respectable tyranny and her mother's subservience to lead a life that defies all conventions. As she moves through the horrors of school, university, enforced asylum and later breakdown she gains a faith in her ability to control her own being, to live apart from circumstance.

Criena Rohan

These contemporary writers were not the only writers to challenge the conventions of the patriarchal society. Ten years earlier, Criena Rohan's two novels,

Kate Grenville
(*National Library of Australia*)

The Delinquents (1962) and *Down by the Dockside* (1963), had altered the conventions of the social realist novel with their vivid portrayals of life in Melbourne's waterside suburbs. Rohan's description of warm Irish working-class vitality has much in common with Ruth Park's portrayal of life in Sydney's slums during the Depression. While Park emphasises the capacity of the mothers to sustain their families through emotional and financial turmoil, Rohan writes of the daughters who challenge this conventional role with their insistence on their right to love as they choose.

Rohan's novels are set during the Depression and Second World War. The younger writers who have followed her example have been concerned with the dilemmas of love and freedom from the point of view of young women and mothers in a contemporary society that has loosened the conventions without providing the structures of forms and ideas that would support the new freedom. At the same time, several women writers have during the last decade or so been publishing fiction that has placed the woman's situation in a wider perspective. These writers challenge conventions not so much by their form as by the context in which they place women's experience.

Georgia Savage

Georgia Savage's *Slate and Me and Blanche McBride* (McPhee Gribble/Penguin, Ringwood, 1983) is a novel, often comic, in the genre of the chase or quest. It changes the genre, however, in the same way that the victim changes her captors. Blanche McBride, unwitting witness of a bank robbery, is taken from her convent by the bankrobber brothers as a hostage, but becomes first their ally in their flight and then mistress of their affections. The convent from which she escapes is a symbol of repression. The wide plains and shanty settlements along the Darling, where they at first seek refuge, and the hill country of north-eastern Victoria where they eventually find sanctuary, are symbols of the freedom they seek.

The brothers dream of money and cars, but Blanche imparts to them a higher vision where body, spirit and nature are one. These dreams drive all three to the margins of society, where the fringe dwellers along the Darling are the only people to give them welcome. The fugitives are able to preserve their freedom only at the cost of violence, to others and themselves. Their society of three is inherently un-stable as the brothers have to choose between a growing love for Blanche and their loyalty to each other. They try to remove the threat presented by Blanche by cutting her long red hair in a symbolic act of rape. Their assault, however, functions for her as a rite of passage to maturity, and from this point she dominates them, her sexuality destroying their brotherhood. The code of mateship is no longer adequate, and security is impossible outside society. At the end, the police destroy their society, and Blanche is left with only the memory on which to build a future, ironically with the policeman. Their marriage can be read as a symbolic restoration to society of the principle of freedom.

Elizabeth Jolley

One of the most remarkable of the women writers who have commanded attention in the past decade is Elizabeth Jolley, whose novels combine a gothic interest in the extraordinary with a capacity for depicting ordinary life on the margins of Western Australian society. Her work places issues of female sexuality, including lesbian relationships, in the con-text of the universal struggle to survive and establish patterns in life. Her characters encompass retired schoolteachers, cleaning women, nurses and a range of misfits. They have in common an insecurity, a need to belong, that gives them both an off-centred view of society and a need to find a stake of their own within it.

These characteristics of her fiction appear in her first collection of stories, *Five Acre Virgin* (Fremantle Arts Centre Press, Fremantle, 1976; reprinted by the same publisher in *Stories*, 1987). The story 'Shepherd on the Roof', a monologue by a woman injured in a car accident and looking back on the events leading up to it and their place in her life, sums it up in her reflection on her inability to have boots made to her order: 'I suppose there is only one length and narrowness we can have made to measure. About these measurements there is never any doubt. Human beings deny each other so many things but this is the one thing one person cannot deny another' (p. 73). The story itself is about her husband's denials of care or responsibility to others, contrasted with her own frustrated attempts to nurture. The story

Elizabeth Jolley
(*Photo: Tania Young*)

does not allot blame, except to the condition of life. In 'The Jarrah Thieves', however, she does suggest an alternative possibility. This story centres on a youth who is uncomprehending, but nevertheless accepted into the life of his tough old aunt and the men she employs in her timber-getting business. Their thieving is a simple gift to a woman who has a family and no husband to support, and whose own giving to life is marked by the constant increase in her family. The youth, an idealist whose understand-ing is limited to books, feels compelled to disclose the crime to his aunt, who reveals her own under-standing and acceptance of the necessities of living. With her timber-getters, she enjoys a life that has been produced, not learned or imposed.

The first six stories in this collection constitute an unfinished novel through their discontinuous narra-tive. At its centre is a marginal family, rather like the fringe dwellers of Georgia Savage's *Slate and Me and Blanche McBride*. The family is seen, however, from within, from the perspective of the daughter and, through her eyes, of the mother. At the centre of the stories is the 'Five Acre Virgin' of the title — five acres of virgin scrub. In the story of this name, the mother takes her lodger, a doctor of dubious standing, out to view this scrub with a view to purchase. Instead of doing so, he runs off with Aunty Shovell, a woman whose largeness of character fits the notion of a five acre virgin, only slightly used. The ownership of land is, however, central to the mother's need for security. She holds on to a similar piece of scrub owned by her father, and even when she sells it after his death she contrives to keep possession of it for herself. Only when her children remove her to an old people's home does the family leave this land.

The security of this land enables the mother to keep her shiftless family together. After she is moved into the home, the family degenerates, until by a stroke of good fortune the son wins title to the home itself. By this time, however, the mother is beyond knowing, the son is caught up in criminality, and the daughter is left wondering if she will ever see him again. The search for freedom from the land and from all ties has destroyed the basis on which the mother was able to preserve their freedom.

This contrast between the need for security and the desire for freedom runs through Jolley's work. The two are at times reconciled in the Australian bush, which with its unmade quality still allows room for the individual to live on it without being possessed. The unity of people and land is in turn a symbol of the unity the individual seeks with another to complete her life. Yet both relationships are threatened by the demand of people to dominate each other. The holiday place in 'Shepherd on the Roof' becomes just another scene of domestic conflict, and the point from which tragedy is precipitated.

The roughness of the Australian bush, the unfinished quality of life that allows people to create themselves, becomes itself a source of conflict, as people attempt to impose their schemes on it or reject it in favour of the imagined sophistication of Europe or America. Migrants refuse to come to terms with their new land, natives try to escape it for overseas. In *Miss Peabody's Inheritance* (University of Queensland Press, St Lucia, 1983), the two are brought together through Miss Peabody's link to her European correspondent. Europe, however, threatens to take her over, making her a figment in another person's tale. This threat becomes a reality in *The Newspaper of Claremont Street* (Fremantle Arts Centre Press, Fremantle, 1981), where the cleaning woman's European employer comes close to taking over both her dreams and her life. In this novel, which completes the story of the search for security from *Five Acre Virgin*, the unity the two women offer each other as a refuge from their loneliness and a strength against the outside world becomes a power struggle that must destroy one of them. The need for acceptance is contradicted by the inability to give. Women, from whom the most is demanded, are the most frequent victims of this contradiction.

Jessica Anderson

Anderson also writes of women who find themselves forced by the pressures of society to tolerate the intolerable. *Tirra Lirra by the River* (Macmillan, Melbourne, 1978) opens with the return of Nora Porteous from London to the house in Brisbane where she had lived as a child. She tries to pick up the strands of living again in a community where she finds 'I shall be compelled to explain my every facetious remark, in which I shall not find even *one person* to whom I can say anything I please' (p. 23). Nora recalls her past life, and particularly the marriage in which she had been trapped with Colin Porteous and his mother.

As a girl, Nora falls in love with the possibility of beauty, symbolised by Tennyson's Sir Lancelot, whom she imagines appearing by the Brisbane river to free her into another world. Instead, she marries Porteous, who uses his money, his mother, and particularly his sexual power to deny Nora any possibility of an independent life. Porteous first belittles her as frigid, and then for being a whore, until she finds: 'I had grown to hate the physical bond between us, and the moment when we got into bed, and lay down side by side, was for me a moment of intense and bitter misery' (p. 59). The tyranny is complete. She cannot escape even into language, for she has no appropriate correspondents and is denied the opportunity of mixing with the artists near whom she had lived at the start of her marriage. When she does write to a school friend, her letters are banal, because, as she later realises, 'I was lying' (p. 58). Her mother-in-law converts language into another weapon of oppression, and Nora is driven into the meaningless repetition of French grammar from her husband's textbook as her only refuge. When finally he brings home a mistress and throws Nora out to the accusation that she is a woman who takes her husband's 'hard-earned money' and gives it to 'queenie boys', his destruction of the marriage is complete.

Like Savage or Jolley, Anderson presents a woman's experience, but the context is not merely paternalism but a world ruled by logic and money to the exclusion of beauty and completeness. Nora's vision of Lancelot is never released because she is never able to develop her talents beyond embroidery and dress-making. Her sister pursues a vision of practical beauty through the well-composted garden, but leaves behind only a more intense green and a memory of herself as a sad eccentric. The kindliness of the neighbours becomes a tiresome intrusion. Yet, despite these failures of vision, Anderson's novel leaves the visions themselves intact. Lancelot may yet come to Brisbane and free the feminine spirit required to bring men and women to completion.

Aboriginal Writers

Although women may have been undervalued in Australian society, and their concerns pushed to the margins of public attention, women's writing has been important since the time of the gold-rushes. The place of women has been of substantial interest to both men and women writers. By contrast, the Aboriginal people have been pushed beyond the margins of society. Aboriginal writers have been almost unknown, and Aborigines themselves have appeared in fiction and popular culture mainly as figures of fun or menace. Occasionally a poet such as Henry Kendall has treated their passing as a subject of pathos and, still more rarely, writers like Katharine Susannah Prichard or Xavier Herbert have seen the tragedy of their situation. In the present generation, however, Aborigines have been asserting their right to determine their own condition, and Aboriginal writers have emerged who speak both for and to their own people.

This writing presents an immediate problem to the white reader. Properly speaking, it is not part of Australian literature, which is a transplanted offshoot of European culture, but constitutes a new and independent literature in English. Aboriginal writing is to be considered alongside the writing of New Zealand Maoris, black Africans or West Indians. These are all peoples who have been colonised and now find themselves forced to use the language of the colonists to express their own condition. Yet, just as white writers in Australia have had to adapt English to its new circumstances, so black writers in all countries have changed the language as they have made it speak of their particular experience. This experience, however, continues to be circumscribed by the whites, and so even when Aboriginal writers speak to their own people the white community forms part of the dialogue. Reading this work is a training in the art of listening.

Even the use of the term 'Aboriginal literature' can be misleading. There are great differences among the Aboriginal people between those communities living a fully urban life, those on the fringes of white society, and those still able to maintain traditional ways. These differences are reflected in the language, which ranges from the original tongues through dialectal forms of English to common Australian speech. Even the term Aboriginal is rejected by some as a European classification which gives them identity only in relation to white society. They prefer such indigenous words as Koorie or Murrie. Unfortunately, in white writing these can appear diminishing or patronising. As Aboriginal writing in English develops and consolidates new terms may emerge, but for the present Aboriginal seems the preferable term for whites to use.

Sue Hampton and Kate Llewellyn open their *Australian Women Poets* with two poems by Aboriginal women. These were collected and translated by the anthropologist Catherine Berndt. Both are songs from an oral tradition, and are therefore double translations. First, the transcription of the Aboriginal language into words on a page removes it from the context of performance and its association with dance and ritual as well as with a particular situation. Second, the translation of these words into English alters the rhythms and the resulting text lacks the associations the words would carry for an Aboriginal speaker. Yet even through these barriers the poems still speak to us of their singers' grief and anger. The first shows how the traditional culture supported the individual through personal tragedy; the second reveals the breakdown of this culture under white influence and shows the emptiness that remains.

Paddy Roe

A sustained attempt to convey both the idiom and the context of Aboriginal narrative has been made in *Gularabulu*, a book of contemporary tales told by Paddy Roe and edited by Stephen Muecke (Fremantle Arts Centre Press, Fremantle, 1983). The tales include 'trustori', events that have involved Roe himself; 'devil stori', or tales of the supernatural; and 'bugaregara', or tales from the Dreaming. The narratives are printed as they were told, divided into lines to indicates breaks in the flow, with dashes to indicate the length of pauses and repeated letters to indicate the dwelling on the sound that indicates time passing. Remarks by Muecke or other listeners during the narration are also included in the written record. The result can appear disjointed, even comically illiterate, unless we read it aloud, when its rhythms lead us into the patterns of thinking of a non-literate culture. Roe offers these tales as a gift from his culture to the world:

> Children, women, anybody.
> See, this is the thing they used to tell us:
> Story, and we know

> Roe, *Gularabulu*, p. i.

To see this world, we must also hear the patterns of sound that weave past and present, individual and landscape, into a unity that has been broken by the analytical and linear habits of thought in cultures based on writing.

The tale of 'Langurr', the possum, for example, is a story of the Dreamtime narrated in a manner that brings it vividly into the present of the listeners, who are referred to particular trees as the site of the events and involved in the drama of the plot and its resolution. It enables us to see both land and life as shaped by a past that continues living. The 'trustori' and 'devil stori', on the other hand, relate episodes the present back to this older pattern. The whole collection of tales thus reproduces the culture that sustains the narrator in his environment.

B. Wongar

The work of B. Wongar is a more controversial attempt by a white observer to reproduce the Aboriginal culture. Wongar is apparently the pen-name of Streten Bozic, an anthropologist who was born in Yugoslavia and immigrated to Australia in 1960. His writings carry a powerful emotional sense of the isolation of people actually or potentially separated from their past, but his frequent resolution of the problem in ritual bloodshed seems to do violence to the Aboriginal culture.

Oodgeroo Noonuccal (Kath Walker)

One of the first Aboriginal poets to command general attention was Kath Walker, who is now known by her Aboriginal name Oodgeroo Noonuccal. Her collection, *My People* (Jacaranda, Milton, Queensland, 1970), which brings together poems from her first two volumes, is dedicated to 'the Brisbane Aboriginal and Island Council, whose policy is self-determination'. The poems, however, are generally directed to the

Oodgeroo Noonuccal (Kath Walker)
(*The Age*)

white community in a spirit of reconciliation and an appeal for understanding. The first poem in the volume concludes with the couplet:

I'm international, never mind place;
I'm for humanity, all one race.

Walker, *My People*, P. 1.

This sentiment animates the whole collection, but the rather glib expression raises the issue of how we should read the poetry. It is a demand for attention rather than, as we have become used to in European poetry, a reflexive pondering of a situation. It needs the immediacy given by singing and recitation.

In some of Walker's poems, where she concentrates on the situation without comment, the very simplicity of the language makes its points with telling force. Thus, when the speaker addresses the 'Holy men' who came to teach the Aborigines, the colloquial rhyme strips away the pretensions of the white missionaries who came to teach them:

'. . . to obey
Laws of God and laws of Mammon . . .'
And we answered, 'No more gammon,
If you have to teach the light,
Teach us first to read and write.'

Walker, *My People*, p. 26.

The rhymes turn the missionaries' words back on themselves.

Other poems convey a whole situation in the weight of their imagery. The 'Dawn Wail for the Dead' (p. 7) conveys the intensity of grief and the renewal of life that enables us to bear it. The images of the camp awakening in the new day carry the reader through the emotions into the whole life of the people. The young girl in 'Nona' (p. 31) is fully present at the 'happy chattering evening meal', as are the men and women with their contrasting reactions to her simple ornaments and unconscious beauty. In a poem like 'Gooboora, the Silent Pool' (p. 71), the invocation of the past goes beyond sorrow to a sense of the loss for all of humankind in the passing of the clans that once filled the place with the lightness of 'their hearts in the dance and the game'. Similarly, the poems where she addresses a particular person make their didactic point implicitly by the fulness with which she brings that person before us.

Grief and hope are the two poles of Kath Walker's poetry. Anger breaks through only occasionally to destroy any complacent belief in the reader that the writer offers purely a literary experience.

Faith Bandler

Grief and anger are the starting points of Faith Bandler's *Wacvie* (Rigby, Adelaide, 1977). In this work she tells without bitterness the story of her father's life from his seizure from the island of Ambrym, through his time as a slave on Queensland sugar plantations to his escape to freedom and establishment of his own farm and family. The book deals with disruption and rebuilding, and contrasts the timeless life of the Pacific Islanders with their later slavery to time and greed, and the callousness of the whites to the determination of the Islanders to keep their own humanity. Yet the author's anger at injustice is subdued to an irony that makes it more effective by emphasising the sorrow of human loss and the strength her people discover in themselves.

Walker and Bandler have written for whites as much as for their own people. Their work asks white readers to see, to understand and to learn. The Aboriginal poets Jack Davis and Kevin Gilbert, however, speak directly from the anger that is both the subject and the motive. They demand attention as they assert their identity. Their poetry expresses contempt for white exploiters and compassion for the victims. It does not, however, achieve the sustained power of Gilbert's collection of prose narratives in *Living Black* (Allen Lane/Penguin, Ringwood, 1977).

Kevin Gilbert

Like the tales in *Gularabulu*, Gilbert's tales give black Australians their own voice. Gilbert presents a series of interviews with black men and women from all around Australia. These people tell the stories of their lives and offer their opinions on the situation of the Aborigines. While Roe's words place his own experience within the context of tradition, Gilbert tries to detach the lives of his people from the myths and traditions that obscure present reality for blacks and whites alike. In particular, he wants to free his people from sentimental illusions by showing the conflicts and divisions within their own community. He intervenes in the interviews, not only to seek clarity but to direct the speaker's attention to particular issues. By his commentaries, and his arrangement of the material, he presents a continuing debate about Aborigines and their experience of history. The book is thus not merely a narrative of injustice, but a portrait of a community rebuilding itself from the fragments it has been left.

Although the words of the book are entirely those of living witnesses, their experience encompasses the disintegration of families at the hands of missionaries and government officials, detribalisation, the denial of identity by various acts of official protection, the sexual exploitation of women and the difficulties of living between worlds, and the social and political struggles to fight back and assert their own identity. The book is not, however, a mere sociological treatise or political tract. The words define a reality that constantly presses on the lives of the speakers, and provide the standards of humanity by which the oppression of their circumstances can be judged.

Horrie Saunders' story, for example, is a tale of social disintegration that is not redeemed by the courage of his own struggle and his success in overcoming poverty, hostility and officialdom. This success only makes sadder the hopelessness he sees around him among his own people, who lack either the strength, the understanding or the opportunity to follow his example. Yet, for all the misery he describes, the story is not hopeless. In describing the source of his own strength he makes it available to be renewed in the lives of others.

Saunders' strength comes, ultimately, not just from his own character, but from his boyhood memories of those intervals of time when his community was at home with itself and its environment:

> Yes! It was something we lived for. Christmas is coming . . . we're going to the beach. Just that natural way of living. We hunted, we swam, we caught worms for bait, we fished at night, the mothers cooked damper in the ashes, we'd come home 'n roast oysters in the fires, joked 'n sang. We went to the bush 'n got honey out of the trees, cooked Christmas pudding in big tins . . .

> Gilbert, *Living Black*, p. 43.

Nature in this passage is not merely a given environment, but a harmony made from the whole life of the community, and therefore able to sustain that life even in adversity. The memory is the more intense because of the speaker's recognition that the spirit of this community has gone, that 'our people lost it when they took Saltwater away from 'em.' 'They barred us from the camping area then and mucked up the place and that was it' (p. 43). The simple statements of fact both condemn the destruction of a spirit of place and keep alive that spirit against the future and against the other evidences of destruction amidst which he lives. Like the other people whom Gilbert interviews, by putting his life into words he starts the task of building a new community to replace the one that has been taken from them.

If the need for this new community arises from despair, the driving force behind its creation is anger. The speakers use their words not merely to tell their story, but with an urgency born of the need to compel people to listen — to teach the whites what they have done, and to tell the blacks what they must do. This urgency burns through Gilbert's story of his own life. It is an intense monologue that rises from childhood memories of comfort and delight through a series of anecdotes of exclusion, frustration and repression to a savage account of his imprisonment in Grafton gaol. He then turns his story back to the origin of white settlement in the need to dominate. He relates the bashings in Grafton to the flogging of the convicts, contrasting the behaviour of the gaoler with the horror of the Aboriginal witnesses, 'screaming frantically and throwing sticks at the flogger'. Gilbert identifies both episodes of cruelty as expressions of the continuing insistence of white society on control rather than understanding:

> . . . you haven't grown in stature to match this country yet. You are still the alien, the outsider and only when you embrace the whole of this country, every sacred living thing upon it and in it and around it, will you grow and survive, because only those who love the land and love justice will ultimately hold the land.

> Gilbert, *Living Black*, p. 245.

The book does not, however, wait on white enlightenment or conceal the complicity of the blacks in their own disintegration. In the final interview in the collection Gilbert returns to his Grandfather Koori, who rounds on the black people themselves. His message is that although the white man has broken

their community, they must remake it for themselves. They have in themselves the power to build
an Aboriginality that every person on earth can
share. The alternative, the closing image of the book,
is that their spirit will die out 'till there is nothing left
. . . like the coals of a long-dead campfire' (p. 305).
This takes the book beyond Grandfather Koori's
anger at his own people and at the whites who have
destroyed them, and beyond the anger that has run
like a current through the whole book, to a spirit of
hope. The hope stems from visions of a past on which
Aborigines can build a future that will redeem them
from injustice.

Mudrooroo Narogin (Colin Johnson)

Colin Johnson's fiction moves back towards a similar
vision of the past. His first novel, *Wildcat Falling*
(Angus & Robertson, Sydney, 1965), is a piece of
social realist fiction describing the life of a part-
Aboriginal boy growing up on the fringes of white
society. The act of violence towards which he falls
is, however, also the occasion of his recovery of
an identity he has lost through his mother's rejection
of Aboriginal ways and his own exclusion from all
social ties. The novel thus places the question of the
Aborigines as a social problem in a wider context.
The story the narrator tells of his descent into crime
is also the tale of a quest for a ground for his being.
At the end, through the agency of the old Aborigine
who extends help to him, he finds his ground in the
country itself.

However, despite the ending, Johnson's first book
remains an expression of need rather than of discovery. After a long interval, he returns to this theme
in the novel *Long Live Sandawara* (Quartet, South
Yarra, 1979). This book similarly deals with a delin-
quent, but this time with one who has discovered his
past in the person of the warrior Sandawara, and
whose career of crime is the first stage of a campaign
to win back from the whites the land Sandawara had
fought to keep. The narrative alternates between
the account of Sandawara's original campaign in the
desert and the attempts of Alan, the youth who becomes the new Sandawara, to restore dignity and
purpose to his tiny band of urban drifters. Alan's
political idealism, the desperate passion of Rob and
Rita, Rob's delight in cookery, Gary's plans for a
band, all bring some temporary coherence to his

household of the hopeless. These ideals cannot,
however, defeat the madness, narcissism and longing
for oblivion that dominate the characters and are
expressed in their orgiastic sex and the pointless
carnage with which the novel ends. The disintegrating
forces of the city allow only violence to survive.

In *Doctor Wooreddy's Prescription for Enduring the
Ending of the World* (Hyland House, South Yarra,
1983) Johnson traces this violence back to its origin
in the original act of white settlement. As a youth, the
hero of the novel, Wooreddy, watches the coming of
the first whites to Tasmania. Although he is fully
initiated, the coming of the white settlers disrupts
his rites of passage and his subsequent marriage to a
'Foreign' woman, that is, a woman from another
tribe. Nevertheless he becomes the custodian of
his people's traditions, the thinker who maintains a
certain independence by learning to comprehend
what is happening to him.

Wooreddy becomes involved in guerrilla warfare,
takes Trugernanna (Truganini) as partner after the
death of his first wife, accompanies George Robinson,
'Protector' of Aborigines, on his attempts to take
the Tasmanians into his custody, is removed to
Robinson's settlement on Flinders Island and finishes
his life near Port Phillip, where he takes part in a
massacre to avenge the rape Trugernanna suffered
during the first days of settlement. The completion
of the cycle, and Wooreddy's mystic acceptance into
the country of Port Phillip, symbolises the passing of
the Aborigines from their own history into a world
that denies them but cannot expunge them from its
memory.

Johnson bases his novel on events that have also
been used by Robert Drewe in his novel *The Savage
Crows* (Collins, Sydney, 1976). While Drewe portrays
the Aborigines as victims and objects of history,
Johnson shows them as the subjects of a tragedy.
They resist and make their own history, although
finally they are destroyed by disease and treachery
outside their control. By combining some historical
characters and prolonging Wooreddy's life to make
him a witness of the last as well as the first stand of
his people, Johnson restores the shape of a tragedy
that has been concealed in accounts that show it only
from the white perspective as the sad passing of a
primitive people.

The progress of the tragedy of Wooreddy and his
people is conveyed through the gradual change of

their language. At first, the sounds the white men make are strange, while their own language is rich with the associations of the land and the myths that give their life its meaning. The whites are fitted into this structure as *num*, or ghosts, but these terms gradually take on a sinister and alienating meaning as the whites bring with them disease and death.

Eventually, Wooreddy's acceptance by the Port Phillip people, and by the sea that has always been his enemy, symbolises his passing into a realm that cannot be destroyed even by the capture of the party and execution of its leaders at the hand of white avengers. Even as he comes to the end of his life and the life of his people, he recognises an encompassing unity of all things. This is symbolised by his discovery of the unity of his element, the land, with *Ria Warrawah*, the sea he had always thought his enemy and the source of the *num* who had come from it to destroy his people.

This mystical unity cannot contradict the record of disintegration that constitutes the narrative of the novel. However, the novel itself reconstitutes the lost world of belief, and thus ensures that the memory of the people who made it remains alive. This world and its people are embodied in the central figure of Johnson's next work, *The Song Circle of Jacky* (Hyland House, South Yarra, 1987). In these poems the despised image of Jacky-Jacky is transformed into a mythical figure bearing the spirit of the land even in his degradation and oppression. Out of a record of defeat Johnson has constructed a figure that has the power to restore unity to the land and its people, black and white. In one section, 'Calcutta Dreaming' (pp. 51–69) the cycle takes us beyond Australia to a Buddhist-influenced vision of a greater unity of all peoples. To achieve such unity, however, the whites must first accept Jacky-Jacky both for what he is and for what they have made him. Rather than bringing the marginal inside the boundaries, they must extend the boundaries so that the marginal becomes central.

Migrant Writers

The white occupation of Australia rests on the doctrine of *terra nullius*, the legal fiction that before European settlement the unknown continent was a land of no one, a blank space on the map awaiting the coming of civilisation to fill its empty spaces. The history of Australian writing is an attempt to justify that doctrine, to fill empty pages with the words that will give legitimacy to white occupation, to make Australians feel at home in the Australian landscape. In the nineteenth century the vehicles for this effort were such myths as the heroic squatter, the oppressed convict and the enduring bushman. Aboriginal writing has contradicted the claims made for these figures, and the validity of the whole tradition, by bringing to the surface the act of oblivion on which they rest. While this contradiction remains, all writing about Australia will be unsatisfactory.

Since the Second World War, however, writers have questioned the tradition on its own grounds as presenting an inadequate map even of the European experience in Australia. Women writers have demonstrated large areas that have been excluded from the Australian consciousness by the form as well as the content of the writing. Writers like White, Keneally and Malouf have recovered a metaphysical dimension, while Moorhouse and Tranter have been among those who have tried to locate the particular Australian experience in the context of the wider world. Still others have seen this global city as the only context of the Australian experience.

Yet as the bounds of Australian writing have extended to embrace the whole experience of the post-industrial world, so Australian writers have increasingly escaped from any clear classification. Recent migrant writers in Australia, for example, have named both the dislocation and alienation that have always been a part of migrant experience, but in the context not just of a separation from their home but a knowledge of the destruction of the home itself. David Martin sounds this note in *Where a Man Belongs* (Cassell Australia, Melbourne, 1969), but at the end of the book his characters leave it behind to step confidently into the clean air of a new country where they can put the past behind them. The theme of loss is, however, more insistent in the stories of Serge Liberman, where the warm if smothering comfort of the home can offer no security against time that inevitably drives the individual into an outside world of loss and disintegration. Survival depends on luck, and the bravura of spirit that is invoked in the dazzling cascades of words with which he confronts fate. His world moves between the poles of a lost past and a vulgar present. The narrator of

'Survivors' in Liberman's *The Life That I Have Led* (Fine-Lit, North Caulfield, 1986) has taken in the one with his mother's milk, which 'expectedly so innocuous, so bland, might already at my birth have been laced with gall', and the other from his own experience. He explains his parents' experience that

> the Russian hearth, the Uzbek ambience, so exotic, so oriental, upon which I had opened my eyes, were not the hearth and ambience of her own origin and becoming, but a derailment in her life — in both their lives, Father's, Mother's — the first of many to which troops Teutonic, moronic and vulpine, the devil at his most bestial beside them a saint, had driven them, the modern spawn of Attila the while reducing to ashes, smoke, dust, soap and decay, and to memory what in my parents' Warsaw had been bustle, breath and industry, what had been humanity, folksiness, God-intoxication and faith, and an innocence that in the blackest nightmare could not have conceived the perditions that a single Austrian dement, a runted swarthy dark-haired dark-hearted dark-souled Schiklgruber was in time to wreak in pursuit of the blue and blond of some fancied and warped and impossible Aryan fiction.
>
> Liberman, *Life*, pp. 65–6.

The exuberant run of words expresses the adolescent fury of the narrator, prompted as much by his immediate sense of deadly embarrassment as by recollections of his parents' lives, but nevertheless places the action of the story in the context not only of the historical crux of the twentieth century but also of the rich way of life he knows only by its absence. By contrast, the suburb in which he moves is characterised by energy without vitality:

> . . . outside the Prince of Wales, closed though it was, a rowdy, joking, back-slapping gaggle of flush-cheeked sweating drinkers had gathered with stubbies, cans and froth-slimed glasses. They were near-facsimiles of each other and templates for numberless clones of beer-gutted mulberry-nosed smoking-drinking hoi-poloi — brick-layers, boiler-makers and wharfies, and mechanics, labourers and workers in mines — the stuff of which, and for whose sake, revolutions in other

places were made, but who in the terrain provincial of *Melbourne parochiale* found religion splendid in trinity divine of footballer, cricketer and horse, who were moved to ecstasy by a ball coursing through goals, who were transported to bliss in a well-hit well-cut homeside run, and were brought unto salvation in a bet redeemed at two hundred to one.

> Liberman, *Life*, p. 70.

The energy with which he enumerates the objects of his detestation implies a contradictory attraction. Nevertheless, the dominant sense of these passages is of the human waste produced by the combination of Holocaust in Europe and human vacuity in Australia. Although the story concludes with the narrator's recovery of his sense of balance, his realisation of his parents' achievement in just surviving, its dominant feeling is the unchanging human misery symbolised by the swirling shapeless masses in Fitzroy Street, 'but one dark tunnel in a huge multi-continental trans-universal network of tunnels along which entire constellations of humanity . . . pitched and scuttled and reeled towards unconsidered perdition' (p. 75). The home offers only occasional and precarious refuge against the joining of Australia to the world in a single vision of futility.

Liberman writes from the point of view of the first generation to grow up in post-war Australia. Peter Skrzynecki writes from the same viewpoint, but his poetry contemplates his parents' fate rather than his own, as he watches them settle in the new land, 'Happy as I have never been' (*Immigrant Chronicle*, University of Queensland Press, St Lucia, 1975, p. 3), while the speaker tries to build a new life without destroying the remnants of the Polish language he has as inheritance from his father. In Antigone Kefala's writing we see the perspective of the migrant woman, separated from her place by distance and from her husband by the duties he can escape from to the cafe and his memories. The story of those who made the decision to migrate and who had the responsibility of raising their families in the new land is told directly in Mary Rose Liverani's *The Winter Sparrows* (Nelson, West Melbourne, 1975). This autobiography gives a warm account of growing up in the poverty of a Glasgow slum, which contrasts with the resistance of the suburban Australia where, nevertheless, the children find a new life. Rosa R. Cappiello's novel, *Oh Lucky Country* (first published in Italian, 1981; English translation by Gaetano Rando, University of Queensland Press, St Lucia, 1984) is, one the other hand, a desperately bitter narrative of the life an Italian finds waiting for her in an Australia where sex offers the only escape from economic exploitation.

Dimitri Tsaloumas

The poetry of Dimitri Tsaloumas takes us into an entirely different world. Although resident in Australia for thirty years, he has until recently written in his native Greek and his work has mainly been translated by others. Tsaloumas writes of experience understood through imagery that has its roots in the Greek countryside and a tradition stretching back to Homer. His poems speak of the solitary condition of man, alleviated only by moments of love and tenderness, the beauty of the seasons and the sharp pleasure of the senses. This individual knowledge is set in the context of the present century, with the false promises of politicians, betrayal of informers, violence and tyranny. Despite Tsaloumas' insistence on the importance of love, the stance underlying his poetry is not the romantic belief in emotion but the harsh fatalism of Homer. His cosmopolitan reach extends not only to the cities of the modern world, but to the endurance of the common people through the whole of time.

Although the poet dreams in his observatory of the ideal city, the observatory is also the tower in which he is imprisoned and from which the only message he can send is the endurance of the inexplicable star:

Know that bitter were the final days upon
    the low stool, and barren
comfort in the nights the inexplicable star,
    this unacceptable insistence.

> Tsaloumas, *The Observatory*,
> University of Queensland Press,
> St Lucia, 1983, p. 151.

Yet this barren comfort, which is all we can hope for, can also take the form of the message that comes to him in his captivity in the South with the assurance that he shall never die, and that he sends back in answer to the mother from whom it came. Its images are the 'wild duck beak straining forward' and the 'hawk beautiful — rising deadly scaling'. The message he sends is that her son

came down to the spray-misted headlands
  of the South and saw the onslaught of waves
    huge as island hills and cried out
The sea! The sea!

> Tsaloumas, *Observatory*, p. 125.

The sea joins past and present, Greece and Australia, in a timeless unity that represents at once constant struggle and the endless journey of hope.

The other side of the migrant experience is given by the relentlessly contemporary Pi 0, whose work is written in the speech rhythms of the inner city where the children of the Mediterranean migrants grew up. At its best, his poetry captures the zest and anger of the back streets. At its worst, it is merely self-regarding.

Other Writers

The rhythms of Pi 0's generation, without the concern for a particular sub-culture, are caught more consistently by his contemporaries Eric Beach and Shelton Lea.

Shelton Lea

Lea's poetry is taut with a violence that emanates from the conflict between his energies seeking release and the social constraints that bind them, allowing only fleeting moments of fulfilment. The poetry repeats them in its fierce alternation between tenderness and savagery:

when the heart soars/and the soul exalts
to the song of broken images and dissolved sound,
i start to look around for angels.
in trams and delicatessens
i find the quintessence of my wordless dreams
in theatres and brothels
i hear the endless echoes of my nightmare
    screams . . .

angels/always gone, just as you turn to catch them
    on the
wing and all you feel is the breath of their passing.
angels/paah . . .

Lea, *The Paradise Poems*, Sea
Horse, Greensborough, 1983,
p. 22.

Eric Beach

Eric Beach similarly conveys the sense of a world
run awry, governed by an insane logic that allows
only the occasional moments when humans can discover themselves. Even amid the junk food and
engine noise of the Hume Highway, his doomwatch
becomes a dawnwatch that uncovers a truth the
watcher shares with all of time:

popped-speed-lights
moon with her thick smoker's cough
woke just as the oil crept across the mud
dawn tuned to some other engine

the first breath stretches interminably
    as a rainbow
herds of thousand mammoths
    collect in my lungs

Beach, 'doomwatch on sydney
road', *A Photo of Some People
in a Football Stadium*, Overland,
Melbourne, 1978, p. 43.

Laurie Clancy

Among fiction writers, fantasy rather than the commonplace has been the rule. Laurie Clancy reveals
the absurdity of our simplest attempts to order our
lives, through the rituals of schooling, social life in
the inner suburbs, or, in his most ambitious work,
the rituals and tragedies of marriage. His novel
Perfect Love (Hyland House, Melbourne, 1983)
shows the ironic failure of the search for a perfect
love through three generations of a Catholic family.
The book is on one level a relentlessly accurate recreation of the life of Nora Quinn, born 1981 and dying
barely fifty years later. The pattern of her life is,
however, an unwitting reproduction of the Australian
᾿ereotypes from Lawson onwards. She marries and
᾿ off to struggle on a poor bush selection, the

farm collapses in the Depression, the family returns
to the city, the husband retreats into alcohol, and the
family eventually drifts apart. The father's attempts
to remove a dunny from a vacant block resembles
the farce of Steele Rudd's cow-cockies. The literary
parallel even extends to the crippled son James who
had read a book and finds God in a globule of spittle.
Nora herself, staunch believer in piety, respectability
and hard work, entrusts her whole life to a wager
on the truth of her church. Yet the absurdity of her
life is also its meaning. The defeated in the novel are
only those who cease to care.

Morris Lurie

Laurie Clancy reveals the absurdity behind the ordinary that alone makes it possible to endure. Morris
Lurie, in a series of works that starts with the urban
comedy of *Rappaport* (Sun Books, Melbourne, 1969
[1966] leads the reader to wonder whether endurance
is even desirable. For Lurie, whose work becomes
increasingly autobiographical in form, the simplest
incident is fraught with disaster. Rappaport is the
survivor, canny enough to convert trouble into opportunity, but the narrators of the later works have
the peculiar talent of finding even happiness unbear-
able. They travel constantly in search of the land of
God's constantly deferred promise. Their comfort is
that they are as little at home in Australia as anywhere else.

Rodney Hall

Hall's work, on the other hand, deals with the frustration of Australia's promises by its own people.
Unlike Lurie's characters, who expect only disaster,
Hall is the eternal romantic, constantly expecting that
love will reveal the place where he will be able 'to
achieve the risk that keeps us human' (*Selected Poems*,
University of Queensland Press, St Lucia, 1975,
p. 27). In *Black Bagatelles* (UQP, St Lucia, 1978) he
conducts an extended dialogue with death that enables him to define the worth of living in the face not
only of time but of all the human betrayals it brings
without destroying the ability of humans to realise
their own values.

His novel, *Just Relations* (Penguin, Ringwood,
1982) brings these concerns together in the story of
a community that has defied history by preserving

the past at the cost of its own future. The people in the novel live in the past of the pioneer settlers and miners who made a tradition continuous with the furthest past of their race. They are, however, interrupted by the determination of the government to bring a road and of a new settler to restore love and the future. Metaphorically, these intrusions represent the ambivalent attempts of the Whitlam government to wake Australia after its long sleep, and the destruction of the community coincides with the dismissal of that government. Nevertheless, the people maintain their life in a kind of underground communion with nature. The land survives the politics. Only in his more recent work, *Kisses of the Enemy* (Penguin, Ringwood, 1987) does the hope of Australians to name their own future seem to be finally defeated by the nameless power of money. Yet even this novel, bleak as it is, finishes with an incomplete sentence. There is always a future.

Peter Carey

Peter Carey and David Foster turn the ordinary world into comic and extraordinary fantasy. Carey's early stories in *The Fat Man in History* (University of Queensland Press, St Lucia, 1974) introduce the reader to a reality in which the one detail grows to become a monstrous whole. In 'Crabs' (pp. 7–21), the protagonist parks in a drive-in only to find it is a single used-car lot without any possible exit. The story is a satire both on our devotion to the automobile and to the privacy in which we try to seal ourselves from the dangers of an anarchic world. In

Peter Carey
(*National Library of Australia*)

the title story (pp. 114–41) the club of fat men becomes itself the secret society that runs the world, embodying a menace that eventually threatens the initiates themselves. In *Bliss* (UQP, St Lucia, 1981), Carey takes the problem of life into a time beyond a death that may or may not be real. In *Illywhacker* (UQP, St Lucia, 1985), the anarchist hero breaks through these constraints with his own audacity only to find he has become the prisoner of his own daring.

David Foster

David Foster, by contrast, takes historical situations that he plumbs to their absurd depths. His novels move across time and space to bring the whole of modern European history into the reality of Australia. His third novel, *Moonlite* (Macmillan, South Melbourne, 1981), starts in the nineteenth century with Finbar McDuffie's arrival on the island of St Kilda and moves to the Victorian gold-fields where Finbar comes to an unwitting end. The barren island of St Kilda provides the setting for the comic encounter between a kind of feudal democracy and the new rights of property that was itself one of the major elements leading to the settlement of Australia. In chasing gold, Finbar acts out the romances of settlement without achieving success. The ideals and delusion of contemporary settlement in the bush become the subject of Foster's *Dogrock* (Penguin, Ringwood, 1985). The quest behind the settlement is the subject of *The Adventures of Christian Rosy Cross* (Penguin, Ringwood, 1986), which is about the original quest for gold by the medieval alchemists. In exploring the nature of alchemy the book identifies the driving force behind modern civilisation and at the same time raises issues of the meaning and application of scientific knowledge that remain constant to the present. The comedy of the book arises from the brutal contradiction between the idealistic professions of the characters and the naked reality of their actions. Christian's own affliction of a continual and gigantic erection may be taken as a symbol of the Western world, while its unfortunate consequences enact a parable of the results of the unrestrained search for personal satisfaction.

Murray Bail

These writers are all in their own ways breaking the bounds of the Australian tradition to show more accurately how our contemporary reality is a product of the forces of expansion and domination that shaped the modern world, and of the violence and disintegration they have produced. Murray Bail, however, reasserts the tradition, demonstrating how it makes and names our consciousness until it completely controls us. In his first collection of stories (*Contemporary Portraits*, 1975; republished as *The Drover's Wife and other stories*, University of Queensland Press, St Lucia, 1984), he has a story called simply 'A, B, C, . . . X, Y, Z'. This is about the frustration of love by insurmountable cultural barriers, but it presents the reader with only a series of scenes, or signs, that suggest this theme. The languages and scripts of Urdu and English are metaphors of the inability of one human being to know another. The librarian's success in Urdu does not open new possibilities so much as isolate her in the only culture to which she belongs. In the same way, the party of Australians who travel the world in Bail's novel *Homesickness* (Macmillan, Melbourne, 1980) remain locked in their own country, able only to translate the rest of the world into a museum display.

In *Holden's Performance* (Penguin, Ringwood, 1987) the central character, Holden Shadbolt, is completely defined by the geography of the cities he lives in and the incidents time brings to him. Rectangular Adelaide, irregular Sydney, beachside Manly, and, finally, circular Canberra control his life and eventually propel him into the dimensionless world of international intelligence. The characteristic activities and artefacts that fill these places make the people, only to destroy them by such coincidences as the precise juxtaposition of a falling trammie and a power pole. Life is reduced to a succession of facts.

Tim Winton

The stories and novels of Tim Winton, the West Australian writer, alternate between the violence of the cities and the attempts of drifters and drop-outs to make a unified life for themselves in the bush. In *Shallows* (Allen & Unwin, Sydney, 1984) these two elements are brought together in the contest between whalers and conservationists that forms the plot of the novel. The blindly swimming whales, their tenderness destined to be wasted, become a metaphor of the civilisation against which his protagonists pit themselves, only to find themselves part of it. In

the bleak title story of his collection *Minimum of Two* (McPhee Gribble/Penguin, Ringwood, 1987), on the other hand, the narrator's attempts to answer violence with violence lead only to his complete destruction. Yet, in the final story in the volume, an account of the difficult birth of the narrator's son, life and human care triumph over the the worst that nature and the officialdom of a technocracy can do. The forces of disintegration are overcome by a love that is not just a discovery, but the product of will and effort.

Fay Zwicky

Fay Zwicky's work deals with the continuity that persists beneath changes of place and history. The title poem of Zwicky's collection *Kaddish* (University of Queensland Press, St Lucia, 1982) is a tribute 'for my Father, born 1903, died at sea, 1967'. The poem takes its title from the Hebrew ceremony of sanctification, which is also a prayer for the dead. In reconstructing her relations with her father, the speaker reconstructs not only their particular lives but their place in history. The Aramaic and Hebrew phrases incorporated in the poem join it back to the Judaic tradition at the centre of Western civilisation, the father's life is linked with the wars in which Australia has defined its identity during this century, and the daughter's ambivalent conflicts with him form part of the struggle for independence from the past and Europe that has shaped this definition. As well as a lament for her father, therefore, the poem can be read as a lament for the old Australia and the coming of the new. The prayer that forms the poem's epigraph, 'Lord of the divided, heal!' is at once a prayer for personal and national wholeness and for unity of the nation with the world.

The speaker's recollection of her father leads her back through memories of his visits, his medical duties, his letters from the war, to the patterns of old song and dance and of household routine that built the structure from which she had to establish her own identity. The rhyme of the house that Jack built becomes a rhyme of his family life, from which he emerges in the figures of laughter and dance:

> laughter
> Shaking in the box of bone, laughter in the dying
> fire, laughter

While the children danced from room to room in
the empty air.

Zwicky, *Kaddish*, p. 3.

The dance of laughter in turn merges into the dance
of all creatures of the earth in fear of the Lord, and
this in turn becomes part of the cycle of history and
the eternal conflict of the father with the mother-
goddess to whom 'the blood of all creatures is due
because she gave it' (p. 4). The speaker owes her
dues to both mother and father, and can only obtain
her identity by refusing both. Yet, without them, she
has no identity. She belongs with

The collective body of the family
The collective body of the race
The collective body of the nation

Zwicky, *Kaddish*, p. 6.

Her life, therefore, can be only a re-enactment of
the cycle, a learning to forgive, and the silence that
comes after forgiveness. Only from that silence,
made from the knowledge of all that has been, can
new life begin.

In her sequence 'Mrs Noah Speaks' (pp. 21–4),
Zwicky suggests both the weariness of the woman
constantly required to tidy up the world and the
necessity to keep going. Naming her dreams and her
tasks, she gives herself the deliverance she seeks.
In her essay 'Living in Western Australia' (*A Nation
Apart*, Longman Cheshire, Melbourne, 1982), she
shows both how the country takes her over and how
she makes it her own. In taking it into herself, she
takes it into the whole of the past that she inherits,
and so changes that past. In the life of all nations,
Australia, oldest of lands and youngest of nations,
begins again the unending task of naming the present
as the future of its own land and people.

Addendum

Four novels that appeared during 1988 suggest a
new direction for Australian fiction. These works are
at once national and cosmopolitan, individual and
political. They are concerned with the philosophical
problem of what truth is and how we can know it.
All of them follow this issue beyond the problem of
knowing another person to the question of how we

know ourselves and what freedom we have in constructing our own lives.

In *Oscar and Lucinda* (UQP, St Lucia, 1988)
Peter Carey returns to the kind of fantasy world that
characterised his short stories. In this novel, however, he projects it into the past, where the details
of ordinary life, viewed from three generations later,
become a fantastic saga of entrapment and escape.

The narrator reconstructs the life of his clerical
great grandfather, his fears and loves, and the story
of the glass church he sailed up the Bellinger River.
Oscar and Lucinda are both addictive gamblers who
play only for the highest stakes: survival, salvation,
love. In their separate lives and joint passion they
relive the history of the white settlement of Australia,
sharing both the empty brutality of the conquerors
and the occasional splendour of their creation. This
is finally symbolised on the overland journey and voyage up the Bellinger of the glass church they have
designed as both celebration and penance. In this
final sequence, the absurdity of their world turns
from comedy to tragedy as human compassion is
defeated by evil.

Both Oscar and Lucinda create themselves in
defiance of the forces of prejudice and repression
that surround them, but these social forces nevertheless confine and warp their lives. The novel traces
the roots of mendacity and injustice in society to the
ancient sins of pride, avarice and wrath.

Three other novels also search for the sources
of social wrong in individual faults.

Rodney Hall's *Captivity Captive* (McPhee Gribble,
Melbourne, 1988) uses an old man's memories to
trace the events leading to a triple murder at the
turn of the century. These events take us into an
introverted society that, unwilling to face the truth
of either its past or its present, turns its lusts on itself in what becomes an orgy of destruction. This
murder in turn becomes a symbol of the new Commonwealth of Australia inaugurated by a people who
have built on the bones of the Aborigines and the
devastation of their land, and who themselves are
destined for the carnage of the Great War.

Mark Henshaw sets his novel, *Out of the Line of
Fire* (Penguin, Ringwood, 1988), after the Second
World War. Its crucial episode is the abduction of
a young woman and the callous indifference with
which her abductor uses the child she bears to him.
This provides the standard against which we measure

both the self-centred behaviour of the characters and the philosophical games they play in avoiding or recovering the truth. As in *Oscar and Lucinda*, the stake in these games is not just life itself, but the values that make life worth living. Individuals are responsible for the whole of their society.

In *Charades* (UQP, St Lucia, 1988), Janette Turner Hospital similarly shows life as a sequence of games. In this case, however, the games serve both to hold death at bay and to reveal the truth. The truth we finally learn is that while facts are always deceptive and contradictory, values remain true. While Charade fails to find any absolute truth about her conception or parentage, she does learn the true nature of all her parents and grandparents and her own lover. At stake in this comedy is her own identity, and with it

the Australia from which she has come and the world of uncertainty and relativity into which she is projected. At the heart of this world, again, is a symbol of absolute truth and horror, the death camps of the Nazis in which fantasy turned into the ultimate evil. Charade becomes the princess who saves her people not only by reversing the old fairy tale, but by accepting responsibility for them.

The question of human responsibility is at the heart of each of these novels. Australia no longer offers a possibility of escape into a new life, but is rather the place where the problems of the old world must be understood and expiated, as a part both of our own history and of our collective responsibility for humanity.

AFTERWORD

Australian writers have always felt themselves uncomfortably impaled on the horns of a dilemma. If they write for a local audience and about their own experience they restrict their scope, but if they unashamedly seek to write for the world they risk losing their own roots. Martin Boyd's novels express this problem as his characters move between England and Australia. Henry Handel Richardson solved it by living in England but writing in detail about Australia. Patrick White does the opposite, staying at home but writing for the world, while Christina Stead lived and wrote around the world but retained an Australian perspective. Many of the most recent generation of Australian writers seem to solve the problem by declaring themselves international and writing without any attempt to relate to specifically Australian experience. On the other hand, migrant writers of this generation have continued to feel the necessity of exploring the conflict between their native traditions and Australian reality.

This stance contrasts with the attitudes of the Aboriginal poets gathered in Kevin Gilbert's collection *Inside Black Australia* (Penguin, Ringwood, 1988). These poets write for their own people, expressing their anger and defiance at their treatment by white Australia. Their verses are made to be used to give their readers confidence in remaking their own identity. Yet this task has concerned all Australian writers from the beginning. Those who wrote for an audience at 'home' in England, and defined the new colony by its lack of comfort and gentility, were defining themselves as a continuing element in English society, but they were also extending the meaning of English society and making it a universal standard of civilisation. In challenging this assumption, nationalist writers from Lawson to Prichard not only made a new image in which Australians could recognise themselves, but also asserted the validity of this image as an integral part of all human experience.

The writers who have subsequently challenged the partiality and exclusions of these images by offering their own have by their writing forced us to recognise different realities of the experience of colonising Australia. Those who now insist on their international context confront us with one result of this colonisation, which has replaced an indigenous culture with a constructed nation, and at the same time has joined this nation inseparably into a global economy and culture. The assertion of local difference and identity is part of this global culture that we share with peoples as diverse as Induits, Basques and Argentinians. It is part of the response to the overriding imperative of the contemporary world, that we learn to live together and separately, maintaining our individuality only as we recognise our commonality.

It is easy to point to a tradition that has now been established in Australian literature. The idea of a tradition is, however, hostile to the understanding of any literature. It necessarily excludes work that does not fit its assumptions, and so inhibits the freedom of writers to tell the truth as they see it, and of readers to use writing as they choose. By suggesting standards and criteria of judgement, it inhibits freedom of response. It is the opposite of an understanding of the past, a recognition that all writing is a response to particular situations and that through it we can understand the struggles that have brought our present consciousness into being and choose the areas of meaning that we need to work for now.

In one sense, all Australian writing is part of new world literature, the literature of displaced peoples and cultures. Aboriginal writers represent a people displaced in their own land; migrant writers adapt by adapting the forms and language of their homelands to their antipodes; the internationalists recolonise the old world, denying its exclusive ownership of any culture and forcing it to admit to the global reality of its own history.

Yet the new world literatures do not themselves constitute a harmonious whole. There are distinctions between the settler literatures of Australia, New Zealand and South Africa, the literatures of displaced and subject peoples in the West Indies, and the literatures of indigenous peoples in Africa, India and the Pacific. Within Australian literature, there are conflicts of power and ownership, between high and popular cultures, between male and female writers, between generations and between metaphor and metonymy, formalism and realism.

These conflicts finally are not literary but political. They represent contending claims for legitimacy, for ownership not just of the right to speak but of the right to live according to our own choices. The traditionalists assert that literature provides universal standards of values on which alone a safe and secure society can be built. It provides readers with access to a tradition that guarantees their humanity. The opposite view is that literature provides a framework that controls and directs the sexuality and the drive for power and autonomy that determine our personal and communal lives. Every literary work is an attempt to free these desires from some constraints so that they can build new orders of individuality or commonality. Conservative literature attempts to build orders that will maintain established values, radical writers try to topple old oppressions and incorporate new values in their structures, but they all are engaged in struggles for power. Australian literature constitutes a struggle to find room in an old continent for old cultures and to enlarge these cultures to accommodate the people at whose cost they were built.

FURTHER READING

These references include critical and historical works related to books discussed in the text, and further works relevant to the themes of the book that there has not been space to discuss in detail. The references are limited to books only. Primary sources of works discussed in the text are not normally repeated here.

General reference

William H. Wilde, Joy Hooton and Barry Andrews, *The Oxford Companion to Australian Literature*, Oxford University Press, Melbourne, 1985. Amazingly comprehensive and accurate, and simply indispensable.

E. Morris Miller and Frederick Macartney, *Australian Literature: a bibliography to 1938, extended to 1950*, Angus & Robertson, Sydney, 1956. Dated but still very useful.

H.M. Green and Dorothy Green, *A History of Australian Literature*, two vols, Angus & Robertson, Sydney, 1985. A revised and updated version of H.M. Green's monumental work.

Graham Johnston, *Annals of Australian Literature*, OUP, Melbourne, 1970. The principal publications of each year, together with an alphabetical index of authors with their works, 1789–1968. The entries for 1968 are limited to authors who have already appeared in a previous year.

Leonie Kramer (ed.), *The Oxford History of Australian Literature*, OUP, Melbourne, 1981. Useful, despite a highly selective critical approach. Excellent bibliography.

Russel Ward, *The Australian Legend*, OUP, Melbourne, 1958. A study of the origins of the democratic and egalitarian elements of the radical nationalist tradition.

Russel Ward, *Australia*, Ure Smith, Sydney and London, 1967. A useful short history.

Russel Ward, *A Nation for a Continent: the history of Australia, 1901–1975*, Heinemann Educational Australia, Richmond, Victoria, 1977.

Russel Ward, *Finding Australia: The History of Australia to 1821*, Heinemann Educational Australia, Richmond, Victoria, 1987. These two volumes are the first of a three-volume general history.

Fred Lock and Alan Lawson, *Australian Literature — a reference guide*, OUP, Melbourne, 1977. A bibliographical guide to sources.

Stuart Macintyre, *The Oxford History of Australia, Volume 4: 1901–1942*, OUP, Melbourne, 1986. The troubled post-nationalist, imperialist and depression decades of Australian history.

C. Manning Clark, *A History of Australia*, Volumes I to VI, Melbourne University Press, Melbourne, 1962–1988. The story from earliest times to the 1930s.

C. Manning Clark, *Short History of Australia*, Macmillan, Melbourne, 1981.

C. Manning Clark, *Select Documents in Australian History*, two vols, Angus and Robertson, Sydney, 1950 and 1977.

Geoffrey Blainey, *The Tyranny of Distance*, Macmillan, Melbourne, 1982 [1966]. Definitive account of the function of distance in Australian history; controversial argument about the reasons for the establishment of the first penal colony.

Geoffrey Blainey, *The Triumph of the Nomads: a history of ancient Australia*, Macmillan, Melbourne, 1975. A recognition of the historical changes of Aboriginal society and its environment.

Humphrey McQueen, *A New Britannia: an argument concerning the social origins of Australian radicalism and nationalism*, Penguin, Ringwood, 1970.

Tim Rouse, *Australian Liberalism and National Character*, Kibble Books, Melbourne, 1978. Like McQueen, Rowse challenges the more comfortable myths of the radical nationalist tradition, particularly as they appear in the work of historians, literary critics and social commentators.

John McLaren (ed.), *A Nation Apart*, Longman Cheshire, 1983. Essays on the Australian environment, people and society at the beginning of the 1980s. Intended to set the agenda for the future, the book represents rather the hopes of the past.

Geoffrey Serle, *From Deserts the Prophets Come: the creative spirit in Australia 1788–1972*, Heinemann, Melbourne, 1973. A general cultural history. Second edition, entitled *The Creative Spirit in Australia: a cultural history*, Heinemann, Melbourne, 1987.

John Carroll (ed.), *Intruders in the Bush: the Australian quest for identity*, OUP, Melbourne, 1982. Essays on the origins and meaning of myths associated with convicts, mateship, pioneering, bushranging, cities and the bush.

Richard White, *Inventing Australia*, Allan & Unwin, Sydney, 1981. Legends and symbols of Australia, and the social movements associated with them.

Anthologies

George Mackaness, *An Anthology of Australian Verse*, Sydney, 1952.

Harry Heseltine (ed.), *Penguin Book of Australian Verse*, Penguin, Ringwood, 1972.

Douglas Stewart and Nancy Keesing (eds.), *Australian Bush Ballads*, Angus & Robertson, Sydney, 1955.

Douglas Stewart and Nancy Keesing (eds.), *Old Bush Songs and Rhymes of Colonial Times*, Angus & Robertson, Sydney, 1957. Enlarged and revised from the collection of A.B. Paterson.

Brian Elliott and Adrian Mitchell, *Bards in the Wilderness*, Nelson, Melbourne, 1970. A collection of poems from the colonial period.

Rodney Hall (ed.), *The Collins Book of Australian Poetry*, Collins, Sydney and London, 1981.

Leonie Kramer and Adrian Mitchell (eds.), *The Oxford Anthology of Australian Literature*, OUP, Melbourne, 1985.

Criticism

John Barnes (ed.), *The Writer in Australia: a collection of literary documents, 1856–1964*, OUP, Melbourne, 1969.

Records the changing attitudes of Australians to their literature.

Ross Gibson, *The Diminishing Paradise: changing literary perceptions of Australia*, Angus & Robertson, Sydney, 1984. Changes from the earliest European images of *Terra Australis* to the middle of the nineteenth century, together with an examination of two of Patrick White's novels about the same subject.

P.R. Eaden and F.H. Meares (eds.), *Mapped but Not Known: the Australian landscape of the imagination*, Wakefield Press, Adelaide, 1986. Essays and poetry about changing Australian perceptions of the landscape.

A.A. Phillips, *The Australian Tradition: studies in a colonial culture*, Cheshire, Melbourne, 1958. Revised edition, Cheshire-Lansdowne, Melbourne, 1966. This includes pioneering studies of Lawson and Furphy and the democratic theme, and the essay on 'The Cultural Cringe' that added a phrase to the Australian language.

A.A. Phillips, *Responses: selected writings*, Australian International Press & Publications, Kew, Victoria, 1978.

Geoffrey Dutton (ed.), *The Literature of Australia*, Penguin, Ringwood, 1976, [1964]. Social, historical and literary background and comment.

W.S. Ramson (ed.), *The Australian Experience: critical essays on Australian novels*, Australian National University Press, Canberra, 1974. From Henry Kingsley to Thomas Keneally.

Harry Haseltine, *The Uncertain Self: essays in Australian literature and criticism*, OUP, Melbourne, 1986. General essays on literature in Australia, together with essays on specific writers from Kendall to Webb. Combines the best of the philosophic, nationalist and biographic traditions of criticism.

Judith Wright, *Preoccupations in Australian Poetry*, OUP, Melbourne, 1965.

Judith Wright, *Because I Was Invited*, OUP, Melbourne, 1975.

Fay Zwicky, *The Lyre in the Pawnshop: essays in literature and survival 1974–1984*, University of Western Australia Press, Perth, 1986. These essays and reviews combine passion and analysis to reveal the relationships between Australia and its writers.

Graeme Turner, *National Fictions: literature, film and the construction of Australian narrative*, Allen & Unwin, Sydney, 1986. A discussion of the way continuing themes and images construct the way Australians see themselves.

J.J. Healy, *Literature and the Aborigine in Australia, 1770–1975*, University of Queensland Press, St Lucia, 1978. A study of the roles given to Aborigines in Australian writing.

G.A. Wilkes, *The Stockyard and the Croquet Lawn*, Edward Arnold, Melbourne, 1981. In a rejoinder to the kind of cultural nationalism represented in the work of such critics as A.A. Phillips and Russel Ward, Wilkes emphasises the importance of the genteel tradition in Australian writing. The writer seems to be simultaneously arguing that the upper class English tradition forms part of the Australian inheritance and that the ordinary Australian shares this tradition.

Prologue

Europe and the new worlds — cultural and economic impacts

Walter Prescott Webb, *The Great Frontier*, London, 1953. Webb's thesis, that Luther provided the spirit for the expansion of Europe, and Columbus the opportunity, has been criticised as simplistic by several of the following authors.

J.H. Elliott, *The Old World and the New 1492–1650*, Cambridge University Press, Cambridge, 1970.

J.H. Elliott, *Imperial Spain, 1469–1716*, Arnold, London, 1963.

A.R. Lewis and T.F. McCann (eds.), *The New World Looks at its History*, Texas University Press, Austin, Texas, 1963.

David Divine, *The Opening of the World*, Collins, London, 1973.

Wayne Franklin, *Discoverers, Explorers, Settlers: the diligent writers of early America*, University of Chicago Press, Chicago and London, 1979. The concepts that determined the way Europeans perceived America.

On European expansion into Asia and the Pacific

Werner P. Friedrich (ed.), *Australia in Western Imaginative Writings, 1600–1960*, University of North Carolina Press, Chapel Hill, NC, 1967. A history of literature and an anthology from writers including de Quiros, Swift, Kingsley, Carboni, Dumas, Twain, Lawrence and Sacchi.

Luis Vaz de Camoens, *The Lusiads (Os Lusiads)*, 1572; translated by William C. Atkinson, Penguin, Harmondsworth, 1980, [1952].

William Dampier, *A New Voyage around the World*, London, 1697.

William Dampier, *A Voyage to New Holland: the English voyage of Discovery to the South Seas in 1699, 1703, 1709*; James Spencer (ed.), Alan Sutton, Gloucester, 1981.

Alan Villiers, *Captain Cook — the Seaman's Seaman*, Penguin, Harmondsworth, 1969 [1967]. Villiers' mastery of the crafts of seamanship and writing enables the reader to appreciate Cook's achievements.

Ernest S. Dodge, *Islands and Empires: western impact on the Pacific and East Asia*, University of Minnesota Press/OUP, St Paul and London, 1976. This volume in the series 'Europe and the World in the Age of Expansion' examines the European expansion into the Pacific and East Asia from the time of Magellan to the beginning of the twentieth century, with a glance at subsequent developments.

O.H.K. Spate, *The Pacific since Magellan*; Vol I, *The Spanish Lake*, ANU Press, Canberra, 1979; Vol 2, *Monopolists and Freebooters*, ANU Press, Canberra, 1983. The second volume deals with the incursions of Dutch and British into the Spanish dominions in America and the Pacific, the trade rivalries and the eventual breakdown of the Spanish empire.

Alan Moorhead, *The Fatal Impact: an account of the invasion of the South Pacific, 1767–1840*, 1966; Penguin, Harmondsworth, 1979, [1968]. A popular and readable introduction to the subject.

A. Grenfell Price, *The Explorations of Captain James Cook in the Pacific, as told by selections from his own journals, 1768–1779*, Angus & Robertson, Sydney, 1969 [1958].

Bernard Smith, *European Vision and the South Pacific*, second edition, Harper and Rowe, Sydney,, 1985 [1960].

On slavery

Eugene Genovese, *Roll, Jordan Roll*, Vintage Books, New York, 1976.

David Brion Davis, *The Problem of Slavery in Western Culture*, Cornell University Press, Ithaca, NY, 1966.

David Brion Davis, *Slavery and Human Progress*, OUP, New York and London, 1984.

Roland Oliver and J.D. Page, *A Short History of Africa*, Penguin, Harmondsworth, 1962.

David Divine, *The Opening of the World*, Collins, London, 1973.

On Aboriginal culture and literature

Roland Robinson, *Black-Feller, White-Feller*, Angus & Robertson, Sydney, 1958.

Roland Robinson, *Alcheringa and Other Aboriginal Poems*, A.H. and A.W. Reed, Sydney, 1970.

Roland Robinson, *Aboriginal Myths and Legends*, Sun Books, Melbourne, 1966.

A.P. Elkin, *Australian Aborigines*, Angus & Robertson, Sydney, 1979.

Berndt, Ronald M., *Love Songs of Arnhem land*, Nelson, Melbourne, 1981.

Chapter 1. 'A Tainted Paradise'

Bernard Smith, *European Vision and the South Pacific*, second edition, Harper and Row, Sydney, 1985 [1960].

Ralph Gustafson, *The Penguin Book of Canadian Verse*, Penguin, Harmondsworth, revised edition, 1978.

Henry Fielding, *Causes of the late Increases of Robberies etc.*, in *Collected Works*, London, 1871.

C. Manning Clark, *Select Documents in Australian History*, two vols, Angus & Robertson, Sydney, 1977.

C. Manning Clark, *Sources of Australian History*, OUP, London, 1957.

John White, *Journal of a Voyage to New South Wales*, London, 1790.

Watkin Tench, *Sydney's First Four Years: a Narrative of the Expedition to Botany Bay, and a Complete Account of Settlement at Port Jackson*, London, 1789 and 1793; with introduction and annotations by L.F. Fitzhardinge, Library of Australian Literature, Sydney, 1979.

David Collins, *An Account of the English Colony in New South Wales*, London, 1798.

Don Charlwood, *The Long Farewell*, Penguin, Ringwood, 1981. Extracts from the diaries of emigrants who travelled to Australia by sailing ship are combined with historical commentary to dramatise the voyage that separated Australia from Britain emotionally as well as spatially.

Robert Dixon, *The Course of Empire: neo-classical culture in New South Wales, 1788–1860*, OUP, Melbourne, 1986. Dixon shows how writing and pictures of the new colony embody the aesthetic principles of the eighteenth century enlightenment and its belief in the historic progress from primitive to civilised that shaped the belief in Australia as the new and greater Britain of the south.

Chapter 2. 'Explorers and Visionaries'

Kathleen Fitzpatrick (ed.), *Australian Explorers*, OUP, London, 1958.

Douglas Stewart and Nancy Keesing (eds.), *Old Bush Songs*, Angus & Robertson, Sydney, 1957.

Paul Carter, *The Road to Botany Bay: an essay in spatial history*, Faber, London and Boston, 1987. This work, published too late to take its argument into due account in this book, examines the journals of discoverers and explorers to cut through the assumptions of history and recover the historical moment. Carter distinguishes between the generalising of the botanists, who reduce the new to the categories of the old, and the particularising of the explorers, who remain open to novelty and the unknown.

Chapter 3. 'New Settlements'

Joseph Holt, *Memoirs*, 1838.

James Hardy Vaux, *Memoirs of James Hardy Vaux*, 1819; ed. Noel McLachlan, London, 1964.

Geoffrey C. Ingleton, *True Patriots All, or, News from Early Australia, as told in a collection of broadsides*, Angus & Robertson, Sydney, 1952.

Henry Savery, *Quintus Servinton — a tale founded upon incidents of real occurrence*, Hobart Town, 1830–31; with an introduction by Cecil H. Hadcraft, Jacaranda, Brisbane, 1962.

Henry Savery, *The Hermit of Van Diemen's Land*, Hobart Town, 1829; with an introduction by Cecil H. Hadcraft, 1964.

Thomas E. Wells (?), *Michael Howe: the last and worst of the bushrangers of Van Diemen's Land*, Hobart Town, 1818; facsimile, with introduction by C. Craig, Hobart, Platypus, 1966.

Edward M. Curr, *Recollections of Squatting in Victoria*, MUP, Melbourne, 1965. Edited version of work first published in 1883.

Chapter 4. 'Far Horizons and Dark Clouds'

Geoffrey Serle, *The Golden Age: a history of the colony of Victoria, 1851–1861*, MUP, Melbourne, 1963.

Geoffrey Serle, *The Rush to Be Rich: a history of the colony of Victoria, 1883–1889*, MUP, Melbourne, 1971.

Leonie Kramer and A.D. Hope (eds.), *Henry Kendall*, Sun Books, Melbourne, 1973.

Adrian Mitchell (ed.), *Charles Harpur*, Sun Books, Melbourne, 1973.

Michael Ackland (ed.), *Charles Harpur: selected poetry and prose*, Penguin, Ringwood, 1986.

Brian Elliott (ed.), *Adam Lindsay Gordon*, Sun Books, Melbourne, 1973.

Alan Brissenden, *Rolf Boldrewood*, OUP, Melbourne 1972.

J.S.D. Mellick, *The Passing Guest, Henry Kingsley in Australia*, UQP, St Lucia, 1983.

Marcus Clarke, *Old Tales from a Young Country*, 1871; facsimile edition, edited by Joan Poole, Sydney University Press, 1972. Fifteen historical tales, most of which were first published in *The Australasian* during the years when *His Natural Life* was appearing as a serial in the *Australasian Journal*. They are drawn from much the same sources as those he used for the novel.

Laurie Hergenham (ed.), *A Colonial City: high and low life — selected journalism of Marcus Clarke*, UQP, St Lucia, 1972. Reports, essays, reviews, commentary and columns from Clarke's Melbourne journalism.

Price Warung (William Astley), *Convict Days*, Australasian Book Society, Sydney, 1960. A reprinting of thirteen stories by Astley, a contemporary of Marcus Clarke whose tales are reworked from records of the convict system.

Price Warung, *Tales of the Convict System*, edited by Barry Andrews, UQP, Brisbane, 1975. For a discussion of Astley's life and work, including his unreliability as an historian, see Barry Andrews, *Price Warung (William Astley)*, Twayne Publishers, Boston, 1976.

Anthony Trollope, *Australia*, edited by P.D. Edwards and R.B. Joyce, UQP, St Lucia, 1967. Selected and edited from Trollope's 1873 account of his travels in Australia and New Zealand, the volume provides the observations of an Englishman on the pastoral society that had developed in Australia. Trollope felt ambivalent to this attempt to recreate the English landed gentry, writing that 'I love the squatter . . . But on principle I take the part of the free-selector.' Trollope possibly met Boldrewood during his travels.

Don Watson, *Caledonia Australis*, Collins, Sydney, 1984. The tragic account of the settlement of eastern Victoria by dispossessed Scottish crofters epitomises the contradictions of imperialist expansion and the metamorphosis of values produced by the antipodean shift.

Chapter 5. 'A Little Radicalism'

Chris Wallace-Crabbe (ed.), *The Australian Nationalists: modern critical essays*, OUP, Melbourne, 1971.

The Bulletin, Centenary issue, Sydney, 29 January 1980.

Patricia Rolfe, *The Journalistic Javelin: an illustrated history of the Bulletin*, Wildcat Press, Sydney, 1979.

Sylvia Lawson, *The Archibald Paradox*, Allen Lane/Penguin, Ringwood, 1983.

Bruce Bennett, *Cross Currents: magazines and newspapers in Australian literature*, Longman Cheshire, Melbourne, 1981. Contains an essay by Elizabeth Webby on literary journalism before *The Bulletin*, and edited extracts from A.G. Stephens's *Bulletin* Diary.

Vane Lindesay, *The Inked-In Image: a survey of Australian comic art*, Heinemann, Melbourne, 1970. Particularly good on the relationship between the *Bulletin* and the tradition of Australian humour in black-and-white art.

A.G. Stephens, *Selected Writings*, edited by Leon Cantrell, Angus & Robertson, Sydney, 1978. Stephens was literary editor of the *Bulletin* and founder of the Red Page. As well as critical essays on contemporary writers, this selection includes essays on writing in general and on work at the *Bulletin* in particular.

Russel Ward, *Penguin Book of Autralian Ballads*, Penguin, Ringwood, 1964.

A.B. Paterson, *Collected Verse*, edited by Frederick T. Macartney, Angus & Robertson, Sydney, 1951.

A.B. Paterson, *Banjo Paterson. Short Stories*, Lansdowne, Sydney, 1981.

Henry Lawson, *Collected Prose*, two vols. Memorial edition edited by Colin Roderick, Angus & Robertson, Sydney, 1972. Vol. 1: *Short Stories and Sketches, 1888–1922*; Vol. 2: *Autobiographical and Other Writings*, 1887–1922. Citations of prose works in the text refer to this edition in which the work is arranged by theme and period.

Henry Lawson, *Henry Lawson; Poems*, edited by Colin Roderick and John Ferguson, Sydney, 1979. A selection of Lawson's best verses. The citations in the text refer to this selection.

Other useful editions of Lawson's work include:

A Camp-fire Yarn: complete works, 1885–1900 and *A Fantasy of Man: complete works 1901–1922*, compiled and edited by Leonard Cronin, with introductions by Brian Kiernan, Lansdowne, Sydney, 1984 — all the work arranged chronologically; *The Essential Henry Lawson*, edited by Brian Kiernan, Currey O'Neil, Melbourne, updated — includes a critical biography and previously unpublished work; *Henry Lawson*, Portable Australian Authors edition, edited by Brian Kiernan, UQP, St Lucia, 1980; *Penguin Henry Lawson Short Stories*, edited by John Barnes, Penguin, Ringwood, 1986.

Critical and biographical works on Lawson include:

Brian Matthews, *The Receding Wave: Henry Lawson's prose*, MUP, Melbourne, 1972.

Brian Matthews, *Louisa*, McPhee-Gribble, Melbourne, 1987. A biography of Lawson's mother.

Denton Prout, *Henry Lawson: the Grey Dreamer*, Rigby, Adelaide, 1963.

John Barnes, *Henry Lawson's Short Stories*, Shillington House, Melbourne, 1985.

C.J. Brennan, *Poems [1913]*, facsimile edition, with an introduction by G.A. Wilkes,, Sydney University Press, 1972. [1914]

G.A. Wilkes, *Joseph Furphy's 'Such Is Life'*, Shillington House, Melbourne, 1985.

John Barnes, *Joseph Furphy*, OUP, Melbourne, 1979.

Chapter 6. 'Reconsiderations'

Dorothy Green: *Ulysses Bound: Henry Handel Richardson and her fiction*, ANU Press, Canberra, 1973.

Vincent Buckley, *Henry Handel Richardson*, OUP, Melbourne, 1970.

Dennis Douglas, *Henry Handel Richardson's 'Maurice Guest'*, Edward Arnold, Melbourne, 1978.

Karen McLeod, *Henry Handel Richardson, a critical study*, Cambridge University Press, Cambridge, 1985.

Rosa Praed, *Lady Bridget in the Never-Never Land*, 1915; with introduction by Pam Gilbert, Pandora Press, London, Sydney and New York, 1987.

A more recent collection of Neilson's poetry is *The Poems of Shaw Neilson*, Angus & Robertson, Sydney, 1965. Previously uncollected poems were published in *Witnesses of Spring*, Angus & Robertson, 1970, edited by Judith Wright.

Chapter 7. 'Renaissance and Revolution'

Stuart Macintyre, *Oxford History of Australia, Vol 4: 1901–1942, The Succeeding Age*, OUP, Melbourne, 1987.

Norman Lindsay, *Bohemians of the Bulletin*, Angus & Robertson, Sydney, 1965.

Douglas Stewart, *Norman Lindsay: a personal memoir*, Angus & Robertson, Sydney, 1975.

Lin Bloomfield (ed.), *The World of Norman Lindsay*, Macmillan, Melbourne, 1979.

A. Grove Day, *Robert D. Fitzgerald*, Twayne Publishers, New York, 1974.

G.A. Wilkes, *R.D. Fitzgerald*, OUP, Melbourne, 1981.

Kenneth Slessor, *Bread and Wine: selected prose*, Angus & Robertson, Sydney, 1970.

Robert D. Fitzgerald, *Of Places and Poetry*, UQP, St Lucia, 1976. Essays on his life and writing.

Max Harris, *Kenneth Slessor*, OUP, Melbourne, 1963.

Ric Throssell, *Wild Weeds and Wind Flowers: the life and letters of Katharine Susannah Prichard*, Angus & Robertson, Sydney, 1975.

Katharine Susannah Prichard, *Straight Left*, articles and addresses on politics, literature and women's affairs from 1910 to 1968, collected and edited by Ric Throssell, Wild and Woolley, Sydney, 1982.

Chapter 8. 'The Test of War'

Kathleen Fitzpatrick, *Martin Boyd*, OUP, Melbourne, 1963.

Brian McFarlane, *Martin Boyd's Langton Novels*, Edward Arnold, Melbourne, 1980.

Martin Boyd, *Day of My Delight*, autobiography, Lansdowne, Melbourne, 1965.

Geoff Page (ed.), *Shadows from Wire*, Penguin, Ringwood, 1983. Anthology of poems of war.

Chris Wallace-Crabbe and Peter Pierce (eds.), *Clubbing of the Gunfire: 100 Australian war poems*, MUP, Melbourne, 1984.

Carl Harrison-Ford, *Fighting Words*, Lothian, Melbourne, 1986. Writings of war.

Chapter 9. 'Sydney or the Bush: savage wilderness'

K.G. Hamilton (ed.), *Studies in the Recent Australian Novel*, UQP, St Lucia, 1978. Critical essays on novels by Herbert, White, Stow, Keneally, Boyd, Porter, Martin and Ireland.

Harry Heseltine, *Xavier Herbert*, OUP, Melbourne, 1973.

Laurie Clancy, *Xavier Herbert*, Twayne Publishers, New York, 1981.

John McLaren, *Xavier Herbert's 'Capricornia' and 'Poor Fellow My Country'*, Shillington House, Melbourne, 1981.

Laurie Clancy, *Christina Stead's 'The Man Who Loved Children' and 'For Love Alone'*, Shillington House, Melbourne, 1981.

R.G. Geering, *Christina Stead: a critical study*, Angus & Robertson, Sydney, 1979.

Chapter 10. 'Realism and Nationalism'

Donald Horne, *The Education of Young Donald*, Sun Books, Melbourne, 1967.

Bernard Smith, *The Boy Adeodatus: the portrait of a lucky young bastard*, Allen Lane/Penguin, Ringwood, 1984.

These two autobiographies give a picture of the intellectual and political ferment of the years before and during the Second World War.

Hume Dow, *Frank Dalby Davison*, OUP, Melbourne, 1971.

David Walker, *Dream and Disillusion: a search for Australian cultural identity*, ANU Press, Canberra, 1976. The lives, hopes and writings of a number of radical thinkers, including Louis Esson and Vance Palmer.

Ian Reid, *Fiction and the Great Depression — Australia and New Zealand 1930–1950*, Edward Arnold, Melbourne, 1979. A comparative study of themes that interested novelists in the two countries and their different ways of treating them.

Chapter 11. 'The Social Realists'

Bernard Smith, *The Antipodean Manifesto: essays in art and history*, OUP, Melbourne, 1976. Essays on individual artists and on the ideas that generated major changes in

Australian art and culture in the years after the Second World War.

Richard Haese, *Rebels and Precursors: Revolutionary years of Australian Art*, Penguin, Ringwood, 1981. The history of the artistic divisions between realists and modernists, including the *Angry Penguins* debates.

John Morrison, *Australian By Choice*, Rigby, Adelaide, 1973. His autobiography.

John Morrison, *The Happy Warrior — selected prose*, Pascoe Publishing, Melbourne, 1987.

Jack Beasley, *Red Letter Days: notes from inside an era*, Australasian Book Society, Sydney, 1979. The story of the society and some of the realist writers it published.

Don Watson, *Brian Fitzpatrick: a radical life*, Hale & Iremonger, Sydney, 1979. Fitzpatrick was at the centre of the cultural and political struggles of the Cold War period.

John Docker, *Australian Cultural Elites: intellectual traditions in Sydney and Melbourne*, Angus & Robertson, Sydney, 1974.

John Docker, *In a Critical Tradition: reading Australian literature*, Penguin, Ringwood, 1984.

Although Docker in these two books discusses writers from Brennan on, he is primarily concerned with literature and its teaching in the context of the political debates of the 1960s. Critical of both the textual critics and the radical nationalists.

K.G. Hamilton (ed.), *Studies in the Recent Australian Novel*, (see Chapter 9).

Ian Turner, *Room for Manoeuvre: writings on history, politics, ideas and play*, edited by Leonie Sandercock and Stephen Murray-Smith, Drummond Publishing, Richmond, Victoria, 1982.

Patrick O'Brien, *The Saviours: an intellectual history of the left in Australia*, Drummond Publishing, Melbourne, 1977. A sceptical, not to say sardonic, account of the left in twentieth century Australia, giving particular attention to the years during and after the Second World War.

Garry Kinnane, *George Johnston: a biography*, Nelson, Melbourne, 1986.

Roger Milliss, *Serpent's Tooth*, Penguin, Ringwood, 1984. Milliss was a member of the Sydney Realist Writers' Group in the 1960s, but this autobiographical novel breaks completely with the realist style to come to terms with the author's own involvement in his father's life of political activism. Each paragraph is written as a single unbroken sentence, conveying the impression of the individual swept away in a constant flow of events. This approach denies the hope of the realists that they could make history, and shows instead history making the person. Yet, paradoxically, it affirms the value of hope.

Stephen Murray-Smith (ed.), *An Overland Muster*, Jacaranda, Brisbane, 1965. Selections from *Overland*.

C.B. Christesen (ed.), *On Native Grounds*, Angus & Robertson, Sydney, 1968. Selections from *Meanjin*.

Chapter 12. 'A Heightened Reality'

Brian Kiernan (ed.), *Considerations — new essays on Kenneth Slessor, Judith Wright and Douglas Stewart*, Angus & Robertson, Sydney, 1977.

Kenneth Mackenzie, *The Poems of Kenneth Mackenzie*, edited by Evan Jones and Geoffrey Little, Angus & Robertson, Sydney, 1972. Mackenzie, who also wrote novels under the name of Seaforth Mackenzie, in his early poetry makes art of sensuous delight in the manner of the early Slessor. In his mature work the delight in the external world known through the senses, above all through love, is at odds with the observation of reason and falls short of the aspirations of the spirit. The loneliness of the self and the knowledge of death, in poems like 'In the Orchard', intensify the poet's awareness of the life he shares with those around him.

David Campbell, *Flame and Shadow: selected stories*, UQP, St Lucia, 1976.

Harry Heseltine (ed.), *A Tribute to David Campbell: a collection of essays*, University of NSW Press, Kensington, NSW, 1987. Essays on Campbell's life and work.

A.D. Hope, *The Cave and the Spring: essays on poetry*, Rigby, Adelaide, 1965. Mainly on the craft, criticism and theory of poetry.

A.D. Hope, *Native Companions: essays and comments on Australian literature 1936–1966*, Angus & Robertson, Sydney, 1974. Reviews and critical opinions, including comments on the Jindyworobaks, Max Harris and Patrick White.

A.D. Hope, *The Pack of Autolycus*, ANU Press, Canberra, 1978. Mainly about European writing, the essays convey Hope's understanding of the relationships between the craft of writing and the world of the imagination it creates.

James McAuley, *The End of Modernity: essays on literature, art and culture*, Angus & Robertson, Sydney, 1959. The essays are linked by the author's conservative and anti-modernist stance.

James McAuley, *The Grammar of the Real: selected prose 1959–1979*, OUP, Melbourne, 1975. Essays ranging over literature from Spenser to modern and European poets, over literary theory and the author's New Guinea experience. The collection reveals McAuley's poetic and intellectual preoccupations with the relationships between art and experience, culture and society, and his consistent opposition of universal values to moral positivism and relativism.

Peter Coleman, *The Heart of James McAuley; life and work of the Australian poet*, Wildcat Press, Sydney, 1980.

Douglas Stewart, *The Flesh and the Spirit*, Angus & Robertson, Sydney, 1948. Reviews and articles from the Red Page of the *Bulletin*.

Judith Wright, *Preoccupations in Australian Poetry*, OUP, Melbourne, 1965. Wright's essays on Australian poets from Harpur to Hope suggest her own poetic principles as well as providing a valuable introduction to the writers she discusses.

Judith Wright, *Because I Was Invited*, OUP, Melbourne, 1975. Essays and talks about poetry, poets, writing and conservation. These writings clarify Wright's mature view that 'The real bearing of literature is not in its structure and language, but in the way it emerges from and reflects on our total situation, as individuals and as societies . . .' (p. viii).

Geoffrey Dutton and Max Harris (eds.), *The Vital Decade*, Sun Books, Melbourne, 1968. Selections from *Australian Letters*.

Peter Coleman, Lee Shrubb and Vivian Smith (eds.), *Quadrant–Twenty-Five Years*, UQP, St Lucia, 1982. Selections from Quadrant.

A.K. Thompson (ed.), *Critical Essays on Judith Wright*, Jacaranda, Brisbane, 1968.

S.P. Walker, *The Poetry of Judith Wright: a search for unity*, Edward Arnold, Melbourne, 1980.

G.A. Wilkes (ed.), *Ten Essays on Patrick White — selected from Southerly (1964–67)*, Angus & Robertson, Sydney, 1970.

R. Shepherd and K. Singh (eds.), *Patrick White: a critical symposium*, Center for Research in the New Literatures in English, Bedford Park, S.A., 1978.

Chapter 13. 'Origins'

Vincent Buckley, *Arcady and Other Places*, MUP, Carlton, 1966. This volume contains the complete sequence of 'Political Poems', whereas the *Selected Poems* include only seven of the eleven.

Anthony J. Hassall, *Strange Country: a study of Randolph Stow*, UQP, St Lucia, 1986.

Chapter 14. 'Otherworlds'

Don'o Kim, *The Chinaman*, Hale & Iremonger, Sydney, 1984. Don'o Kim, an Asian-born Australian writer, in his first English-language novel brings together Eastern and Western traditions in confrontation with nature in the

waters of the Great Barrier Reef. The novel contains three stories: the novel of nuclear devastation being planned by the main character, the Japanese JoBu (Joe); the book he is reading about a Chinese writer discovering Australia's outback; and the story of the pleasure cruise for which he has been engaged as yacht-boy. It opposes three possibilities; Zen Buddhism, or the way of silence and listening; the acquisitive greed and hedonism of Western materialism; the ruthless struggle for existence of the natural world. The three possibilities are variously symbolised by the attitudes of the characters to the yacht, *Quovadis*.

Rosemary Cresswell (ed.), *Home and Away: travel stories*, Penguin, Ringwood, 1987. Recent stories by Australians of adventures abroad. Mostly, these stories deal with Australians defining themselves against their experience abroad, rather than with an interest in origins or in the otherworlds for their own sake. Exceptions are stories by Malouf, who tries to define antipodes of feeling, and Angelo Loukakis, who questions the possibility of identity.

Morris Lurie, *Rappaport*, Sun Books, Melbourne, 1969 [1966]. Rappoport's frenetic energy creates its own world that continues to exist within his head despite the continuing refusals of suburban Melbourne, his antique business, his friends Sally and Friedlander or his car, to match his ambitions. This energy continues to sustain Lurie's later works, as he travels about the world but always finds himself as the only centre of constant disintegration. *Snow Jobs*, Pascoe, Melbourne, 1985, brings together occasional pieces that record the writer's failing encounters with a recalcitrant world.

Barry Oakley, *Wild Ass of a Man*, Cheshire, Melbourne, 1967; *A Salute to the Great McCarthy*, Heinemann, Melbourne, 1970; *Let's Hear It for Prendergast*, Heinemann, Melbourne, 1970. Oakley's characters, like Lurie's, live in a world where only their energy keeps disaster at bay. In *McCarthy* the culture and ambition of football becomes itself a part of the absurd world. Oakley's stories, collected in *Walking Through Tigerland*, UQP, St Lucia, 1977, portray a similar world of absurdity, but in the title story it is given balance by the community of Richmond and the exultant priest who swings wildly on the bells to celebrate its team's premiership. The otherworld is realised in community triumph.

John Hanrahan (ed.), *Gerard Murnane*, Footprint New Writers, Footscray Institute of Technology, 1987. New work, interview, critical essay.

Robert Sellick (ed.), *Gwen Harwood*, Centre for Research in the New Literatures in English, Flinders University, Adelaide, 1987.

Helen Daniel, *Double Agent: David Ireland and his work*, Penguin, Ringwood, 1982.

Helen Daniel, *Liars*, Penguin, Ringwood, 1987. Essays on contemporary novelists, including Peter Mathers, David Foster, David Ireland, Peter Carey, Murray Bail, Nicholas

Hasluck, Eliabeth Jolley and Gerard Murnane. The book combines analysis of the particular writers with discussion, in the form of dialogues, about the larger issues they raise, the engagement of the writers with 'the incapacity of language to deal with the complexities of life'.

Chapter 15. 'New Voices'

Mal Morgan (ed.), *Pie Anthology*, Whole Australian Catalogue, Melbourne, 1974. In both content and lay-out this sums up the idealistic and boundary-breaking spirit of the 1970s, when everything seemed possible. Although mainly poetry, the collection contains some prose and is set in a matrix of illustrations, calligraphy and graphics that offers to wrap the reader in an ecstatic cloud of words, images and sensations.

Kris Hemensley (ed.), *The Ear: The Ear in the Wheatfield 1973–76: a portrait of a magazine*, Rigmarole Books, Melbourne, 1985. Selections from one of the most important of the little magazines of the restless years. *The Ear* was committed to a modernist and international outlook.

Robert Kenny (ed.), *Applestealers*: a collection of the new poetry in Australia, including notes, statements, histories on La Mama, Outback Press, Melbourne, 1974.

Roger McDonald (ed.), *The First Paperback Poets Anthology*, UQP, St Lucia, 1974.

John Tranter (ed.), *The New Australian Poetry*, Makar Press, St Lucia, 1979.

Robert Gray and Geoffrey Lehmann (eds.), *The Younger Australian Poets*, Hale & Iremonger, Sydney, 1983.

Susan Hampton and Kate Llewellyn (eds.), *The Penguin Book of Australian Women Poets*, Penguin, Ringwood, 1986.

Since writing this chapter, Michael Dransfield's work has been published in a single volume: *Collected Poems*, edited by Rodney Hall, UQP, St Lucia, 1987.

Recent work by writers not otherwise discussed in the text:

Autobiography

A.B. Facey, *A Fortunate Life*, Fremantle Arts Centre Press, Fremantle, 1981; Penguin, Ringwood, 1983. The success of this autobiography indicates a renewed and non-polemic interest in the past.

Sally Morgan, *My Place*, Fremantle Arts Centre Press, Fremantle, 1987. This autobiography reads like a mystery novel as the author discovers her past and the past of her Aboriginal forebears. As she persuades her great-uncle,

her mother and her grandmother to tell their stories, she creates her own place and life. Through these the reader is given also an understanding of the role and sufferings of the Aboriginal communities as whites colonised the land and subjected its people. In telling this history, the author restores to her people what has been lost, and so makes a possible future in which this past can belong to all.

Fiction

Paul Radley, *Jack Rivers and Me*, Collins, Sydney, 1982; *My Blue Checker Corker and Me*, Collins, Sydney, 1982; *Good Mates*, Allen & Unwin, Sydney, 1985. Three novels that recreate growing up on the coal-fields between the wars.

Jan McKemmish, *A Gap in the Records*, Sybylla, Melbourne, 1985. A mysterious conspiracy threatens the structures of political power. The novel overturns the conventions of the political thriller and the assumptions of patriarchy in a style that also questions the nature of reality.

Nicholas Jose, *Feathers of Lead*, Penguin, Ringwood, 1986. Short fiction.

Nicholas Jose, *Paper Nautillus*, Penguin, Ringwood, 1987.

Jean Bedford, *Country Girl Again and Other Stories.*, McPhee Gribble/Penguin, Fitzroy/Ringwood, 1985.

Gerard Windsor, *Memories of the Assassination Attempt and Other Stories.*, Penguin, Ringwood 1985. In these stories Windsor places the personal legends people make from the history they survive in a world in which even the inanimate becomes a map of their emotions and frustrations.

Louis Nowra, *The Misery of Beauty*, Angus & Robertson, Sydney, 1981.

Archie Weller, *Day of the Dog*, Pan Books, 1982.

Archie Weller, *Going Home: Stories*, Allen & Unwin, Sydney, 1986.

Beverley Farmer, *Alone*, 1983; *Milk*, 1984; *Home Time*, 1985; McPhee Gribble Penguin, Fitzroy/Ringwood.

Antigone Kefala, *Island*, Hale & Iremonger, Sydney, 1984.

Angelo Loukakis, *Vernacular Dreams*, UQP, St Lucia, 1986.

Lionel Fogarty, *Yoogum-Yoogum*, Penguin, Ringwood, 1982. A novel using the rhythms of urban Aboriginal speech.

Poetry

Philip Martin, *New and Selected Poems*, Longman Cheshire, Melbourne, 1988. This collection from work published over the past twenty years reveals the range of this most urbane of poets. The wit and craft of his work gives form to the deep longing of the speaker for the completion promised but never fully yielded by love, friendship, religion and art.

Sources of illustrations

National Gallery of Australia

Swartte Swaane drift op het Eyland Rottenest, copper engraving (hand col.), 28.4 x 17.7 cm, Rex Nan Kivell Collection No. 2110; Henry Macbeth-Raeburn (b. 1860), *Captain Arthur Phillip, R.N., The Pioneer*, mezzotint (hand col.), 61.5 x 43 cm; James Reid Scott, *Flogging Prisoners, Van Diemen's Land*, pencil drawing, 16.8 x 25 cm; J. Macfarlane, *Sturt's Party Threatened by Blacks, at the Junction of the Murray and Darling*, 1830, engraving, 52.5 x 68.5 cm; Augustus Earle (1793–1838), *Female Penitentiary or Factory, Parramatta*, watercolour, 15.9 x 25.7 cm, Rex Nan Kivell Collection NK 12/47; 'Incidents in the Life of a Selector, *Illustrated Australasian News*, 25 November 1885, p. 200; Catherine Helen Spence (2004/4/260); Nicholas Chevalier (1828–1902), *Return of Burke and Wills to Coopers Creek*, painting, oil on canvas, 89.2 x 120 cm; 'Banjo' Paterson; 'The Drought in the Far North of South Australia', *Illustrated Melbourne Post*, 25 November 1865, p. 168; Joseph Furphy – 'Tom Collins'; Henry Handel Richardson; 'Eureka Stockade', *Illustrated Australasian News*, 1 August 1888, p. 16; *Major Johnston with Quartermaster Laycock*, water colour, 31.2 x 41.3 cm, Rex Nan Kivell Collection; Christina Stead; Vance and Nettie Palmer; No. 200 Palmer Collection; Eleanor Dark, photograph by Olive Cotton; John Morrison; *The Doomed Ship*, Shackleton Expedition 1914–1917, Frank Hurley Collection No. 12; Rosemary Dobson; Thea Astley; Christopher Koch; Blanche d'Alpuget; David Malouf; David Ireland; John Tranter; Kate Grenville; Peter Carey.

Mitchell Library, State Library of New South Wales

Sir Joseph Banks; Norfolk Island Convict Settlement; William Wentworth; National Art Gallery, Sydney.

State Library of Victoria

Hulk *Success*, Hobart (La Trobe Collection); Marcus Clarke; J. F. Archibald, *Life Digest*; Henry Lawson (J. K. Moir Collection); Christopher Brennan (J. K. Moir Collection); John Shaw Neilson (J. K. Moir Collection); Martin Boyd (J. K. Moir Collection); Miles Franklin (J. K. Moir Collection); Rex Ingamells; Alan Marshall (J. K. Moir Collection); J. Macfarlane, *Captain Rossiter Comes to Eyre's Aid* (La Trobe Collection).

State Library of Tasmania

Louisa Anne Meredith (Allport Library and Museum of Fine Arts).

National Film and Sound Archive, Canberra

Scene from *The Sentimental Bloke* by C. J. Dennis.

National Gallery of Victoria

Emanuel Phillips Fox (1865–1915), *The Landing of Captain Cook at Botany Bay, 1770*, oil on canvas, 261.6 x 190.5 cm, Gilbee Bequest.

Fremantle Arts Centre Press

Elizabeth Jolley, photograph by Tania Young.

Historical Resources Centre, Armadale, Victoria

Help Our Boys

Jimera Pty. Ltd., Edgecliff, NSW

Ginger Meggs cartoon

All other source are acknowledged fully in the text.

INDEX

Australian Literature